LIFE
and how to survive it

by the same authors

FAMILIES
and how to survive them

LIFE
and how to survive it

Robin Skynner/John Cleese

Cartoons by
Bud Handelsman

Methuen

To Josh and Ding

First published in Great Britain in 1993
by Methuen London
an imprint of Reed Consumer Books Ltd
Michelin House, 81 Fulham Road, London SW3 6RB
and Auckland, Melbourne, Singapore and Toronto

Reprinted 1993 (three times)

ISBN 0 413 66030 3

A CIP catalogue record for this book
is available at the British Library

Photoset in Great Britain by
Rowland Phototypesetting Ltd
Bury St Edmunds, Suffolk
Printed in England by Clays Ltd, St Ives plc

Contents

Acknowledgements

We would like to thank the following friends and colleagues for sparing time to read and comment on parts of the manuscript, or for providing information and advice; however, responsibility for the views expressed, and for any errors and omissions, remains of course entirely our own:

Douglas Bennett, Vivian Bickford-Smith, Eddie Canfor-Dumas, Roger Clark, Cynthia Cleese, John Crook, James Crowden, Alyce Faye Eichelberger, Ron Eyre, Patrick Gaffney, Merete Gardiner, Peter Haynes, Alan Hutchinson, Iain Johnstone, Peter Kellner, Peter Luff, Jacob Needleman, Helena Norberg-Hodge, Josh Partridge, Philip Philippou, Monty Python, Sogyal Rinpoche, Win Roberts, Denis Robinson, Margaret Robinson, Becky Salter, Andy Sargent, Michael Shamberg, David Skynner, Jane Skynner, Prue Skynner, Ian Stevenson, Takeshi Tamura, Stephen Verney, Nick Wapshott, Tom Wilkinson, Charlotte Wood, John Wood and Irene Young.

We would like to acknowledge the valuable editorial contributions of Ann Mansbridge and David Watson, and in particular of Christopher Falkus, whose creative suggestions were once again immensely helpful. We are also most grateful to June Ansell, Henrietta Williams, Melanie Bowker and Garry Scott-Irvine for their tireless work in typing the original conversations and the many drafts of the text.

We also thank the Mount Nelson Hotel, Capetown, for facilities provided.

Introduction

When we wrote *Families and how to survive them* ten years ago,
we wanted to make intelligible and accessible the psychological
aspects of how families behave and function; what makes some
work and others fail; and how families can move up the scale
towards greater health and happiness. We looked at such
things as how our own family backgrounds dictate not only
our choice of a partner but how the new family relationships
then created tend to perpetuate those backgrounds with their
good and bad characteristics. We looked at family taboos,
repressed emotions, and explored the destructive nature of
feelings shut away 'behind the screen' and not acknowledged
even by ourselves. We explained how these feelings can be
'projected' onto others, our partner or another scapegoat within
the family, who thus acquire from us and automatically enact
the forbidden emotion we unconsciously deny in ourselves.
We explored the make-up of our own personality – the 'child'
within us all which, if it dominates us, can lead to that distorted
view in which we see the world only in terms of ourselves
and our own needs; and the 'parental' part of us which, if it
denies our childlike aspects, can distort our relationships in
equally harmful ways.

These ideas were well received, so much so that *Families*,
gratifyingly, has become established as a virtual text-book not
only in many of the mental health professions but for the
non-professional audience for whom it was written. *Life and
how to survive it* carries the study further. It begins by focusing
on the factors which make for health in individuals and
families, going beyond clinical observation to include the recent
and little-known research now available about exceptionally
healthy families, and then extends and develops the ideas
outside the family context: thus it analyses our behaviour at
work; the behaviour of companies and organisations; the
conduct of societies and social groups; and beyond even that,
the secular and spiritual values by which we connect to each
other and the world. It is a book about the mental health of
individuals and groups operating from the smallest to the
largest of scales.

In the 'Afterthoughts' between the main sections we also
study some related topics, including the connection of
humour and laughter with health; the changing family
relationships now that so many women as well as men go out
to work; the basis of the widening rich–poor divide; and the
place of death in life.

Families and how to survive them and *Life and how to survive it* are two parts of a project on which we began work in the spring of 1980. We wanted to make available to the general public, in a way that was easy to absorb, those aspects of psychological knowledge we had found most helpful ourselves towards making life more understandable, meaningful and enjoyable. While we know that no definitive statement can be made about such a wide range of ideas, at this point they do seem to us to fit together at least enough to clarify many important questions and to stimulate discussion. We therefore offer this book, like *Families* before it, as part of a continuing process of exploration which we hope others will be interested to share. We look forward to the discussions that *Life* may spark off, and though we cannot hope to communicate personally with all those who join in, we have already made arrangements to coordinate any feedback received with the intention of eventually producing an improved version. In any case, we hope that many readers will share some of the great enjoyment we have found in our search for a better understanding of these issues.

1 Anyone for Health?

John While we were writing *Families and how to survive them* you mentioned several times that there had been research done on unusually mentally healthy families.

Robin That's right. They're the quite exceptional ones – the Olympic gold medal winners, as it were.

John It's funny but I've never heard anyone else talk about this.

Robin No that's right, it's hardly mentioned.

John You'd think shrinks would discuss it, but they don't. But then the odd thing about psychiatry is that it's entirely based on the study of people who *aren't* doing very well – folk with 'problems'. I mean, if you wanted to write a book about how to paint, or play chess, or be a good manager, you'd start by studying the people who were good at those things. And you wouldn't expect heavy sales of a book called *Play Championship Golf by Learning the Secrets of the Worst Twenty Players in the World*.

Robin True. Doctors do at least study normal physical function – anatomy, physiology – before going on the wards to study disease. But psychiatrists seem interested almost entirely in people who are abnormal.

John Maybe shrinks veer away from the topic of naturally-very-healthy-folk because they feel as envious of the lucky so-and-so's as we ordinary folk do. So why do *you* know about this research?

Robin I really took up psychiatry in the first place because I was interested in mental *health*, rather than in mental illness.

John Why do you think that was?

Robin As far back as I can remember, I felt I didn't really understand other people. Their behaviour so often didn't make sense to me. At first I assumed it was just because there was something wrong with me, that *I* wasn't normal. So I became curious about what real 'normality' was.

John You mean, you shared the notion, as I think the majority of us do when we're young, that most people are normal, in the sense of well adjusted, grown-up, rational and emotionally stable?

Robin Yes, and I soon began to see that what you have just described wasn't 'normal' at all, in the sense of being that common. So when I started my training, I looked for information about really mentally healthy people and was surprised to find the subject had been almost completely ignored. But much later I discovered two significant projects in America, one at Timberlawn in Dallas, which I visited several times, and one which had looked at a sample of healthy and successful Harvard graduates over a long period.

John Is the information surprising, or obvious, or what?

Robin It's a mixture. Of course, the more familiar you get with it, the more it all begins to fit together, but at the start some of it is even a bit shocking!

John Oh? Well, just to begin with, can you give a general principle that underlies unusually healthy behaviour?

Robin Actually that's quite difficult to do. In fact the book on the first Timberlawn research was called *No Single Thread* just because the researchers couldn't really find a way of expressing simply what unified all their different findings about these families. So we'll just have to take the different aspects one by one. And what I will be telling you is my *own* attempt to put together everything I've learned from many different sources – not only the research studies, but also almost forty years of working to help individuals and families improve their level of health, as well as experience and discussion with colleagues and friends, the family I grew up in, and the family I've been part of as a father. And, of course, what I have understood through my own struggle to become more healthy.

John Well, what is this well-kept secret?

Robin I want to add one more thing before we start off on that. It's this: in trying to describe excellent mental health, and compare it with ill-health, and with the 'average' health in between that most of us enjoy most of the time . . . it's difficult not to talk as if they are quite different from one another, and inhabited by different people. But, in fact, our level of health is changing all the time. We all feel more healthy in our better moments, when we are 'in a good mood', when things are going well, when we feel loved and valued, when we have done our best. And we can all feel less healthy under stress, when our usual sources of support are removed, when we have 'let ourselves down', when we 'get out of bed on the wrong side'. Also, our level of health is not the same in all areas of our functioning. A person who is 'average' overall may be outstandingly healthy in some respects, even though functioning poorly in others.

John And obviously the overall level can change over time, too. Otherwise you'd be out of a job.

Robin I suspect that's the reason for your interest in the subject – as mine was when I came into my profession. You'd like to know *how* to become more healthy!

John Spot on, squire. Can't wait. So if you're finished with all the provisos and qualifications and modifications and caveats . . . please do tell me about these more healthy people and their families. What's the most striking thing about them?

Robin These particularly healthy families are unusually positive in their attitude to life and other people. In general, they give the impression of enjoying themselves, enjoying each other, and especially of reaching out and being friendly to the people around them.

John This will disappoint the British press. So they're nice.

Robin Very much so. On one visit to Timberlawn I took part in their research by watching videotapes of families showing different levels of health, to act as a 'rater' and compare and score them. Of course, the researchers couldn't tell me which they considered to be the most healthy because that would have prejudiced me and spoiled the results, but the differences were very obvious. It was the same with some healthy families that colleagues studied here in England. Whenever I've watched videotapes of such families, I've found myself thinking how enjoyable it would be to live next door to them. You can't help feeling warm and friendly in response to the way they behave. And, in fact, the research shows that they are particularly valued members of their communities.

John Does this mean they get ripped off easily? I mean the world can be a very tough place. Being too open, too optimistic about people can be unrealistic.

Robin Optimistic isn't really the right word because an optimist, or a pessimist, is someone who sees the world in a one-sided way. But one measure of health is the extent to which people see the world as it is, without distorting it to suit their own imaginations, and members of healthy families are in fact very realistic. They know people can be good and bad, so they're not easily deceived. But they accept people as they are, taking the rough with the smooth. And they'll tend to give the benefit of the doubt to people who appear unfriendly at first. They'll reach out to strangers in an open and accepting way and won't immediately withdraw if they don't get a warm response back.

John So, if the seemingly unfriendly neighbour is just a bit *shy*, or has had bad experiences in the past and is just being extra careful . . . that shyness or caution will be overcome by the friendly attitude being offered.

Robin Yes. So these families get positive responses from everyone because their behaviour brings out the best in people.

John But what's so special about that? We all know that if we approach other people positively, they're more likely to be pleasant back. That's 'How to Make Friends and Influence People'.

Robin That's true, but the important thing about these healthy people is not that they're doing something completely different, but that they're able to do it so well and so consistently. What's unusual about them is the *extent* to which they're open and friendly, and also how *natural* it seems to be for them to behave in this way.

John You mean, they're not trying especially hard to be friendly or well mannered?

Robin Exactly, it just doesn't seem like an effort for them. You don't get the impression that they're putting on an act in order to get a rewarding response, as you sometimes do with people who've done courses like the Dale Carnegie training, or who are 'religious' in the sense of trying to be good people by sticking to the rules, by following the book. Really healthy people don't behave as if they're giving goodwill away in the hope of getting it back again – although of course they *do* get it back. It's much more as if they have such an abundance of well-being and enjoyment that they can just afford to be generous, like some very rich people who give large sums to charity knowing that they'll always have enough for themselves anyway so they can scatter it around a bit. It can be described as a 'philosophy of plenty'.

John And of course the reason for a lot of 'good behaviour' is that we want to gain and maintain people's approval. These people sound as though they feel so good they don't need to seek other folk's approval much – their friendliness isn't manipulative.

Robin No, it seems more spontaneous. They'll enjoy the approval of others, of course, but they don't have to set out to get it.

John So how does this very open, spontaneous and friendly behaviour compare with what the rest of us do?

Robin Well, first, take the worst case. In very *un*healthy families, relationships with other people tend to be very bad indeed. It's my experience – and most psychiatrists who are interested in looking below the surface and don't take everything that they are told at face value would agree – that where one or more members of the family are very sick in a psychological sense, that whole family often turns out to have a high level of negative emotions, both towards each other and towards outsiders.

John And where does that leave 'average' folk? Which includes the two of us, right?

Robin Indeed. Well taking 'average' families to be the vast majority of people in the middle of the range, as opposed to the few at the 'very healthy' or 'very unhealthy' ends of it, you won't see the extreme negative emotions I've just described – *except* perhaps *occasionally* under unusual stress or provocation. But you won't find the extraordinary positive attitudes of the very healthy families either – *although* ordinary families may be like that *sometimes*, when they're in a good mood, or on a particular day when things are going well, or when they 'rise to the occasion' in an emergency.

John So what does that mean? What are average families really like?

Robin They have an attitude to human nature which is *basically* a bit mistrustful. Of course, this is carefully disguised most of the time. But, underlying the outward expression of politeness or friendliness, there's nearly always a somewhat cautious, guarded, calculating attitude. It's as if we feel that the supply of good things is quite limited, so we have to be constantly on the look-out to see no one else takes our share. There's more of a 'what's in it for me' attitude, even with a spouse or a child, let alone a neighbour or a stranger. Relationships are fundamentally viewed almost as if they are business arrangements, with the people involved watching to make sure they're getting exactly as much out as they put in, or even hoping they might get a bit more, make a little profit.

John Yes, well it's not particularly pleasant to admit, but I've begun to realise that that's how I operate most of the time – unless I'm in a very good mood. Most days I try to be reasonably friendly and encouraging to other people, but if I don't fairly rapidly get some positive feedback, I have no inclination to continue being 'nice'. I just switch off and preserve a minimal courtesy. And again, as you describe, when I'm under a lot of stress, I notice I get very 'business-like' in my personal relationships: 'Now I've done this, and this, and that, what have you done?' Still, I suppose these attitudes just get handed down the generations. Most people I know can remember their parents saying: 'After all I've done for you . . .' or 'You'll appreciate me when I've gone . . .' But you're saying the really healthy families just don't do this.

Robin They don't seem to keep score, make accounts, or keep an eye on the emotional books to make sure they balance. As I said, they behave as if they have such an abundance of goodwill and enjoyment that they can give freely just because they *feel* like doing so, without any element of calculation.

John So . . . that's the first characteristic of these extremely healthy families. What's the second?

Robin The second important feature is a lot more surprising. I remember that when I first read about it, it gave me quite a shock, and it was a while before I got used to the idea. The 'love' these families have in such abundance is rather different from what the rest of us mean by the word.

John How so?

Robin Well, one meaning of 'love' is a desire for closeness. But closeness can mean two things. It can mean enjoyment of intimacy or it can mean dependency, feelings of being attached to another person in such a way that we find it quite hard to do without them. Indeed, for some people, it can even mean clinging, needing each other badly all the time, with a lot of suffering when the other person isn't around – which, of course, causes possessiveness and jealousy.

John So what's so surprising about the 'love' of the healthy families?

Robin It involves closeness *and* distance. They're capable of great intimacy and affection; but they also feel self-sufficient and confident and free, so they don't need each other desperately. When they're apart, they can cope perfectly well; indeed, they can enjoy themselves thoroughly!

John They don't 'miss' each other?

Robin Well, it all depends what you mean by 'miss'. They'll certainly remember the partner warmly; they'll enjoy thinking about them and the good feelings that arouses. But they won't 'miss' them in the sense of feeling miserable, of not being able to enjoy the other good things which are there in front of them at the moment.

John So to what extent are they really emotionally independent, in the sense of not 'needing' each other?

Robin The happiness the relationship brings is a luxury, a bonus. So the rest of their life isn't spoiled by fear it might go wrong, by worry about how they would manage if they lost their partner. And of course, the more you can enjoy life and feel confident when you're on your own, the more interesting a person you become, and the more you have available to share with the partner when you meet up again.

John And again, if a couple *are* emotionally independent, when they're *together* they won't feel constricted by each other's needs – they won't have to be careful what they say or do in case it threatens those needs – so they'll be freer to be themselves.

Robin And that's the same as giving the other members of the family the space to do their own thing too, so they don't hang around each other like dogs around a dinner table, worried they might miss something.

John Right. So what effect does this have on intimacy?

Robin Well, just because they *can* take space for themselves when they feel like it, without their loved ones trying to cling to them or make them feel guilty, it feels safe to give themselves to great closeness and intimacy at other times.

John You mean there's no fear that if they get too close, they won't be able to separate again, and get their independence back afterwards.

Robin Exactly. It looks paradoxical at first, but really it's obvious that the more 'separateness' you put on one side of the scales, the more 'togetherness' you can put on the other side.

John Whereas the more you 'need' other people, the more you have to control them?

Robin Inevitably. By contrast, the more confident you are in your ability to cope on your own, the less you need to control your partner. You can enjoy each other, instead of just feeling needy and worrying they won't give you what you want! And then all this enjoyment will sustain you both, and give you even more confidence when you're apart. An upward spiral, instead of a downward one, a 'vicious circle' based on clinging dependence.

John Can you describe this dependence spiral a bit more?

Robin Well, when a relationship is based on anxious need, each partner will be trying to hold onto the other by showing they can't do without them. For this to be convincing, they mustn't appear to enjoy themselves much when they're apart. So they give up more and more of their separate interests and friends, which gradually *makes* them more needy and helpless!

John Giving up their independent activities increasingly paralyses them?

Robin And the relationship itself becomes more and more constricted and boring.

John I remember encountering this idea of emotional independence when I was first in your group in 1975 and being, well . . . almost appalled that needing someone desperately was not considered the touchstone of true love!

Robin Do you remember what appalled you?

John Well, first of all, the equation of true love with deep emotional need seemed almost sacred. I had a huge emotional commitment to the idea. And yet it had never been taught to me, never spelled out. It was part of the conditioning that I'd received from my lower middle-class English background. Then, the alternative – a more separate and emotionally self-confident attitude – seemed positively callous. Nothing to do with 'love' at all!

Robin That's what I meant when I said some of this stuff seems shocking. It's how I felt when I read the very first study of exceptional health that I ever came across when I was still a student thirty-five years ago. To illustrate the point, the article mentioned that when a husband or wife in one of these families died, the other partner would mourn the loss very deeply for a time, but would then recover well . . . and would build new relationships and continue life without much difficulty. I remember I found the thought painful; it struck a chill into me. I sensed that it must be true; but it took me a long time to come round to the idea that it was actually very healthy.

John It all strikes at the idea of romantic love, doesn't it? Being 'made for each other', 'I'd die without you', 'You're the only one in the world for me' . . . all that kind of thing.

Robin Yes. Some couples in therapy will bitterly resist, for *years* even, this idea that it's possible to be really independent *and* also deeply involved with one another, because they find it so hard to accept that the two aspects can go together.

John Well now, what implications does 'emotional independence' have for fidelity? Do people who need each other less, play around more?

Robin My experience of more healthy couples is that they are more committed – but from choice. They don't play around because they don't want to, and one reason for that is that they *could if they wanted to*. As the actor Paul Newman said when asked why he seemed to be so committed to his wife, Joanne Woodward: 'Why have hamburger out when you can have steak at home?' And the research findings support this. They show a pattern of long-term marital fidelity in the healthiest couples.

John Really.

Robin Which compares with one 1992 estimate of infidelity in the British population as a whole – most of whom will be mid-range – of at least 40 per cent for women and 75 per cent for men . . .

John I know you think fidelity is important. But why? Is it because infidelity inevitably leads to lying, which destroys trust and intimacy?

Robin Lying means you can't be open, can't be fully yourself, and that obviously makes real intimacy impossible. If people are really healthy, they will therefore be straight about other attractions they may feel. And because they aren't possessive and clinging, there would be no reason why feeling 'turned on' by members of the opposite sex other than their partner should cause problems; indeed, I would expect it to enhance the relationship, make them more aware of, and turned on by each other. But actually having another sexual relationship is another matter, because this would prevent either relationship from reaching its full possibility. It's *possible* to ride two motorbikes at the same time – you see it done in circuses sometimes – but not as well or as enjoyably as you can ride one! So I would expect more healthy couples to make a choice, not out of guilt or fear of the partner's reaction, but because the existing relationship is so rich and they want to preserve it and make it richer.

John Interesting. Well I'm not going to try to argue the merits of emotional dependence, because I've been so completely converted to your point of view, that all I seem to observe now is how much unhappiness the idealisation of dependence brings. Just take the Great Love Stories – *Romeo and Juliet*, *La Traviata*, *Anna Karenina*, *Carmen*, *Antony and Cleopatra*, *Aida*, *Doctor Zhivago*, *Tristan and Isolde*, *Brief Encounter*. Mention them to people and a dreamy radiance passes across their face and they say: 'Oh, they're wonderful aren't they, so romantic.'

Well, they're *not* wonderful. They are tales of almost
unmitigated misery. There's not ten minutes of good, everyday
happiness and fun in any of them. The lovers usually get one
dollop of over-the-top ecstasy and apart from that it's
wall-to-wall suffering. They get stabbed, walled up in tombs,
they throw themselves under trains, or commit suicide with
asps, they poison themselves and die of consumption or
renounce each other in agony. They're convinced they can only
find happiness with one other person, whom they
deliberately choose on grounds of unavailability. So, Doctor,
why do you think all this dependence and its consequent
suffering is equated with true love?

Robin Well, after all, the first love we experience, for our
mothers, *is* like that. At the beginning of our lives we *are*
completely dependent, so we do suffer badly if mother isn't
there when we need her. And though we'll naturally always
need love and support, if we don't grow out of this kind of
childish demand we'll go on treating our lovers in the same
way, trying to make them care for us like parents and feeling
threatened when they don't.

John And this kind of love makes us feel 'special', doesn't it?
As babies do, with all that exclusive attention. But really healthy

families obviously don't believe that suffering adds significance to their lives.

Robin No. As they're not so needy, they won't need to justify childish demands by suffering terribly when they aren't met.

John Now, let me ask you something that has puzzled me a lot. Even the healthiest people are occasionally going to need emotional support to get through some particularly difficult period. And being healthy they won't have any problem about asking for it when they do need it, and their partner, being healthy, won't have any problem about giving it to them. So what's the difference between this, and people 'clinging' to each other?

Robin If they're healthy, both partners can ask straightforwardly for support when they need it, and can accept a refusal with good grace when the partner sometimes can't provide it. The relationship isn't based on pretence, on imagination. There isn't a struggle going on – as there is with less healthy people – where each is trying to manipulate the partner into meeting their own demands, while avoiding feeling obliged to give anything back by each trying to show that they are the most needy. Most of the time, healthy people will be able to get support, and give it back, whenever it's required. That's precisely *why* they don't have to cling and demonstrate desperate need to get their requirements met.

John This is why they seem to get over a bereavement and remarry quicker than less healthy people?

Robin Basically, yes. But there are several factors at work here. First, because of their warmth and friendliness, they'll have a wide circle of friends, a big emotional support-system, so they won't feel suddenly marooned with all their supplies of love cut off. Second, the grief they suffer is more likely to be due to compassion for the partner, rather than concern about themselves, because they already have the confidence of knowing that they can manage well on their own.

John Yes, but surely they'll feel an even deeper grief, just because the relationship has been so exceptionally happy.

Robin Well there's an odd paradox here. It's often easier to accept the loss of a relationship or an experience that has been very good than it is to recover from an unsatisfactory one.

John Ah! I think I know what you mean. In the past I've sometimes found it difficult to let go of relationships which have never really worked because . . . it's as though there's been a compulsion to return to them again and again just to prove that they *could* work!

Robin Exactly. Whereas, if something has been good, and you feel happy and fulfilled even thinking about it, it can be easier to accept that you can't go on having it forever. Because you've had so much already, and the good memory of that sustains you! For example, when my wife, Prue, died five years ago, I found that the sorrow I felt about losing her also had a joyful quality in it when I remembered the good life that we had had together. It not only made the sorrow bearable, but in some ways it was like another good experience of her.

John . . . You know, when Graham Chapman died, I found myself reviewing my Monty Python days and realising, much more clearly than I had for years, just how enjoyable they'd been.

Robin Indeed. Paradoxically it's easier to let go of a relationship that's been really good, because the memory of it is positive; so you don't feel guilty about it not working and you're not still trying to put it right. And again very healthy people find it easier to grieve than we mid-range folk. Indeed, they may feel an even deeper grief just because they can go unreservedly down into the emotions to do with loss . . . and of course, that will mean that they will recover more quickly and be up and off again, getting on with life and enjoying it much sooner than average people might think seemly. Because, as we said in *Families*, it's by mourning a loss that you recover from it.

John Whereas people who are very frightened of sadness may use all their defences to avoid feeling it, and therefore take years and years to get over the loss?

Robin If indeed they ever do at all.

John Could you tell me how far you feel you've recovered from Prue's death?

Robin About two years after her death I felt a big increase in liveliness and enjoyment and realised that, as the books on bereavement tell you to expect, the shock had led to a temporary depression of my energy in a physical sense. But as you know, we tried together to face the likelihood of her death, without shrinking from the pain of it, right from the beginning of her illness two years earlier. Because of this I seemed prepared psychologically when it came and coped with it much better than I had expected. As I said, the pleasure of the good life we had experienced together seemed to counteract the grief. Sometimes I would feel myself sliding towards very negative feelings, but then I'd realise that these were all really forms of self-pity, and therefore completely destructive. They were all about myself and nothing to do with her. So I didn't give them any encouragement.

John But hang on a minute Robin. If grieving is the natural human reaction to loss and the way of recovering from it, how do you distinguish between this kind of sadness . . . and self-pity?

Robin Grief is when you accept the loss. You don't shrink from the natural suffering it causes you and you're concerned more about the person who has died than about yourself. You let the pain act on you, let it change you. Then it forces you to let go. By contrast, self-pity is what you feel when you *don't* accept the loss. Instead of letting the experience change *you* you're wanting the *world* to be different; you want the clock to be put back as if the loss hadn't happened. Unfortunately, a lot of books on bereavement don't make that difference clear; they can make it appear as if self-pity is a virtue.

John This may seem an odd question, but . . . did you ever feel that you should have been suffering *more*?

Robin I think I might have done if I hadn't been so familiar with the idea that you don't have to be endlessly incapacitated by grief. But I think some people were a bit shocked that I seemed to be suffering less than they'd expected!

John You mean, they thought you were being callous because you weren't making more fuss?

Robin Yes, and I'm pretty sure their disapproval would have affected me – perhaps made me feel guilty – and pushed me towards wallowing in self-pity, thinking it was the right thing to do.

John Did many people disapprove of your lack of suffering?

Robin I remember *you* certainly didn't! In fact *most* people were pleased for me, even if they were a bit surprised. Perhaps it helped them feel they might be able to cope when they came to face a similar loss themselves. And I felt these people cared about *me* rather than about themselves and about justifying their beliefs.

John Why do you think some people didn't approve?

Robin Those who were shocked that I wasn't suffering more – the ones I knew well that is – were people I already knew to be rather cut off from their feelings, scared of facing up to their own death, or of losing their partner, so my situation put the wind up them. If I'd been more upset, I think *they* would have felt better . . . because they would have been able to keep all the feelings of loss focused on me and away from themselves . . . and *then* they could concentrate on feeling sorry for me instead of worried about how they would cope when they came to it.

John Ah. Feelings of loss were so frightening to them, that they wanted you to carry all such feelings for them?

Robin Yes. In fact, when I was with these people, I tended to feel worse. They clearly thought they were 'supporting' me by talking about how terrible it must be, and feeling sorry for me . . . but I experienced it as if they were 'laying a trip on me'. So being with them was a real struggle. In fact, if I resisted their 'support', it seemed to make them very uncomfortable. Because then they had to deal with the uncomfortable feelings I wouldn't carry for them, and they couldn't avoid noticing they couldn't handle them.

John So there was a kind of struggle between you to see who was going to carry the uncomfortable feelings – and they felt bad if you wouldn't shoulder them all.

Robin That's how it appeared.

John OK. Now, where are we? Prue's death came up because you said that the second characteristic of the extremely healthy families is that they love each other in an unusually independent way. Now, what's the next characteristic of these lucky people?

Robin Well, the next two features are connected, and we should deal with them together. They're both to do with how decisions are taken in the family.

John How the power is distributed?

Robin In a sense, yes. Now the first of these features is the position of very clear authority that the parents take in the family. There's no question about the fact that they're in charge, that they're responsible for the children, and that the children have to do what they're told, ultimately.

John I'm surprised. It sounds very old-fashioned.

Robin Now listen to the second half of it. In these families, it's anything but 'children must be seen and not heard'. The children are always consulted very fully – even the youngest one – before the parents take a decision. Everyone in the family is encouraged to have their say. In fact, the children are free to discuss not just the decisions, but even how the parents use their authority in taking them! So, as you guess, children in these families have pretty outspoken views, and the parents enjoy and approve of that. It's the way they want the family to be.

John But if the whole family *can't* work out an agreement . . .

Robin . . . or if there's an emergency, the children are expected to shut up and do what they're told when it comes to the crunch.

John How do the children feel about those occasions?

Robin The striking thing is that, perhaps just because they're normally so fully consulted, they are prepared to accept the parents' authority. Even when it really goes against their wishes.

John But I bet they have to learn that. It's not a kid's instinctive response, is it?

Robin No, that's right. When children are very young, they'll do their best to manipulate their parents if they can get away with it. They'll try to get one parent on their side. But with these very healthy families the coalition between the parents is so strong that the children can't divide them. Manipulation doesn't work, so the kids can relax in the knowledge that they can give their opinion but must hand over the responsibility of the final decision to their parents. Even working with families I saw professionally, the children would always accept the parents' authority once I had helped them to take charge in this way, and appeared happy that they now knew where they stood. Indeed, when asked what they thought the parents should do to solve the family problem they had all come about, they would often request this stronger alliance themselves.

John So, the children can express exactly how they feel, but they aren't given too much power.

Robin Not more than they are ready for. And that's one reason why they grow up healthy in a psychological sense. Children who can 'divide and conquer' by playing one parent off against the other get frightened, not only of the power it gives them, but also of the damage they might be allowed to do to their parents' relationship and to the family's stability. So they end up insecure and anxious, while the fact they've not experienced consistent control makes it hard for them to develop self-discipline.

John Well, let me ask you more about this strong parental coalition. How is the power distributed between the man and the woman?

Robin One of the most interesting findings is that in these families, Mum and Dad share power pretty equally.

John This will please the feminists and all their supporters.

Robin And the masculinists, I hope. What may please them even more is that the Timberlawn research team has found big changes in male and female roles and relationships as time has passed. In their first book, back in 1976, they reported that there wasn't one couple which didn't show the traditional pattern of very different male and female gender roles, with the man but not the woman as the wage-earner. But in their most recent report on very healthy families, studying couples born in the early sixties, they found that two-thirds of the women were working and some took the more executive role in the partnership.

John In that case, answer this point, Mr Shrink. I've heard you say in the past that you've noticed that it's best when the *father* takes the main responsibility for good order and discipline in the family.

Robin Yes, for a long time I seemed to believe contradictory things about this! Sometimes I would treat family problems as if I believed the father should be in charge – in the sense of his having the casting vote when there was no other way of settling a disagreement. I reached that conclusion because, when we began treating the whole family by seeing them all together, almost half the problems they came with were quickly solved once we got the father to take over the main responsibility for control and discipline from the mother, but couldn't be solved unless we brought that change about. Yet with some families, I'd act as if I believed the parents should share the power equally.

John So, intuitively you handled different families differently, but you couldn't explain why?

Robin Yes, and it was the research on the exceptionally healthy families which cleared up my confusion. It explained that both of these apparently contradictory approaches could be right. Which one worked best depended on the level of mental health of the family. The research made it clear that even a rigid military-style hierarchy, with either the father or the mother as a kind of dictator, is at least an improvement on the terrible chaos and confusion that reigns in the most unhealthy families – the ones professionals call 'borderline' or 'multi-problem'.

John Because you've got to have some kind of order before you can sort anything out.

Robin Yes. But of course that authoritarian behaviour should only be a half-way stage to something better. I realised that the families where I got good results from putting the father in charge were the more disorganised, sicker ones which, for example, I had encountered frequently in my work in poor districts of the East End of London. Though, of course, I treated some professional families of this kind too . . .

John Newspaper owners, dictators, film directors . . .

Robin Often people at the head of huge organisations, certainly, like government ministers and captains of industry.

John People who've been driven to seek great power, because that power enables them to avoid experiences that they couldn't cope with. That is, experiences that would force them to acknowledge their psychological problems?

Robin Certainly. One of the great advantages of being the big panjandrum, totally in charge of everything and everybody, is that *you can always have your own way.* You're *never frustrated.* And if you are really a grown-up baby and unable to cope with the slightest frustration, then being powerful at work where subordinates dance attendance on you makes you feel strong and shelters you from having to face that childish weakness.

John So would you try to put someone like that in charge of the family?

Robin I'd probably encourage them to take more family responsibility, because such people often leave all that to the mother, and behave at home like another child themselves. Then the mother gets no real support, becomes overloaded and the children take advantage. Of course, I would have to help the father get more genuine confidence and control of himself first, before he could play more part.

John So some of the families you saw were chaotic and needed someone to be put clearly in charge.

Robin Yes, but many of the families which came to see me were much more healthy than that. They would be complaining of more minor problems; the family was often well organised and efficient and its members quite successful in the outside world. But often everyone was over-inhibited and simply not *enjoying* life. They weren't having much fun. So with families like these, the mid-range ones, I had to concentrate on getting them to relax the rules and to develop a more democratic structure, a freer and less rigid way of operating. And that often meant helping the parents to be more equal and to share power.

John So, instinctively, you tried to establish order where there was chaos; and then, once order was established, you tried to introduce more democracy. It sounds like a history of politics.

Robin Well I think the same principles apply with groups of any size, yes. As we'll be finding out later on, in Chapter 3!

John I want to know a little more about this balance between the parents. What does the research say about the way that the mother helps a child's development, compared with the father?

Robin At the risk of stating the obvious, my clinical experience certainly obliges me to say that, in general, mothers seem better at giving nurture, support and comfort, at accepting and loving their children unconditionally so that they grow up to accept and value themselves. And fathers, in general, seem better at giving a more objective, detached love which is more conditional, in the sense of requiring the child to develop self-discipline and to learn to fit in socially. I think this follows logically from the fact that in most families, the mother has from the beginning a more intimate relationship with the children, and the father is emotionally more distant and living more in the outside world. But there are many exceptions; a minority of mothers are fatherly, and some men more motherly than most women. So I'm only talking in a general way.

John Yes, but does the healthy family research say anything else about this?

Robin Some of the findings are rather unexpected. For example, in one study, the autonomy of the children – that is, their confidence and ability to function independently – was linked particularly with the *mother's* role.

John Really. Fostering independence in the outside world?

Robin Yes. If she had achieved a high level of autonomy herself, this would give permission to the children to follow her example.

John 'Autonomy' meaning the opposite of 'dependence'?

Robin More or less. But the research showed that even if the mother wasn't very autonomous, she could still do a good job of raising confident and independent children, if she got enough love and support herself.

John So a fairly dependent parent can raise children more autonomous than themselves, provided they have a supportive relationship?

Robin Yes they can.

John Good. Well I hope that's what I'm doing!

Robin You see, if you're prepared to acknowledge your personal problems, then those problems can be contained. And they don't spill over on to the children.

John I always find that thought encouraging, and quite an incentive, too! Now if the mother is especially linked with the children's autonomy, what does the father particularly influence?

Robin This bit of research found the father influenced the family's ability to communicate freely about their feelings, and therefore to solve problems. This ability to face up to conflicts seemed to depend on a general feeling of security, especially the confidence that it was safe to say what one truly felt, even if it might upset people. So families which were good at overcoming emotional difficulties turned out to have fathers who had a warm and spontaneous relationship with their children. Whereas the families that were bad at this had fathers who were usually rigid and distant.

John Well, I must say I'd have guessed things would be the other way round, with the mother having the greater effect on communication, and the father on autonomy.

Robin I think most people would. But it makes sense to me the way it is. The mother's example here is about *individual* autonomy; the father's takes this a step further, to include support for the autonomy of the family group as a whole.

John Well, that was a digression from the subject of how parental power is exercised in very healthy families, with the children having a very full say, but genuinely accepting the parents' ultimate authority just because they are so well consulted, and also because if they try to split the parental coalition, they fail. What's the next characteristic of these obnoxiously healthy families?

Robin They communicate well. They're straightforward – direct and open and honest with each other.

John Hardly a surprise. Ideally we'd all like to function like that, so perhaps the interesting part is – how do they manage it?

Robin Well, there are a number of reasons which of course partly interlock. First of all, in these healthy families, there's a belief that people's basic needs and drives are not evil! No human feeling needs to be a cause of shame. Therefore, the children experience no need to hide things, to confuse, distort, or otherwise cloud what they experience. Sexuality, anger, envy, they're all regarded as a natural part of human experience. Similarly – and the importance of this will be more obvious later – it's accepted that they'll feel ambivalence about people or events, including their parents – that is, positive and negative feelings about them at the same time.

John Is it as obvious as this: they learn to be open because they don't feel they have to hide anything?

Robin And also because these families have great respect for everybody's world view. Each person's subjective opinion is given house-room, and people are allowed to disagree. There's not some 'family view' that they all have to adhere to, like a 'party line' in politics.

John Obviously this is linked with the last characteristic, too: non-authoritarian parents.

Robin And then, third, these families manage to resolve their conflicts as they arise. So that's another reason not to be frightened to disagree with people, and to communicate what you really think . . .

John You mean, where families have a history of lingering, chronic resentment due to unresolved conflicts, family members will end up keeping their feelings to themselves so as not to make things worse? In fact, if you don't admit problems, they stay unexpressed and therefore unresolved.

Robin That's right. So in these healthy families with their open communication, everyone knows where they stand. They get a good idea of what others in the family want, how they feel, what they enjoy and what things they're unhappy about.

John And I suppose constantly hearing exactly how everyone else is feeling teaches them to understand others better. So they'll become good at tuning in to people's feelings.

Robin That's right. So they avoid many of the things that you see in less healthy families, like people speaking for each other, with everybody mind-reading everybody else and getting it wrong! All the research, like my own clinical experience, indicates that this freedom to be yourself, to express your innermost feelings is very characteristic of the best-functioning families.

John Well, it all sounds very nice. It's just a pity it isn't more interesting.

Robin Still, there is a slight surprise in all this. To an outsider listening to their conversation, very healthy families are less easy to understand than average ones.

John Less? Because?

Robin Their conversation is quicker, more complicated. They interrupt and finish each other's sentences. There are big jumps from one idea to another idea as though bits of the argument are missed out.

John But it's only outsiders that find it confusing?

Robin Exactly. The conversation isn't as tidy and logical and carefully structured as it can be with somewhat less healthy families, nearer the middle of the range. Ideas are coming so thick and fast that they keep interrupting and capping each other's statements. They can do that because everyone grasps what other people are trying to say before they've finished saying it.

John Because they understand each other so well.

Robin Right. So what looks like lack of control is actually a sign of their unusually good communication.

John I see. I think I was just beginning to wonder if these extremely healthy folk might seem just a tiny bit colourless, with all this suffocating honesty and goodwill. After all, they say that the Devil has all the best jokes.

Robin Sorry to disappoint you, but the individuals in these families are unusually alive, with fun and energy and wit and jokes and good humour. One of the research teams used a wonderful image to describe their impression while watching these very healthy families. They compared it with watching a three-ring circus!

John So much going on, and yet all somehow under control . . .

Robin That's exactly how they described it. Many different things happening, all at once, at full blast. Yet everyone taking it in their stride, despite the fact that to us it would seem to be on the edge of confusion.

John Well, I'm feeling confused, just trying to picture it. This is yet another of those reminders of my undistinguished position on the mental health ladder. If I ever got into the middle of this kind of family, I'd either have to take charge, calm things down and get a bit of order into proceedings . . . or I'd have to pop into a quick coma.

Robin Can you describe why?

John I think so. Anxiety. The first thought would be that the neighbours would complain. But it's not only that. I'd get anxious simply because there was so much going on, so many stimuli, so much energy, so much that could go wrong at any moment! In other words, I'd feel things were out of control.

Robin Interesting that you say that. It's probably how most mid-range people react. The better I've come to understand these findings, the more I've come to think that healthy people live more fully because they're able to use more of themselves. They seem able to handle comfortably parts of their personality that the rest of us – I mean more ordinary, mid-range people – are scared of, and therefore suppress, keep under tight control, keep the brakes on. I once suggested to the Timberlawn researchers that perhaps one big difference in very healthy people is that they can be more comfortable with their 'madness' than the rest of us. But of course, for them it isn't 'madness', but just the wilder, more spontaneous reactions that we keep under tight control in case they get out of hand. They can handle it all, and put it all to use.

John A 'circus' is a nice analogy for that – we can enjoy the excitement of seeing wild animals, because circus people know how to handle them. And my experience of therapy is that the bits of myself I thought were 'slightly strange', and therefore better kept nailed down and out of sight, turned out to be just those qualities I needed and always thought I lacked.

Robin I think everyone in therapy has that experience. For example, there was quite a strong streak of violence in my family background. My paternal grandfather certainly had quite violent moods and could be scary in expressing them, and my father held his feelings tightly in check but at times would explode. So I grew up feeling very uncomfortable about anger, and tried not to be like either of them. When I had therapy later in life I realised how aggressive I was underneath the surface, and as I accepted these feelings they turned into a powerful source of energy.

John Well, what is it about the upbringing of extremely healthy folk that allows them to live in a circus without feeling anxiety?

Robin It's presumably because there's been so much trust and confidence and mutual support. When you're given a lot of freedom and encouragement, yet also feel contained and supported, you learn to express your energy outwardly, fully and freely, without fearing the consequences.

John You mean children don't have to suppress spontaneity for fear of 'upsetting people'.

Robin Yes. People give each other space, allow them to be what they are and develop their own unique personalities, as far as that's possible without encroaching on the rights of others. They're not forced tightly into a mould of family values and expectations.

John That feels very right. Sometimes when I get very excited about something, I notice I feel almost as if I'm being physically squeezed, as though there's a kind of inward pressure on me. Is that because I never really learned that it was quite safe to let all my energy out?

Robin Probably. And that's a particular problem in Britain, isn't it, especially among middle-class people who are expected to keep a tight rein on emotions.

John So . . . these healthy families have very good, open communication, even though it looks a bit rowdy and out of control to normal people. You know, I'm getting a teensy-weensy bit bored with hearing how wonderful these people are. Is there any slightly bad news about them – that they die young, or get dropsy, or support Arsenal? Even a tendency to early hair loss would help me through this little fit of envy. Go on, say something about them that will cheer us all up. Make it up if you have to. *Please* . . .

Robin Over 90 per cent of them can fly.

John . . . No, I wanted you to make something up that was . . . oh, never mind. Well now Robin, what's the next characteristic that these admirable, friendly, joyous, generous-hearted, bandy-legged, poxy little slimeballs display?

Robin Well, the next feature is they're very realistic and practical, which I've already mentioned briefly. They see the world more or less as it is, rather than living in dreams and fantasies about themselves, and about other people.

John Ah! Are you implying they're not very idealistic?

Robin Well it all depends what you mean by 'idealistic'. They have a strong sense of values, but what they will be trying to achieve will be realistic. And because they're so down-to-earth, they'll be more likely to achieve what they're aiming for. For two reasons. Not only will they want things they have a good chance of getting, but they will also see clearly how to go about getting them.

John So what's the reason that they are able to perceive the world so clearly?

Robin Well, we have to go back to the idea of mental maps that we talked about in *Families* – the pictures or models or theories we form in our heads to guide us in dealing with the world. If the map in your head is a really accurate representation of the world around you, and where you are in that world . . . you're going to know how to get from A to B.

John You mean if you're clear, say, about how much power you have in a situation, you're not going to miscalculate by thinking you're more powerful than you really are; at the same time, you're not going to underestimate your strength and miss out on something that you could get.

Robin That's the idea. Take emotions, for example. If there's anger, or fear, or sadness, or envy around . . . healthy folks are clear about how much of it is theirs, and how much is other people's. So they behave appropriately. They don't 'lay trips' on other people – which can set off those downward spirals of bad behaviour which make life much more difficult.

John To use our favourite bit of jargon, they don't 'deny' any of their emotions, and then 'project' them onto other people.

Robin Right.

John But what's the reason that these healthies don't do this, when most of us do – at least a bit?

Robin Well, if you remember, emotions get denied because, as a child grows up, it discovers that these emotions are not acceptable to the family. But one characteristic of healthy families is that all kinds of emotions can be admitted and faced up to. They know that 'there's good and bad in all of us', as my uncle Fred used to put it. So, in healthy families, members can acknowledge their own anger, or jealousy, or sexual feelings without fearing they'll be rejected. And they feel free to discuss what they and others are feeling. The researchers have a marvellous way of describing the effects of this. They refer to the process as a 'powerful training programme, in defining where one's skin ends and another's begins'.

John So their perception of what's going on between people will be accurate.

Robin Yes. And as they can take responsibility for their own feelings, they don't try to blame other people for them. So they are bound to get on better with one another . . .

John I work with someone from a healthy family like this, and she is quicker to admit mistakes than anyone I've met. Party politics would be a dead duck if these people were in charge.

Robin And of course, if you can see your own limitations, you'll be more understanding of the limitations of others. So you won't start thinking they're more wonderful than they are and therefore finish up being disappointed in them. And you don't exaggerate the bad things either, so you won't behave in a provocative way yourself as if you're expecting trouble, and thereby create the trouble unnecessarily.

John Right. So, to sum up, the children in really healthy families grow up knowing all their emotions are fundamentally acceptable, and therefore gain a very realistic perception of the world, which enables them to deal with it really effectively. Sounds pretty good to me. OK, Doctor, what comes next? And how many more characteristics are you going to give?

Robin At this stage, only one more. It's the remarkable ability the most healthy families have to deal with change. Most of us find anything more than a moderate degree of change disturbing and stressful. But these families not only seem at ease with quite big changes, but even seem to enjoy them, indeed to thrive on them.

John You mean, they don't have a problem with adjusting their mental maps fast enough to stay in step with what's happening.

Robin Whereas most of us can't keep changing our ideas and expectations fast enough, so things take us by surprise, and we tend to get a bit off-balance and disappointed that events never quite turn out the way we expected.

John So again, what do they know that we don't?

Robin Well, do you remember from *Families* what makes it easier for people to cope with stressful change?

John I think so. If we suffer a really big, jolting change, we're obviously not able to adapt to the new circumstances immediately. Similarly, if we've had too many smaller-sized changes too close together, we may also feel overwhelmed. Either way, we need three things to help us cope. First, there's rest – a period of time when we are relieved of as many demands as possible, so that we can catch up with the backlog of readjustment.

Robin Good.

John Second, as we have to adapt our mental map to the changed world around us, we'll need advice and information from people who've been through a similar experience and know how to cope with it.

Robin Two out of three. And third and most important?

John Emotional support. In the same way that a child can be calmed just by being held or even by being near its mother, we get something incredibly important, but almost impossible to define, from being around people who love us – that's from simply being in their presence, over and above their looking after us or giving us advice.

Robin Well, let's take them one at a time. The healthy families will be clear about their emotional needs so they won't have any hesitation about stopping to take a rest if they need to, or asking for help and advice when they want that. But I think it's the last of these three factors, the degree of emotional support that they can draw on, which mainly accounts for the ease with which they deal with change. The researchers noted three different kinds of support that all contributed to this resilience. The first was the good relationships that the family members enjoyed with each other. The second came from their good connections in the community, due to their friendly behaviour in the past. And third, they seem to be particularly good at drawing support from the biggest system of all . . .

John You talk in riddles, Sire.

Robin Just preparing you for a particularly important nugget of information. For me, the most striking finding in the research is that the most healthy families of all gain great emotional support from some kind of transcendent value system. By that the researchers meant a set of values and beliefs which gives a sense of meaning and purpose going beyond just the welfare of themselves, or even of their family.

John Religion you mean?

Robin Often the value system came from that, yes. Many of these families were committed members of a church, or held to one of the traditional religious beliefs. But it didn't have to be that. Sometimes the 'transcendent' values were not so much religious as connected with some broader humanitarian cause. What seemed to matter was that their greatest source of value came from something much bigger than themselves, beyond even their family, something which provided a feeling of meaning and purpose which could survive loss and change of all kinds. Including the death of loved ones – even of a spouse, or a child – or the thought of their own eventual extinction.

John So, they can handle even the nastiest kinds of change, because they're plugged into a larger and more permanent source of emotional support than just human relationships can provide?

Robin Yes. People can lose all their loved ones, as in a war or a terrible event like the Holocaust. Yet among those at least fortunate enough to escape death, many are severely damaged emotionally by a devastating experience like that, while a few – amazingly – are somehow even able to grow and gain strength by the way they engage with it. They are somehow carried through it all by the values they live by – what people usually call 'faith'.

John Victor Frankl, the psychiatrist, went through Auschwitz and Dachau and realised that many people, who had been lucky to survive, had been sustained by a faith which enabled them to retain a sense of meaningfulness even during such an appalling experience. So he devoted the rest of his life to developing a method of therapy – logotherapy – which concerned itself with helping people to discover such a sense of meaning for themselves.

Robin Another psychologist, Bruno Bettelheim, also went through a horrific time in a Nazi concentration camp. He coped and grew through it too, and went on to apply what he had learned to the treatment of children who had been severely damaged psychologically. His books are immensely moving and inspiring.

John . . . I've suddenly remembered what you once said, when I was in your group – that when patients began to show interest in some values beyond themselves, it was usually an indication that they'd started on the road to a healthier way of functioning.

Robin Yes, I did find that. And it was all the more striking because I was still quite hostile to religious ideas at the time I first noticed it.

John Do you think it's possible for someone to be very mentally healthy without the sense that there's something bigger and more important than themselves?

Robin I think it's impossible, almost by definition. But this is such an important question that I'd like to deal with it later on, when we talk about beliefs and value systems in Chapter 4.

John OK. Well, we've just been talking about the ability of these extremely healthy families to cope with change. So we've listed all the main characteristics of these families. Now, being only a mid-range creature myself, I feel the need for a nice, clear, organised, slightly over-orderly recapitulation of what you've said. So I'm going to attempt that, even though some readers of *Families* found my summings-up irritating. I suppose they were the very healthy ones.

Robin No, *they* just skipped them.

John And appreciated, of course, that some readers found them useful. Here we go then. Attention, all anal-retentives!

The first feature of these Happy Valley Folk is their basic positive and friendly attitude; the second is their degree of emotional independence, which allows them both intimacy and separateness, and to move easily between the two; the third is the family structure, with the parents in a strong and equal coalition, prepared to lay down the law if they have to, but always consulting very fully with the children first; the next is the family's very free and open communication, based on the children's sense that no feelings they experience are unacceptable or forbidden, giving a feeling of freedom and lots of fun and high spirits; the fifth is their ability to perceive the world very clearly, based on the fact that they can accept all their own feelings and therefore don't need to project them onto other people; and finally they can cope quite readily with change that would floor the rest of us, because they enjoy an extraordinary emotional support derived from a transcendent value system. Have I missed anything?

Robin No, that pretty well covers the main points.

John You know, I suddenly had a mental picture of all our readers staring at the ceiling, thinking 'Who on earth do I know who's like *that*?'

Robin Well, how many Olympic gold medallists do you know?

John OK. Now to put what you've been telling me into perspective, I want you to compare this very healthy family behaviour with both typical mid-range behaviour, and with positively unhealthy behaviour. Which should you deal with first?

Robin For clarity's sake let's start at the unhealthy end of the spectrum. Relationships in those families are very controlling and engulfing, with each family member behaving in a very demanding and possessive way towards the others. There's a lack of respect for any person's separate identity, because no one even knows what it means. They'll try to read each other's minds, and feel they have the right to probe into each other's affairs as much as they like.

John So presumably they have a very shaky sense of their own identity.

Robin Of course. Each one finds it hard to tell where their own personality ends and that of the next person begins.

John Or, in terms of mental maps, their individual maps are very unclear, with uncertain boundaries between their own emotions and everyone else's.

Robin That's right. They're not clear where their own edges are so they'll imagine, all the time, that others are experiencing feelings which are really their own, but which they're suppressing and denying.

John And if they deny certain feelings in themselves they'll project them onto the other family members, and then think the others are actually feeling them instead.

Robin And to make this chaotic situation even worse . . .
because everybody's boundaries are so fuzzy and uncertain,
all the family members are very vulnerable to emotional
'atmospheres' and easily soak up each other's feelings when
these become at all strong. Indeed, in families like this it is
regarded as a form of love to do so.

John So really no individual family member ever really knows
clearly what he or she is feeling.

Robin That's it. If anyone starts to have independent thoughts,
or doesn't follow the family 'party line', they'll be regarded
as traitors. Which means they'll experience violent disapproval
from other family members until they fall into line again. But
– and I can't emphasise this too strongly – they'll see this
possessiveness, this need to control each other, as something
positive . . . as 'love'.

John But will they in reality be experiencing many positive and
friendly feelings to others or to each other?

Robin It's what they understand by love, the best they can do.
But it's more a kind of desperate need for support and acceptance,
so it will show itself through a lot of demands, possessiveness,

jealousy. They're clinging together more out of fear of abandonment than the kind of love which seeks the welfare of others.

John Because they don't feel they can cope on their own? Clinging together gives some sense of security, like people adrift in a lifeboat?

Robin Yes, that's it. So it's not surprising that the onset of a breakdown in a member of such a family is usually connected with events which signify a separation of some kind. For example, becoming sexually mature, getting a girlfriend or a boyfriend, or leaving home for university, or for a job. Or, of course, a death in the family.

John So the great sin is to be different.

Robin Hang on. Not different but *separate*. Independent, autonomous, free . . .

John I don't get the distinction.

Robin Well, instead of being separate individuals with lives of their own, they end up playing roles which fit in with the needs of the family. For example, one of them may be the 'bad one', the scapegoat.

John Ah. The scapegoat's different, but not separate. Got it. Sorry.

Robin The situation is the complete opposite of the very healthy families, where all human emotions are acceptable. Here, in these unhealthy families, they can't admit to any imperfections in themselves, because no one ever gets the loving support and acceptance from others that would enable them to accept themselves. As a result, they feel deep down that they're worthless and hopeless, which means in turn that they create an impossibly demanding world for themselves, a world for which they can never feel good enough. So in order to feel better they try to turn that situation on its head by projecting all their faults onto others – sometimes onto a scapegoat in the family, sometimes onto some outside person or group.

John They have to blame each other constantly to try to feel good about themselves.

Robin So there's a game of 'pass the parcel' going on the whole time, with everyone trying to get rid of their own problems and weaknesses onto someone else. The ones who are less good at getting rid of the 'parcel' may end up with it on their own lap, carrying the blame for everything that goes wrong in the whole family, while everyone else can feel that any problems are absolutely nothing to do with them. Where this 'scapegoating' is extreme, the person cast in that role can end up in a mental hospital.

John . . . It's hard not to feel anger towards the family. But that's just joining in the paranoid system on the scapegoat's side. After all, they have no idea what they're doing, have they?

Robin Not really. Given their level of health, it all follows inevitably. They can't help it. And when you study them closely enough, you see that even the most destructive families are trying to preserve something good, even if it's at this terrible cost of loading all the blame and hate onto one individual who often ends up being the 'sick' one. They're all trying to keep the 'goodness' in the family totally disconnected from the 'badness' . . .

John Because they fear that otherwise the 'badness' will contaminate the 'goodness' and turn that into 'badness' as well?

Robin Yes. So when you ask the parents to come with the whole family for treatment they often won't bring the 'good' one for fear that member will be harmed. And interestingly there's also a core of altruism and self-sacrifice in the scapegoat's behaviour. It's a lot easier to work professionally with a family like this when you realise that the 'sick one' senses that playing their scapegoat role is often preventing even worse things from happening, like the destruction of the marriage and break-up of the family.

John And all of this occurs because on their mental maps the boundaries are so unclear?

Robin That's one factor. But all the other aspects of unhealthy family functioning are contributing.

John And they're the opposite, all the way down the line, of the very healthy characteristics?

Robin Yes. It's hardly necessary to go through each point, but, if the parental attitudes are rigid, negative and critical, the children will conceal their real feelings, communication will be restricted and there won't be much spontaneity and fun. There won't be a warm and strong parental coalition, and the children will be able to play one parent off against the other and won't get the clear, consistent control they need to develop confidence and self-discipline themselves. The parents will be jealous and possessive, which will make it hard for the children to grow away, make good relationships outside the family and establish their own independent lives – unless they make a violent break from the parents. And so on. The details are different in each case, but each failure adds to all the others, in a vicious spiral.

John OK. Well, now let's move on from the most unhealthy and talk about all the people in the middle. Ordinary persons. Not sick, not eccentrically healthy, but nice, 'normal', averagely pathological folk. Tell us about us, Robin.

Robin Well, it's easy enough to understand what 'normal' means once you've grasped the principles by which people function at the healthy and unhealthy ends of the scale. 'Normal' people are simply in between the two!

John We're somewhere on the road from one to the other.

Robin Yes. We've escaped from the confusion and fuzzy boundaries of the most unhealthy level and achieved a certain clarity about who and what we are. We can see other people as separate, with feelings of their own. And we've learned to control ourselves, to fit into society and play some part in it.

John 'We' are also the vast majority of people on the planet?

Robin Well, yes. Some societies show a higher level of mental health than others – we'll talk about that in Chapter 3. But in the developed nations at least, research suggests that there's about 20 per cent at the bottom of the scale who find life a major struggle. Then there's about 20 per cent up the other end who function well.

John Wait a moment. These are not the *exceptionally* healthy people you've been talking about.

Robin No. Probably only a quarter of this top 20 per cent function *exceptionally* well. The Timberlawn researchers called these 'optimal'.

John OK. So that leaves . . .

Robin The great mass of all the rest of us – the 60 per cent in the middle. The ones we call 'mid-range'.

John Which covers everyone from the folk who are having almost as much of a struggle as the least healthy, right up to the people who just fail to make it into the top 20 per cent?

Robin Yes.

John But can you really say anything useful about such a wide spectrum of people?

Robin You can make some generalisations, even though you have to allow for whether they are higher or lower in that mid-range part of the scale.

John OK. So is there a key idea to the general psychology of mid-range families?

Robin Yes. Rigidity.

John Well, you go on, and I'll try to relax and move up the spectrum a bit.

Robin Let's go back to the concept of people having mental maps that represent the world, more clearly or less clearly, and how it works. As we've seen, members of the least healthy families have very fuzzy ideas about where their own personalities end and those of others begin. Well, we average people have avoided that degree of confusion. We've reached a higher degree of stability by being clearer about who and what we are, which feelings belong to us – where our 'boundaries' are. We therefore possess a more clear and consistent idea of our own identity. We've achieved some stability, clarity and order.

John And no society could work without that. So that's good.

Robin Yes. But the trouble is, deep down we're not really confident about our ability to hang on to what we've gained. We're still anxious that we might lose that stability and clarity if we don't hold on to it tightly. So everything in us – our attitudes, opinions, ideas, beliefs, principles – are kept firmly nailed down, as it were, in case it all comes loose and starts floating about again. Think what it's like when you're mastering some new skill. At first you can do it only if you concentrate and give it all your attention, because you easily slip back into making mistakes. You feel good while you're getting it right, but it's still a big struggle to maintain it. You can't relax, it isn't exactly fun.

John It's like acting a scene before you really know the words. You're always thinking ahead, or checking that you haven't just gone wrong! You feel that if you ever relaxed for a moment, you'd blow it!

Robin That's it.

John And you're saying that's a bit how we mid-range folk experience life? Average health is always being a bit watchful, and seldom totally relaxing? Whereas the 'very' healthy families have mastered life-skills to a point where they're so confident that they can let go and simply enjoy what they experience?

Robin Exactly. They've plenty of energy and attention left over to spend on just having fun. Like that moment when we're learning how to dance, when we suddenly realise that we're enjoying talking to our partner instead of just thinking about our feet!

John And are you saying mid-range people fear they may slip back towards fuzziness and confusion if they relax their guard and don't work hard at being definite and certain about things?

Robin Yes. And also, the order and clarity they've reached has been achieved by tight control, by rigid suppression of any strong, potentially disturbing feelings. They've walled themselves off to some extent, constantly keeping a distance from emotions, both positive and negative, which they might not be able to control. One way to achieve that safety is by keeping an emotional distance from others.

John So we can't afford to be as open as the most healthy folk.

Robin No. We may have very good manners and a basic goodwill, but underlying that will be a certain amount of suspicion, or at the very least marked caution. Compared with the very healthies, who have all that friendliness and goodwill in such abundance, people like us feel we don't want to give too much away in case we find we haven't got enough for ourselves.

John It's a little bit more calculating. We wonder if we're getting as much back as we're putting out?

Robin And in close relationships too, mid-rangers still need to keep their distance in order to maintain their boundaries, so they're rather cut off from each other emotionally; they find it hard to be sensitive and to tune in to each other's feelings.

John Real intimacy is scary, because it can't be controlled?

Robin Yes. That's why in mid-range couples you usually see a sharp division between the sexes. Quite often there's not much understanding and enjoyment of the opposite sex, except in bed. And even then she'll often complain that he's only interested in the physical part of it and doesn't get emotionally involved, while he'll say that she's mainly interested in the cuddling and doesn't let herself go physically. So, because sexual pleasure is such a powerful emotion, which could threaten the uncertain self-control, it tends to be kept safely shut off in a separate compartment, away from tenderness and other forms of love and enjoyment. As a result, the sexes will seem a bit like different species to each other, and both partners can feel vaguely disappointed with the relationship. Though frequently – even with couples just below the most healthy level – the women feel more disappointed than the men.

John Why so?

Robin Because the relationship between the man and the woman tends to be traditional, unequal, instead of being equal as it is with the very healthy families. The woman has been programmed to be one-down, and to let the man be one-up. So he's having a better time and she's having a raw deal, as the feminists rightly complain.

John Now if there's this disappointment with the relationship, these parents won't form quite such a strong coalition, from the point of view of managing the children.

Robin That's one result. Or it may go further than that. If the marriage is unsatisfactory enough, a spouse may look to one of the children for the closeness and understanding they're missing from the partner. That will thoroughly upset the balance of the family and lay a heavy burden on the child concerned. It's also more likely that a spouse, especially the one who gets excluded in this way, will feel a need for some sexually charged friendship with a person outside the family. Which may lead to an affair, and threaten the marriage and family stability.

John All right. Now if there isn't quite the same warmth or equality between the partners as with the most healthy families, what's their attitude to 'love'?

Robin Well, 'love' in average families doesn't mean total possession and control in the way it does in very sick families. But people at this mid-range level don't feel too secure about getting their needs met, nor about looking after their own needs by themselves when they have to. So there's a strong tendency to want to control the partner – to keep them dependent so there's no danger they'll leave.

John How?

Robin Usually, they'll both be careful not to show their own ability to function well on their own, for fear it will encourage the partner to become more independent too. In the end the danger is that they each come to *believe themselves* that they can't function without the partner, and become increasingly clinging and dependent! So at this level 'love' comes to mean needing someone so much that you can't imagine living without them.

John But the effect of feminism has been to make women far more independent. Has this increased the level of health of couples in general?

Robin Where women are genuinely more independent – rather than just taking a rebellious instead of a submissive stance, which is still a form of dependence – my impression is definitely of much more healthy functioning. This makes a far richer relationship possible, but *both* partners have to become more independent for this to happen. The trouble is that the woman's emancipation often uncovers the man's denied dependence on her, which she previously colluded in and didn't challenge. If he can face that, and grow as she has done, then the relationship can become better and better. I've tried to do that personally, and am grateful for the benefits these changes have brought me. Unfortunately, a lot of men have not risen sufficiently to the challenge, but instead have either tried to resist and disqualify the woman's growth, or withdrawn and refused to engage, or reversed roles and become passive and submissive themselves. All this tends to lead to worsening relationships and ultimately divorce.

John To return to the rigidity of the mid-range family, what effect does all this have on the children?

Robin Well, of course, there'll be a huge variation in that. But family members won't feel as 'free' as the very healthy families do. Because of the greater emphasis on stability and caution, there'll be more pressure on each family member to behave conventionally, to do 'what's expected'. So the parents and the children may all end up playing 'roles' which don't fulfil their real natures.

John The children won't feel free to make real choices? They're more likely to feel that they have to fit in?

Robin That's likely, yes. One response is to conform. But the other is to rebel and swing right in the other direction . . . which may be better than just falling into step, but also may be a very long and time-consuming way of getting where you'd really like to be. After all, rebellion is almost as rigid a reaction as conformity. You're still defining your life in terms of other people's values and expectations, rather than becoming independent and living in terms of what you've discovered for yourself.

John But to get through life, you have to take on 'roles'.

Robin Indeed. But in the healthiest families children grow up with a strong sense of who they are, and they're comfortable with that. So they'll be able to play a part when it's socially useful to do so, but can then drop it again when it's no longer necessary.

John They don't confuse themselves with these 'roles'.

Robin And by contrast, mid-range folk are more likely to identify themselves with their roles and to feel lost when they can't follow one of these automatic social patterns. Their lives tend to become more and more limited by them.

John Mid-range children will therefore grow up more likely to take on the sexual stereotypes, being 'Rambos' or 'Bimbos'.

Robin Yes. And therefore more likely to find themselves locked into rival camps, experiencing the boring old Sex War. They'll be frightened that if they change roles to take over the partner's usual tasks for some reason, they'll get stuck and never get back again!

John At the same time, the traditional roles would provide a way for the 'averages' to keep a bit more distance. Which they might prefer since intimacy's a bit dodgy.

Robin That's true. They're not secure enough in their manhood and womanhood to let themselves be really close and open to one another. Whereas in the most healthy families, husbands and wives can be real friends as well as lovers.

John You said that power is shared by husband and wife in the most healthy families. What happens in the mid-rangers?

Robin It's more of a hierarchy, with one of the parents holding the reins. In the upper mid-range families the other parent accepts the position of second-in-command, and that can work reasonably well as far as the children are concerned because there are clear, agreed rules and they know where they stand. But in the lower mid-range you find a lot of conflict and competition between the parents for the number one position, which faces the children with problems of divided loyalty and inconsistent guidelines.

John Now, with the changes in traditional sexual roles and an increasing divorce rate, there are more and more one-parent families. Are the children worse off because of that?

Robin Well, I've no doubt that two parents who are both healthy and happy, and get on well together and agree basically over the management of the children, is the *ideal* arrangement. But as I've made clear, the reality is often very different from that; and there's evidence that children can lose more by living with two unhappy, warring parents who stay together 'for the good of the children', than by living with one of those parents who is happier because of a separation – provided the parents put the children's welfare first and cooperate well to maintain the children's contact with both of them. Of course, all the levels-of-health principles apply here too. If the head of a one-parent family has lost their partner because of their own psychological problems, those problems will still be there to cause trouble after the separation. Someone who's basically hostile to the opposite sex will tend to undermine their child's relationship not only with the other parent, but with substitute parent-figures after the separation too; while a parent who had a loving relationship with their partner, but was bereaved, will make sure such substitutes are available.

John Moving on . . . next on the list is communication. That's going to be more controlled and careful. Not very circus-like.

Robin Not least because the children will have discovered that not all their emotions or reactions are acceptable. So they'll have learned to repress them for fear of rejection by the family, instead of being allowed to experience and express them in such a way that they can learn to control them.

John Now, the next one on the list of healthy family characteristics is . . . seeing the world realistically.

Robin Well, average, mid-range people will have a much better and more accurate view of the world than the least healthy; but they'll also differ from the very healthy in their greater tendency to blame others, both inside and outside the family. So, they'll project a lot of their denied feelings onto other people.

John They're more likely to be prejudiced against other groups?

Robin Certainly, and the further down the mid-range, the more so.

John In what other ways will this less clear view of reality show itself?

Robin In similar ways to what you find in really unhealthy families, though to a lesser degree. They are much less comfortable with novelty and uncertainty than the 'very healthies', and therefore tend to cling to established ideas and beliefs rather than revising these constantly in the light of fresh experience. They'll continue to believe in their old 'mental maps', regardless of the evidence, instead of being interested mainly in the 'territory' and treating the 'map' as if it is secondary, just a temporary approximation. So they will 'stick to their principles', hold rigidly to a particular policy or party affiliation or to racial and class prejudices, even when events contradict these. They also usually maintain a rather idealised picture of their own family, shaped by the emotions they typically avoid and deny, which distorts their ability to see themselves clearly. Like 'we're never jealous in our family', 'we're all very close', or 'we're really landed gentry even though we've lost all our land and our money'.

John So how are mid-rangers going to function out in the real world, for example, at work?

Robin Well, the research shows that people at the top of the mid-range can be very successful at work. They're decent, responsible folk, and they see the world reasonably clearly. Moreover, they can be highly efficient at seeing things get done.

John But are they as good as the very healthy at dealing with people?

Robin No. They tend to be task-orientated and to find dealing with co-workers more of a source of frustration and irritation. Which naturally prevents them from getting the best out of other people. Whereas the fathers from the healthiest families are said to 'thrive on persuasion' at work: that is, they derive great satisfaction from motivating others to excel.

John In other words, they really like working with people, whereas the more 'average' fathers are more likely to experience others as 'getting in the way'!

Robin And obviously, if they feel like that they won't be able to collaborate well with colleagues. But we can deal with this in more detail in Chapter 2.

John OK. So finally . . . how do we mid-rangers cope with change? This overall rigidity you're describing is going to hold people back from adapting to it easily.

Robin Again, they're in between the very healthy, who thrive on change and adjust readily, and the really unhealthy, who can't cope with it at all and almost 'try to stop time'. To take the most extreme example, the loss of a family member through death; they won't be able to mourn and then adjust and move on freely like the very healthy. But they also won't deny the loss altogether like the least healthy. They'll adjust to the loss, but slowly and with difficulty. One compromise is to transfer the feelings for the lost person onto another family member – who may then be adversely affected by being treated not as themselves but as someone else.

John And as we're talking about the 60 per cent in the middle of the population it's easy to see why we're all rather conservative in our own attitudes.

Robin And that's going to seem very normal.

John I must say, the more I think about the very healthy folk the more strongly I get a sense of how their characteristics somehow all connect. It's strange . . . hard to express just in words . . . but it just feels that any one of them wouldn't really be possible without all the others.

Robin Remember that the research team which studied the *exceptionally* healthy families called their book *No Single Thread*, to make it absolutely clear that there wasn't just one 'miracle ingredient' which made the unusual health possible.

John No, but it's more than that. It's a sense of how each factor facilitates all the others, and is in turn dependent upon them all. I mean you can start anywhere. Take the children growing up knowing that all their emotions are acceptable. Obviously, this helps them to communicate more openly. So other people will be more open with them in response. So they will learn much more about what people are like. So that will mean their perception of the world will be better. Which makes them realistic. Which will mean their expectations won't be disappointed much. So they'll enjoy life more, feel good and will therefore be more open to other people. It just goes round and round.

Robin It does indeed. Here's another positive circle that connects the different characteristics. Because the children are consulted as much as possible by the parents, they're learning not just how to be open, and what other people think and feel, but also to respect other people's subjective views. Which will increase each individual's sense of identity and separateness. So they learn a greater degree of emotional independence. So they feel freer to be themselves, they're not trying to 'fit in', to 'toe the family party line'. So they're able to be unrestrained and joyful and enjoy being part of the 'circus'.

John And if you're part of a circus, where everyone's enjoying themselves, you feel confident. So the occasional problem doesn't seem threatening. So you don't have to hide negative feelings. So arguments and conflicts occur, but they get solved because the general context is warm and supportive, *and* the 'three-ring circus' atmosphere means everyone's playful, which makes them more creative in coming up with possible solutions to a conflict! So the family becomes even better at solving conflicts, and even more relaxed about negative feelings. So they become even more unrestrained and have even more fun.

Robin Which makes them even more open, which makes them even more comfortable to be themselves, which means they become even more confident about being 'separate', and about allowing everyone else separateness.

John Which means they can also risk giving themselves up to great intimacy, so they can get great support and pleasure from each other, which makes them feel even more confident, which helps them to handle any changes that occur. So knowing they can take on anything that happens, they become even less restrained, and so on and so on and so on. Sickening, isn't it?

Robin There's one other aspect that's probably obvious, but I'll mention it anyway. You see, because the spouses are acting as equal partners, they're sending a powerful message to the children which will help them to form equal partnerships themselves when they grow up, instead of slipping back into the mid-range pattern where spouses tend to be dominant or submissive towards one another.

John Hum. I'm still being amazed at how interlinked it all is.

Robin That's because the family is an interconnected system.

John What on earth does *that* mean?

Robin Well . . . the old way of thinking about cause and effect was that it was like a line of railway trucks in a shunting yard, colliding one after the other. But about forty years ago, people in many different branches of science began to be more interested in studying the *whole* rather than just the *parts*, using a wider focus to look at *relationships between things* rather than a narrow focus just on the *bits and pieces*.

John A 'whole' being what you refer to as a 'system'?

Robin That's right. And as they studied systems, of all different types – from weapons guidance systems, to computers, to families – researchers began to see that everything was much more connected and interdependent than they had realised. Instead of a system working like the line of railway trucks, it was now pictured more in terms of a central heating system, where the boiler, when it got hot, turned the thermostat off, which led it to go cold, which turned the thermostat on again, keeping the temperature steady.

John A family's like a homeostatic system with a huge number of interconnected variables?

Robin Well not necessarily homeostatic! In some systems, if turning one thing on turns other things on as well, rather than off, you have something more like panic building up in a crowd where the fear gets multiplied as each person's screaming affects all the others in an escalating chain-reaction, or a similar increasing chain-reaction in a nuclear explosion. But either way, cause and effect in a system were more often found to be connected in a *circular* way.

John So as far as families are concerned, does this mean that serious problems might be caused by quite small things, multiplied over and over by a 'vicious circle'?

Robin Exactly. That's the good news which family therapy discovered when it employed this systemic way of thinking. The good news is that you can break those 'vicious circles' which spiral down into greater unhappiness, and turn them into 'virtuous circles' going the other way. Which means that very small practical changes can continue to multiply into greatly increased happiness.

John Fascinating. I know that family therapy often yields very quick results. This is why.

Robin It's one reason, yes. Another is that you are drawing on the intelligence of the whole family. Each member will have noticed things that others haven't spotted about the way family problems start. So you are getting much more information. Often it's one of the children – a brother or sister who is not regarded as a problem by the parents – who sees the cause of the problem better than anyone else. And with the whole family there, you can get everyone to cooperate in solving the problem once it's understood.

John Well after that commercial, back to families who don't need therapy. With all these healthy characteristics connected in this circular way, are there any that aren't connected with others?

Robin Probably not. The healthiest families showed all these variables to some extent. But . . . there were significant differences in the degree to which they were all found in each family.

John So there was no 'one way', but a different 'mix' in each case?

Robin That's right.

John I'm thinking of what Tolstoy says at the beginning of *Anna Karenina*. 'All happy families resemble one another; each unhappy family is unhappy in its own way.'

Robin Yes, basically I think that's right. Of course each family is unique, just as every fingerprint is unique. But very healthy families seem to operate on the principles I've been outlining. And the number of ways you can get something right is obviously very much smaller than the number of ways you can get it wrong.

John Clever Leo. He was always good on statistics. Well now, Robin, you've been chatting on and on about these so-called healthy families, cheerfully offending all those of our readers who up to now had thought they were pretty healthy themselves, thank you. So they're hopping up and down, absolutely furious with me for not asking you tough, probing hard-nosed questions about your evidence. So what research is there to back up what you're saying?

Robin Well, as I said at the start, the interest in healthy families is pretty new so there isn't a great deal. And what does exist is complicated by the fact that the researchers are all using words in rather different ways, and measuring and studying slightly different things.

John You mean they don't agree on what's 'healthy'?

Robin In some ways that's true, but provided you make allowances for the different things they're all studying under different labels, there's really no significant disagreement at all.

John Really?

Robin And that's true not only of the more formal *research*, but also of the conclusions of all the main family *therapists* based on their practical experience of working with families. It certainly chimes with everything I've learned from clinical work. I don't know of a single feature that any one researcher or therapist says is vital for health, which is denied by other experts in the field. In fact the level of agreement is astonishing. Froma Walsh, in *Normal Family Processes*, an excellent book in which she reviews the literature on the subject, says that '. . . the various family models are remarkably free of any major contradiction or inconsistency' and 'No theorist states explicitly or implies that a variable deemed essential to a well-functioning family by another theorist either makes no difference to or is inversely related to normal functioning.'

John What sort of research? Can you give me an example?

Robin Well apart from the Timberlawn projects I've mentioned, and my own observations and those of my colleagues with whom I've discussed this subject, there is the study of exceptional Harvard students. The work is described by George Vaillant in the book *Adaptation for Life*. It followed these students over no less than thirty years, using regular questionnaires and follow-up interviews.

John How did they choose the students in the first place?

Robin They started with several hundred male students and then excluded any with academic, physical or psychological problems. Then college deans selected from the remainder the ones who seemed to them most 'sound' – ones who were able to 'paddle their own canoe'. This left ninety-five.

John There was a big emphasis on independence?

Robin Yes. And on achievement, on those who could compete successfully. In later life, they were generally the most occupationally successful of all the Harvard students of that period. But qualities like a capacity for intimacy were not valued highly in choosing them.

John Well-adapted hedonists were of no interest?

Robin Probably not. So the sample was all male and very WASP. Nevertheless, 70 per cent of them thought of themselves as 'liberal' in the general sense, and 90 per cent were anti-Vietnam war by 1967.

John So . . . question number one. How 'healthy' were these chaps, do you think?

Robin I mentioned earlier that you could say about 20 per cent of the general population are mentally healthy. Well, Vaillant reckoned that about 80 per cent of his lot would fall into that top, healthy 20 per cent slice. Some mistakes were made in the original selection so the rest were less healthy than that. But of course, they all had their vulnerabilities. At the end of the study, Vaillant says that: 'None had survived the game of life without pain, effort and anxiety'!

John But what did the study look at?

Robin They compared the students to try to discover what influences seemed to contribute to mental health and success in coping with life. In particular, Vaillant looked at the ways these men behaved when they found themselves in stressful situations, and analysed what kind of defences they used.

John 'Defences'? You're not trying to slip a bit of jargon in, are you, Doctor?

Robin I'll wash my mouth out. You're right, it's a technical word which means the methods people use to cope with painful situations, so as not to get so emotionally overloaded that they might not be able to manage.

John Does that mean a defence is a way of avoiding facing the truth, and therefore a 'bad thing'?

Robin Not necessarily. We all have to use defences of some kind as the pressures build up. What's important is whether we use healthier or unhealthier defences. So Vaillant decided he was going to study a variety of different kinds of defences, and he divided those into immature defences, neurotic defences and mature defences.

John 'Immature' being less healthy than 'neurotic'?

Robin Yes.

John OK. Here we go. So, starting at the bottom . . . what's an immature defence?

Robin It's a way of avoiding difficulty and discomfort, by pretending things are different from the way they really are. For example, *fantasy* – living in a 'Walter Mitty' dream world where you imagine you are successful and popular, instead of making real efforts to make friends and succeed at a job. Or *projection* and *paranoia* – saying your own limitations are really other people's, or at any rate, blaming your limitations on them. Or *masochism* and *hypochondria* – trying to get what you want by manipulating others to give it to you, instead of taking responsibility for your own life. Or *acting-out*, which means giving in to your impulses without any reflection about their meaning or their consequences, so that you don't suffer any conflict or frustration.

John Is there anything in common among people who use these 'immature' defences?

Robin Yes. They don't feel they've got any problems themselves! So, first, they don't get better. For example, fantasy cuts people off from help. Vaillant found that not one person who used fantasy a lot had any close friends, while few kept in contact with their families. Second, they can cause a lot of problems to others! Acting-out and paranoia are common in criminals and, interestingly, also in revolutionaries who may externalise their inner conflicts into political struggles. And, of course, these defences are found in increasingly extreme form as you go down towards the bottom of the health scale, towards real madness. Vaillant didn't include that fourth group of 'psychotic' defences, right at the bottom, because there was no one in the study as unhealthy as that.

John OK. Now, next category. What are 'neurotic' defences?

Robin They're ways of trying to cope with unusual stress and anxiety which are typically used by mid-range people. So while they involve distorting or not fully facing up to reality, they at least pay some heed to the needs of others, thus helping us to fit into society. For instance, *repression* means pushing uncomfortable ideas and thoughts to the back of the mind where we pretend they don't exist most of the time – 'behind the screen' as we put it in *Families*. Very similar are *isolation* and *intellectualisation*. In the first, we repress the thought but not the feeling – we might feel anxious without knowing why, for example. In the second, we do the opposite and remember the thought but forget the feeling connected with it – we might imagine doing something violent without the violent feeling that would normally accompany that. In *displacement* we shuffle around our thoughts and feelings; a man might be angry with his boss, but avoid the danger that the boss might notice it and fire him by feeling angry with his wife instead. And finally *reaction formation*, which is a kind of leaning over backwards to avoid feeling some feared emotion or impulse, by emphasising the opposite one. For examples, we might adopt an uptight, prudish attitude to keep our sexual feelings in check, or a touchy pacifism to build up a barrier against our own repressed but violent anger.

John What's the harm in all these mid-range defences, if they help to show consideration for others?

Robin The problem with them is that they all damp down our emotional response and therefore lead to a somewhat flat, joyless, tightly controlled kind of life.

John All right. Now the sixty-four-thousand-dollar question: What are the *mature* ways of dealing with real stress?

Robin Well, one of them is *anticipation*. You reduce the stress of some difficult challenge by anticipating what it will be like and preparing for how you are going to deal with it. Then, because you've done your homework, as it were, you can relax a bit, because you're more confident you can cope. For example, having 'insight' into yourself helps you to predict how you may respond and to consider the consequences – it's one way that psychotherapy makes people's lives more effective and enjoyable. Then there's *suppression* – instead of repressing a frightening feeling and pushing it right out of awareness, you hold it in check and bear the discomfort of *feeling* it. That means you're more likely to be able to work out how to handle it, given a bit of time.

John Sounds a rather dreary and pudding-like approach.

Robin I think the word 'suppression' is an unfortunate choice, because it does carry associations of heaviness and passivity. Whereas really, it means being able to hold your fire, to wait and choose the right moment. Containing the emotion like this can actually increase its strength, so you can feel very alive, full of energy, while you wait, choosing the moment to let the emotion explode into action. But to go on. Next there's *sublimation*, finding other ways of expressing problematic emotions and impulses which not only feel satisfying, but which are socially acceptable and perhaps creative. One example is *altruism* which can be seen as vicarious pleasure – enjoying doing for others what you would enjoy being done for you. We can enjoy giving our children experiences we would like ourselves. But best of all, you'll be pleased to hear, is *humour*! You feel things to the full; there's no shrinking from full consciousness of the painful facts of life; but you master them by turning it all into pleasure and fun!

John The best! Isn't that nice.

Robin Vaillant quotes Freud as saying: 'Humour can be regarded as the highest of these defensive processes'!

John Splendid. But wait! Here's the one-hundred-and-twenty-eight-thousand-dollar question: if using mature defences means not avoiding reality, not avoiding our own uncomfortable or destructive feelings by projecting them onto other people, but on the contrary taking the full blast of life in the face . . . does this make these 'mature' people happier, or simply more responsible?

Robin Oh, definitely happier! When Vaillant interviewed all these men twenty-five years after they had left Harvard, he asked them a lot of questions about happiness – about their jobs, their health, their marriages, and particularly whether the 'present time' was the happiest period in their lives. And what he found was that happiness was four times as common in the men who used the more mature defences.

John So tell me more about these four-times-happier fellows. They're the healthiest, right.

Robin Yes. They weren't necessarily the richest, of course, or the most powerful. But over 90 per cent of them said that their job satisfied them; in other words they were doing something they really enjoyed doing, rather than because it gave them status. Then again, they tended to have a lot of friends, in marked contrast to most of the men with 'immature' defences. They were able to take full vacations – 60 per cent of the 'immatures' couldn't do that – and a lot of the 'matures' were able to be aggressive with other people, if that was necessary. Only 6 per cent of the 'immatures' reported themselves as able to do so! And, you'll be pleased to know, the 'matures' mostly enjoyed competitive sports!

John Talking of them, what about marriages?

Robin Well, if there was any one main indicator of mental health, it was the ability to stay happily married over a long period of time.

John Never mind . . .

Robin Twenty-eight out of the thirty 'most mature' had established stable marriages before thirty and remained married after fifty.

John All right, don't go on about it.

Robin However . . . Vaillant does say: 'It is not that divorce is unhealthy or bad, but that loving people for long periods of time is good'.

John I think that is very beautifully put. By which I mean that it makes me feel better.

Robin Finally, the 'most mature' even had a mortality rate that was half that of their classmates!

John Life is unfair isn't it? You'd think suffering would have its compensations.

Robin Well, unnecessary suffering – being a hypochondriac for example – certainly does have some compensations. We can persuade others to let us off things we don't want to do; or more to the point, persuade ourselves to let ourselves off doing them, whatever others say. But the cost to our energy and well-being are enormous, far outweighing any advantage, and if we carry on doing this long enough we can actually *make* ourselves ill.

John Still, it all reminds me of the Woody Allen joke: 'Why do Jewish men always die before their wives? – Because they want to.'
So let's see where we are. We've looked at exceptional mental health from the point of view of how healthy families function, and then of how healthy individuals handle stressful situations. And the two basically seem to fit, don't they? They both emphasise the benefits of facing reality squarely.

Robin The same principles apply in so many ways. Tolerance and absence of scapegoating in the family, and self-acceptance and absence of rigid repression in the individual. Open communication in the family, and openness in the individual towards all aspects of his or her personality. All leading in both cases to integration and harmony combined with freedom.

John But they do give markedly different perspectives – which is good. I mean, when you're discussing something complex, it always seems useful to slice it several different ways, because each facet throws new light on to the matter and helps you to grasp the central idea in a more complete way.

Robin Yes. This is what I was trying to say about the validity of the research. Whatever the merits of particular bits of information, what is most convincing to me is the way all the evidence – from studying individuals, groups or families, and from many different angles – fits together and make sense of things which before were incomprehensible.

John Now, Robin, I want you to tell me how you'd slice this mental health thing. What's your personal take on it?

Robin Taking all this information together with everything I've learned from clinical work with different kinds of people, there is another way of looking at health which I've found very helpful. It links the 'healthy family' research up with family therapy, and with psychoanalysis, and with the ideas that Eric Berne used in *Games People Play*, which made sense of psychology to a lot of ordinary people.

John The book caused a stir in the sixties, didn't it? It became the bible of Transactional Analysis, which has been used a great deal since in training business executives.

Robin That's right. As you know, Berne had this idea that we can get stuck in parts of our personality, rather than using the whole of it. For example, if we want to be dependent and irresponsible, or are frightened of sex, we can use the child-like parts of ourselves; so we avoid developing the more grown-up, responsible aspects of ourselves – even to the point of denying we have them in us. On the other hand, if we are frightened of being vulnerable and helpless, or of feeling uncertainty, we can disown the childish parts and put all our energy and attention into the grown-up, responsible parts of ourselves.

John The first corresponds to what Berne calls the 'Child' in us, and the second to what he calls the 'Parent'?

Robin Yes. So we can spend most of our life in just one of these parts of ourselves, and relate to other people through it, while virtually closing the other parts down. Either way, we can't function on our own because half the total machinery that we need for coping with life isn't operating.

John Someone who is functioning on the basis just of their 'Child' will always be wanting someone else to look after them?

Robin That's it. And someone who is only owning the 'Parent' part of themselves will be needing someone to *look after*.

John I can see how the first of those works, but I've never been really clear about the second. Why do the people who've concentrated on their grown-upness have to look after somebody else?

Robin They've shut down the more spontaneous, lively, emotional part of themselves and know they're missing something vital in life; so they are drawn to people who can express that aspect, even though they disapprove of it. Also, as long as they arrange to be in a situation where they can focus on child-like behaviour outside themselves, in someone else, their own childishness – which for them is taboo – is less likely to emerge from behind their screen.

John And a really adult person?

Robin A really mature person isn't stuck in either position. He or she can use and enjoy both the child-like and the parental parts of themselves. In other words, where both parts are integrated and working together you've got a proper 'adult'! But where a person just has half their personality in running order, they'll be drawn to someone who has only the other half operating. Then, between them, they have available all the psychological equipment needed for life.

John They'll have to choose a partner who complements them in this way . . .

Robin So someone operating mainly through the child part of themselves – an alcoholic for example – will seek out a so-called 'rescuer' – someone who is uncomfortable with being dependent and has therefore denied the child-like part of themselves. And the rescuer needs the contact with the child-like person, in order to cope with their denied dependence by dealing with it vicariously! To put it another way, each needs someone else to 'carry' the part of themselves they are uncomfortable with, and want to avoid by off-loading it.

John So presumably couples like this will find it impossible to feel emotionally independent of one another?

Robin Yes. It's as if each person contains a part of the other. So if they separate they feel as if they've lost a part of themselves, though of course they can't understand why they feel so bad.

John Do these 'Parent' and 'Child' parts correspond roughly with the 'Super-ego' and the 'Id' that Freud talked about?

Robin They're similar in some ways. Freud, of course, thought of people as made up of three parts; Id, Ego and Super-ego. But yes, the Id is the spontaneous, unrestrained instincts and desires that we associate with childhood. And the Super-ego has similarities to Berne's 'Parent', being made up of all the social rules and values and prohibitions learned from parental figures in childhood; a kind of parent sitting on one's shoulder telling one what one should and shouldn't do.

John So what's the Ego doing?

Robin That's the executive machinery which tries to find acceptable compromises between Id and Super-ego, between the more childish and the more parental parts. What it's trying to achieve corresponds roughly with Berne's 'Adult'. Or to put it yet another way, and very roughly: Id, Ego, and Super-ego correspond to what we mean in ordinary language by Desire, Self-Control and Conscience.

John I think I understand this roughly, except for one thing. Are you identifying 'feeling' – the emotional life of a person – only with the child part of them? Does this mean there are no adult emotions?

Robin A person who is capable only of emotions and desires, and has no self-control or sense of responsibility towards others, surely *is* still operating like a child, whatever their age. But if the other parts of the self develop as we grow older, the emotional life will change and become less extreme and violent, more subtle and rich.

John Very interesting. Now remind me, what has all this got to do with mental health?

Robin Where there's a high level of health, these three aspects of the personality are all well developed – the person is aware of them all, and can use them all. Such a person is in touch with their emotional life, can feel deeply and be spontaneous and creative. And they can do that because they feel safe – confident that they can control those feelings when they need to. Also, they have a clear idea of what's acceptable and not acceptable in society, what will do good or cause harm to others and themselves. In other words, they've got engines to drive the ship, a wheel and rudder to steer it, and a chart to help them to navigate it to where they want to go. And because they have these three aspects of the personality available and connected up inside themselves, they can function adequately in life on their own when they need to. Which is what we mean when we say they are healthy. . . .

John So, if you'll allow me a stunning insight, being unhealthy means not having all three parts available?

Robin Yes. You've rumbled it. Unhealthy families need each other so much because no one has all three bits operating properly. These three parts are all split up among the different members. One member, perhaps a child or teenager, may have plenty of emotion and spontaneity, and provide a feeling of life for the family, but be unable to control it. Father may be strong enough to help them control it, but too irresponsible to bother.

John He's got the Ego, or adult, functioning, but no Super-ego, or parent.

Robin And mother may be too weak to do the controlling, but may have a strong sense, which all the others lack, of what's socially acceptable.

John Yes, that's clear. So?

Robin Well, when I was developing my methods of family therapy I realised that this explained why we could help some people by individual psychotherapy, and why we got nowhere with others unless we saw the whole family together.

John Ah. I'm getting it. You mean the ones where individual therapy worked had all these three parts of the personality already connected up and working, if not in balance. . . . But when different people in the family were 'carrying' different functions, you had to see them together, in order to get them to share them round, so that each individual member was carrying some of all three?

Robin Exactly. If you wanted to get anywhere, you obviously had to get the *problem*, and the *concern* about the problem, and the *ability to do something about it*, all together in the room at the same time! I called that connecting-up of the three functions the Minimum Sufficient Network – you had to have all those parts in working order and joined up for intelligent action of any kind to happen. If that network was in one person, they could operate independently and you could work with them alone. But in other cases you could only have that Minimum Sufficient Network available if you had three or more people in the room, and connected them up to each other by talking to them.

John Most enlightening. And the most horrible bit of jargon yet, too.

Robin I hate it myself, but it was the best I could think of at the time. If you like, let's call them the Three Basic Bits.

John That's much better. Dr Skynner's Three Basic Bits. So your way of slicing mental health is to look at it from the point of view of integrating the Basic Bits of the personality.

Robin It's just one more aspect of mental health, but it was tremendously helpful to us in choosing the right kind of therapy for the people who came to see us. And made it much more successful.

John Well I think we've flogged the question 'what is real mental health?' to death. So it's high time to get on to the two-hundred-and-fifty-six-thousand-dollar question. Fanfare please. Thank you. Here it is: since 80 per cent of the people on the face of the planet aren't particularly healthy, and most of the remaining 20 per cent aren't *very* healthy . . . why isn't everyone running around crying: 'I'd like to get healthier'? Any hints?

Robin Well, I'm afraid there's a catch. And the catch is that every level of mental health has its own, different, value system.

John And the value system typical of each level of mental health will lay out what is healthy and what isn't?

Robin That's right. And – surprise, surprise – each level claims that its own characteristics are the most healthy ones, and that the characteristics of all other levels – those above, as well as those below – are less healthy.

John . . . In exactly the same way that you and I both disliked the idea of 'separateness' in a loving relationship when we first came across it, and found it uncaring, if not callous.

Robin Just so.

John Ah. So everyone is reassured by their own value system that they're as healthy as they can be.

Robin Let me give you some examples. At the lower end of the health scale, families with a schizophrenic member will usually see themselves as perfectly all right apart from that person. In my experience, when you interview them it's often hard to get them to admit to any problems at all, even of the kind that average people take for granted. In other words, they present themselves as extraordinarily healthy.

John Except of course for the one who's gone 'bad' or gone 'mad' – the family scapegoat.

Robin Yes. It's as if that person contains all the problems in the family, so everyone else can be almost perfect.

John Almost perfect. Right. So moving up the mental health scale, who are the next lot and how does their value system justify their behaviour?

Robin Well paranoids would, for example, justify genocide by the idea that they are purifying the human race.

John Murder, terrorism and expropriation become 'ethnic cleansing' . . .

Robin And like the Mafia, they'll put an enormously high value on loyalty, but no value at all on anyone outside 'the family'.

John How would they see their behaviour to non-family members?

Robin They'd first justify it by saying that they are just looking after their own families and they might claim they were toughening people up, teaching them about reality.

John Doing the sucker a good turn by not giving him an even break.

Robin Something like that. And then if they're a little bit healthier, but still basically operating in a paranoid way, they'll be very attracted by the idea of the survival of the fittest.

John Like ruthless people in business, or politicians who have little concern about those who can't look after themselves very well in a meritocracy.

Robin Now moving a little further up the scale we come next to depressives. They'll put a very high value on kindness, and sensitivity, and tolerance and understanding. But they'll tend to disapprove of confrontation and direct, forceful criticism.

John They'll tend to see ordinary healthy assertiveness as unpleasantly aggressive? And confidence as arrogance?

Robin So they'll be likely to admire and indeed justify certain kinds of weakness.

John Their great heroes and heroines will be folk who suffered a lot, writers with consumption, political martyrs, misunderstood thinkers. There was a lot of that kind of thinking in my English private school in the fifties. Captain Scott and General Gordon, for example . . . rather unhappy, solitary men with dodgy sex lives who achieved spectacular failures. I got the impression they were to be specially revered; happy and successful folk seemed in contrast rather superficial and inconsiderate.

Robin And of course anger tends to be taboo for depressives . . . unless expressed against authority, or on behalf of others. And violence of any kind at all.

John All right. Who's next after depressives?

Robin Moving up the scale, we reach obsessional people. They'll put a very high value on order, cleanliness, control and conscience. They'll be uncomfortable with spontaneity, either their own or other people's.

John Their heroes will be administrators, accountants, traffic wardens and linguistic philosophers.

Robin That's the idea. And of course they give great importance to hard work and tend to be less at ease when they haven't got things to do, or if there's humour about, or when people are being high-spirited.

John Enjoying yourself too much is seen as self-indulgent. So, we've talked about the self-justifying value systems of schizophrenic folk, of paranoid folk, of depressive folk, and of obsessional folk. Now further up the scale we find mid-range people like us. How do we see ourselves?

Robin Well, of course I'm ignoring the huge overlap between all these levels, but we mid-rangers are usually more aware of our limitations, and more able to accept responsibility for ourselves, our emotions and our own problems. But because we are in a big majority, and in the absence of any criteria by which to judge ourselves differently, we tend to regard our way of operating as absolutely 'normal' and 'natural' and 'healthy'.

John So we also see ourselves as the healthiest, and everyone else as operating at a lower level.

Robin That's right.

John OK, so how would we 'normal' chaps and chapesses view the characteristics of the 'very healthy' persons?

Robin I think we'd find their openness and warmth rather odd at first, and might start wondering, 'What are they up to? What are they hoping to get out of this?' And we'd probably imagine that they were rather naïve, and feel a bit sorry for them because they might be easily conned. At any rate we'd be likely to think they were taking rather foolish risks, being too trusting, not protecting their own interests enough. But then, we'd almost certainly see their emotional independence and capacity for separateness as a lack of caring, as rather selfish, and as a sign of not being really involved and loving. As regards discipline, we'd probably feel that the parents were being too indulgent with the children in asking their opinions so fully, but at the same time we'd probably be puzzled that the children accepted the parents' decisions so cheerfully. We'd almost certainly feel that the 'healthies' discussed some things that were better not talked about, or at least were rather tactless or insensitive, in the way that they were able to voice their negative feelings. And we'd certainly find the lively 'three-ring-circus' atmosphere too chaotic and disorderly and worry that things would get out of control, or that they were out of control already! And we'd probably feel that some of their views on life were rather harsh and bleak, that they showed a tough and very unromantic attitude towards illusions that we value highly. We'd also be confused and critical that the 'healthies' handled change so well, because in mid-range families it's a great compliment to be told, 'You've never changed,' or 'You're just the same person you've always been.'

John That's right. It's a strange compliment isn't it? 'You've been on the planet all these years and you've learned absolutely nothing. You're fantastic!' But why are we so critical of people's ability to change?

Robin Well, what the mid-range family doesn't like is this: that the person has done it on their own – it's their own personal improvement. The change is not family property, as it were, so when people change it feels threatening to the clinging 'togetherness' that the rest of the family equate with love.

John Well, here's a paradox. If mid-range people, who after all form the bulk of the population, feel this way, then the healthies should be unpopular! Yet you said they get on strikingly well with their neighbours.

Robin I think they'd be sufficiently sensitive and considerate about the feelings of others to fit their behaviour to the company they're in.

John You mean they'd make their behaviour more mid-range!

Robin In mid-range company, yes. They'd choose to 'do as Rome does', rather than push their philosophy of life down other people's throats.

John So you'd never notice they were 'healthies'. All right. Now finally, the 'very healthies'. Do they also regard their own level of mental health as being the best?

Robin Well the healthier people are, the more they are willing to admit to their limitations and so the more open they are to the possibility of improvement. For example, by later middle age, 40 per cent of the Harvard Study subjects had visited psychiatrists because of one problem or another.

John That's amazingly high. I mean the whole group had been originally chosen as the most healthy and independent students.

Robin Yes. Of course in some parts of America, visiting a shrink is accepted as a normal thing to do, like visiting a dentist. But it shows how very open the most healthy men were to trying to improve the way they functioned, despite their very high level of success.

John That's actually been your experience, has it – that people who are more healthy are quite happy about seeking help if they need it temporarily, and that the less healthy are more resistant?

Robin Certainly. And it follows from what I said about the different types of defences. People who are really crazy, or who are using 'immature defences', can't face reality and tend to live in fantasy instead. They'll blame others for everything that goes wrong, so they won't see any need to change themselves. It's the people with neurotic defences, who are aware of their inner difficulties and struggling with these, though in ways that are often ineffective and lead to a lot of pain, who are more likely to see the need for therapy for themselves.

John They'll tend to be mid-range?

Robin Yes. And the more healthy they are, the more likely they will be to seek out therapy of some kind if they need it – unless, that is, they already understand themselves pretty well and can get whatever help they need from friends. It's notable that the *most healthy* Harvard Study men – the ones who used 'mature' defences – never sought any kind of psychiatric help at all.

John Well, after hearing endlessly about these exceptionally healthy folk, and feeling lingeringly envious throughout, I want to know how they get where they are . . .

Robin Well, we saw with the Timberlawn research that if children grow up around very healthy parents, they are likely to inherit the same healthy attitudes. Similarly, with the Harvard Study men, Vaillant compared those who'd experienced loving parental care with those who'd come from a bleak and unloving childhood. The differences between the two groups were very striking. The former had five times the chance of being in the 'most healthy' group and were five times less likely to suffer any mental illness. The latter lacked friends to a most noticeable extent, were frozen up emotionally, were more demanding and self-centred and mistrustful; and just as they'd been unable to play as children, they still couldn't play and enjoy themselves as adults. Also, the children of the least healthy were eight times more likely to be delinquent, or to need psychiatric hospitalisation.

John So to sum up, you're saying that the best way to achieve a high degree of mental health is to be born into a very healthy family.

Robin Bravo! You've got it!

John Well, thank you very much. That's most helpful. And encouraging, too. Just choose the right parents. Simple as that. You should write a 'Teach Yourself' book about it.

Robin Well, wait a moment. I said that was 'the best way' . . .

John . . . Go on, cheer me up.

Robin I will.

John Undisillusion me in that wonderfully wise way of yours . . .

Robin The Harvard Study also shows that by the time people with unsatisfactory childhoods reach the age of fifty, they can be functioning just as healthily as people from very happy family backgrounds. By that age, the researchers couldn't guess what kind of background they'd grown up in, from how they were currently functioning.

John Really?

Robin Encouraging, isn't it!

John I've suddenly remembered what you said in *Families* – that if you've missed out on a stage of your development, you can go back and learn it again *if* you admit that you need to do so.

Robin I'm convinced that's true. Provided only, as you say, that we don't hide from ourselves the fact of whatever it is we lacked – and the weakness that results. If the Harvard Study men who had difficult childhoods, and who showed the effects as young adults, could improve so much that by the age of fifty you couldn't tell them apart from men with happier childhoods, then they must have been getting experiences in between that were remedying the deprivation.

John And since they were originally selected as part of a particularly healthy group of people, they would have been less likely to deny they had any problems – less likely to hide them 'behind the screen'. So they'd be more likely than most to find the experiences that would put them right.

Robin That's how I would explain it, yes.

John So, here's the one-million-and-twenty-four-thousand-dollar question. If you're just mid-range, or *even*, I suppose, quite healthy . . . and you want to get healthier – and happier – what's the trick?

Robin Well, I'm intending to deal with that in stupefying detail in the last chapter. But first, I want to look at very healthy families again.

John We've done them to death, haven't we?

Robin I'm talking about much, much bigger families.

Afterthought:
You've Got to Laugh

John Comics are always a bit unsure of their status, so it's reassuring to know that humour and laughter are characteristic of exceptionally healthy families. And also that psychiatrists regard the use of humour as a 'mature' way of dealing with problems.

Robin I thought you'd like that.

John How do you explain it, as a shrink? Is laughter a cause of the healthiness, or an effect of it, just the froth on the beer, as it were?

Robin I'd say it's both. We have to look at it in a circular way. Confidence, relaxation, playfulness, creativeness, fun, bubbliness, the feeling of having time to enjoy things, they're all aspects of the same very healthy state of mind. Each one strengthens and reinforces all the others, and in turn is encouraged by them. It's a 'virtuous circle'.

John That's the opposite of a 'vicious circle' or 'downward spiral'.

Robin Right. But you're supposed to be the expert on humour and laughter. What do you make of it all?

John Well the only thing I know for sure is that a discussion of the subject always disappoints people because they think for some reason that it's going to be 'funny', rather as though lectures on Ibsen will be dramatic, or analyses of Bach's music will produce semi-mystical states. But I'll essay a couple of thoughts if you promise not to expect entertainment.

Robin Get on with it.

John Well, for a start, humour is a long way from being the same as laughter, which complicates things. There's a lot of reasons why we laugh and several of them are nothing to do with humour at all.

Robin You mean when we laugh out of pure joy.

John Yes, as when we see people we're very fond of whom we haven't seen for a long time. There's lots of laughter, but nothing very funny is being said. Then I've noticed that occasionally we laugh out of pure delight with something. An act of breathtaking gracefulness, or of astounding dexterity, or the first sight of great art or scenery, or the first taste of a quite extraordinary wine or a particularly fine bit of cooking. A reaction like that has nothing to do with humour, just with acknowledgement of perfection. Then again, I've noticed that if you play with a small child, and you do the same thing two or three times and then the next time you do something different, the child will laugh. So sometimes I think we laugh at something because it's unexpected, it's different from what we'd anticipated.

Robin And of course we also laugh when we're relieved, don't we? Something alarming happens, and a few seconds later we realise there's been no damage, nobody's hurt, and we laugh.

John And I remember J. B. Priestley once saying about a man who was well known for his loud, shoulder-heaving laughter: 'No one with a sense of humour laughs as much as that.' Because we can *force* laughter for many reasons – to create a friendly atmosphere, to cover up embarrassment, to try to dispel anxiety, especially to show other people – and ourselves – that we *have* a sense of humour. Even when we don't. *That* produces the loudest laughter . . .

Robin And then there's nasty laughter. When someone's triumphed over a person they really don't like; or when someone unpopular has made a fool of themselves and people laugh scornfully at them, to rub in their embarrassment of humiliation; or when teasing suddenly stops being good-natured and becomes deliberately hurtful.

John And then there's one other kind of laughter we mustn't ignore. The kind produced by something funny. So, Robin, why is the human race the only species of God's creatures that laughs? Apart from gasteropods, of course.

Robin Well apart from all the health reasons, I believe it serves one other major purpose. But it requires a bit of a detour to explain it.

John Carry on. The reader can always skip.

Robin Well, Darwin had some interesting things to say about laughter.

John Funny man, Chas.

Robin As you know, his idea of evolution arose from his observations of similarities and differences in the form and function of animals' bodies. Well he got interested, later on, in the way that different emotions were expressed by different bodily shapes, and patterns of tension.

John Posture you mean?

Robin Posture, stance, facial expression . . . all the physical manifestations of different emotions.

John You mean how we can more or less tell someone's mood by the way they look.

Robin More than that. A physiologist called Nina Bull wrote a book called *The Attitude Theory of Emotion* describing experiments where people had been hypnotised and told to assume the posture typical of a certain emotion. Then they were told to feel the opposite emotion *without moving* – without changing the position of their body or the tension in their muscles.

John And could they?

Robin They couldn't! Not one person, for example, succeeded in hanging on to the depressive posture, while at the same time managing to feel confident and cheerful. Nor, the other way round: nobody could change to feeling miserable, while retaining a buoyant, bouncy stance. Yet the moment they were allowed to *change* the position of their bodies, they could obey the command of the hypnotist to change to the opposite emotion almost every time.

John How did she explain that?

Robin She said that an emotion was a preparation for action – a 'postural set'.

John 'Set'?

Robin Yes, 'set'. You know . . . Get ready . . . Get *set* . . . GO! When the referee starts the race by saying that, 'Get Set' means that the runners' muscles should be tensioned up in the way they will be when running, but without actually starting to run. It's action in storage, as it were. And as you know when you've taken part in a race, that's when you feel the most intense emotion. Once you begin to run all the energy goes into movement. Emotions are intimately linked with particular postures and muscular tensions.

John So?

Robin Well, here's Darwin's observation: *laughter* occurs when two incongruous ideas set off two contradictory postures or tension patterns in the muscles, corresponding to two contradictory emotions.

John You mean . . . a *collision of different tensions* in the muscles *caused by two contradicting emotions or ideas* triggers laughter.

Robin *If* the person is surprised, Darwin emphasised. Then, he said, you get 'a convulsive discharge of muscular energy'!

John Well it certainly releases tension and relaxes us. But why does he emphasise surprise?

Robin I think it's because if we aren't taken by surprise, we can protect ourselves against the loss of control that the explosion brings about.

John Yes, because laughter's *involuntary*, isn't it? It's very hard to laugh convincingly if you're faking it. OK. Very interesting. But what's all this got to do with the purpose of laughter?

Robin Well to explain that I need to tell you first about the two different ways in which we all relate to the world. Basically we function in two modes: 'open' and 'closed'.

John . . . All right, I'll ask. What's the 'open' mode?

Robin That's the mode we're in when we open ourselves up to the world, take in new information, and let it change our internal maps to make them more comprehensive and accurate; so that they reflect even better how the world really is, and how we can work to get what we want from it.

John And the 'closed'?

Robin We move into the 'closed' mode when some action has to be taken. We give our attention to achieving some particular goal. So temporarily we narrow our focus and stop taking in all the information around us.

John Yes. If you're attacking a machine-gun nest, you shouldn't make a particular effort to enjoy the scenery.

Robin Right. Or even to see the funny side of what you're doing. So although the 'open' mode sounds rather attractive when I describe it . . .

John . . . because it conveys greater awareness, greater open-mindedness, greater relaxation, a more humorous and philosophical approach and so on . . .

Robin . . . we need the closed mode too, on every occasion when we need to act.

John So, to be really effective we need to be able to alternate between the two modes. Well . . . *how* do we switch between modes?

Robin Well, moving from the open to the closed mode is easier. It's more or less done for us. Perhaps some outside event alerts us to the fact that action's necessary. Someone rings the doorbell, or the baby starts crying, or the house catches fire – you're triggered into the 'closed' mode in order to deal with the situation.

John Or you simply come to a decision you've been pondering, and consciously switch to the closed mode to implement it. OK. No problem, squire. But how about going the other way – from 'closed' to 'open'?

Robin Well that seems to be much more difficult. Once we're in the closed mode, we find it hard to let go and relax into the open mode again.

John That's true. Once I'm focused and directed, and experiencing that slight but pleasurable anxiety you get when you're 'getting on with things', but also feeling some time pressure, I tend to run on like that for the rest of the day, even if I *really* need to stop, step back and take a wider view of what I'm doing to see if I'm still on track to achieve my goals.

Robin Yes. When you're in the closed mode you need to remember the old IBM slogan: 'Don't confuse activity with achievement.'

John Because pulling back to examine your activity can feel . . . *indulgent*. 'There's no time for that, we must press on!'

Robin That's the whole problem with the closed mode. Once we're in it, we *are* closed off to the kind of information that might jolt us out of it. It's like being on automatic pilot. Which we are, of course, we're just following the programme which began with a particular postural set or emotion, and which was triggered in the first place by some demand for action.

John Yes, so it's actually uncomfortable to have to admit any disturbing new information. We don't really want to think, and risk having to question our activity.

Robin So we can't actually *learn* anything now. We can only add details to what we already know; but we need to be in the open mode if we're to change our ideas, look for new solutions, reassess our aims.

John So, Doctor, how do we escape from the closed mode?

Robin Well, occasionally certain strong positive emotions can stop us in our tracks and make us open and reflective. Experiencing awe and wonder have that effect, whether it's in a religious context, or just the sight of great beauty, or possibly witnessing some moving event. The postural changes associated with those emotions are more towards relaxation, and widening our awareness rather than focusing it.

John We are left 'open-mouthed' . . .

Robin Yes, such experiences dissolve tensions and leave us 'slack' and receptive. Also, surprisingly, so can bewilderment and confusion *if* we can avoid reacting to them with anxiety. They can leave us in the 'open' mode, in which we're more likely to find the answer to whatever is baffling us. But these experiences are rather rare . . .

John Ah ha! We're coming to the end of this interminable digression. You are about to say that ordinary, common-or-garden laughter is the easiest way for us to get into the open mode.

Robin You've got it.

John So I could now explain the value of jokes to a Swiss banker in terms of their usefulness in facilitating problem solving.

Robin In fact, you could.

John I'm more important than I thought!

Robin Perhaps. Do you remember that after-dinner speech you gave at that banquet to celebrate the thirtieth anniversary of the Association of Child Psychology and Psychiatry? I had given my little spiel about the ideas behind *Families*, and after I'd finished, and you got up, I was able to watch the reaction of the audience.

John Typical psychiatrist – watching the audience instead of the performance.

Robin Well, I'd seen your performance before. But the audience reaction was very interesting, in the light of what we are talking about. At first, people looked uncertain. They didn't know whether to expect another serious talk, or a Monty Python sketch. Then: 'Everyone knows,' you said, 'that you psychiatrists are *all completely mad.*' I saw the jaws drop as they rocked back on their heels, insofar as it's possible to do that sitting tightly packed and digesting bellyfuls of banquet.

Should they pretend to take this in good part, be good sports, treat it as a joke? There was a gasp of nervous laughter, which was cut short as you continued '. . . And the wonderful thing is that you *don't mind being mad at all*. In fact, you *like* it! Because it helps you to understand your patients, and to help them to understand themselves. Such courage! Such altruism! How I *admire* you all for that!' As you said this, the faces of the audience oscillated between opposing emotions, alternately stiffening in rejection, then relaxing and opening up in laughter. I could see their faces twitching as people wondered whether it would be better to pretend to be more dignified and normal than usual, or to be a bit mad; some were evidently trying to be both at the same time – but was that possible? They would return to fixed and solemn postures and look serious one moment, trying to 'understand' what you *really* meant by what you were saying. The next moment you would paradox them again and the audience would explode in amusement, like a bird-dog trying to stand motionless, pointing at a pheasant, while its behind is being repeatedly tickled with a feather.

John I can hardly remember it. I have to do these things off the cuff and am never quite sure what I've said afterwards.

Robin Which is very 'open' mode, isn't it? That's probably why you're able to switch the audience into the open mode too. And that's why it was so fascinating to watch it, because the audience kept trying to get into the closed mode where they could have some comfortable, clear-cut attitude to the things you were saying – for or against, agreeing or critical, contented or discontented, one thing *or* the other. But your paradoxical combination of criticism and admiration produced these explosions of laughter and made it impossible for them to do that. So they had to put the stuff 'on hold' and ponder it later.

John Of course, I've suddenly remembered your doing exactly the same thing in our group. We'd all be sitting there trying to 'understand' something you'd said, struggling to get our tight, anxious, grasping little minds round one of your nuggets, and you'd suddenly lean back and say: 'I sometimes wonder if there's anything in this psychiatry nonsense' . . . and we'd all go slack-jawed. And I can see now that in that bewildered, but not unhappy, state, we might have been able to take in something new; in a way that we couldn't if our minds were rushing round in their usual tight little circles.

Robin Do you think this is why Video Arts uses humour in their management and sales training films?

John Well, we'd nearly all been teachers so we knew that laughter helped to keep people interested and on their toes. We also knew that you could put across *ordinary* factual information *without* that. But we slowly came to see that if we were trying to change people's attitudes and behaviour – stuff with strong emotional aspects – then humour seemed vital in helping us to achieve those changes.

Robin That's what I mean. It helps us to become more flexible when we are rigidly 'set' in some strong emotional attitude. When we laugh, we become free, loose, and unbolted, ready to move in any direction. Like a tennis player dancing from foot to foot when waiting to receive a service.

John I interviewed the Dalai Lama last year, and I asked him about humour. Because the first time that I'd met him I wasn't sure what to say. I hadn't met many Dalai Lamas in Weston-super-Mare and I didn't know whether you were supposed to say: 'That's a nice pair of sandals, where did you get them?' or: 'Is this your best incarnation so far?' I just looked at him and after a moment we just started to laugh and we laughed for about two minutes. I don't know still what we were laughing at but I know that it felt absolutely wonderful.

Robin He always looks very good-humoured in the photographs.

John So I asked him why Tibetan Buddhists laugh so much, and he said: 'Sometimes I find it useful you see, to make jokes, then your brain becomes a little more open. It's helpful to get new ideas. If you think with too much seriousness, your brain somehow is closed.'

Robin Well, there you are! He's saying the same thing, only wonderfully simply and clearly. Now, what are *your* thoughts on laughter?

John I suppose I have a few. But the difficulty is finding some explanation that covers everything from puns and jokes through farce and slapstick to high comedy and satire.

Robin Have you come across any theory you like?

John Nearly all of them contain the idea that something is 'funny' because two frameworks of reference that are normally quite separate are suddenly brought together in a way that seems, momentarily, to connect them.

Robin Well that's a perfect fit with Darwin's theory of 'two incongruous ideas'!

John Absolutely. So let's work through the types of humour.

Robin It certainly explains puns – it's exactly what they are.

John And I think it explains almost all the *jokes* I can think of, like the old story of the woman doing research into sexual behaviour who stops, among other people, an airline pilot, and asks him when he last had sexual intercourse. And the airline pilot replies: 'Nineteen fifty-nine.' And the researcher, knowing airline pilots, is surprised and queries this, whereupon the pilot, glancing at his watch, says: 'Well, it's only twenty-one fifteen now.'

Robin So the two frameworks are the twenty-four-hour clock, and the way we express what year it is, and suddenly they collide . . .

John And there's another major factor here. You'll always laugh more at the joke about the airline pilot than you will at a pun because there's much more emotion attached. There's sexual curiosity, and sexual embarrassment, and perhaps anxiety about the intimate nature of the question and so on.

Robin And the greater the build-up of emotion, the more laughter there's likely to be.

John Exactly. I think Arthur Koestler put this best. He said that in any joke, the punchline derails a trainload of emotion that has been set in motion by the first part of the joke. So jokes arouse and build up the audience's emotions, plus of course *anxiety* about those emotions . . . and then the punchline reveals those emotions to have been inappropriate and their energy discharges in laughter. That's why people laugh so much at sex jokes, even though so few of them are funny. It's also why people tend to tell jokes about unpopular people or out-groups. Even if the joke is genuinely funny, the resentment adds to the trainload of feeling and increases the size of the laugh.

Robin Because all humour cuts people down to size. Even when it's warm and affectionate rather than hostile, as in friendly teasing, it's still a bit painful for that reason.

John No. It's essentially critical and you just can't escape from that fact.

Robin So that's why it works so well in deflating pomposity.

John That's right. The more inflated the person, the more laughter there is available when you deliver the pin-prick.

Robin And of course that's why self-important people are so scared to be in a humorous atmosphere. They just know what's in store for them. So they demand solemnity, because that keeps them *safe*!

John But they *call* it 'seriousness' – which tricks people! I have a speech about the importance of not confusing being 'serious' with being solemn; because some folk have been conned by the pompous view, and don't see you can have a thoroughly serious conversation while laughing a lot.

Robin Some people think there's something unreal about humour. But I think Arthur Miller was right when he said: 'Comedy is probably a better balance of the way life is. It's full of absurdities, and you can't have too many absurdities in a tragedy, or it gets funny.'

John And great jokes aren't just profound, they're also persuasive. Because if you laugh at a joke you acknowledge the truth of the point it's making.

Robin And the more important the subject of the joke, the bigger the laugh, because there's more emotion involved. But it's not just the amount of emotion that determines the size of the laugh. To go back to Charles Darwin yet again . . . you remember he talked about the need for surprise. Well, the greater the surprise in a joke, the more rapidly the derailment takes place and so the bigger the laugh must be.

John I'm sure that's why timing is so crucial in comedy. You have to take that into account in any analysis because some people can tell the best joke in the world to complete silence! Timing is about achieving the maximum load of emotion and the maximum suddenness of derailment.

Robin So what are the tricks to maximise surprise?

John First of all, the more original the joke, the greater the surprise. Then you build up an expectation that something *different* will happen. Comedy writers talk about the Rule of Three, because once something's happened twice, there's an expectation it will happen a third time; so when it doesn't you have more surprise and more laughter. *Just* like the example I gave of making a young child laugh! Of course, there are lots of other ways to create expectation. Familiar situations will do that. If a man walks into a hearing appliance shop and says: 'Good day. I'm interested in buying a hearing aid,' and the man behind the counter says: '. . . I'm sorry. I didn't quite catch that', it's funny because we particularly assume someone in such a shop will have normal hearing. It wouldn't be funny in a butcher's shop. Then you can set a comedy series in a setting as obvious and unimaginative as a hotel. The advantage is that everyone's been in a hotel and knows what's *supposed* to happen! Then again, you can create an expectation simply by twisting a very well known phrase. So when Mort Sahl said that President Eisenhower had delusions of competence, the audience laughed, because even in the split second they heard the word delusion, they had formed an expectation, of hearing 'grandeur' and so could be surprised.

Robin OK. So you've talked about two independent frameworks of reference coming together, and the fact that the greater the emotion attached to this coming together, and the greater the surprise and suddenness with which the coming together occurs, the greater the laughter. But we've only been talking about jokes. How well does it explain the kind of comedy we see on stage, TV and film?

John May I say, first of all, how nice it is to have you doing the summings-up for once. Next, the simple answer is I don't know. I haven't thought it out. Obviously there's exactly the same need for surprise, so timing is just as important. So far as emotion is concerned, it's much easier with people acting out the scene because we can see and hear the emotions – we don't have to imagine them. I'm sure that the vital need for believability in comedy is that it increases the degree of emotion that the audience experiences in the situation. The moment you cease to believe in the way that a character is behaving, either because it's not credibly written, or because he's acting badly, you lose your intense involvement with the action, and your laughter will never be as loud or enjoyable again. There's little emotion to be 'derailed' and the play just becomes 'jokes'. But when you come on to the two frameworks bit . . . I'm just going to have to ask you to put that on hold, and stay in the open mode while I rattle on about Henri Bergson.

Robin The French philosopher who wrote *Le Rire*.

John Yes. He came up with the explanation I've found most useful in looking at comedy over the past twenty-five years. He said, to boil it right down, that laughter is a social sanction against inflexible behaviour, which requires a momentary anaesthesia of the heart.

Robin And you twit me for using jargon.

John I know. I'm going to break it down. Start with the comment about inflexible behaviour. Bergson says that people are funniest when their behaviour becomes most mechanical. And I think that's spot on. The most obvious example is obsessional behaviour. It's nearly always funny. Do you know that Barry Humphries story about the man who gets shipwrecked on a desert island and the only other survivors are a pig and a dog?

Robin No.

John Well after a few weeks his libido is building up and of course there's nowhere for it to go. And then the man starts noticing that the pig is better looking than he'd realised. So he decides to get on friendlier terms with it. But each time he tries to get closer to the pig, the dog leaps out of the undergrowth at him and barks and the pig runs away. This goes on for several weeks until one evening he decides to make a particular effort to get to know the pig. And he's sitting there figuring out how to do it and the most beautiful woman suddenly wades ashore. She's stunning. She's five foot ten, blonde, and magnificently built. And of course she doesn't have a stitch on. And she walks up the beach towards him and she smiles at him and she says: 'Hello. Is there anything at all that I can do for you?' And he says: 'Yes. Could you hold this dog for a few minutes?' Now, what's so funny there is that he's become completely inflexible. Once his libido has become directed at the pig, he's incapable of responding flexibly when a better offer turns up. Isn't that how you'd define an obsession?

Robin Yes, obsessional people are rigid, 'set' in their ways. They repeat the same old patterns of behaviour over and over without being able to stop; like when a needle gets stuck in a particular groove of a gramophone record and keeps on playing the same bit of the tune.

John Then take all the light-bulb jokes. Each one is about a class of people who behave inflexibly when confronted with having to screw in a light bulb – the Poles stand on a table and then turn the table; the Jewish mother expects to be left in the dark; the women's libbers make a documentary about it; the London cab-driver says: 'What, all the way up there as well as back down empty?'; the actor says: '*I* could have done that.' It's why stereotype jokes work. They assume inflexibility, which is funny.

Robin It's the contrast between the inflexible behaviour and the behaviour that would be appropriate to the situation. Again, it's the contradiction, the collision between the expectation about what will happen, and what actually happens.

John And even the hint of an obsession can be funny. At the beginning of *Doctor Strangelove*, when Sterling Hayden first mentions 'vital bodily fluids', the whole audience twitches, and then laughs, because they know that it's some strange obsession, inappropriate in a man who can launch a nuclear attack. And I remember a Rowan Atkinson sketch about mountaineers preparing for an ascent, and one of them keeps on bringing up the subject of mintcake. And after a time, you realise he's only going up the North Face of the Eiger because he wants to eat mintcake. He's not the slightest bit interested in climbing, it's mintcake that he's after. And of course he could eat mintcake without doing any mountaineering at all, but the two are so inflexibly associated in his mind, he doesn't think of that.

Robin But this idea about inflexible behaviour goes much wider than obsessions?

John Oh yes. I just started with them as the most obvious examples. Now my observation of emotion in comedy situations is this: if a comic actor reacts to something with an appropriate emotion it's not funny. But the moment that the actor becomes *stuck* in that emotion – that is, when the emotion persists in them after the moment when it was appropriate – *then* we're into 'funny'. For example, Basil Fawlty's anger is mostly inappropriate. He has very little flexibility in his emotional responses. His range goes from irritation, through indignation, ordinary resentment, crossness, anger and quivering rage to gibbering fury. Like late Thatcher. And it's that mechanical inflexible unvarying recourse to anger that makes him funny. Similarly, Jack Benny built into his character the trait of miserliness. When he was confronted by a man with a gun who demanded 'Your money or your life!', it took about four minutes for Benny to make up his mind. It's the same with any of the 'Deadly Sins'.

Robin Even in real life we can laugh at some dreadful experience we've had, *after it's over*! While we're in it, we're gripped by some emotion like anxiety or anger or embarrassment, and can't see the funny side of it at all. Then, later, we do, because we're no longer in the emotion's power. We're flexible again.

John James Thurber says: 'Humour is emotional chaos recalled in tranquility.'

Robin Lovely! So . . . if responding to different situations again and again with the same inappropriate emotion is mechanical and therefore funny . . . can a *'good'* emotion be funny?

John I think so. If it's inappropriate to the situation, or disproportionately great or small. In *A Fish called Wanda*, Michael Palin played an animal lover called Ken. What was funny about the character was not that he loved animals; it was that he loved them much, much, *much* more than he loved human beings.

Robin And even when people love other human beings, it can be a source of amusement to onlookers if they are so overboard about each other that they are oblivious to their surroundings and the kind of behaviour that's appropriate.

John Of course there's a whole vein of humour which consists of laughing at stupidity. But every example of that that I can think of boils down to a simple lack of mental flexibility. And can you think of any way in which someone who is flexible can be funny?

Robin Well yes. It's funny when someone is inflexibly flexible, when they go to ridiculous extremes in adapting to others. But that's *in*flexibility again.

John Somebody once said to me: 'Show me a sitcom about St Francis of Assisi, and I'll show you a bummer.' If you portrayed Christ, or the Buddha, you simply couldn't make them funny, because they would always respond flexibly, whatever happened.

Robin So if you're saying that inflexibility is funny, where does the 'two frameworks' idea fit in?

John I suppose if there are two frameworks they must be (a) the inflexibility of someone stuck in his thinking or feeling, and (b) the flexible behaviour of a really well adjusted human being. Ah! I've got it! Of course, *once* you've laughed at someone being stuck in an emotion, it's not really very funny if he simply goes on being stuck in it. The way you'd make that funny is to have him then appear to revert to more flexible behaviour, and *then* to return to the inflexible behaviour *again*! So it's the oscillation between the two that keeps us laughing. The one framework of inflexibility isn't enough.

Robin Yes. The essential thing is that 'explosion in the muscles', caused by two incompatible emotions or expectations, which loosens up the pattern in which we've become set. I know you're talking about humour rather than laughter, but I think that all humour has that same effect, even if it's on a smaller scale – a chuckle, or a smile.

John I'm rather pleased that Bergson's idea fits with the idea of the two frameworks, because somehow they both always felt right to me. But so far we've only looked at the first part of what Bergson said. The second part states that before we can laugh at something, we need to experience 'a momentary anaesthesia of the heart'.

Robin I don't believe you can laugh at someone without standing back and being a bit detached for a moment, which I suppose involves some temporary withdrawal of sympathy from them.

John That's right. If we're too concerned that someone is unhappy, or physically hurt, or in danger, we certainly can't laugh.

Robin They can experience some of that provided the audience knows they're fundamentally 'all right'.

John Yes. We can laugh at Harold Lloyd hanging onto the hand of a clock umpteen storeys up because deep down we simply know he's not going to fall to his death – even though he's arousing terrible anxiety. And each moment when he slips we gasp because, at that instant, we forget for a split-second that he's really safe. In all those early silent movies, people are getting kicked and hit and run over and you never worry about them at all.

Robin Whereas if it happened in real life, it would be impossible to laugh at them.

John Yes, so an audience has to be able to remember that it's 'pretend'! Then emotionally they stand back a little from the actors' experiences – in fact, treat the whole thing rather more as though it's a cartoon. Take Michael Palin killing the dogs in *A Fish called Wanda*. In real life people would have been absolutely horrified. But in the cinema, they scream with laughter because it's the *idea* of it they're laughing at, just as they're amused by Jerry running over Tom with a steamroller.

Robin Ah, but didn't you have to re-shoot one of the shots where the dog got squashed?

John Yes! The first close-up we did had been lovingly decorated by Charlie Crichton, the director, with a small handful of entrails from the local butcher. When we showed the audience this shot, they gasped. Their instinctive reaction of horror overrode their ability to laugh at the abstract idea. So we replaced the 'bloody dog' with a shot of a ridiculous, completely unbelievable straw-woven dog without any ketchup at all and then they howled. And again I don't think the audience would have laughed if the dogs had been anything other than those awful, hairy, yappy little insects that nobody thinks are real dogs anyway. It's very hard to know what people will take.

Robin And, of course, each person has a different threshold, so even if you get it right for most people, a few will always be offended.

John Yes, and it's extraordinarily difficult – I don't know why – to sound at all reasonable and sympathetic when you have to defend a joke against the accusation that it is cruel and callous. Even though you know that an hour earlier it made an entire audience rock.

Robin Why not point out that you can withdraw some sympathy from a character without withdrawing *all* of it.

John Go on.

Robin Many believe that it's helpful to be completely and absolutely sympathetic when someone's in difficulty. In my experience that's usually not true, except at moments of extreme crisis. Loving behaviour consists in being able to support people, while also being willing to challenge and criticise when that's appropriate. After all, we all know how healthy it is to be able to laugh at ourselves. Yet that doesn't mean we're totally unsympathetic to ourselves, does it?

John No, and I remember your saying when I was in your group, that when people started laughing at themselves, they were beginning to get better.

Robin That's certainly my experience. We need to stand back and find a little distance from our behaviour, to take ourselves less seriously, if we're to learn and change for the better. And humour gives us that distance. It's like teasing. When you tease someone, you are often alluding to some part of their behaviour which is problematic and which they need to look at. If it's done with real affection, the person concerned will often examine themselves afterwards, and change as a result of what they see. But if it's done with no affection at all, it's experienced as persecutory; the person concerned won't be able to see the funny side, or take the criticism on board, or change, because it's too painful.

John Interesting. All comics know that they're funnier if they have some affection for their victims. So the anaesthesia of the heart, as Bergson says, can only be *momentary*. All right. Now: the third and last part of Bergson's definition. He calls laughter a social sanction. Meaning that it's a reaction of a social group. I've never really understood this.

Robin What's the problem?

John Well I know that you do laugh more when you're in groups. Laughter is infectious and all that. And I know that laughter increases the cohesion within a group. Think how politicians make an audience feel good by making jokes about opposing parties. Incidentally, do you know which group of people always has the best jokes?

Robin No.

John Salesmen! They know how quickly rapport will be created if they can make a potential buyer laugh. But then I always get bothered that all this nice cosy cohesion in a group is usually bought at the expense of out-groups. Because there's another kind of laughter which in recent years I've come to value far more. And that's the laughter that says 'Yes, that's funny, and it's funny because I recognise that this behaviour is something I share, something that we *all* share because it's intrinsic to being human. It's how people are.' Now that is definitely the best kind of laughter, and yet when you laugh like that, there's no out-group at all. I'm afraid I find it rather confusing.

Robin I think I can give you a clue here. Do you remember what conclusion we came to about mental health at the end of the first chapter?

John You mean that the least healthy people are paranoid and need other people to blame and hate, but the most healthy people are 'affiliative'.

Robin Yes. Well I'm suggesting that humour, like all other aspects of human behaviour, can be looked at in the same way. That is, any given piece of humour or laughter can be placed at some point on the spectrum between most paranoid and most affiliative. For example, take the nastiest kind of racial jokes. They'll be ways in which one group expresses its hostility towards another, so those jokes belong down the most paranoid end of the spectrum. Whereas the jokes you describe in which people acknowledge they are laughing at failures which are common to all human beings, part of the human condition, would be right up at the healthiest end of the spectrum.

John Then there's not really an out-group at all – the humour is saying: 'Isn't it hilarious that this is what *all* we human beings are really like, despite our pretensions.'

Robin And of course the same jokes can be told with quite different intentions; and heard and understood in different ways too.

John Yes, and some 'insult' jokes *are* very funny. How we feel about them might depend on whether they were told primarily for their aggressive content, or because of their intrinsic funniness. But it would be dreadful to censor them all just because paranoids use them unhealthily. After all, they can use *any* humour in a paranoid way.

Robin Indeed. Think of how we've observed people responding to Basil Fawlty. Some people laugh at him as though the way he behaves has absolutely nothing to do with them – they think they're a different species! Others can acknowledge, while laughing, that they sometimes feel a bit as he does. The second attitude is much healthier and belongs up the healthy end of the spectrum with the other 'isn't the human condition hilarious?' jokes.

John I must say your idea is a bit of a revelation. I remember Jonathan Miller saying that true humour produces great intimacy. Now I see why. Because the best humour emphasises the similarities between people, not the differences.

Robin That's humour's greatest value, I believe. Not just for the pleasure and sense of well-being it brings us, but the way it can remind us day after day of the limitations we all have simply because we're human beings – *and* of how easily we *forget* that!

2 Look Mummy, I'm Chairman of International Consolidated

John So what is this about 'much bigger families'?

Robin Well, as we grow up we're repeatedly moving from smaller to larger systems. Even in the family, Mum will probably be the main influence on us in the first year or two, and we'll be strongly affected by her attitudes and blind spots. But after that Dad will become equally influential, and even though his attitudes may be similar in many ways there'll also be differences which will counteract some of Mum's biases. Later on, brothers and sisters, and the extended family, and then neighbours and friends have a similar balancing effect, all tending to save us from being pressured into copying the prejudices and blind spots of any one person or sub-group.

John And after that we join groups like sports teams, clubs and bands, and become part of organisations like schools and universities and later of companies, government bureaucracies, the armed forces or whatever. So these are the 'bigger families' – these larger systems?

Robin Yes. And as we move out into bigger and bigger systems all the time, there are greater and greater opportunities for fresh information to reach us, different ways of seeing things to those we were limited to in our families. So provided we've been prepared for the change to each bigger system by our experience in the smaller one before, and can therefore cope with the increased stress it brings, each move out into the wider world brings with it a new chance of learning things we've missed out on so far, and therefore of greater health.

John I still remember the feeling of the first day at a new school, of excitement just balancing the terror, the intensity of the experience giving you more impressions and memories than you normally get in six months. What they'd now label 'the steepest part of the learning curve'.

Robin I can remember the stress I felt undergoing some of those changes to bigger systems, too. Particularly going away to boarding school at fifteen, which I chose to do when I had the opportunity, because I had been very unhappy at a boarding school previously – so unhappy I'd been eventually taken away from it. So I wanted to prove to myself that I could do it! My home hadn't really prepared me for either of these experiences of separation, but this second time I went away I coped and eventually enjoyed it – though I felt desperate for a time – and it gave me a confidence I would never otherwise have found. Another big change was volunteering in World War Two, when I was eighteen, to train as a pilot in the RAF; that was pretty stressful at first but when I began to get a handle on it and enjoy it, it really opened up the world for me. Of course, a wartime situation like that pitchforks people into experiences that widen their horizons and leads them to grow in ways they might otherwise have avoided.

John So you're saying that life is a series of lessons, where we learn to cope with new situations, provided we get enough guidance and emotional support to sustain us through the stress.

Robin Yes.

John What's the most recent thing you've been learning?

Robin Well, it's horse-riding, since you ask. My partner, Josh, arranged a 'surprise' for me last week and told me to drive up the M1. Eventually we arrived at a riding-school, of all things, where she had arranged lessons for us both. I thought I was too old, and too scared, to start riding but it was tremendous fun and I was soon feeling like a cowboy, spurring it on and shouting at it to make it go faster. Another good example of being pitchforked into doing something you would otherwise have avoided!

John In the last month I've had the completely new experience of having our family group widened by the arrival of elder daughter's first really grown-up boyfriend. 'Dilapidated Patriarch Nears Cemetery' would be a suitable headline you'd guess, but strangely it's had the effect of making me feel more irresponsible!

Robin Always something new. And this is what education

really is, of course, it's not just something we receive at school. It should go on all our lives, till the time we die.

John I love what Charles Handy says: 'Learning is not just knowing the answers. That is Mastermind learning at best . . . learning is measured only by a growth experience . . . learning is not finding out what other people already know, it is solving our own problems for our own purposes . . .'

Robin I believe the most important learning is finding out the limitations of what we know. Unless we know the boundaries of it, we're not curious and won't feel a need to learn.

John Nevertheless a lot of education – of a more and less academic variety – does go on at school. Can we assume that some schools are more 'healthy', and turn out more healthy children, while others are less successful in this respect?

Robin There's been quite a bit of research done on this – comparing different schools to see what kind of environment turns out pupils who function best, not only from the point of view of academic attainment, but also of their general behaviour, regular attendance, tendency to continue their studies beyond the legally enforced limit, and amount of delinquency. It's been shown that all these factors connect with one another – and, of course, with the way the school is run.

John So how do these good schools operate?

Robin Surprise, surprise! In a similar way to the very healthy families!

John Tell me more.

Robin The fundamental principle is an affiliative attitude. There is a benign, supportive, caring attitude, not only towards the pupils but also to the school buildings and the general environment. But the growth and achievement of the children is a primary aim. The children are respected as individuals, and the school involves them by giving them responsibility for running things as far as possible, and caring for their surroundings. Some schools even have pupil representatives as governors. And there is easy, open communication between staff and pupils, so the children know they can always consult the teachers about their problems.

John What about the 'discipline' side of things?

Robin That follows the pattern of the healthy families, too. In the most successful schools there is a good balance between structure and freedom. Although the teachers treat the pupils with respect and listen to them, they are expected to work and there is a high expectation of achievement. The children are 'stretched' – something that I've always noticed that children enjoy – and adults for that matter!

John I know from my own two years as a teacher that kids hate two things: being bored, and inconsistent discipline. And they hate them so much that they'll do anything – including armed insurrection – to get either situation remedied.

Robin So the teachers set a good example by preparing thoroughly for classes, to keep pupils engaged in productive activities and prevent chaotic situations developing.

John And if there's bad behaviour?

Robin Usually, the teachers are able to spot trouble coming and will deal firmly with it, if necessary by punishment. But, in general, criticism and punishment was found not to be the most effective approach – in fact, in schools where there was a lot of it, behaviour was worse – and as far as possible the approach is based on encouragement and praise.

John Would you agree that 'praise is the best motivator'?

Robin Yes. There has been very extensive research which shows that to be true. But I think most of us know it for ourselves. Encouragement, support and interest from a parent or teacher who likes us generates keenness and energy of a more complete and sustained kind, compared with fear of punishment. It helps us to give the whole of ourselves to the task, rather than just dodging criticisms.

John That has to be right, doesn't it? To build on what people have got *right*, not to shake their confidence by immediately zooming in on what they've got *wrong*. Yet every adult I know has horror-story memories of nasty things teachers said to them – gratuitous negative remarks that even from the *teacher's* point of view were completely counter-productive. But perhaps some teachers are fearful that a child whose confidence is growing won't behave so well and will be harder to control.

Robin That'll be true of a bad teacher who has to control through fear. But with teachers who are respected, confident children will behave even more positively.

John It's not that children mind criticism, is it, if there's some *warmth and involvement* in it? When one teacher described my attempt at a rugby tackle as 'dancing about like a disabled fairy'

I enjoyed it, *even* at that moment! But when a science teacher said 'Your housemaster says you're clever – I just can't see it myself,' I think it slightly damaged my confidence in physics forever. But I digress . . .

Robin Not really. By and large, it's been found that children behave according to what is expected of them: they will be responsible and hard-working if they are treated as if that's natural: or irresponsible and badly behaved if teachers expect them to be like that.

John And cleverer, if that's expected of them too?

Robin Well, yes. If their potential abilities are recognised and they are helped to develop them, they will do their best.

John But now, the good results these successful schools achieved depended a lot on the kind of children who came to the school in the first place, didn't they?

Robin To a surprising extent that wasn't true at all! If there was a very high intake of dull, less promising pupils it was understandably harder to create an atmosphere of pride and enjoyment of achievement, but it didn't alter the exceptional character of the school. Even the quality of the buildings and other physical facilities doesn't seem to have much effect, *if* the psychological attitudes are right. In fact I can remember from my time as director of a child guidance clinic in a very deprived area of London, that two schools had every practical advantage, while a third was scattered in a number of old buildings and took the most difficult pupils which the heads of the two other schools tried to avoid . . . *yet* that third school outshone the other two in most of these qualities I've mentioned.

John I know of one town where the most undisciplined school is the brand new comprehensive. So how about the behaviour of kids who'd be expected to be difficult?

Robin In the best schools even a high intake of socially disadvantaged children is not associated with delinquency, although research shows a strong connection between those things on an individual level.

John You mean the good influence of the school can overcome the statistical tendency, as it were?

Robin Yes.

John Presumably because these good schools provide pupils with the substitute experiences that enable them to learn things their families couldn't help with?

Robin Probably, yes. You see, as there's more open communication, and as children are more accepted and respected for what they *are*, rather than being expected to fit into a mould, the staff would be more able to see the emotional needs of the children. And as the staff have such a constructive attitude, and are comfortable with being *either* encouraging and supportive, *or* tough and firm when that's necessary, the odds are that some staff members will end up giving the kind of relationship each child needs in order to repair whatever gap there is in his or her social learning.

John So what happens when children encounter a less healthy system?

Robin When that happens we tend to recreate our family pattern. If we come from an unhealthy family, the way we dealt with it is the only one we know. If we then move into another unhealthy system we will behave as we did in our family and the system will be likely to give a similar negative reaction. If we were made a scapegoat, or a 'mother's darling', in our family, we'll trigger the same kind of response in the new system and the pattern will be confirmed and is intensified. But if the school is more healthy, and is not controlled by our manipulation, we learn new ways of relating, new views of ourselves and of others.

John I've just thought of an interesting point. Could it actually be a disadvantage to the child if its parents have too much say in choosing the school? I mean, won't they try to pick a school which has the same problems as themselves?

Robin Well, yes; I'm afraid there's some truth in that – at least where the parents are unhealthy. For example, parents who have a problem over accepting authority and have never learned to accept 'no' for an answer will tend to choose a very permissive school, and the child won't learn to fit in there either. I remember treating a teenage boy where the father was very passive and withdrawn. The son's bad behaviour was an obvious attempt to provoke his father, to get him to be more firm and help the boy to control himself better. But instead they sent him to a well-known progressive school, where he behaved in a similar way. When the headmaster complained about it, I explained that the boy was wanting the staff to provide the firmness lacking at home. And the head said: 'I'd better go and ask my wife about that'! He was as feeble as the father.

John And presumably conventional schools could be chosen for equally bad reasons. Parents who are very inhibited about showing affection to their children will choose uptight schools where any expression of warmth and tenderness is highly disapproved of; very driven parents will approve of extremely competitive schools.

Robin Absolutely. I'm sure that was the basis of the harsh conditions the British public school system imposed until recent times. But fortunately nowadays we're less uncomfortable about showing feelings, and so don't feel obliged to train our children not to show them either.

John All right. Now school is the first organisation we encounter as we venture beyond our family. The next, for most of us, is the workplace, isn't it? So if we now move on to talk about the bigger families at work, how much do healthy family characteristics apply there?

Robin It's a continuation of the same process – learning to cope with bigger systems and increasingly complex relationships. The challenges involved in starting work are similar in some ways to those you've faced earlier, but the demands are tougher, you're on the line, it's less forgiving than home and school. You're faced with more realistic assessment and feedback about yourself and your performance; if you fail you may get fired. So there are greater risks, but there are vastly greater possibilities. You can't end up as the father of the family you grew up in, and you won't be made headteacher of your school no matter how well you do in your A-levels, but you *can* become chairperson of your company. So work brings a new discipline.

John How do you mean exactly?

Robin It's tougher. Simple as that. There are greater anxieties about failure, but also the chance of achievement, and the confidence and self-respect that brings. In turn, this will change the home relationships; most of us have experienced the difference in the way parents treat us when we start a job and become independent. And someone who accepts and rises to challenges at work will develop greater courage and competence and so more true authority, thereby gaining the genuine respect of their partner and children, and providing a source of confidence and stability for the family. So in various ways work is essential to psychological development.

John Learning to be part of a team, dealing with rivalry and issues of envy, accepting you have to be disliked sometimes, taking difficult decisions which affect other people's lives . . .

Robin Balancing the demands of home and of work, dealing with stressful situations, learning how to present yourself in public, the lot!

John All right. Now moving on from the value of work . . . when people choose a particular job, how much are psychological factors affecting that choice?

Robin Very strongly. People tend to be drawn to their type of work – and to organisations that are compatible with their own psychology – quite automatically, in the same way that they choose their partner. Of course, as in getting married, there are lots of other factors influencing the decision too, but the search for a psychological 'fit' at a deep level is always there, though most people are more or less unaware of it.

John You mean they'll try to choose an organisation that's like the family they grew up in?

Robin Yes, in the sense of one that operates at a similar level of health, according to the principles we discussed in Chapter 1. So a more healthy person will tend to pick a more healthy work-environment; a less healthy person will be drawn to a less healthy situation.

John Now when we talked about different kinds of marriages in *Families*, you said there could be different solutions depending on whether a person wanted to stay the same, or change and grow more healthy. Is it the same when a person chooses an organisation?

Robin Yes. At the lowest level of health, the person's choice will be based on the need to deny their own problems and to put the blame for them on someone else. So a very bad-tempered person will be more *comfortable* in an organisation where there's a bad-tempered boss and generally negative, adversarial relationships. Then even though people like that always find themselves in a negative, hostile mood, they can believe it's a 'natural reaction' to the unpleasant work situation.

John Nothing to do with them *really* . . . they'd be all sweetness and light if only they worked in a different place. It's like the *Who's Afraid of Virginia Woolf* marriage where both partners can believe they'd be happy if only they had married someone else . . .

Robin Yes, though they would actually feel *worse* in a more positive situation! Because then they'd have to face up to what they're really like, and admit that the problem lay in themselves.

John Now there was another healthier kind of psychological arrangement by which couples could avoid facing their problems – the *Doll's House* marriage where the relationship was more cooperative and positive, but where the spouses carried certain personality functions for each other, and so avoided having to change at all.

Robin The same thing occurs in choosing work. People can pick a company where the structure and values are similar to the pattern in their family, so that there's no questioning of those attitudes, as everyone takes it for granted that they're right. That way, people won't feel any pressure to change and can comfortably avoid facing their problems.

John Can you give some examples?

Robin Let's take someone who has grown up in a family where people don't trust emotions, and where relationships are rather distant; they'll be more comfortable working in data processing, where the main need is to use the mind and there's not a lot of emotional interaction with people. Take someone else from a home where control and order and tidiness are the essential things; they'll fit naturally into a job as an accountant or civil servant. Someone from a family where there's quite a lot of anger, but open aggression is frowned on, will be at home working as a barrister where aggressive questioning is essential, but where it's all within a framework of rules and under the control of a father-figure. And someone from a deprived family, but where no one could *admit* to being needy, won't have to face that deprivation if they become a social worker, or join one of the other helping services. There's nothing *wrong* with these choices, you understand! For the very reason the type of work fits their habitual pattern, such people are likely to do it well and enjoy it. But they may not get the kind of emotional challenge that would help them grow.

John Now, beyond Virginia Woolf and *The Doll's House*, there was a third kind of marriage where the partners chose each other in order to help themselves and become more healthy.

Robin Exactly the same can happen when we choose our type of work, and select a particular organisation. So young people who feel they aren't tough enough, haven't enough self-discipline or ability to cope with adversity, can join the armed services, or the police.

John Not because these organisations are above-averagely healthy in a general, overall sense, though.

Robin No, although individual parts of them might be. It's that every type of work will require particular kinds of competence, and for people who lack those skills and abilities, joining such an organisation can enable them to become more adequate in those respects. Of course, the organisation itself may *over-emphasise* these capacities, and in that way be somewhat 'unhealthy'. But that needn't prevent some individuals from benefiting from what the organisation is good at. As I said, you can use an organisation to blame someone else for your troubles, or to remain comfortable and avoid change, or to grow and become more healthy. It all depends on you, on your attitude, how you approach it.

John Could you become more healthy by working with an organisation which is less healthy than you are?

Robin Yes, that is possible, because you can learn something from everyone and every situation. You can even use a bad experience to become better at coping with bad experiences! But I think that what you'd learn might be very limited. To get the greatest benefit you need to find an organisation that is overall functioning at a healthier level than yourself.

John All right. But supposing someone who's from a family that isn't really very healthy finds themselves in the middle of an organisation that's running on very healthy principles. How are they going to feel?

Robin Not great! For example when Charles Schreiber took over an unhealthy firm and announced he was abolishing 'clocking', they threatened to go on strike – they assumed he must be trying to fiddle their pay! Well, in a healthy organisation more allowances will be made for people's limitations and weaknesses, and there'll be more support. So over time, people who are less healthy will tend to get more healthy. But it's obviously a matter of degree: if the discrepancy between the levels of health which the organisation, and the employee, are operating at is too great the employee will find it just too uncomfortable.

John In what way?

Robin Well, if there's a lot of freedom and scope for initiative, they might feel insecure and worried that no one is telling them what to do.

John And I suppose the confidence and liveliness of their colleagues could make them feel inadequate.

Robin And the open communication would feel threatening – they might get some constructive criticism that feels too close to the bone. Being insulted and shouted at is easier for some people because then they can distance themselves and feel that their critic has been 'rude'. So they can dismiss the criticism instead of asking themselves whether it's true.

John An unhealthy company gives people more ready-made excuses if they fail?

Robin Yes. In fact a friend of mine, who runs some companies along unusually healthy lines, told me that he had great trouble with a few people who were much less healthy than the rest of his employees. They left, but seemed to protect themselves from facing the fact that the company was too healthy for them by becoming quite paranoid and inventing extraordinary stories in order to create reasons for leaving it.

John I see. Now, finally, what about the situation where a person from a not really very healthy family finds themselves in an organisation that doesn't work in a very healthy way, either. Is this a perfect fit?

Robin Certainly neither will help the other to become more healthy, but otherwise it could be fine for both. Less healthy people have their own strengths and skills which those more fortunate may lack. A deprived child who has learned to cope with very little support may survive better in a tough situation like working for Robert Maxwell than a person who's had it easy in an affectionate, affluent family. And in an organisation that's run dishonestly, it may be an advantage to be able to lie and cover your tracks.

John OK. Well in case our readers want to find, or avoid, a healthy organisation, let's start examining them and find out what makes them healthy. I suppose we're talking about companies, hospitals, government bureaucracies . . .

Robin Most of the research is based on companies. It's certainly easier to see which ones work and which don't.

John But does that mean you're taking only financial success as the criterion of health? That doesn't sound right.

Robin No, it's *long-term* financial success that I'm taking as the main criterion. Because a certain kind of charismatic leader can run a financially successful company on thoroughly unhealthy principles for a time. But only for a time. Then the chickens always come home to roost, and the longer the firm's been run in an unhealthy way, the bigger the flocks are!

John OK. So . . . how are we going to start examining these healthy organisations?

Robin I suggest we go through the characteristics of the healthy families, and see how the organisations compare.

John Really! I'm surprised. You feel that companies are enough like families for us to be able to compare them usefully?

Robin Yes, on the whole they are. You remember in *Families* how we said that people with similar family backgrounds were almost automatically attracted to each other, and that they would often marry, and then bring up children in the same mould, who would be attracted eventually to someone of a similar mould, and have children . . . etc, etc, etc?

John Yes. Are you telling me that the people who start a business are going to hire people who are like themselves?

Robin And who will in turn hire people like themselves? Certainly. There's a very strong tendency for that to happen.

John Well I know many businessmen say that each organisation has a personality of its own, but it hadn't occurred to me it was the personality of the founder . . .

Robin Obviously a powerful new personality may come in and change the feeling of the company. But then the company will come to resemble *them*. Either way, over time the people further down the hierarchy will usually come to reflect the attitudes, the values, the philosophy of those at the top.

John So organisations will have attitudes, ways of doing things, values, that are very like a family's?

Robin Indeed. The corporate culture parallels a family's personality in many ways.

John So from the point of view of the person who's thinking of working in this organisation, is he or she going to be drawn towards it?

Robin If it fits, it'll be like strangers across a crowded room!

John Oh come on!

Robin No! You remember how much information people can pick up from each other, unconsciously, leading to an immediate sense that someone is right or not right. And if someone is being considered for a place in an organisation at a relatively important level, there's going to be a lot of exchange of information first, and plenty of opportunity for each side to be unconsciously guided by these kinds of intuitions.

John As well as by the more conscious and rational stuff.

Robin Of course, all that will be going on too. But the unconscious stuff is very powerful just because it *is unconscious*. Remember what I explained about 'falling in love'.

John Well how about at the bottom of organisations? Not that much care is taken in hiring people at that level, unless you're Nissan.

Robin No, but those same unconscious factors are still influencing the choice, even if it's to a smaller extent. Of course at that level, people aren't going to affect the personality of the organisation much. And if they don't feel comfortable they'll leave. But if it fits them, if the atmosphere feels right and 'familiar', they'll be influenced by it increasingly, and they'll come to correspond more and more to the organisation's personality as they get promoted higher.

John So basically, if the organisation operates in a similar way to how your family worked, you'll fit in.

Robin Yes. If the basic attitudes are similar to those you learned in your family, you'll 'feel at home'.

John And similarly, they're more likely to accept and approve of you, because you're the kind of person they can understand, and so they'll have expectations of the way you'll behave. Are you saying you'll enter the organisation with unconscious expectations of how it will work?

Robin Yes.

John So what happens if those expectations turn out to be wrong?

Robin As with a couple, there'll be conflict, perhaps to an extent that the person may leave. Or they may settle down to a rather stuck, stalemate relationship where both sides are dissatisfied, but they grumble along. Or as in a healthy marriage, the person may change to fit the values of the organisation better, and may in turn even change it a bit too!

John So how can someone who's reading this tell how well they fit their organisation?

Robin They can check themselves against the 'healthy family' characteristics we listed in the last section; then check their organisation against the 'healthy organisation' characteristics we're just about to give them; and then see how they match each other!

John OK. Well let's do as you suggest, and go through the list of healthy family characteristics seeing how much they apply to organisations . . . first, do these so-called healthy organisations have an 'Affiliative Attitude'?

Robin There's no question that the most successful companies operate on this basis, whether you're talking about customers, employees, distributors, suppliers or whoever.

John Take customers first.

Robin In manufacturing, the attitude towards customers starts with the product. The most successful companies expect 100 per cent reliability from their products. There's no tolerance of even the occasional defect or 'reasonable' failure! Of course, it's an objective that's impossible to achieve completely, but if you aim for that, you're more likely to get the best result possible.

John When I first heard about this 'zero defect' policy I really couldn't see that such a way of thinking quite made sense. Then somebody asked me what I thought of a firm called Supermarvellex who believe in a minimum standard of 98 per cent. This sounds admirable. It means that no metre ruler leaves their factory unless it is at least 98cm long. Then I was asked how I would feel if the London Underground announced a target for next year of only fifty fires in tunnels and an absolute maximum of twenty deaths. And a management consultant friend of mine tells me that companies who budget for absentees get as much as they budget for.

Robin Well the 'zero defect' policy certainly works for customers. The smartest organisations have found that people will pay and will go on paying for quality. So Tesco, for example, now plough their profits back into quality, and never into lower prices.

John In one business training video that I made on achieving 100 per cent quality we taught that it is only possible if each part of the process is constantly studied and improved in the light of feedback from everyone connected with it – all of whom are constantly involved and consulted.

Robin An early advocate of ideas like this was the American Alfred Deming. He was pretty much ignored in the United States but found that his ideas were taken up enthusiastically by Japan after 1945 – he is regarded there as one of the main reasons for their huge industrial success. He believed that an endless striving for improved quality would not just make customers return with further orders, but would even lead them to boast about the product, thus bringing friends with them. Only when US firms were being wiped out because American consumers were finding many Japanese products to be better did some of them begin listening to what Deming had to say.

John It's an amazing thought, but Nissan is now a major British exporter! Every day Nissan supervisors meet their teams for ten minutes to discuss any aspect of improving their work. Everything is based on a concept of 'Get the process right and the bottom line will come right in the end'. In fact, Nissan have a near obsession with getting the relationship right between the supervisor and the team.

Robin And such firms have a philosophy of service to the customer which seems to go far beyond 'rational' business considerations. So when something does go wrong in, say, a product of a US firm like Caterpillar Tractor or IBM, or a British firm like JCB or ICL, tremendous efforts are made to replace or fix it in the shortest possible time, as though there was a war on and victory was hanging in the balance. Firms like these will send someone out, often someone quite senior, at great expense without seeming to take money into account at all.

John Yes. And if a mistake is rectified really well, you can turn the disappointed and probably antagonistic person who is complaining into a lifelong customer. Because most people don't enjoy complaining, and anticipate trouble when they do;

so if you greet them warmly, listen carefully to the problem and then really put it right for them, they feel a tremendous relief and gratitude – probably more than if the product worked properly in the first place.

Robin Everyone takes it for granted that Marks & Spencer will always change anything that's brought back, without any resistance or questioning. So people don't have to worry about making a mistake; they can buy with more confidence and so end up buying more.

John Now, moving on from customers, you said the Affiliative Attitude also applies to employees.

Robin It's certainly very evident in the attitude of responsibility towards the employees. Everyone knows about the large Japanese firms' policy of lifetime employment, but there are many Western firms – Hewlett Packard is one, and United Biscuits is another – which go to enormous trouble, apparently contrary to their immediate financial interest, to protect the workforce from redundancy. Companies like these see the need to provide new jobs for people who would otherwise become redundant, as a reason for diversifying their operations. In addition they look after their employees in an astonishingly wide number of other ways, from health schemes and providing help with housing, right through to sports and social facilities that seem to have almost no bearing whatsoever on making the company more profitable. The effect of all this is to generate a high level of loyalty and commitment in the workforce, so that everyone contributes more towards the success of the firm. Look at the difference in staff turnover rates in the different stores.

John But some would say this kind of benevolence is paternalistic – essentially manipulative – and that people are not naturally altruistic in this way.

Robin I would see it as showing a natural human responsibility towards one another, with the more senior, stronger people taking a correspondingly greater share of the load while they are in that favoured position. Like the old British army principle that an officer doesn't start to eat until his men have been provided for. That's no different from the way a good family operates, except that the degree of intimacy and mutual responsibility is less.

John And children and adolescents have some responsibility towards the family too, don't they? Perhaps this suspicious attitude towards the people at the top assumes that management and workforce are basically different types of people.

Robin Exactly. Because people prefer working at a really good, friendly, well-organised place. They enjoy it more.

John I just want to query this again. In these top organisations, this so-called Affiliative Attitude goes beyond rational business considerations?

Robin So it seems. It's just like the healthy families' affiliative behaviour. These healthy companies simply don't seem to be doing it just for what they get back. They behave this way because that's what they believe in.

John Put like that it almost sounds like a spiritual belief . . .

Robin Often it is. If you look at the companies which are successful in the really long term, which survive and continue to maintain their excellent qualities beyond the loss of the founder or original guiding spirit, you'll usually find that some of the values on which that person was operating were 'spiritual'.

John In what sense?

Robin Well of course it can involve membership of a particular religious movement. Thomas J. Watson, the founder of IBM, explicitly based his business philosophy on Christian values, even if they were at a pretty prosaic, Dale Carnegie level. Konosuke Matsushita, the founder of the huge Japanese electrical manufacturing conglomerate of that name, was deeply impressed by a Japanese religious movement and systematically tried to apply its principles to the development of his company. Then obviously there were the great Quaker families – Cadbury, Fry, Rowntree and Kellogg. But what's more important than a specific creed is the way the founder 'lives' according to certain ethical principles – which are probably common to all the great religions and philosophies of the world.

John So what matters is the way they behave, rather than their belief system?

Robin That's right. So the main influence on them is likely to have been the family they grew up in, though they may have encountered good influences later in life – at school, at work, or from a mentor, or even from some spiritual source. But some will operate on these unusually good values without having thought a great deal about where they've come from!

John They just have a very positive view of what people are capable of if they're trusted, motivated, and working in enjoyable conditions.

Robin And they'd take it for granted that honesty, giving good value, and providing good service are all worthwhile things *in themselves*.

John And they're good business tactics, too. So, I suppose the difference between someone who 'believes' in these values and someone who just tries to put them into operation because they're profitable, is that the latter is not going to hold on to those principles with the same conviction and tenacity when things are going against him, when they're not 'working' in cash terms. He'll be tempted to cut corners in a crisis, and people will sense that about him. And then he will never get quite the same affiliative response from them as the person who gives good value and service come hell or high water, no matter what it seems to cost.

Robin In fact, there's someone in Japan who tries to run an operation very like Marks & Spencer in this country, but who is very frustrated that he can't make the same profits. And every time he meets someone who has knowledge about Marks & Spencer, he pumps them for information about how it is Marks & Spencer are doing better than he is, so that he can make more money himself. But it never does him any good because Marks & Spencer don't make their exceptional profit from the narrow, wholly selfish kind of attitude which that question comes from.

John Woolworths now tell this story about themselves. A few years ago they tried to be more like Marks & Spencer and bought all their staff new smart overalls to raise morale. Only the overalls didn't have pockets – the staff could use the pockets for stealing, you see! The result was: worse morale. Because, one, removing pockets doesn't actually stop you from stealing, though if you're that way inclined it may help to put the idea in your mind! And, two, everyone who realised what the thinking had been was insulted.

Robin That's a marvellous example of how people can always pick up, in some very subtle way, whether an act has a genuine Affiliative Attitude behind it or whether it is in fact manipulative.

John I find it incredibly encouraging that genuinely generous behaviour also brings in the right results. Machiavelli must be turning in his grave. But these 'beliefs' that you're talking about, they're not expressed in spiritual terms?

Robin Not usually. Mostly the leaders have the aim that their companies should be 'the best': and they value their employees very highly as individuals. If you've flown on Delta Airlines or Virgin Atlantic, you'll have noticed there's a special attention and relaxed friendliness shown to passengers. It comes from the importance they've given to good relationships between management and staff, which in turn builds a high team spirit and a strong sense of pride and enjoyment in their work and the way they relate to customers. The research shows that where you have this kind of dedication to achieving high standards by bringing out the best in people, the employees come to have an explicit belief in the importance of the company's economic growth and profit.

John Yes, it follows from each person feeling that he or she is valued. Because if you feel you're making a valuable contribution and that it's being recognised . . . then you can take pleasure in the success of your company, because its success becomes your own. If a film crew has really enjoyed working on a film, they take a surprising pleasure if its box office returns are good.

Robin But of course to get this feeling in an organisation the people at the top have to be 'team players'. Because only leaders with this Affiliative Attitude will possess the great managerial skill of getting the best out of the 'ordinary' people in the organisation – who've been called the '60 per cent with 50 per cent ability'. And 'getting the best out of them' is all about seeing the best *in* them, expecting it, and knowing how to draw it out, by stretching employees to develop their capacity, rewarding their successes, and enhancing competence and self-respect. Which all leads to pride in your work, and more enjoyment.

John The trouble is, if people haven't had this experience, they won't believe it's possible.

Robin No, and unhealthy managers don't believe that 'the best' is actually in their employees at all. If you haven't come from a particularly healthy family, you'll need experience to show you that all this is possible.

John OK, and I feel quite excited and want to shout 'Ra ra ra!' but then I think . . . 'Wait a moment, aren't people going to take advantage of this kind of system?' At school I was taught that if people were treated like this they'd get 'slack'.

Robin That's not what generally happens in practice. Other things being equal, when management act from generosity and trust towards others, it tends to arouse the same attitudes in response. Remember the 'philosophy of plenty' we talked about? If one person displays it, the other will usually respond. For instance, such companies don't use time-clocks and other checks to make sure people are earning the money they are paid. They rely instead on employees repaying them for the trust and goodwill shown them, for treating them as responsible adults. And it works. There's been some research showing that only between 3 per cent and 8 per cent of employees actually abuse this trust.

John But what about bosses who say the way to keep people 'on their toes' is to make sure they know they'll be sacked if their work isn't up to scratch?

Robin That's one way of achieving high standards, it's true. But just by itself it causes a lot of anxiety, creates tension, and spoils good relations between management and workforce. Also, it encourages people to conceal mistakes, and inhibits creativity. The more positive approach I'm describing works better. After all, if people's work slips below the required standard, an Affiliative Attitude doesn't mean that you don't mention it!

John I worked with Video Arts, the management and sales training film company, and I remember a film we did about this. The basic idea is that every job has a 'standard' of performance that is objectively measured. Then if an employee's work falls below it, they discuss it with their manager, so that the causes for the shortfall can be identified. Next, ways of improving performance are explored and agreed. But the problem is approached cooperatively. It's not a question of the manager shouting: 'Pull your socks up'; it's more: 'We have this objective problem. How can we get the work back up to standard?' And of course it doesn't exclude the possibility of firing somebody if they can't meet the standard. Because if they can't, someone else must do the job.

Robin In fact, though it's painful to be told one's work is falling short, most people eventually feel grateful to the kind of boss who points it out, but puts the emphasis on helping them to become more competent. And of course there's the question of how the standard itself has been arrived at. If it was originally agreed between the employee and the company after discussion, the employee will be far more committed to it.

John That was the other lesson in the film!

Robin It's certainly a trusting and cooperative process, but it doesn't mean that work isn't monitored efficiently. In fact in a cooperative atmosphere it's *more easily* monitored, so problems are identified sooner.

John All right. Now moving beyond customers and employers, how does this Affiliative Attitude apply to distributors and suppliers?

Robin It's the same there. McDonalds, Nissan and Marks & Spencer are outstanding examples, as they take a helpful and encouraging attitude towards their suppliers. Of course they expect very high quality and won't be satisfied with less – otherwise they let themselves and their customers down – but they maintain close relationships with suppliers and work with them to help them achieve the required standard. They even show the same kind of concern in the working conditions in their suppliers' firms as they do in their own. Apparently a former Chairman and CEO of M&S, Marcus Sieff, when he was visiting a supplier, always asked to see the toilets; he knew they would give him an accurate impression of how much trouble the supplier was taking over good working conditions.

John So these healthy companies display our so-called Affiliative Attitude not just towards customers, but towards all the various groups they deal with and they do so because they 'believe in' openness and cooperation as a way of life, rather than just because this way of behaving happens also to bring the best results!

Robin That's certainly the impression one gets.

John All right. Well, let's now move on to the second thing on the list of characteristics of healthy families – love! Discuss, please.

Robin If you remember, the most surprising thing about love in the healthy families was how much it was to do with independence and separateness; how the couple, after coming together and sharing great intimacy, can then separate again and operate independently with great confidence.

John Not needing to cling together and control each other, yes.

Robin Well with organisations there's a real parallel. It's very striking how the most successful companies give independence to people, how they empower them to get on with things by allowing them to operate with surprisingly little supervision. And of course some successful companies dispense with supervision completely by franchising parts of their business! Milk delivery companies have franchised the milk rounds.

John I suppose this is not so surprising really. We all know, in badly-run organisations the leadership's trying to control everyone because they can't be trusted to get anything right.

So there they all are, clinging together for security and nobody can actually do anything . . .

Robin Just like an anxious, depressed, unhappy family.

John Like some Hollywood films too. There'll be a flock of 'producers', all being very excited and drawing big salaries, but none of them ever expressing a clear point of view, least of all in front of the others and they'll be very 'supportive', without actually doing anything except keeping an eye on the rest of the flock, until one day . . . at the same *split second* the whole pack of them will say: 'It's a disaster *and* I saw it coming, too!' The next stage is known as 'Hunt for the Guilty' and they're quite good at that. But their primary skill is always to be indistinguishable in opinion from everyone else.

Robin Well, in contrast, the healthy companies have tremendous respect for individuality and independence. For a start, the leaders themselves are often chosen precisely for their unconventional – indeed convention-challenging – qualities, which means that the yes-persons are likely to get spotted and shaken up rather early on in their careers. And this unconventionality is held to be an important part of their company ethos, enshrined in stories of earlier successful innovators who were regarded as mavericks in their time. In the same way, unconventional attitudes are respected and sought out when recruiting new staff. And once they're part of the company, individuals of this kind are protected and supported, and indeed often championed by one of the senior people.

John Despite the fact that mavericks are often 'trouble'?

Robin Exactly.

John Yes, I remember Tony Jay, who was an executive at the BBC for years, telling me that each head of department has to make a basic choice between a smooth-running, cooperative, friendly and well-ordered department, or one that produces good programmes.

Robin Alas, nice conventional people don't tend to be so creative. So the healthy companies are very happy to buy creativity and innovation, at the price of a little nuisance.

John But wait a moment. So far we've just been talking about individuals. But most individuals can achieve very little *on their own*. You have to cooperate to get anything major done. So surely these companies can't organise themselves around individuals?

Robin No indeed. But this respect for independence and separateness results in the whole organisational structure being based on Schumacher's principle: 'Small is Beautiful'.

John Bigger than one, but still 'Small'?

Robin Yes. So no matter how big the firm, work groups are kept to a size where they can really operate as teams.

John Yes, but what size?

Robin Round about ten. Then everybody can know each other really well. And, as I say, each of these small groups is allowed to function with a great deal of independence.

John It's interesting, this figure of ten. In *Corporation Man* Tony Jay points out that the basic infantry unit has a strength of about ten – whether you're talking about the US army, the British army, the Roman army or even Genghis Khan's! Squads in team sports are around this number, too, juries are twelve, the Jewish prayer group is ten . . .

Robin The 'quality circles' some companies use to explore ideas aren't allowed to get much bigger.

John In a well-organised movie there are between seven and ten key jobs. There were only twelve apostles!

Robin My therapy groups were usually about eight!

John It's as though humans are wired so that they can cooperate best, and indeed develop an almost instinctive understanding, provided they work in groups not bigger than, say, at the outside fifteen.

Robin Yes, if you can keep a group under that number, you get all the advantages of family-style communication, so it can respond very fast to what's going on.

John But Robin, if a group is really going to act quickly in this independent kind of way, they've got to have the confidence to do that. And that can only come from the people at the top.

Robin Absolutely. In the most successful companies the leadership encourages people to try things, instead of having every new thought discussed and reported upon and sent up and down the hierarchy for comment and approval.

John But how can you do this without completely losing control?

Robin Rather like the way the healthy families do it. It's a system called loose/tight control. The leadership exercises *very* *strict* control over a *small* number of absolutely crucial 'regulators', but gives as much freedom as possible apart from that.

John What kind of things do they regulate?

Robin They're almost always to do with money. After all, ultimately, the only thing that's going to stop the business is bankruptcy. Otherwise it goes on operating, even if it needs improvement.

John So the 'tight' bits of loose/tight control are mainly financial?

Robin Yes, provided that these few regulators are adhered to – and this is continually checked – the rest of the group operation can be run in a relatively 'loose' way. And even financially, provided the groups get the big sums right, they can play around a bit with everything else. Head Office won't make a fuss if a group pinches some money from one budget, and uses it in another, because they want to try something new without getting permission from above. It's called bootlegging, and they're almost *encouraged* to behave in this kind of way – in the sense that those in charge turn a blind eye to such practices.

John Well, if most of the control is as loose as this, what's the leadership doing?

Robin Apart from monitoring the 'crucial' regulators, the chain of command is there more for guidance, with leaders tending to listen and suggest rather than give orders. General Sir John Hackett used to refer to the chain-of-command in the army as a chain-of-confidence!

John So control – or power, or decision making, or authority, whatever you want to call it – is a *shared, company-wide function*.

Robin Of course, to some extent this is always the case in any organisation. Even in a prison, some decisions and jobs are delegated to trusties. The 'healthy' successful companies recognise this reality and explicitly acknowledge and extend it, designing a company structure to make the best possible use of the fact.

John So obviously if control is this 'loose', they're not frightened of people making mistakes.

Robin No. It's absolutely accepted that a reasonable proportion of mistakes are going to be made, if people are getting on with the job in this independent and healthy way.

John They must have heard the old English proverb, 'He who does not make mistakes is unlikely to make *anything*'.

Robin Very good. In fact, in the healthiest companies the taboo is not on mistakes. It's on *concealing* them!

John Because if they're concealed, they can't be put right. That remarkable man Sir Peter Parker, who ran British Rail, once said: 'If someone comes to the door of my office and says: "I screwed up" I say: "Come on in!"'

Robin But leaders have to work hard to get that message across. It's so hard for us to have confidence to admit mistakes. All our training teaches us to conceal them.

John I have a speech about the importance of allowing mistakes to be made, and after I finish so many people come up and tell me they agree, but *if only* I could tell their boss . . . yet fear of mistakes leads to such unhealthy behaviour, with people spending their day scattering memos around to establish overwhelming documentary evidence that they're not to blame for anything.

Robin While drawing salaries which they can't risk losing by making a mistake and getting fired.

John These past few years I've noticed that when companies approach me about working for them, it takes about three phone calls to find out whether they're running on this kind of fear. And if they are I just walk away. Because it's not just that projects never happen easily with such companies; they don't really happen at all. That is, you can never find out afterwards whether what you did worked, because they don't really know themselves. Nobody at the top seems to want to make up their mind and say 'Good 'n' Bad' because if they did, that would establish criteria that could then be used to point out *other* mistakes, which they want to conceal – *if* they're mistakes, that is, which they're not quite sure about.

Robin I recognise what you're saying from the consultancy work I've done with companies. Well, it's the opposite in the confident companies. People take decisions and act precisely because they're expected to! And if they get it wrong, that's clear because the criteria are clear. Which means any errors can be corrected straight away.

John In my speech I suggest our role model should be Gordon, the Guided Missile. He checks his course every split second, and corrects it every other split second. So . . . apart from encouraging independent behaviour in the teams that the company's organised around, are there other ways the best organisation can be said to respect individuality?

Robin There is one other very distinctive way in which they do this. They are interested in all the facets of each individual's personality.

John You mean, not just the bit people usually bring to work?

Robin Right. Let me tell you how Tom Peters, who co-wrote *In Search of Excellence*, puts this. Talking to groups of business executives, he will tell them they'd get a big surprise if they were to ask ten of their employees what they do in their spare time. They might find, he says, that a couple of them were deacons in their church and that one of them, whom they thought couldn't count, was the church treasurer. A couple more might be experts in electronics, another might have built his own boat. A sixth might run the local dramatic society, with the seventh a lead actress. Number eight might organise the local youth club, and the ninth could be a graphics artist who had exhibited widely. Only number ten might not show some high similar level of competence. And Peters ends by telling the business people in his audience that their employees are all intelligent, caring, creative, thoughtful, talented and energetic individuals 'except for the eight hours they are working for you!'

John That's so appallingly accurate. Once we get the message our talents aren't wanted, it's quite depressing how easily we accept a narrower role. We just give up on the bits of us that aren't made welcome. Think how sheep-like we become when we fall into the hands of an airline. A stewardess once told me she'd been taught that passengers check in their brains with their luggage. I agreed that was true but pointed out that it was a direct result of how they treated us.

Robin Let me tell you another story.

John Oh goody.

Robin It's about the 'Basic Bits' we mentioned in Chapter 1 – the three main parts of the personality.

John Parent, Adult, Child. Or, Super-ego, Ego, Id. I'm sitting comfortably.

Robin Back in the sixties, there was a fascinating study done by Isabel Menzies on the nursing system in British hospitals. Management were very concerned about low morale and high staff turnover. So she was asked to investigate. I'm sure I don't need to emphasise that work in a hospital requires people to cope with high levels of anxiety, because of the responsibility involved. Your product is healthy people, and your failures are dead people, so you really do have to aim for zero defect! Now what Menzies found was very interesting. She discovered that the organisation was such that no member of the nursing staff was able to use the whole of themselves in their job. Instead of each person being able to tap into all three of their Basic Bits, these Basic Bits were shared out among different levels of the hierarchy. All the 'responsibility' was on the shoulders of the matron and sisters, who were expected to be serious and severe and were regarded as fierce and strict dragons. Whereas all the fun and playfulness and liveliness was carried by the student nurses, who were regarded as immature children.

John And therefore treated as 'irresponsible' and 'unreliable'?

Robin Precisely. Their natural liveliness, openness and warmth were viewed with disapproval, so they had to suppress it. But they weren't given a chance to use their capacity for responsibility either. So they were deprived of the enjoyment of exercising their more grown-up aspects too. And, of course, the hospital lost the benefit of these aspects as well . . .

John Whereas the dragons couldn't have any fun!

Robin They had to maintain very tight control of everything, and because of that, of themselves too. So they lost out on enjoyment of the more sensitive, feeling side of their personalities. Which meant the patients lost out too, by not receiving that more sympathetic, human form of contact.

John And the nurses in between?

Robin They were 'pig-in-the-middle'. Since the nursing sisters were carrying all the authority and control, and the student nurses all the natural human feeling, the ordinary nurses were deprived both of the enjoyment that goes with taking responsibility, and of the pleasure of sharing spontaneous feelings with the patients and with each other. So they were left just with executive functions, doing exactly what they were told rather mechanically, without showing what they felt or 'wasting' time making patients feel happier. And also walking a tightrope, fearful of challenging the authority of the seniors on the one hand and of being thought childish and irresponsible on the other.

John So really, each of the three groups was operating on just one of the Basic Bits, and not really using the other two. The sisters were carrying all the 'Super-ego' or Parent functions. The ordinary nurses were carrying the executive 'Ego' or Adult functions. And the students were landed with all the 'Id' or Child functions.

Robin Another way of putting it is that each group was perceiving certain aspects of their own personalities as if they were only in other members of the nursing team. They were all locked into fixed, limited roles, hedged about with restrictions, and none of them was really able to meet the patients' needs properly.

John Why had it been organised in this rigid way?

Robin The system was overtly designed out of concern to protect patients against mistakes being made; but instead of reducing the nurses' anxiety it had the effect of preventing it from being expressed and recognised. So none of the nurses was able to ask for and get proper support and guidance in dealing with the fears and stress their difficult job aroused. So the risk of breakdown were vastly increased. And this was a major reason for the huge turnover and wastage of trainees.

John So the rigidity of the system, which was intended to exclude mistakes and reduce anxiety actually rendered it very inefficient.

Robin Because nobody could use the whole range of their personalities and their skills. So the lesson is this. The more that organisations recognise people as individuals, the more those people are able to contribute: the wise and responsible bits, the ordinary competent bits, and the playful, creative, enjoying bits. For example, Avon Rubber closed one factory and started up another up the road, using the same employees but working in the way we're describing. As a result, productivity and quality have spectacularly improved.

John Fascinating. So to sum up . . . in healthy organisations, 'love' manifests itself as: respect and consideration for individuals; a willingness to employ unconventional types of person, even in high positions; and a very non-controlling attitude towards the small groups into which the healthiest organisations structure themselves.

Robin What's the next healthy family characteristic? I've forgotten where we've got to . . .

John It's . . . two factors together: the clear authority of the parents; and the full consultation of the children.

Robin That's right. In the healthy families the parents try to negotiate with the children as far as possible; but are prepared, if necessary, to accept responsibility and take decisions that the children don't like. Well, in the healthiest organisations we see an exactly parallel process! For a start they're almost fanatical about consultation.

John What's the business thinking behind this fanaticism?

Robin If there's one idea above all the others, I think it's the determination of the management to *use the intelligence of the whole system*.

John Oh, I like that.

Robin Instead of just using the intelligence of the people at the top, and treating everyone else as an instrument for carrying out their orders. We've already been talking about one aspect of this really – the high degree of autonomy given to the smallish groups in successful organisations.

John Encouraging these groups to take decisions and put them into effect themselves is even better than consultation!

Robin But, where decisions have to be taken at a higher level, everyone affected gets to put in their fourpenny-worth.

John . . . And it's obvious that any organisation run this way will be more intelligent than one where everything's decided by the board. Because the people who know what's wrong with the mailroom are the ones who work there, and the folk who really know about the problems with the product are the sales-persons and the service engineers. So if you can only gather all their intelligence before you take a decision, you're going to have a huge competitive edge over the companies that are drawing only on the knowledge and ideas of the headquarters group.

Robin It's a major reason for the success of Japanese companies like Honda, which has produced the best-selling car in the USA three years running. But now General Motors has finally caught on and set up a separate company to build a new car called the Saturn. The workforce is divided into teams of between six and fifteen people, each of which has its own budget, hires any new members required, organises its own training, plans its own work and monitors its own quality. People working there love the arrangement and the project is immensely successful! By involving everyone in this way you constantly draw on all the information, and all the interpretations, and all the ideas for possible responses, in the decision-making process. And there's another equally important aspect.

John I know what you're going to say! Years ago I was researching a film for Video Arts on Decision Making and the more I talked to experienced managers, the more I became convinced that getting the decision right *wasn't* the hardest part! That was getting peoples' *commitment* to it, *if they didn't agree with it*! And the more I explained this, the clearer it became that the key was consultation. Because if people have been invited to give their opinions, and *really* feel they have been *listened to* . . . then, even if they don't agree with the final decision, they won't obstruct it. They'll be much more likely to say, 'All right, what I had to say was listened to and treated seriously. So although I think the decision's wrong and I don't agree with it, I'll give it a go.'

Robin That's right. And for us in the West, I think there's a very important lesson in the immense trouble the Japanese take over the process of securing agreement to a plan. They involve everyone in repeated discussions which go on for an unbelievable time . . .

John Yes, I remember some of the British executives at Sony telling me that when they first went to Japan they just couldn't believe how undirected and discursive the meetings were.

Robin Well, the Japanese reckon that it's time well spent.

John Our trouble in the West is that there's always such a sense of time pressure. In meetings people often feel they don't have the right to express worries or objections. It feels as though to do so would be 'negative', or would hold things up. And what they have to say may be very important but because, perhaps, they can't articulate it clearly, or the Chairman's looking impatient, they keep their mouth shut, and a serious problem may be overlooked as a result.

Robin The Japanese, on the other hand, deliberately allow the time for these kinds of objections to emerge, to make sure they can be taken into account; instead of skating over them, so that they grow beneath the surface and create unforeseen obstacles later. This may cause delays in starting, but it means they ensure everyone is as committed as possible to the plan, so that all the psychological resistance that we in the West would meet at a later stage has already been ironed out. The other advantage is that, from a practical point of view, everyone's had a chance to query the plan from every technical angle, so that they really understand exactly what their bit of the job is, and how it fits in with everybody else's. Sir John Harvey-Jones, the ex-Chairman of ICI, described the process of building two identical paraxylene plants, one in Japan, and one in the UK. The Japanese were still having their endless discussions four months after the British began to build. But once the Japanese started, as Harvey-Jones puts it, 'they moved like greased lightning' and finished their plant seven months earlier than the British. What's more it all worked from day one, whereas when the British plant finally opened seven months later, it went through three months of teething troubles!

John I feel quite worried. When I wrote a Video Arts film on Meetings, we advised that the chairperson should indicate for certain agenda items the number of minutes allowed for discussion. I'm very uncomfortable with that now and believe that should only happen with trivia. OK, some of the time that kind of chairing is right; but some meetings should be *open-ended*, so that vague and unformulated thoughts have time to emerge and clarify, whether they're faint stirrings of disquiet, or creative ideas that can't be forced.

Robin And it's not just a question of time, is it? It's also about the atmosphere created by the chairperson. Are people being encouraged to keep their minds ajar? It's fine for everyone to come to the meeting with clear ideas – that helps everyone else's to become more defined too. But if people have become too identified with their own ideas, correct decision making gets subordinated to a battle between egos.

John There's a motto for meetings: 'Cooperation between people, competition between ideas'.

Robin Lovely. The chairperson's job is to try to achieve exactly that.

John But there's a slightly different problem, too. If you're consulting people to get criticism of something that's been decided and done – to see if it needs to be changed – it's a tricky business getting them to tell you what they really think. My experience is that people have been brought up to think that you won't like criticism, yet their view may be vital to you. So I use subterfuge. At trial screenings of my movies, to get the real criticism that will enable me to re-edit properly, I no longer say: 'What didn't you like?' because people won't tell me if I ask them like that; I've learned to say: 'If I was making this again from the beginning, what two bits of advice would you give me?' That way people can sound positive while expressing thoughts that are in fact critical. So the great problem is: unless you really want criticism, you won't get it; if you're just pretending, people pick up that hidden message and don't give honest feedback. Management consultants know they're sometimes employed to agree with the board – and if times are hard they do!

Robin The Japanese have a clever way of dealing with reluctance to criticise. After a discussion, when the time comes to decide on the action to take, the leader will invite everyone there to give their opinion but *beginning with the most junior person* and working up the scale of seniority. That way no one has to disagree with someone more senior, and there's less likelihood that they will just parrot what the boss thinks. Finally, the leader's job is to arrive at a decision based as far as possible on the consensus.

John Brilliant. Because we can only improve things through feedback. The snag is: the better the feedback, the more it hurts! I think in the West we're very aware of this; people are loath to speak up because they think nobody will listen.

Robin Sir John Harvey-Jones says: 'Yes-men come cheap. What we're looking for is what I call Constructive No-men.'

John OK. Now I'm getting a little bit lost. We're talking about criticism, and how it's absolutely pointless consulting people if you don't want your ego ruffled. And that came from the fact that the healthiest organisations always consult very fully before reaching decisions. And that related to the way very healthy parents consult their children. But we haven't really dealt with the other side of that coin – the clear authority of the parents.

Robin Well we've mentioned one important aspect: as with the families, the thorough consultation means that the decisions eventually taken are accepted better even when they're not agreed with.

John Oh, that's true.

Robin But we also need to bring in here what we were saying earlier about the small, largely autonomous groups that the healthy organisations encourage. The authority of the leaders is also accepted because they *delegate as much as they possibly can downwards*. They retain only those decision-making powers they have to, the ones that can't be delegated down a level.

John Yes, I can sense how this enhances the leaders' authority. If people are trusted this much, they're more likely to listen attentively to authority in those areas where it *is* asserted.

Robin Why do you sense that?

John Because if you're entrusted with what you can handle, you get a clearer feeling for what's outside your competence – at least for the time being.

Robin I'm sure that's right. So if there's a crisis the leadership won't be afraid to use their authority and take charge more fully if that becomes necessary. They'll pull the reins in a bit. But as soon as the crisis passes, the really healthy company will relax the tighter control back to the previous level.

John So the degree of authority necessary is variable.

Robin Yes. That flexibility is vital. Being able to let go of the reins, and pick them up again, as required. The principle is: don't exercise more control than is necessary at any given moment.

John Which again reinforces the whole system. A group can get on with its job with confidence, and take a few risks because: first, they know exactly what requirements they have to fulfil; second, they therefore know exactly how much freedom of action they have; third, they're actively encouraged to get on with it; and fourth, they have the additional confidence that comes from knowing there's a safety net, because the people in charge will take much tighter control if things begin to go wrong.

Robin That's true, isn't it? We're all much more prepared to try something new if we know that someone we trust is in charge – in a way, it's what therapy's about. The therapist is trying to give patients new experiences, new ways of looking at things which are alarming to them just because they are so new. But patients can risk trying the new experience if they can trust the therapist to contain the situation, to provide the safety net. Just like in a healthy family, where you can see the toddlers becoming more and more confident precisely because they can trust the parents to exercise firm control if necessary to stop them from going too far.

John I find this very interesting, because all our attitudes to authority go very deep, don't they? Some people are basically 'for' it, some basically 'against' it. Yet in these healthy organisations people accept 'authority' quite willingly, because it's being exercised well. But when it's *not*, people spot the fact pretty quickly, begin to resent it and become obstructive; which, to the authoritarian-minded, looks like further proof that their subordinates are difficult and uncooperative and untrustworthy; which obviously justifies a more authoritarian approach; which in turn makes everyone even more resentful and obstructive, and so on and so on. In other words, whatever the leaders believe about their subordinates, will be proved true for them because it's a self-fulfilling prophecy: each different type of leadership behaviour produces the response that it predicts.

Robin Yes, the management theorist Douglas McGregor demonstrated that back in 1960 with his 'Theory X' and 'Theory Y'. 'Theory X' was the widely-held belief that the average human being disliked work and would avoid it unless controlled and coerced. That attitude inevitably leads to the autocratic type of management, and the resistant, uncooperative response to it you've just described, with the vicious circle of more control – more resistance.

John And theory Y?

Robin That said people like to exercise their intelligence and skills, welcome responsibility, and more often than not are highly creative and resourceful in helping to solve organisational problems; and that if only management believed this, it would lead to cooperation and good morale.

John So what did McGregor demonstrate?

Robin Well, it's rather amusing. When McGregor became president of a college and tried to put his ideas into practice, he thought at first that by following Theory Y completely he would avoid discord and confrontation. But he ended up realising that there were times when he had no alternative but to use his power, and lay down the law. In short, there's a place for authority, as well as for consultation, and the balance has to be adjusted to fit the current need. Just like the healthy families. And the healthy organisations know this, and see no contradiction in being firmly authoritative at times even if their general aim is closer to Theory Y.

John Which brings us neatly to the next topic in the healthy family characteristics: good, open communication.

Robin Well, the healthy organisations fall over themselves to encourage this.

John . . . Can't you say something a bit more surprising than that, Robin? You know. 'They always hire a couple of pathological liars, specially trained by Robert Maxwell, to keep everyone on their toes.' Or, 'Heads of Department have to say the *exact* opposite of what they mean on Thursday mornings.' Something like that?

Robin . . . Well what's surprising is that . . .

John *Very* surprising?

Robin . . . *Fairly* surprising . . . is that they encourage communication, even when it doesn't have any clear or immediate objective.

John That's better. You mean it's regarded as a good thing in itself, full stop.

Robin Healthy organisations know there's always something worth talking about. So companies are run in such a way as to push people into contact with each other.

John How?

Robin Say, using big long tables in dining rooms, to bring about unexpected meetings and cross-conversations, instead of small tables, which lead to the same small groups sitting together regularly. Providing spare rooms for people to meet and talk informally. And managers will be constantly on walkabout, chatting with the workforce and answering questions and noting comments, instead of being closeted in a separate office or shut away in a headquarters building. MBWA, it's called – Management by Walking About!

John There is a lovely story about encouraging people to talk to each other. Oliver Blandford, who ran Upper Clyde Shipbuilders a couple of decades ago, had a problem with absenteeism, so he pinned up a notice with the names of absentees, arranged under the names of their respective foremen. Naturally, some foremen had a lot more absentees than others. When they complained about being criticised, Blandford told them: 'It's not criticism. I just thought you'd like to know which foremen have the fewest absentees so that you can ask them what they're doing that you're not.'

Robin Very good. Following the same principle management will provide funds for running all kinds of social groups, however unrelated to the company's business activities they may be! It's realised that friendships and conversations are likely to develop which will benefit the company in the long run.

John That is interesting, this trust in informal communication.

Robin And it's striking how much they distrust more formal administrative machinery – the kind of committees which are set up to solve a problem but which take on a life of their own and become part of some executive's expanding empire.

So instead of committees, small one-off brainstorming sessions are preferred; and for major problems ad hoc working parties will be set up, but the number of members involved is kept limited, and they're encouraged to bring themselves to a close as soon as possible by not being given too much administrative or secretarial support, in case they start generating paperwork instead of practical proposals.

John There's a real mistrust of bureaucracy.

Robin They're always trying to cut it down, to optimise communication. And there's a major *structural* way of doing that, too: minimising the number of levels in the hierarchy of the organisation. Because inevitably every extra layer in the hierarchy slows down communication, and so delays reaction to the outside world. Often the extra layer isn't necessary. For example, Wal-Mart, the retailing outfit based in Arkansas, has a turnover of around $30 billion, and only three layers in its hierarchy! Some organisations that size have as many as ten. British Steel at one point had a printed organisation chart which stretched right across an ordinary-size office!

John So these organisations believe strongly in communication. They certainly believe in encouraging plenty of it *upwards* – we've talked all about consultation – but what about *downwards*? What kind of information does the leadership want everyone to have?

Robin Very wide. Not just matters of immediate relevance to their jobs, but also information about how the company is doing, what its future plans are, what changes are being contemplated – in other words, they're trying to give everyone as wide a perspective on the business as they can.

John Aren't there some things they don't want communicated?

Robin How do you mean?

John Stuff they'd rather keep secret.

Robin Yes, but in the past companies have been far more secretive than they needed to be. The present tendency is swinging very much in the other direction. Tom Peters lists only three kinds of legitimate areas of secrecy: some personnel information, because that's for the benefit of the workforce; patent information, because that's part of the company's competitive advantage; and would-be acquisition information, because that's the way the marketplace operates. But he feels this is about all that management should keep to themselves. There's a lot of research showing employees want more information, are able to understand it, and do treat it responsibly.

John Well I'm delighted to hear all this, because one always feels that openness is preferable, and it's marvellous that it seems to work. But just from one's own experience, it requires a constant effort, doesn't it? It's the most natural human failing to forget to tell other people what we're doing and thinking. Rather as though we expect others to pick it all up by ESP.

Robin I'm sure that's why these healthy organisations harp on and on about it, constantly trying to keep the notion at the front of everyone's mind.

John But there are other blocks to open communication, too. We hold back because sharing information can mean sharing our power. And sharing our ideas can expose us to ridicule, if people don't think they're any good. There's a general fear that we may not be 'right', and that people will think less of us.

Robin That's true. So it's all the more important that the attitudes of the boss, and the kind of work atmosphere that he or she produces, should work to reverse that feeling and encourage participation.

John When we were setting up *A Fish called Wanda*, I thought about how to do this. So first, I very consciously tried to make all the individuals feel confident, trusted, really good about themselves. That wasn't so difficult because they'd all been hand-picked and my feelings were genuine. So it was just a question of making sure that they knew how I felt. I hoped this would free them to say anything that came into their head, to anybody, without feeling they had to check every thought before expressing it, in case it was 'wrong' or 'silly'. But more than that, I tried to break down the barriers caused by the lines of demarcation between people's jobs – you know how territorial people can get, professionally speaking. It's a defence: nobody questions anyone else's area of expertise, to make sure nobody else questions theirs! I'd decided to try to remove this block to good communication by setting an example! So from the start I asked everyone for suggestions on the script. At the first read-through, the assistant director suggested a very good line, so I just crossed out the one I'd written and wrote in his. Some of the folk there were pretty startled – expecially the Americans. But then it energised everyone. But the point is that inviting people into my territory meant that they didn't resist me if I trespassed into theirs. It was like a deal. They weren't territorial because I wasn't.

Twenty-four people contributed dialogue to the movie, and I could stick my oar in everywhere without folk getting defensive . . .

Robin I remember when I visited the set, I found myself grinning a lot. There was a very relaxed atmosphere, a bit like a big, happy family. Maybe what you'd learned about the research was being put into practice.

John Well, that's what I was trying to do. What's next on the list of characteristics? Ah, yes, very apt. The so-called Three-Ring Circus – the sense of freedom and fun, individuality and creativity, all somehow held together.

Robin Well it's surprising how much fun is being had in the most effective organisations! All the different factors we've mentioned are going to encourage it. There's the loose structure with the semi-autonomous groups kept to a size small enough to maximise interaction, mutual support and enjoyment. Then the leadership, which really trusts them to get on with it and encourages them to innovate. All this will give them confidence. Furthermore, the work groups know that if anything starts going seriously wrong, top management will step in. That leads to more confidence. Then there's the easy, open, informal communication, and the tolerance of the odd mistake. More confidence still! And there are some mavericks around having off-the-wall ideas and stimulating original thinking in others, despite being a bit difficult and behaving a little oddly. The whole atmosphere is encouraging people not to hold back – to take action and try things out.

John More than that! People become much more creative in an atmosphere like this. Because when we're confident we become more playful, and I'm entirely sure that playfulness and creativity are indistinguishable. There's some very impressive research done by Donald MacKinnon at Berkeley University in the seventies, where he examined several professions to discover what made people creative. He found that the behaviour of those rated 'most creative' displayed two characteristics: one, they had a greater facility for switching themselves into a playful, 'child-like' mode; and two, they were prepared to ponder problems for much longer periods before resolving them. Now, not only does confidence lead to playfulness and thus to creativity; it also enables us to think for longer before making up our minds, because it helps us to tolerate better the feelings of anxiety that bubble inside us while we postpone a resolution. So instilling confidence in employees increases their creativity in both ways.

Robin Listen to what Akio Morita of Sony said recently: 'The human infant is born curious, but that natural curiosity gradually drains away as they grow older. I consider it my job to do everything I can to nurture the curiosity of the people I work with, because at Sony we know that a terrific new idea is more likely to happen in an open, free and trusting atmosphere than where everything is calculated, every action analysed, and every responsibility assigned by an organisational chart.'

John Spot on. Unfortunately not everybody realises that you don't come up with the best ideas by working logically from existing ideas and methods – what Edward de Bono calls 'digging the same hole deeper'. On the contrary, you throw everything into question, just go wherever your imagination takes you, and accept that a lot of the stuff that comes out doesn't make sense.

Robin Or *rather* . . . it doesn't at first, but it's amazing, later on, how often you see that the nonsense has a kind of meaning, a shape to it which you weren't aware of at the time.

John We've learned, when we get stuck writing this book, just to say the first thing that comes into our heads. And even now, we still usually feel we're wasting time, just wandering aimlessly all over the place.

Robin But later on in the conversation, or after it has been typed out and we can get a bird's-eye view of it, we almost always suddenly see in it a pattern that we were quite unaware of at the time, which is pointing us towards an answer.

John The odd thing for me is how long it's taken me to trust this process, considering I'm supposed to be 'creative'. But I *did* with comedy. There I was able to brainstorm without expecting anything to make sense straight away. After all, I grew up thinking important problems had to be solved by the usual logical-critical kind of thinking we're taught in our Western culture. The idea of putting that approach *on hold* when dealing with *serious* questions seemed almost alarming! It's as though I felt that 'thinking' wasn't really valid, if I didn't know *how* I was doing it!

Robin It is astonishing how little we know about how we arrive at new ideas – which of course can only happen when we are in a creative and playful mode. When we try to put the process under the microscope and 'explain' it, we find ourselves automatically back in the logical-critical mode again; the process we're trying to study has vanished.

John Psychologists studied creativity a lot in the sixties and seventies, but then got stuck. They reached a point beyond which they just couldn't explain it.

Robin But of course, in solving problems, we need both these modes. In other words, after you've done some play-thinking, you've got to switch to the logical mode, and analyse. Then you hit some new problems. So you switch back to playing again, and then after a bit back to logical criticism of the latest stuff you've come up with. On and on until you think your idea is worth trying out in action.

John But once you've decided what to do, you've just got to do it!

Robin Agreed. But then, once you've carried out your action, and collected the feedback and analysed it to see whether you're on the right track, you must then switch back to the brainstorming mode to see if you can come up with a next step that's better than the one you've already got in mind.

John Like Gordon the Guided Missile. So the secret is not the ability to play, nor the ability to act decisively; the secret is being able to switch between the two as appropriate. And the structure of healthy organisations, with their 'Three-Ring Circus' atmosphere, gives people the confidence to do that. Because when we lack confidence we neither act decisively, nor do we trust our creativity.

Robin There's only one problem: you have to learn *when* and *how* to switch from one mode to the other – which takes time. That's why the selection and training of the facilitators who run quality circles is so important.

John OK. Let's move on to the last-but-one characteristic of the healthiest families: their realistic perception of what's going on . . .

Robin Yes. They see the world with great clarity. They don't have illusions about it being better or worse than it actually is. And not only do they have a good mental map of the world; they've got *themselves* on it too.

John Ah, yes! In the right place, and about the right size, too. So they're likely to get what they want out of life.

Robin And there's one other aspect of these healthy organisations' attitude to gathering information. They love new ideas and they don't care where they come from.

John Yes! I remember a British businessman telling me that he'd joined a new company and suggested a way of doing things that had been successful in his last company. But the Chairman shook his head and said: 'NIH.' That was the end of the matter. And my friend asked after the meeting, 'What's NIH?' and was told: 'Not invented here.'

Robin By contrast, these really healthy organisations are great borrowers.

John 'Borrowers'! I like that. Comics 'steal', artists 'are influenced by', businessmen 'borrow'. Very good.

Robin Hush. Think of the Japanese! They've never had inhibitions about . . .

John Careful!

Robin . . . about taking over Western industrial know-how – from the time they began to open up to the world after 1868 – and then steadily improving on it. It's a major reason why their companies are world-beaters.

John That's 'scientific', isn't it? Not pretending to know more than you do.

Robin Yes, putting the main value on reality, rather than on self-importance and face-saving.

John And you know, if you examine how respect for reality, for the truth, is sometimes lost even in science, it's always because the personalities, the 'egos' of individuals get in the way. Somebody becomes attached to an idea and stops listening to the evidence. Everything in these companies is encouraging people to remain open-minded, to keep looking for new evidence, and to revise their ideas constantly.

Robin Because they'll have reasonable expectations to start with, and they'll see the most sensible way of realising those expectations.

John So the same will apply to these healthy organisations, obviously . . .

Robin Yes. In fact there's not much more to say about this.

John You'll find something.

Robin . . . I think it's only interesting to understand how the organisation comes to see the world so clearly. And that's by being open to all the information it can get about three things: itself; the world outside; and the relationship between the two.

John Well we've gone on enough about how these companies maximise the flow of information inside themselves. But what about information from the outside?

Robin Let me give you a simple example. In 1976, the CBI completely changed its attitude to employee involvement because it had studied research which proved that the process increases profitability.

John Splendid.

Robin Of course in a healthy organisation everyone recognises the need to pay constant attention to feedback, but had it struck you how much *more* feedback they're getting, than they would in an ordinary organisation?

John . . . Oh, you mean because they're doing so much more?

Robin Yes. These small groups which are exploring and trying things out are like groups of scientists carrying out more and more experiments to find out about the world. As *In Search of Excellence* put it, each try 'is simply a tiny completed action, a test that helps you learn something, just as in high-school chemistry'.

John In a sense, these healthy organisations are thoroughly scientific?

Robin According to the latest understanding of 'scientific', they certainly are.

A new bit of information at the chemistry department.

John I made a film about Budgeting once and was struck by what a scientific attitude it embodied. The old-fashioned attitude to budgets was this: look at the figures for the previous year, estimate a budget, put it in the safe, and forget about it! But now it's regarded as a vital management tool. So first, the figures are estimated very, very carefully. Then, as operating figures come in, they're vigorously compared with the budgeted ones. Any mismatch is regarded as crucial information from the outside world that something has gone wrong and needs to be investigated, with a view to changing the company's behaviour, to get it back on track. Apparently, unhealthy companies prefer not to have such information and actively seek not to get it.

Robin Like ostriches with their heads in the sand.

John OK. Now we move on to the last item on the list. Change.

Robin Well the more I learned about these successful organisations, the more I was amazed at their capacity to cope with it. They all treat change as the norm, unlike the unhealthy organisations who think of it at best as an unpleasant annual exercise. So all their thinking is geared to innovation, both in the way that they operate, and also in the nature of their products and services, always with an eye to matching the altering requirements of the outside world.

John Sounds pretty demanding!

Robin It's true that some experts, like Peter Drucker and Abraham Maslow, have noted that it can put too much stress on weaker members of the organisation. But most people enjoy some change. In fact, they go to a lot of trouble to get enough of it, even when sometimes they can't cope with it very well! Most of us want holidays for that reason, though our mid-range difficulty over coping with change often turns holidays into a stress and makes us quite relieved to get back to the daily grind. But effective organisations, like healthy families, seem able to make change enjoyable and stimulating. I think there are several reasons why the people working in them feel it's safe to change: because the people in charge are really competent; because there's lots of mutual support; because change is seen as normal and necessary, rather than as an uncomfortable interlude to be avoided as far as possible; and because by getting used to coping with change, you become more confident and relaxed about it, and as a result handle it better.

John There's something else about change in organisations that intrigues me. When we were talking about families I thought of their ability to cope with change as a kind of by-product of all their other healthy characteristics. But with organisations I suspect it's the other way round! It's been the very need to cope with change that's forced these organisations to acquire all the other healthy characteristics.

Robin I think that's true. You can't buck the market. Ultimately we have to adjust to the larger system of which we're a part.

John Because most of this stuff is relatively recent, isn't it? When I started making Video Arts films twenty years ago there wasn't a great emphasis on listening to people, and delegating responsibility to them, and treating them as complete human beings! But now all our films are about that.

Robin It's part of a change that's been taking place throughout society – a change in our whole way of seeing and thinking about things, towards seeing better how everything is *connected*.

John But it's not that the ideas are that new. Last week I read a piece written in 1961 by one R. Likert for *New Patterns of Management* which contains a great deal of what we've been talking about. But I don't think many people were interested thirty years ago. It's the awe-inspiring speed with which the world now changes that's forced us to get healthier . . .

Robin In fact, many of the main principles of healthy functioning that we're talking about were clearly expressed by Mary Parker Follett, who died in 1933! She was far ahead of her time, preaching in an almost completely male-dominated industrial world, which focused narrowly on the task and ignored the human element. Her wisdom – extraordinary at that time – was clearly influenced by her different view, both as a woman, and through her practice of social work before she began studying industry. Which goes to show how important it is to have both male *and* female minds contributing to policy at a high level. Still, just the need to survive in the present industrial world is bringing that greater balance about now, thank goodness. And don't forget this: *most of us are mid-range* and therefore a bit rigid; it's only natural that we need a strong push from the outside world to make us accept a life of constant change – even if it then helps us to become healthier individuals.

John . . . Just glancing back over these healthy organisation characteristics . . . as with the families, my mind is boggled again by the way in which they all interact.

Robin Well, as with a family, you're dealing with a system; that is, a number of parts connected together to make a whole. It's really one interconnected process you're looking at. But by breaking it down and looking at it from different – and basically artificial! – points of view it's easier to understand it. And to change it if you want to do so.

John I see that, but it's astonishing how everything connects with everything else. For example, the fact that there's confidence and no great fear of making mistakes allows communication to be much freer; one result of which is that the information is maximised; which means that a work-team will improve its understanding of what it's trying to do; which means that its attempts are going to have the maximum chance of success; which will in turn reduce the number of real mistakes they make; which reinforces their original confidence.

Robin Or, respect for the working group's separateness means the leadership minimises the number of regulators; this increases the working group's sense of being trusted; this encourages them, in turn, to communicate more freely with the leadership; which increases the leadership's tendency to respect the autonomy of the working group; which increases the working group's acceptance of the leadership's authority on the occasions when it is exercised.

John Every aspect reinforces and strengthens every other aspect . . .

Robin And here's the exciting thing about that: a small improvement in any one aspect in fact *multiplies itself* by affecting all the others, and can therefore lead to a huge improvement in the organisation. Just as with families, very small interventions can have big results, provided you get it right. It took Izuzu just five years to achieve a huge culture change at the General Motors van plant at Luton.

John Provided you get it *right*. Because unfortunately it works in the other direction too. The arrival of one full-blown paranoid manipulator, or one total incompetent, can have an equally big effect.

Robin Well, I think you're being a bit pessimistic there. Because it depends on the level of health at which the system is already operating. In an organisation which is chaotic and confused, with poor communication, a high level of distrust and generally low confidence or shared sense of responsibility, a person like that can certainly do considerable harm. But the more healthy the organisation is already, the less effect an unhealthy new member will have. It's like physical health: the more healthy we are, the more resistant we are to infection or stress, and the more quickly we cope and recover from any injury. In just the same way, these principles we've been talking about ensure that a healthy organisation copes rapidly with stresses and threats of all kinds, and that it learns and gets even stronger in the process!

Afterthought:
All Work and No Play

John I want to ask you more about the value of work. You've already described how it draws us out to engage with a bigger system, and the psychological advantages that brings.

Robin That's one important effect of it.

John But there must be many other ways of arranging for ourselves to have those sorts of experiences. In the classical world, when work was considered something that slaves did, I suppose politics and the military offered those kind of challenges. But let's face it, for most of the last two thousand years the people at the top of the pile wouldn't look at anything that you or I would call 'work'. At the beginning of this century even middle-class folk 'with a private income' saw no reason to get a job. So why is work considered so important now? Why do so many people organise their entire lives around it, and in particular why do women now attach such high importance to it too? What's so fulfilling about it?

Robin Well to start with, in modern times work has become more connected with power and status. And the rigid role division where only men's work, away from home, earned money and was considered important, was a major reason why men wielded more power than women. So securing equal access to jobs was a natural part of women's drive to obtain equal status.

John And I suppose a hundred years ago your place in the hierarchy was pretty much established, and if it was a reasonably high place you didn't have to do anything to justify it. Whereas nowadays, with meritocratic ideas much more dominant, your status depends on being reasonably successful professionally.

Robin Yes. The change is a natural consequence of the democratic shift of power away from an aristocratic elite towards the middle class.

John But you started by talking about status. What about income – that's what work is for many people, isn't it?

Robin Well, we all have to earn enough to meet our needs and responsibilities, that's true. But it's not the reason most people choose their jobs or the main satisfaction they get out of it. I'm sure most of us would be glad to settle for a bit less in the way of money, if it gave us the chance of greater satisfaction, combined with happiness from our home life and leisure.

John Do you still think that money is not the primary concern in this country after all the changes Mrs Thatcher wrought in this sphere?

Robin She certainly did her best to move it towards a more selfish and mercenary society, and I'm afraid she succeeded to quite an extent. But in my experience a preoccupation with money makes people less, rather than more happy.

John I hope that's right. I shall never forget asking a house-parent at my elder daughter's school about all the pupils who returned. I was curious to know whether any grouping seemed either happier or less happy than the average. 'Only one lot,' I was told, 'the ones who go into the City. They are generally less happy.'

Robin I can believe it. But the trouble at the moment is that we are *all* locked into a system in which work is given too high a priority.

John Exactly! I feel this very strongly and that's why I want to find out more. If I look at my own life I find generally that the happiest *and* the most deeply satisfying parts of it are not those connected with work. Studying, talking with friends, meditating, keeping a journal, spending time with my family, looking at paintings – all these activities are much more rewarding to me most of the time than my work activities. I'm conscious of this, and yet I'm always too busy. In other words, the old protestant work ethic is driving me, despite the fact that I genuinely believe it to be fundamentally neurotic. So is it?

Robin I wouldn't disagree. Of course it has very positive spin-offs in our great scientific and artistic and industrial achievements, but it needs balancing with other values based more on human relationships, personal development and enjoyment of life. Otherwise it just legitimises greed and selfishness in those who are affluent, and justifies their exploitation of those who are not.

John But where does this work ethic come from?

Robin From several sources. But I think this over-emphasis on work is especially based on a fear of pleasure and of what pleasure may lead to – 'the Devil finds work for idle hands . . .'

John That seems an incredibly potent force in early puritanism. I think it's a fairly well-known passage of Benjamin Franklin's, but it's worth quoting what he wrote in 1748: 'Remember, that *time* is money. He that can earn ten shillings a day by his labour, and goes abroad, or sits idle, one half of that day, though he spends but sixpence during his diversion or idleness, ought not to reckon *that* the only expense; he has really spent, or rather thrown away, five shillings besides.'

Robin Not an easy man to work for.

John But I suspect that workaholism is performing a number of other functions for us that we might not want to admit openly. For example, I think it gives a sense of purpose for people, doesn't it? I mean the hardest issues in life – why we're here, what we are really like as people, whether we're getting our relationships with our loved ones right – they are all pretty daunting and since we arrived on the planet without being given a booklet outlining the rules of the game, questions that we often prefer to shy away from. So instead, we can concentrate on the quarterly figures for South-East Sales, or the next promotion or salary increase. In other words, work can provide us with a purpose that we'd lack otherwise in our lives.

Robin Indeed. Though the problem is that it's a limited, narrow purpose. It locks us into the closed mode, focused on some immediate goal with our minds shut to wider questions and interests. It's as if we've got blinkers on; and it's only when these emotional blinkers are torn off by some emotional upheaval – like the breakdown of a marriage, a life-threatening illness or the death of a child – that we realise we've been wasting a lot of our life up to that point.

John And then again, work helps us to structure our time, doesn't it? It helps us to overcome the kind of anxiety we can feel on holiday when we don't have to do anything!

Robin True. And similarly the loss of that structure is a major reason for the difficulties many people experience when they retire and can't cope with the freedom, space and time it gives them.

John The bottom line is that I've suspected for many years that a great number of very busy people are busy because they can't handle not being busy! They're frightened to be quiet. To quote Pascal, 'man's greatest problem is that he cannot sit quietly in a room on his own'. Discuss.

Robin I think there's a simple reason for that. In Western society we don't get much help or support towards getting to know ourselves at a deep level, towards finding that deep sense of inner life and enjoyment and meaning which is much better understood and supported in the East. Instead, if we are in danger of having any interesting feelings of this sort, most of our relatives will suggest we read a book or go for a nice walk. And people go on rescuing us from feelings of this kind throughout life, because they themselves are scared of being more in touch with themselves. So there's a tremendous social pressure in our Western nations to keep us floating on the surface of ourselves, avoiding asking any really profound questions, or allowing ourselves any profound experiences.

John So . . . *apart* from status and income, and apart from keeping us occupied so that we don't have to deal with profundities, what's the real purpose of work in your opinion? What's its essential value?

Robin Apart from the points we've just discussed, I think that work actually makes us more *healthy*, and for a reason other than those we discussed about moving into bigger systems. I believe that good work makes us more integrated, more 'together'.

John How so?

Robin Well let me tell you about a contemporary of Sigmund Freud – the French psychiatrist Pierre Janet. In many ways Janet's ideas were similar to Freud's. In fact it was Janet who coined the word 'subconscious', and he also anticipated Freud in showing that symptoms could be cured by restoring deeply-buried ideas and feelings to consciousness through what he called 'psychological analysis'. But he was also interested in people's capacity for *attention*, a subject ignored by almost everyone else.

John You mean, how well people could concentrate on something?

Robin Yes. He was interested in it because he believed that emotions got split off – or 'put behind the screen' as we've expressed it – more easily in people whose power of attention was poor, because it meant that their ability to 'hold things together in their minds' was weak.

John You mean that Janet believed that a low level of mental health, as we're expressing it, is due to weak powers of concentration.

Robin Yes, difficulty in paying attention in a sustained way – being 'dreamy' or 'vague' or 'scattered'. He believed that the difficulty patients found in 'getting their act together' and achieving emotional balance and control was due to this.

John So where does work come in?

Robin For Janet the main bit of his treatment lay in developing and extending the power of attention through finding the right kind of work.

John Fascinating. I've never heard this before.

Robin No, not many people know about him, even in my profession. Although Janet's ideas in many ways anticipated Freud's, it was Freud who came to command the attention of both the profession and the public. Unfortunately, Janet's work has been largely ignored. And the same is true to a lesser extent of another of Freud's contemporaries – Alfred Adler – who emphasised the need we all have, for mental health, to feel we are playing a useful part in the community. Work is one way in which we experience this positive feeling, though of course there are other ways too.

John Final question about the value of work. Apart from status, and apart from increasing our mental health, and apart from distracting us from the ineffable . . . if we genuinely have a purpose in our life, what other value does work have for us?

Robin There's great pleasure in the exercise of any skill – partly because you have to be in a state of concentrated attention to do something well, and being highly attentive to what you are doing is extremely enjoyable in itself. We all understand that from our leisure activities – it's a big part of the enjoyment of games and sports, whether it's skiing, or fishing, or playing darts. For a moment we are 'all there', completely in the present, tuned up like a musical instrument, vividly aware of what we are doing, and consequently *feeling very alive*. And if we give that same kind of attention to our work, we can make it equally enjoyable.

John All right. So having explored the value of work to my satisfaction, here's the big question. What's the ideal balance between work and non-work?

Robin I think the ideal is to enjoy both so much that you hardly notice when you cross the boundary from one to the other.

John You really think that's possible?

Robin It's easier for some people than others, of course. My work as a shrink has been so interesting that I've never experienced it as any kind of imposition; I'm enjoying getting to know people, and learning more about life whether I'm sitting with a group of patients, or with my family, or with friends. My partner, Josh, who is a painter, experiences her life in that way too – she seems to be enjoying herself in the same kind of way whether she's at work or not.

John But you're lucky. You've both got interesting jobs.

Robin Well, admittedly it's easier to give your full attention to your work if you are naturally interested in it. But it's the focused attention which is the reason for the enjoyment. And if it's easier for us, remember that we both chose our careers deliberately, not placing too high an emphasis on income, and we made sacrifices and worked hard to get where we are. Many jobs in my profession are dead boring, and I gave many things up to end up doing what I enjoy.

John So folk who choose their job largely for financial reasons – for the highest possible income – are less likely to find enjoyment, and therefore more likely to experience work as very different from non-work?

Robin I think the key is that you have to be able to find ways to generate that enjoyable high level of attention. And that's always possible if you use your work as an opportunity for learning and growing. In fact, if you manage to do this it may help you to develop the habit of using the rest of your time in a similarly positive and enjoyable way.

John All right. There's one more question concerning the balance between work and the home which concerns many people. Do you think that a couple can successfully bring up children, when both partners are keenly pursuing careers? Or do you think the family needs a 'home-maker', no matter whether it's a her or a him?

Robin I don't think there should be any problem at all when the children are of school age, at least. Indeed children are likely to benefit if both parents are getting the stimulus and support of outside activities, because they'll be more lively and cheerful and interesting as a result and so have more to give each other and the children. And as the healthy family research shows, relationships work best when there is enough space as well as enough togetherness.

John Fair enough. But what about the situation before children reach school age?

Robin Well, where it's possible I've no doubt at all that children benefit immensely from having one parent there full time, for at least the first couple of years – or better still, three. Perhaps ideally, five.

John Why do you feel that?

Robin It would take a long time to go into all the evidence, but it's well established that children develop the greatest sense of confidence and trust if they can form a stable attachment in their earliest years to a person who is reliably available.

John But supposing that's not possible, or even that both parents want so badly to work that they're simply not prepared to stay at home during the children's early years.

Robin In some cases a child will be better off with parents who are fulfilled and happy because they are working, than in the care of one of them who is at home all the time but depressed because of that. And I think the quality of the parents' relationship to the child is even more important than the amount of time they are there. Also, even if the time is limited, it won't matter too much as long as good quality and consistent love and care is provided from some other reliably available person who can form a long-term relationship – a granny or a nanny, or an au pair or whatever. And incidentally, the more people there are sharing in this supportive role, as well as the main person, the better. But of course, I can only generalise. I've seen very good results with mothers who've been working throughout, and bad results with mothers who are at home all the time.

John So apart from the case of young children there's no reason why anyone has to be at home full time.

Robin Not unless the couple prefers that arrangement.

John And supposing both partners are in demanding jobs.

Robin Well, then I would emphasise that they should both share the home-making and child-care tasks fairly, and not with the man just helping out – nor the woman either. I'm glad to say this seems to be happening more and more these days, at least with younger people.

John But there are always going to be conflicting demands from work and from home. How can a couple reduce the friction this causes?

Robin The key fact is this: if both partners, and their families, are together for enough *quality* time, then absences and crises can be easily coped with. So the main thing is for the partners to put the family first, as far as possible, while accepting that work demands will interfere with that quite often and will have to be dealt with. The reason I suggest putting the *family* first is that work demands tend to put us into a closed mode of thinking, where it's hard to remember other things. So the bias must be towards the family, to compensate for the fact that work is bound to eat into family time.

John And where couples have chosen that one partner shall be a home-maker, what can the 'worker', as it were, do to help?

Robin The single best thing is to send the home-maker off on a nice holiday occasionally, by offering to look after the home and the children for a week. In my experience nothing else demonstrates so effectively what the home-maker's job involves; and though it may be a bit daunting at first because the 'worker' has so little experience of it, they usually enjoy it, especially the new deeper relationship which develops with the children, as a result. It also brings the couple closer, and often a marriage will change gear after one of these episodes.

John But if the home-maker is the mother, will she feel the father can be trusted with complete responsibility for the children?

Robin Absolutely not! When the time comes to hand the kids over and leave, the mothers are usually reluctant to grasp their freedom because they fear that the children will be eating nothing but baked-beans-on-toast while watching endless cartoons on the telly. And there'll be some of that, and lots of other things that mother might disapprove of, but the kids will be doing it with Dad and they all have a terrific time together. As long as it's only a week, no one will die of having too few vegetables.

John One thing that makes this balance between the couples harder, is the relative reluctance of most employers to pay much attention to the importance of people's home lives.

Robin Well, as we've seen, in the healthier organisations they treat people much more as complete individuals, and take much more account of the whole of their employees' lives. But all employers need to give more value and consideration towards such things. Which perhaps means that the ideal employer would be a woman! Anyway, in practical terms firms need more women in senior positions to carry these broader values into the workplace. And men, of course, who'll listen to them . . .

John There's one worry in all this. Britain started the industrial revolution and seems to me to have gone right through the work ethic and out the other side. If we really achieved a thoroughly healthy and balanced attitude towards work, isn't there a danger that a bunch of insecure, highly anxious, over-competitive and thoroughly unhealthy nations might wipe us out economically?

Robin If we became less efficient that might happen. But if we get a healthier balance as a result of taking on all these other healthy characteristics, then as we've seen from the research we'll become more, and not less effective in the economic sphere.

3 Let Me Go Forward: Together, by Myself . . .

John So, we've looked at groups of the corporation-institution-hospital size. What's the next level up?

Robin We should move up the scale to society.

John You mean countries, nations?

Robin Yes in the main. But also groups – for example ethnic groups – within countries. By 'society' I mean a network of families whose behaviour is connected and coordinated through shared ideas, values, traditions, obligations and institutions, extending over whole life-cycles. The size can be anything from a small tribe to a superpower. A society includes all kinds of people, of all ages, and of different levels of intelligence and health.

John How much of your healthy family stuff is going to apply at the society level?

Robin Plenty!

John You really believe there are major similarities between families and societies?

Robin Yes, I do. Of course each society will usually contain the entire range of families from sick to very healthy, so you would expect the mental health of all *societies* to be roughly the same: average, mid-range. But like individuals and families, their overall level of health is affected by external stresses and strains and by their philosophy of life, the values that guide them. So some societies are more affiliative and cooperative, others foster antagonism and violence; some respect individuality and difference, others demand uniformity; some encourage freedom of speech and frank questioning of government policy, others impose censorship and execute people for such criticism.

John Nevertheless, we're going to have terrible problems when we try to compare the levels of mental health of different societies, aren't we? I mean if each family develops a moral code that justifies its level of mental health as being the best possible, it's going to be crazy discussing different cultures. Nobody's ever going to agree on the criteria.

Robin Well, the two of us might! And after all, no one has any final answers on this subject. We won't be saying we're 'right', we're just hoping the knowledge we already have about families and organisations might also apply on an even bigger scale. If it starts other people talking, and we can say a few useful things that someone else may be able to take further, I'll be quite happy.

John . . . Fair enough. How do we start?

Robin Well it may be easier to get some agreement about the sickest end of the spectrum. What would you say was the worst possible kind of society?

John Off the top of the head, I guess I'd proffer Nazi Germany.

Robin And what would you say made Nazi Germany the worst?

John Well, the whole system was based on terror. No kind of difference was allowed; uniformity was imposed – if the top man raised his right arm, everyone else had to do so or get beaten up – there was no discussion allowed, let alone criticism. Everyone was encouraged to spy on their neighbours, and children were rewarded for betraying their parents. The worst off were the racial groups like the Jews and the Gypsies, who were systematically used as scapegoats, and initially persecuted and then eventually murdered in millions – along with other 'undesirables' like open homosexuals and the mentally handicapped. All forms of creativity were suppressed and art became state propaganda. And of course, any country that hadn't been subordinated was treated as an enemy, undermined, attacked and then incorporated. In a nutshell, Doctor, the Nazis scored rather low on Affiliative Attitude.

Robin Redeeming features?

John Now that's an interesting question . . . well, the trains ran on time.

Robin Go on.

John And I suppose . . . in a society like that, if you do what you're told and keep your nose clean, you can get along quite nicely, materially speaking. *If* you're from the right race, of course.

Robin And . . . ?

John Well, now I come to think of it . . . *provided* you show no signs of thinking for yourself, I suppose things are quite well organised. There's plenty to eat and drink, and the houses are in good repair, and there's certainly full employment and a very good welfare system and pensions . . . and, I don't want to sound as though I'm warming to the subject, but in some senses, their performance in the war was pretty extraordinary. I mean, by the end of 1941, they were controlling pretty well the whole of continental Europe. And certainly their fighting forces performed well, with discipline, and efficiency, and sometimes great self-sacrifice. And of course their industry performed superbly too: the speed with which they could get a bombed factory restarted was extraordinary. And for the right people, with blond hair and blue eyes, there was a powerful sense of identity with the Fatherland. So I suppose you're making me realise by your Socratic questioning that although Nazi Germany was morally appalling, there could be places that would actually be *worse* to live in.

Robin Not morally worse, simply worse from the point of view of surviving. I mean, if law and order has utterly broken down, if there are violent gangs on the rampage, if there's no supply of food, water, medicine, electricity or anything . . . then *everyone* is having a terrible time, and no one can improve their lot in any way at all.

John Yes, that's obvious, isn't it? I suppose the 'Complete Chaos' scenario hadn't occurred to me because I tend to think of European history, and things haven't usually got *quite* that bad here. I guess there was the sort of chaos you're talking about in parts of Germany during the Thirty Years War, parts of England during the Civil War, parts of France during the Great Terror . . . in fact in *some* parts of any country where there's war, as in Yugoslavia now . . .

Robin And also, perhaps, even during the early years of the Weimar Republic, when people were pushing their money around in wheelbarrows because hyper-inflation was pushing prices up literally by the hour. But it's always happening somewhere. As we're speaking, Mogadishu, the capital of Somalia, is operating at this chaotic level and I've just been watching a television news report illustrating how the army has lost the ability to impose any kind of order and discipline to the extent that little bands of soldiers in armoured vehicles are driving around the capital shooting at whatever takes their fancy, in particular any civilians who look as if they have anything worth taking. An eight-year-old girl has just been shot because she was carrying a bag of rice.

John . . . Yes, I agree. Certain kinds of prolonged chaos are worse even than organised wickedness. But this was obvious to you, wasn't it? Is that because of your work with families?

Robin Yes, that's why I almost instinctively think in this way. As I think I said earlier, you can talk about families, roughly speaking, as operating on three different levels. These are regularly described in the kind of research we talked about earlier, and in my work in family therapy I came to very similar conclusions. The levels correspond to different stages of development that children go through on the way to growing up. At the bottom level, the level of health experienced by the sickest families, there are very fuzzy, unclear, overlapping boundaries, and nobody quite knows where they are, or who they are, any of the time. Then, slightly better but still at a lower level, there's some order and structure, members of the family know where they are, but at the price of having very, very rigid boundaries, and very fixed and limited identities. These identities are 'protected' by emotional distance, a rigid hierarchy, and an intense, violent, punitive type of control. If you were classifying societies on the family scale, the Nazis would fit on this authoritarian level, which incidentally is also characterised by scapegoating.

John And if we move up above the authoritarian level?

Robin Well, then we start getting into the healthier mid-range areas, where people have a fair amount of mutual regard and respect for each other's individuality, and an ability to be a little more flexible with their boundaries. Then finally, at the higher levels you'll remember how it's easy for the parents to overlap in function, to listen to the children and consult with them, and to 'hang loose' and have a very open emotional relationship because they are secure and no longer need these rigid boundaries. This means people have more tolerance of others' separateness and difference. So these upper levels of health correspond more to a well-functioning democracy.

John Do you think these three levels correspond roughly to chaotic societies, totalitarian societies and democratic societies?

Robin Yes, I believe they're rather similar. Of course, at the authoritarian level, the authority can be malevolent, as in a fascist dictatorship, or relatively benign – Cromwell for instance – and that will make a huge difference. Also, a high degree of mental health can be prevalent in societies we might label as 'primitive'. But basically, in more highly developed societies the greater choice, responsibility and freedom accorded to individuals tends to foster mental health. At the same time, when democratic nations use the CIA and MI5 to behave like Big Brother we should not hesitate to see that it corresponds to behaviour in the sickest societies.

John So does this all imply that the form of government needs to be appropriate to the stage of development of the people concerned?

Robin Of course.

John So that democracy is not necessarily the best form of government for everyone.

Robin No. Some societies may need to pass through a transitional stage first.

John That seems a bit shocking!

Robin Well, to go back for a moment to the family analogy, if I'm dealing with a chaotic family, the first thing they may need is some order to reduce the high level of anxiety they typically feel; and you can't give a chaotic family more order by making it operate more democratically! So you have to boost the authority of whoever is most likely to be able to exercise it. But if I'm dealing with a family where there's enough stability then I can try to free them up, by encouraging more democratic ways of operating, because they already have a sufficient degree of order.

John I'm reminded of some stories a few years ago about Russian defectors to the United States, who discovered that they just couldn't handle all the freedom – they had to return to Russia.

Robin And remember how difficult it is for people to come out of prison back into society, and how they need a transitional period of being made more independent again – and these are people who functioned in society, after a fashion, before being imprisoned.

John So it may take time to develop the right conditions for democracy . . .

Robin Yes, and the fact that it takes time is often forgotten, because people tend to talk about politics and social issues in absolute terms, as if you can just decide what to do and then do it; when in fact we are always dealing with developmental processes that may be quite slow like human beings growing up. Think how many centuries it took to develop what we would now recognise as democracy in the West.

John History books used to date the first English parliament as Simon de Montfort's in 1265, and younger women were finally given the vote in 1928. Six hundred and sixty-three years.

Robin It's interesting to think how fast development has been in black Africa. European nations bequeathed democratic institutions at the time of African Independence, and most of them pretty soon reverted to one-party states. But in the last two years, around seventeen African states have moved towards multi-party democracy. It takes time – but not necessarily that much.

John It certainly explains why revolutions which topple tyrants so often become tyrannical themselves. If a populace simply isn't used to more democratic methods of functioning, then removing an authoritarian ruler can create a vacuum which gets filled by another totalitarian. So you get Robespierre following the Bourbons, Lenin following the Romanovs and Cromwell after Charles I.

Robin Yes. If you try to move to a more open and democratic system too quickly you can end up with something even more authoritarian than before.

John So before people can move from an authoritarian system to a more democratic one, they need a period of relative stability during which the beginnings of democratic attitudes and skills can develop?

Robin Indeed. Even on the smaller scale of *institutions* I have worked in, it has always interested me that you can't make the transition to democracy in a totally democratic way. It seems to require something like a period of benevolent dictatorship under a person who *believes* in democracy and is able to relinquish power at the right moments. Which is, I suppose, exactly what all good parents do to help their children grow up.

John So the English parliamentary tradition begins to develop under Elizabeth and James I, is put into cold storage under Charles I and Cromwell, but then revives during the relatively calm twenty-five years of Charles II's reign, so that by the Glorious Revolution of 1688 we're capable of running a democratic system. At least in the sense that the king had to rule via his ministers who, even if not exactly elected, at any rate needed the cooperation and consent of regular parliaments to operate.

Robin Yes, but we mustn't make the mistake of thinking that a nation achieves some degree of mental health and then simply maintains it. Just as individuals' level of mental health will go up and down a bit, depending on how favourable or stressful their circumstances are, the same will happen to nations.

John Are you saying the style of government they need will vary too?

Robin Certainly. The obvious example is war. Nobody questions that the government has to be given greater powers then, because decisions have to be made more quickly, plans have to be kept secret and strategic priorities enforced. We know we have to sacrifice some freedom and individuality as the price of united, disciplined action.

John Yes. It doesn't make a great deal of sense to give the enemy the benefit of the doubt, or to allow each platoon to vote whether to attack a machine-gun post. So under war conditions, some 'healthy' behaviour should be discouraged.

Robin Yes. What I've been describing as exceptionally healthy behaviour certainly should be. Which is why dictatorships are notoriously efficient at the start of wars. The first few moves are obvious, so there's tremendous speed and efficiency because everyone's getting on with their job and nobody's arguing. But of course, the longer the war goes on, the less efficient and the more crazy the leadership becomes, because it has cut itself off from the feedback it needs to respond appropriately to what's happening. So you get Hitler's refusal to face the fact of the failure of the Russian campaign, despite all the evidence that it was doomed from the time of Stalingrad.

John So you need to hang on to some health . . .

Robin Yes, even in wartime, it pays to stay *as democratic as possible* – to remain open to incoming information and to listen to criticisms of official policy.

John And then the moment the war is over, you can throw out the authoritarian types who've been so useful, and install people who are temperamentally more suited to democratic government. As in 1945, out with Churchill, in with Attlee.

Robin That's right. And nations will always, over the years, experience fluctuations in confidence or anxiety, and government should be responsive to this. For example, I believe the more authoritarian style of Mrs Thatcher was chosen by the electorate when there was a general feeling that Britain was falling apart, going down the tubes economically, because the unions had become too powerful and because the welfare state and nationalised industries were sliding out of control.

John The same happened in America where the electorate chose the ultra-conservative Ronald Reagan to replace Jimmy Carter, who was making everyone nervous, particularly after he claimed he'd been attacked in his canoe by a rabbit.

Robin In fact, something rather fascinating happened at that time. Media professionals were initially appalled by the ignorance and lack of grasp that Reagan displayed at press conferences. But they found that reporting this simply made them very unpopular with the nation. They were called unpatriotic! Middle America didn't want to hear anything that would shake their confidence in Reagan – because it was a time when confidence in Presidents had been shaken once too often, by Nixon and Ford and finally the hostage debacle under Carter.

John So Reagan could present himself as embodying family values despite the fact he was alienated from all his children, and as a symbol of the return to traditional standards, although more than two hundred of his appointees were eventually charged with fraud.

Robin But they called him 'The Great Communicator', and he was brilliant at playing that particular part of the leadership role – holding people together in a consensus by appealing to common concerns and values – even though so much of what he was saying was hopelessly wrong.

John Because it was a time of little dissent, or questioning of values. Whereas, when the First World economies were flourishing in the sixties, society was able to tolerate all the diverse social movements that flowered at that time, all of them questioning authority and tradition, because there was an underlying feeling of confidence.

Robin Just like families. When they feel strong they can allow a lot of freedom, diversity and disagreement; and when they're under threat, or the parents are weak, they show a much more rigid structure.

John Now, although democracy may not yet be appropriate for every society, we've nevertheless been assuming that it's the most desirable system, simply because it's how healthier families operate. Let's examine it further. Why is it the best system for the people in it?

Robin Well, to answer that, I need to go right back to what we were saying at the end of Chapter 1. Do you remember what I was saying about the Basic Bits?

John You were saying that people function at their best, are healthiest, when they are in touch with, and can draw upon the different facets of their personality: the more child-like, spontaneous and playful ones; the more practical and organisational aspects; and the more conscientious, responsible, sober and parental aspects.

Robin That's right. Health means having all these different bits available within you, and not needing to hand some of them over to other people to perform for you. You remember how Isabel Menzies discovered that the hospital department functioned badly because the Super-ego functions were projected upwards into the matron and sisters, who were seen as fierce and strict; and the Id or emotional functions were projected downwards into the student nurses, who were seen as childish, irresponsible and unreliable.

John And that meant that the group in the middle – the trained nurses – felt the squeeze. They'd been deprived of a sense of responsibility for their actions because that had been projected upwards, and of any sense of fun or enjoyment, because that was projected downwards.

Robin So everyone lost out on the arrangement. No one could use the whole range of their personalities and skills. Well, exactly the same principles apply on a bigger scale too. When you have authoritarian leadership, control and responsibility and confidence get projected upwards onto the leaders. So if you want to make people lose their wits and self-respect, and feel credulous and dependent, you organise a Nuremburg rally.

John With your leader spotlighted and surrounded by all the symbols of power, with a huge mass of people looking up at him.

Robin And that's why all totalitarian leaders do it, fascist or communist. Hitler, Mussolini, Stalin, Ceausescu, Kim Il Sung, Saddam Hussein . . . the purpose is precisely to encourage splitting off and projecting some of the Basic Bits. So that the public increasingly feel like helpless dependent children, and so actually want to hand over more and more power to the leader or leadership group. And the bad news is . . . the larger the group, the stronger this tendency is!

John So a dictator is deliberately taking people's confidence and intelligence away from them.

Robin It's as if they lose their intelligence, their conscience, their values, and their sense of responsibility – as if they made a present of them to the leader without realising this has happened, and without necessarily being forced to do so. They become zombies, through this projection process.

John But you don't have to be a totalitarian leader to take advantage of this.

Robin Certainly not! If the leader is clever about the way they arrange encounters with the public, they can rely on this splitting and projection to work automatically to make people hand more power over to them. And in the same way that competence and responsibility get projected upwards, those qualities which are *unacceptable* to the leader get projected *downwards* onto the people at the bottom of the pile.

John That's going to create or accentuate social divisions, and stir up conflict and hatred towards the poor or minorities. In extreme cases, persecutions.

Robin Exactly. It's all part of the same psychological process.

John I think that kind of social division has been encouraged in quite damaging ways in the last decade in the USA and in Britain. I wonder if Reagan and Thatcher were using this mechanism – even if unconsciously. They both rigidly controlled their contact with the media; and Mrs Thatcher got away with being much more authoritarian than other Prime Ministers. And both of them created unsympathetic and even punishing attitudes towards those at the bottom of the pile.

Robin They certainly both *spoke* as if they felt most unsympathetic towards the people who had the least resources – as if it was their own fault and they were not worth helping.

John It seems to me that this was the period during which the so-called 'underclass' became so split off from the rest of society.

Robin . . . Nevertheless, my point is that this splitting process is minimised in the West because in democracies, the distance between leader and led is normally reduced. You can see politicians on television, or hear them on radio, not just in ideal conditions where they can present the positive side only but, warts and all, under attack in public debate where their limitations can be exposed. And newspapers present an even more unflattering picture, constantly highlighting any weaknesses, especially in cartoons! And there's also much more personal contact with a greater number of the public.

John This was also true of Gorbachev, as he tried to move the Soviet Union towards a more democratic model. Instead of those mysterious figures taking the salute at the May Day Parade, you saw him chancing his arm, arguing in the Russian parliament, or even going on walkabout, despite the risk.

Robin Funnily enough, though, I think Gorbachev is a striking example of a leader who didn't realise that it isn't possible to go straight from an authoritarian regime to democracy. So he tried to accelerate the delegation of power to the people too quickly; as you'll remember, I forecast it would only be possible if he held on to enough power to steer the process through the inevitable conflicts and clashes of personal interests. However, on principle I do believe that the more a government delegates responsibility and decision-making powers – what European politicians are now calling 'subsidiarity' – the more responsible and competent the population will become.

John So democracy helps us grow up!

Robin Yes, but it's not good only because it has that effect on each individual. Society itself functions best when as many of its members as possible are autonomous – behaving independently and able to contribute something to the whole organisation.

John You mean it's at its most efficient then.

Robin Yes. So individuals get more benefit from it for that reason too.

John . . . We're back to the principle of using the intelligence of the whole system.

Robin Exactly. So a society where the poorer people, or the younger generation, are treated like inadequate children, while only the rich and middle-aged have power, is not going to be efficient.

John: After all, the communist world fell apart because they were trying to run everything according to some central plan, dreamed up by a few senior party members. But no small group is capable of taking account of the vastly complex inter-relationships in a society of millions of people.

Robin Whereas the capitalist system, with its market economy, sets up rules where everyone is motivated to use his or her intelligence in their own local sphere, because it's in their self-interest to do so. They must act intelligently if they are to survive. So we're talking about the same principle that we found with the most successful and healthy corporations: the most effective arrangement has to be one which provides some kind of order, *some set of broad basic rules . . . within which each individual can use his or her intelligence as fully as possible.*

John Provided those broad basic rules take social considerations into account?

Robin I agree.

John But there seem to me to be two absolutely insuperable problems.

Robin The first is . . . ?

John . . . that we're talking about society and that the people in charge of that are politicians.

Robin So?

John Well . . . I met J. B. Priestley a few times, and I've never forgotten his saying, 'The trouble with democracy is that it means that the people at the top are all power-seekers. The only way to have someone normal in charge is to have a hereditary monarchy.' Now I'm not sure about the second part, but I'm absolutely sure the first bit is true. And people who spent their working lives seeking power are going to be the last ones that want to surrender it. Their essential quality surely is that they want to control other people. I mean, Mrs Thatcher became Prime Minister proclaiming her belief in freedom, but when it came to the crunch, she just couldn't allow people to do things in ways she didn't approve of. No politician wants people going off and improving things by applying principles which aren't in the party manifesto. I remember some thoroughly decent Labour friends of mine in the early seventies telling me that the examination results in the comprehensive school they controlled were so bad they had to hush them up, otherwise there'd be pressure to change the system. Which leads on to another aspect of the desire to control: nobody likes criticism, and the vast majority of politicians use any influence they have to stifle it. Look at the way Harold Wilson, and then shortly afterwards, Mrs Thatcher, both quarrelled with the BBC. So surely politicians are the very last people who are going to give up their hard-earned power in order to trust the intelligence of the whole system?

Robin It's not surprising that people who want power for its own sake just can't bear to be criticised. You see, the trouble is that politics, like my profession, attracts a lot of people who have serious problems themselves, but don't want to face that painful fact and try to change.

John But it's not just in the world of politics that people who are in charge don't want to surrender their control . . . at the top of bureaucracies, pressure groups, businesses, trade unions, professional associations and so on you generally find driving and controlling types – the kind who feel they have to take responsibility for everything because they can't trust anyone else to make decisions, or to carry them out either. In addition to them there are all the Fundamentalists, whether Christian, Islamic, Jewish, Hindu, Dutch Reform or Born-Again

Obsessionals, all of whom are trying to impose their value systems on everyone else via legislation, or, if necessary, violence. And then there's quite a large group called Parents, who almost without exception try to go on controlling their children many decades after it's appropriate. As someone once put it, 'A mother spends the first twenty years of her son's life helping him to grow up, and he spends the rest of her life trying to convince her that he has.' I could go on . . .

Robin I'm sure. But I think I've got the message. You see, what all these people have in common is this: they don't want to change. So it's much more comfortable to try to *change everyone else instead*, on the principle that everyone else must be out of step. This is why they are so preoccupied with controlling others – it's because they can't control themselves.

John You mean if they just stood in the middle of other folk *without* trying to control them, they would start experiencing feelings that they couldn't really cope with, that would make them too uncomfortable?

Robin That's it.

John That's why everybody seems to be trying to control everyone else, *especially* the politicians?

Robin Not everybody, just people who are less healthy. Healthy people will be more interested in controlling themselves.

John Well, this all being the case . . . what chance is there of moving towards a healthier society where we can use the intelligence of the whole system?

Robin I believe it *is* happening, slowly but steadily. Inevitably, it is so gradual that we don't realise it's going on until we look back; it's like watching the grass growing. In my lifetime tremendous changes have taken place, like the acceptance of greater equality and participation of women, awareness of global issues, of the interconnectedness of human life the whole world over, and of the consequences of pollution and neglect of the balance of nature to name only a few.

John I know there's truth in that, but at the same time I feel that the only hope of these healthier ways of thinking coming through to the political decision makers is from the business world. The splendid thing about business people is they're not very ideological – they're more pragmatic. They like things that work. And if enough of them see that these healthy ways of operating are successful in business . . .

Robin . . . I agree they'll be able to bring those same ideas to the bigger scale of society.

John I can't see it happening any other way. Unless . . .

Robin What?

John Unless everybody reads this book and does exactly what we say, and stops trying to control everyone else and we could all live happily ever after. Under the Liberal Democrats, of course. And then they'd all put huge statues of us up in all the big cities, saying how we'd told everyone to be more self-effacing and modest. That would be nice, wouldn't it?

Robin Very nice. As long as you do what *I* say, of course. Now you were saying, there were *two* insuperable problems to having a society in which individuals can use their intelligence as fully as possible. What's the other?

John Well, we've agreed that they can only do that within the framework of a few basic rules. And in a modern society, you'll never get people to agree on those rules, what with Islamic Fundamentalists saying that Democracy is Atheism, with the Politically Correct saying you have to refer to girls as 'pre-women', and with Presidents Bush and Saddam claiming to have won the same war.

Robin But we don't have to get them to agree. That's the nice thing about writing a book. We just have to see if we can agree ourselves.

John I'd forgotten. What a relief! Even so . . . I know that *my* prejudices will intrude. I mean if you start suggesting Britain needs a bit more Swiss open-heartedness, or a more Latin attitude towards corruption, or more Swedish *joie de vivre* – or even that we should try to learn from the French how to be the centre of the universe . . . I have to say that my judgement might be clouded by the red mist of chauvinism – a word of French derivation interestingly enough.

Robin Well, I was going to suggest that we look at different societies to help us figure out what values we like best, and should incorporate in our basic rules . . . so perhaps it will help if we start on some more unfamiliar societies, where our prejudices won't intrude so automatically.

John Good idea. Let's start at the worst end again. Tell me about a bad and unfamiliar society.

Robin Well one leaps to mind immediately whose values became, well, just about as bad as you can get. It's an African tribe that was studied in depth by the anthropologist, Colin Turnbull, who lived among them and shared their life for a bit.

John Is this the Ik?

Robin That's right. They live in the mountainous north-east corner of Uganda, near the borders with Kenya and Sudan.

John Didn't Peter Brook produce a play about them?

Robin He did. Like Turnbull, Brook felt that what had happened to the Ik held a vital lesson for us all.

John So presumably they didn't start out 'bad'?

Robin Oh no. Originally they were a tribe of nomadic hunter-gatherers who had always been free to roam around in search of food in a large area, which is now divided up into the three countries I've mentioned.

John Everything was OK then?

Robin Yes, in those days the men played the main role in the hunting, but the women and children all joined in driving the animals towards the men who used nets and weapons to catch and kill the animals. And the women all shared the task of gathering vegetable foods.

John So they were cooperative?

Robin Very much so, like all people living this kind of life are said to be – generous, affectionate, honest and compassionate.

John So . . . what changed?

Robin Well, when the African colonies became independent nations so that frontiers became more important, and big areas were set aside as nature reserves, this tribe couldn't continue their nomadic life. So the Ik ended up confined to a barren mountain area, where food and even water were very hard to come by.

John So their lifestyle completely altered, and they didn't have the skills that might have helped with the change.

Robin So their condition became more impossible, and they began to starve. As a result, the social structure changed and became more and more and more negative.

John Didn't they become totally obsessed with food?

Robin That was the key to it, yes.

John The only time that I ever fasted properly I found that when I woke up after the third night, I had been dreaming about lamb chops. The image stayed with me for about fifteen minutes – these incredibly succulent char-grilled delicacies, surrounded by mountains of sweet young bright green peas. I'd never dreamed about food before, and I haven't since. But the degree to which it obsessed me after only three days of hunger astounded me.

Robin Well, it took on a tragic dimension for the Ik. For instance, on the occasions when a hunt was successful, or some other source of food happened to be discovered, there was no impulse to share it. In fact, any good fortune of this kind was hidden from others, because if it became public knowledge there was an obligation to share. So those who made the kill, or the discovery, would just gorge themselves and then take the rest to sell at the police post.

John But what about sharing it with their family?

Robin Even that was regarded as the greatest foolishness!

John Good God. So I suppose this refusal to share food meant they lost the capacity to cooperate in other ways . . .

Robin I'm afraid that's right. As they became more and more selfish and individualistic, concern for others and the desire to care for them completely broke down.

John They still cared for their children?

Robin Not really. The parents showed little interest in their offspring, after the mother had finished breast-feeding. By the time the children were three, they'd be pushed out of the house to fend for themselves.

John They weren't even allowed into the house?

Robin No. If it rained, they might be allowed to sit in the doorway of their parents' house, but that was it. Otherwise the children had to make shelters for themselves.

John Were the children able to cooperate at all between themselves?

Robin They formed groups of different ages, for self-preservation against other groups of children, since they'd be unlikely to survive alone. Rather like rival gangs in big cities. There was a lot of violence, and friendships were brief because they would turn on each other.

John And old people?

Robin They were even more harshly treated than the children. They were the ones least able to get any food, so they'd be starving. And while old people were actually dying, the others would snatch their possessions and clothes, and even food from their mouths.

John So they'd lost *any* kind of fellow feeling?

Robin Almost all of them had, yes. You see, their life was so dreadful, there was so much to grieve about, and so little to enjoy, that they learned to repress practically all their capacity to feel.

John I remember in *Families* you made the point that you couldn't repress one emotion without repressing them all.

Robin Correct. Turnbull said that it was hard to detect any emotion at all among the Ik. In fact, he called them 'the loveless people'. He says they behaved as if it was important not to love anyone, and he thought this protected them from pain and sorrow they would otherwise have suffered. In his own words: 'I had seen little of what I could even call affection. I had seen things that made me want to cry . . . but I had never seen an Ik anywhere near tears or sorrow, only the children's tears of anger, malice and hate.' And again: 'I had seen no sign of family life such as is found almost everywhere else in the world. I had seen no sign of love, with its willingness to sacrifice, its willingness to accept that we are not complete by ourselves, but need to be joined to others.'

John And did the Ik treat Turnbull in the same way as they treated each other?

Robin They did indeed. So it's not surprising that he found living among them extremely painful. Most of the time they enjoyed frustrating him by preventing him from getting from them the knowledge he had come to seek. They would talk a different language to exclude him. Even when he once sat for three days by a water-hole with a group of Ik, there was silence throughout. Really, they were just showing him what it felt like to be one of them: completely isolated, each on his or her own.

John So he actually felt like them?

Robin More than that. Turnbull was very honest about this and says that as time went on, he was disturbed to find that he was beginning to behave like the Ik, too, in order to protect himself. Increasingly he found himself in a chronic bad humour, withdrawing into isolation and silence, and, believe it or not, actually experiencing pleasure at shutting others out and eating in isolation.

John He'd become really identified with them.

Robin Yes. I think it would be impossible to resist doing so.

John I notice a mention of the word 'pleasure'. But it was pleasure at making others feel worse than yourself.

Robin Yes. That's a further aspect. The Ik did seem to get most of what little enjoyment they had from watching other people having unpleasant experiences. For example, someone falling over, who was too weak to get up again, might be taunted and humiliated. Old people who could only crawl would be pushed over as a form of amusement.

John Ah now, that *is* fun . . .

Robin Shut up. Turnbull adds that more than once the tribe tried to lead him to his death, just for amusement. And worst of all, they would watch a child crawling towards the fire, without stopping it or even warning it, but waiting keenly for the moment when it would touch the flames. Then they would burst into laughter when it burnt itself.

John Well now, I can really understand the development of callousness. I can see that even in my everyday life: the more stressed I get, the less I am able to worry about how other people are feeling. But I don't understand what you've just been telling me, which is out-and-out cruelty. What's the point?

Robin Probably several things. First, it takes some strength of character – that is, a good level of health – to be able to endure adversity yourself while others are in happier circumstances, without wishing they were suffering equally. Otherwise, there is a natural tendency to lessen your own pain by spreading it around, and the worse you feel yourself, the nastier you want to be to others. That works best if you can make others feel much *more* pain than you do, so you can feel lucky by comparison, and that's easier to achieve with babies, old people, and any other people who are weak and vulnerable.

John OK. So taking all this behaviour into account, how would you put their moral code into words?

Robin 'Every man for himself.' It's an extreme form of a code that's increasingly common in our own society. It's no different, except in degree, from 'free enterprise' carried to its limits; or where those in work are quite content to see a lot of other people remaining unemployed, rather than sharing their own jobs and accepting less money.

John I suppose you could say that the behaviour of the Ik made sense in evolutionary terms, given their situation.

Robin Turnbull came to that conclusion himself. The most vital thing for the continuation of the *tribe* was for the healthy adults to survive. They were the ones best able to cope and they could always have more children later.

John Now tell me about a society which operates right at the other end of the mental health spectrum.

Robin Well, let's talk about Ladakh. We went there recently so we have some first-hand experience.

John Yes, it's right up in the north of India, but culturally it's Tibetan Buddhist. It's about the only area where that culture still exists, since the Chinese have been systematically destroying the culture inside Tibet itself – by the rather efficient process of murdering a million and a half Tibetans and resettling Chinese in Tibet to outnumber the indigenous population.

Robin And the fact that Ladakh was also under threat from the Chinese, so that the Indian government put it off limits to foreigners, helped to protect their old way of life from outside influences until it was opened to visitors in the mid-seventies. At that time a researcher called Helena Norberg-Hodge began visiting it and she said the people were the happiest, most contented ones she had encountered anywhere, and that there probably wasn't another place in the world that could compare with it. Other visitors found the same story: an astonishingly open, cheerful, honest people, smiling, friendly, and helpful, who seemed to enjoy life and possess the secret of getting on well with each other. There seemed to be so much laughter and *joie de vivre* coming from a deep feeling of peace and contentment.

John Well, in 1990, you and I were still very impressed by the great sense of equality and mutual respect.

Robin Despite the fact that there's a clear hierarchy, with an aristocracy that is recognised by everyone.

John Yes, but there's no sense of the classes being divided, is there?

Robin That's true. Everyone speaks their mind with confidence, and gets listened to with respect. In fact, it's quite clear that Ladakhis are respected for what they are in themselves, not for their position or possessions.

John I remember passing a tiny hut and being told it was the prison. There was just about enough room for four people to play cards in it. Our hosts explained the prison was empty for most of the time because crime of any kind was very rare and violent crime virtually non-existent. The only real use for the prison was for someone to spend the night if they'd drunk too much Chang and needed to sober up. So why do you think Ladakh works so well?

Robin Well, those who've studied it carefully seem to agree that a major reason is the good balance they've achieved between individual independence and a sense of communal responsibility. One expert said that Ladakh was close to the 'rural utopia' that Ghandi was aiming for.

John But what strikes one is their cooperativeness rather than their competitiveness.

Robin Except when they play polo, when it's no holds barred! So they *can* be competitive, but their basic values are orientated towards mutual help and maintaining good relationships. So disputes get settled easily.

John What do you think is the starting point for this cooperativeness?

Robin Well, the Ladakhi value system is eastern, and profoundly influenced by Buddhism. So they operate on the principle that we are all inter-dependent – that everything and everybody is connected, and that relationships are essentially harmonious if people remain open and honest with one another. Norberg-Hodge said that she 'had never met people who seemed so healthy, emotionally so secure, as the Ladakhis . . .' and she believes that 'the most important factor is the sense that you are part of something much larger than yourself, that you are inextricably connected to your surroundings'.

John Whereas our Western view of the world emphasises the separateness of everything from everything else. So we feel separate. We experience ourselves as separate from others and from nature.

Robin And yet we don't feel comfortable and confident with that separateness. We often feel cut-off, lonely, alienated. By contrast Norberg-Hodge says she 'found the Ladakhis less emotionally dependent than we are in industrial society. There is love and friendship, but it is not intense and grasping, not a possession of one person by another'. She believes that the reason is that they live in a healthy society that 'encourages close social ties and independence, granting each individual a net of unconditional emotional support'. And that 'with this nurturing framework individuals feel secure enough to become quite free and independent'.

John And there's something very reassuring about them. Apart from their cheerfulness and friendliness and vitality, they seem perfectly *ordinary*! Ladakh is *not* Shangri-La.

Robin No, it isn't perfect, as we saw. John Crook, who led our little party and who has been to Ladakh many times, shares the positive view of the Ladakhis, but he's found that they have their strains and their stresses too, and that sometimes relationships break up. It's just that they seem to handle it all better than we do. He also said that although there was a very high level of mutual aid and cooperation in the villages, with good ways of resolving disputes, warm friendliness and a remarkable capacity to endure hardship, there was a cost. For example, he thought that being expected to be so pleasant could disguise underlying tensions, so that their reactions didn't always feel authentic. And the possibility of not being able to return some act of generosity could make them anxious. Interestingly enough, that's very similar to the price the Japanese pay for their remarkable social cohesion. But all in all, he was very impressed with the high levels of intimacy the Ladakhis could sustain.

John Yes, I remember when I told my mother how much I liked Ladakhis, she said she'd always like the darkies, too. I digress. So everyone who has spent time there seems to agree that this is a remarkably healthy culture. And when you check it against the features you describe for the exceptionally healthy families, it does seem to match them all pretty well. They show a strong Affiliative Attitude and cooperate well in groups, yet they're also very independent and respect each other's individuality.

Robin And there is a clear social structure, yet the relationships are very democratic.

John Communication is good and even nineteenth-century travellers to the region described them as 'a truth-telling people'. They are lively, spontaneous and seem to enjoy life a lot.

Robin And they face the harsh realities of life in that high-altitude desert cheerfully. They cope well with change, like loss and death. The parallels are very striking . . .

John Do you think we may be idealising them?

Robin No. The evidence is very strong. And anthropologists have shown very clearly that 'primitive' life is often much more healthy, judged by the principles of health we've been talking about, than our own. For instance Turnbull says: 'In terms of a conscious dedication to human relationships that are both affective and effective, the primitive is ahead of us all the way.' From earliest childhood, throughout every stage of life, this social know-how and understanding is passed on to everyone in a practical way through continual social training. Almost everything that happens – formal education, social events, work, games, and of course rituals – contribute something towards this understanding. Turnbull cites a children's game played in a very cooperative tribe called the Mbuti, who live in North-Eastern Zaire. A number of children will climb a young, springy tree until enough of them are at the top for their weight to bend it over so they're quite near the ground again. Now, the point of the game is for everyone to let go simultaneously and drop to the ground together. If one of them hangs on too long, they'll get tossed up by the tree into the air – a mistake they won't be keen to repeat. In this way people *grasp the need to play their part*; and they learn how to play it in the most effective way so that everyone benefits, including themselves. By contrast, in the West we do almost nothing to bring about this social consciousness and understanding of society as a whole, or to develop competence in fulfilling our part in it and a sense of responsibility about our doing so.

John But you know, here's the puzzle. This, Doctor, is the enigma wrapped in a paradox. These wonderful, simple, happy, uncomplicated societies – the ones we think we envy – never seem to be able to resist materialistic corruption when it's offered to them. Western individualism and materialism must go against their deepest sense of value, but these simpler societies usually grab at it with both hands, even though they must know that it's a route that will lead them to lose most of what is special in their community. Can you think of a single healthy society which has chosen not to follow the path of greater materialism?

Robin Not really. Certainly not Ladakh. Now that the Ladakhis have come into contact with people from the West it has made them begin to feel poor by comparison. So their feeling of self-respect is changing, as they begin to doubt themselves, and feel inferior. There's an increasing emphasis on money and material gain. Where visitors were treated as guests in every house when the area was first opened up, Ladakhis in contact with visitors now are more concerned with money. There are increasing signs of people becoming less generous, charging high prices, and even of theft where Western influences have been strongest. And where that's the case, people are beginning to develop our Western tensions and instabilities, like restlessness, aggressiveness, and depression. There's even a little alcoholism, and the Ladakhis are not looking after the old in the way that they used to.

John Perhaps it's hard to resist the lure of Western values if you don't see where they're leading . . .

Robin Well, if we can't resist them ourselves, despite all the evils they lead to – constantly rising crime rates, social unrest and alienation, increasing break-up of marriages and families, child abuse, forests dying from acid rain, one Chernobyl disaster already with world-wide effects and plenty more disasters ready to happen, holes in the ozone layer so we're asked to wear hats and dark glasses instead of enjoying the sun, the destruction of wildlife, of the beauty of nature and even of the trees that produce the oxygen we breathe – if *we* still haven't got the message we can hardly blame people like the Ladakhis, who see the watches and transistor radios but aren't told about the down-side consequences of it all, and who take what we say at face value because they are still open and trusting while we are so untrustworthy and can't even face the truth about ourselves . . .

John You know, it's suddenly struck me that we're talking about 'Western materialism' and 'Western values' as though the West has always been like this. But actually the West underwent exactly the same process we've just been describing – exactly the same transition from a communal and cooperative society to an individualistic and competitive one.

Robin Go on . . .

John I mean the change from Medieval Christendom to Modern Europe. Just because it happened a long time ago, we forget it's the same process. If we go back to the Middle Ages, we find a simple cooperative culture in Europe.

Robin What would you say was the basic idea underlying it?

John Oh, the easy ones first, eh? Well, I suppose it's all based on the unquestioned assumption that society is the way it is because God ordered it thus. So everyone and everything is in their rightful place. Therefore there's absolutely no point in trying to move up or down the hierarchy, and not much point in changing anything at all!

Robin Not exactly a recipe for encouraging competition.

John No, because each person is so identified with his or her role in the social order, that they think of themselves as a member of a guild, or a knight, or an artisan, or a peasant, and *not* as an individual who happens to hold this position. So it wouldn't occur to them to change. And, there are rules and obligations determining almost everything. They can't even dress or eat as they like.

Robin How's society organised?

John Well, the feudal hierarchy is a network of obligations, going both ways. OK, the king is top dog, but even he's expected to consult the magnates – the Magna Carta is a memo of this. So wherever you are in the set-up, you owe dues to your superior, but he has defined obligations towards you too. So land, the only real source of wealth, is very hard to buy or sell, because each patch is encumbered by all the various rights that people have in it.

Robin And business?

John Well nobody can make very much money. The Church fixes a 'fair price' for everything and there are rules to tell you where you have to sell it. If you're a tradesman, you must belong to a guild, which blocks most competition among its members by forcing them to share trade secrets and the buying

of raw materials. In addition, of course, usury is forbidden –
to protect those in need from exploitation. In a nutshell, the
key is that economic principles are completely subordinate to
human needs; as Richard Tawney puts it: 'It is right for a man
to seek such wealth as is necessary for a livelihood. To seek more
is avarice . . . a deadly sin.'

Robin So morality dominates even economic issues because, for
most people, heaven and hell are realities.

John Yes, the Church, which is supra-national, fosters a sense
of guilt for crowd-control purposes. It's also amazingly powerful.
It owns a third of the land, controls communication – the pulpit
was the medieval newscast – and it makes it clear that you can
only communicate with God through its officials. Services are
in an incomprehensible language, there are no holy texts
available that you can think about on your own, and the way
to escape guilt is by doing a deal with a priest.

Robin And all learning is controlled by the Church too.

John Although even there, thinking for yourself is an alien
concept, because all arguments are settled by reference to
authorities – preferably Aristotle, but a Founding Father will
do. They tell it the way it is, and no arguing. So discussion
consists of trading quotes and pointing at the spiritual ranking
system.

Robin So it simply doesn't occur to people to check anything
against reality?

John No because nobody who is well educated has much
interest in the real world out there: they're concerned only with
the important matters of theology and metaphysics.

Robin So there's no science.

John As a result, technical innovation takes epochs. Similarly,
in art and architecture people carefully copy earlier masters,
who themselves copied earlier masters. And, of course, nobody
needs to sign their work. God knows who did it.

Robin Does this mean that people didn't really think about
themselves much – you know, to try to analyse themselves?

John I get the impression that such an idea wouldn't occur to
them. They simply didn't have the habits of introspection that
we take for granted nowadays. As Erich Fromm puts it,
'Awareness of one's individual self . . . of others . . . and of
the world as separate entities, had not yet fully developed.' So
if you don't see yourself as separate from everything around

you, you can't really think about yourself in any objective
– or even subjective – way!

Robin True. You wouldn't be on the agenda as a separate item.

John I mean I've often noticed that I'm most introspective when
I'm unsure or doubtful about something. Fromm points out
that medieval man was 'rooted in a structuralised whole and
thus life had a meaning which left no place, and no need, for
doubt'.

Robin So the other side of the coin of people's lack of awareness
of themselves was a tremendous sense of belonging, of
security.

John Which is hard for us to understand now – a bit like trying
to imagine how people looked at paintings before perspective
had been discovered.

Robin And approximately when was this medieval world
you're describing?

John Oh dear. Well there seem to be very unresolved
arguments between historians about when things were like
this, and by what dates certain traits had developed. A brilliant
group of Oxford historians headed by Alan Macfarlane
claimed that England was an extraordinarily individualistic
society by 1300! But several respected older historians think

the individualisation process was happening two or three hundred years later. Then again, in Italy during the Renaissance, individualism was much more confined to the very wealthy, with the masses remaining rather undifferentiated; whereas in northern Europe it was part of the culture right down to the lower middle class. So what I'm trying to describe is a sort of idealised picture of medieval communalism, guaranteed to annoy any proper historian.

Robin In order to make a clearer contrast with 'Modern Europe'?

John Exactly. And, to highlight the complete change that's taken place I'd characterise 'Modern Europe' as a variety of early-nineteenth-century Northern Protestant Europe to highlight the complete change that's taken place.

Robin So what's the essence of this Modern Europe of yours about which you do not wish to be asked anything in too much detail?

John Well, because people are now more aware of themselves as individuals, they feel more separate from the rest of the world, which allows them to view it in a much more objective way. Jacob Burckhardt, the great historian of the Renaissance, says that a veil of illusion had melted into air.

Robin Now the essence of the medieval world was that it was all ordered by God . . .

John Right. Well the result of folk viewing the world more objectively is that they're finding out how it works. So after Galileo and Descartes and Newton, God's glory is seen to be His Plan for the Universe – in other words, the laws of science. He's not in everyday control of things any more; he's a non-executive God. So there's no fixed order of things, apart from these laws.

Robin So it's not ungodly to better yourself. Whereas the medieval Church was stifling competition, this view is actually promoting it!

John In addition, people are also looking more objectively at *themselves*, and are deciding that many of their needs are valid, not just a manifestation of sin! Which means that it's moral to satisfy those needs – the pursuit of happiness is not sinful any more.

Robin So where's the Church in all this?

John The church services and the holy scriptures are in people's native tongues, so now everyone can discuss theology and make up their own mind. The direct contact between each person and God is emphasised so each person is now primarily answerable to their Maker.

Robin Personal conscience becomes important.

John Right. And the Protestant work ethic develops rapidly with its extraordinary emphasis on accumulating personal wealth – not for spending yet, but because it's a measure of your industry, thrift and efficiency. 'The Devil makes work for idle hands,' and 'Time is money.'

Robin So the Christian Church says that capitalism is totally acceptable, usury is therefore fine, there's no such thing as an unfair price, and a man can pay the lowest wages he can get away with.

John Indeed, the Church is so capitalistic that later on, when legislation is introduced in the House of Lords to put some limits on the use of child labour, the *Bishops* vote it down!

Robin What about the rights that poorer country folk used to have in their lord's lands?

John They're gone, so these folk have to move to the towns in search of work and become the cheap source of labour the capitalists require. So the landowners now have the freedom to exploit their land for maximum profit.

Robin So in all these ways, economic behaviour is no longer just an aspect of personal conduct.

John That's right. There's now an impersonal power about economic laws that puts them above human consideration.

Robin People are saying for the first time: 'Sorry, but that's business!'

John Right. And another aspect of all this individualistic behaviour is the explosion of creativity. Scientists are not just discovering, they're inventing. The technological revolution is amazing. And art is becoming more and more inventive and individual too. It's easier to recognise each artist's personal style, and none of them would think of leaving a painting unsigned!

Robin What about personal life?

John Well, the movement to the towns is breaking up the extended family. Also, there's more individual choice in marriage. The relationship seems a bit more romantic and a bit less business-like. Above all, privacy exists! People now choose to spend time on their own, reading and painting and keeping diaries and thinking about their own lives.

Robin So how have people's lives changed since medieval times?

John Each individual has made a huge gain in self-awareness, in knowledge of the world, and in freedom. And he or she has done that at the cost of a tremendous loss of security, economic and emotional.

Robin In other words, all the aspects of medieval life that can be viewed as constraints on freedom, were at the same time sources of connection and support for the individual.

John Freedom brings aloneness. So, Mr Shrink, is there a parallel here with the experience of each child as it grows up and away from its family?

Robin There is indeed. Growing from infancy to adulthood – in modern society at least – is a process where the initial oneness between mother and child is steadily replaced by increased autonomy and independence, but at the cost of greater separateness, feeling alone and having to look after yourself. You see it particularly in the toddler refusing to do what it is told and demanding to do things itself. And that growing away from dependence and security is a strong pressure again in adolescence. If you remember, in *Families* I said that one meaning of the myth of the Garden of Eden – Adam and Eve disobeying God and getting thrown out – was about this weaning process.

John All right. Well, now I need to stop for a moment to think where we are. We'd been looking at some simple and cooperative societies and noticing how Westernisation has moved them in a more individual and competitive direction. And then . . . we traced that process as it happened in the West a few hundred years ago . . .

Robin Wait a moment. Why did you choose the early nineteenth century? Is that when individualism was at its height?

John I think that's when you get the clearest picture of it. After then people are becoming much more aware of all the casualties that the system produces. So ideas and political movements start developing to counteract the rampant capitalism. At first, most of the amelioration is carried out by private voluntary groups; but gradually the state takes over more and more control, and attitudes become very politicised.

Robin And so, as people further down the social hierarchy start getting votes, the process accelerates.

John The socialist ideas which develop have two manifestations. One is Communism, which was intended as a complete replacement for capitalism, but which proved quite unable to deal with the complexities of modern markets . . .

Robin As the collapse of the Soviet bloc has displayed for all to see . . .

John . . . As well as being in practice, morally disgusting. I mean, the notion of Communism has great moral validity – it's very Christian in some aspects. Indeed, when people revile it, I think of G. K. Chesterton's remark about Christianity: 'It hasn't failed, it has simply never been practised.' The trouble was that the theory behind it was utterly paranoid: Working Class – Good. Bourgeoisie – Bad. As Bertrand Russell once pointed out, if that is the case, why change the system to give the working class all the advantages that made the bourgeoisie so bad? So this paranoid theory attracted paranoid types who always outnumbered the genuinely communally-minded ones. And this was made worse by the fact that power corrupts, and that one-party Communism had no 'checks and balances'. In fact, it deliberately got rid of them. Loyalty to the party was the greatest virtue. Result: collapse of stout Communist party.

Robin Right. Now you just said there were *two* manifestations of Socialism.

John Well, where some Socialist ideas were incorporated into the capitalist system, a great deal was accomplished. No one would seriously argue now that there's no need for a welfare state, in the way that the Conservatives argued against the National Health Service Act in the 1940s.

Robin But Socialism proved no good as far as creating wealth was concerned, did it? Bureaucrats not only can't run entrepreneurial operations; they tend to obstruct those who can.

John True. In the mid-seventies I asked a professor at the London Business School why the British economy had been in trouble since 1945, and he said: 'It's supposed to be a mixed economy, but the private part of it has never been allowed to work properly.' And, although I voted Labour several times, I couldn't really see how you encouraged investment by making people pay 98 per cent tax on the income from it.

Robin So now, there's a very wide acceptance that only capitalism delivers the goods.

John And hand-in-hand with capitalism comes Liberal Democracy. I know that South Korea and Singapore are hardly paragons of democratic virtue *yet*, but the adoption of free market principles seems to lead inexorably to other freedoms, of a social and political nature. So at present, as Francis Fukuyama, the American historian, says: 'We have trouble imagining . . . a future that is not essentially democratic and capitalist'.

Robin Well, even if that is true, it certainly doesn't mean we are experiencing just one type of society, does it? After all, it strikes me that the two most successful Liberal Democracies in the world are at either end of the individualistic–communal spectrum we've been examining in this chapter.

John You mean America and Japan?

Robin Yes. The United States with its long tradition of rugged individualism; and Japan, which operates through a highly communal structure and with an exceptionally consensual style.

John You mean, if we examine each, we may be able to see more clearly which facets of individualism we like, and which facets of a more communal culture we prefer. Then we could see whether any mix between them would give our Liberal Democracy the best of both worlds.

Robin Exactly.

John Well I've spent over three years of my life in the United States, and have always made it a point of principle to marry American women. Shall I start?

Robin Fire away.

John Well, first a disclaimer. The people I like best in the world are Americans who've spent time in Europe. *And* Europeans who've spent time in America. I believe we need to incorporate each other's qualities. So what I'll say refers to pure, unadulterated America.

Robin So when you went there thirty years ago, what first struck you?

John The energy and the rudeness. But then, I was in New York. Even so, I soon began to see how cultural was my judgement of 'rudeness'. A lot of it, I realised, was simply directness of a kind I just wasn't used to. If an American wants the salt, they say: 'Pass the salt, please.' Now, believe it or not, to an Englishman, this can actually sound rude! A bit blunt, and rather graceless. We're more used to: 'I'm so sorry to trouble you, but I wonder if I might be so bold as to ask you if you could see your way clear, if it's not too inconvenient, to consider the possibility of, as it were, not to put too fine a point on it, passing the salt, or not, as the case may be.' I'm sure it's because we English have such an exaggerated fear of provoking anger, that we try to ward off any possibility of it by behaving in an absurdly vague and apologetic way. Maybe we're so tightly packed together on our island that we grow up with the sense that we have to keep our elbows in at all times or fighting will break out. Rather as the Japanese, crammed together on their islands, have also developed an exaggerated courteous formality.

Robin But we often enjoy it when American visitors show their directness and start a conversation on a train, where otherwise we'd all be studiously ignoring each other. It brings us to life.

John That's right. And American energy seems to me to arise from them not holding themselves in like us: they feel they've got space, and they're not frightened of anger. Sometimes to the point that any refinement at all can be seen as decadent! As one young Californian said: 'Good taste is what you finish up with when you've run out of energy!'

Robin It's the choice every society has to make, isn't it? Either we inhibit our spontaneous feelings so that we don't upset others, which can make us rather lifeless and boring; or we go for vitality and freedom and accept that we are going to have more social strife.

John So because they're not basically uncomfortable with anger, many Americans can be assertive in the healthiest way – friendly, yet effective.

Robin Remember that the research showed that healthy people seemed to be more comfortable with aggressive and competitive feeling. I must say I enjoy and admire it – though I might feel differently if someone had tried to mug me during a visit there!

John *That's* the down-side . . . this lack of inhibition about anger easily overbalances into violence. And I mean the full spectrum of violence, all the way from the usual violence of ordinary business executive language – they have an infinite number of expressions conveying the degree of violence that they intend to do to one another's bottoms – through the unending violence on television and in movies, via the national sport of American football which is, quite simply, the most violent game ever devised, all the way to crime statistics which deteriorate so fast that by the time you've quoted them, they're out of date.

Robin In my practice of couple therapy, where a quarter of my patients have always been American, I find this puts a huge strain on the men who feel they've got to live up to this macho image. And paradoxically it gives the women enormous power because they can humiliate the men by indicating they're not powerful and tough enough. I find this tends to wreck their relationships more than anything else.

John Three other aspects of American life fascinated me on those visits. One was their attitude to money. I realised that the possession of money actually conveyed moral status. I can still remember what a shock it was, because I'd grown up with the idea that there was no connection between wealth and moral status whatsoever. In fact, if anything, it was a slightly negative relationship: very rich people were probably greedy. But in America, it didn't seem to matter how disreputable were the means by which you'd made your pile; once you had 'made it', you were a Shining Beacon Guiding Others on the Path.

Robin And more than that, in the US someone who has made a lot of money is listened to with respect on matters completely unrelated to the skills which enabled them to accumulate wealth. Like Ross Perot . . .

John Second was their dislike of hierarchy. Not surprising, considering that it was the hierarchies that caused most of them to leave Europe. But Americans often seem to find even hierarchies of knowledge or understanding offensive; they feel it's bad that any idea can't be grasped immediately by a complete beginner. This begets an extreme kind of relativism that not only leads to the outer reaches of Political Correctness, but also to the refusal to resist any manifestation of the youth culture. Which is why American culture slides remorselessly in that direction.

Robin I agree, their dislike of hierarchy makes total sense in terms of their history. And there's a very attractive side to it – like the way people from all walks of life will strike up a conversation with you without consideration of 'class' and 'social position' getting in the way as it would in England. But hierarchy is a fact of life. You can't get rid of it, and in some ways they've created even more extreme forms, like the concept of 'celebrity' and the 'star' system in the movies. Instead of hierarchies of excellence they have hierarchies based on publicity, outward show, whoever can make the most noise.

John The third I noticed when I invited some people to an extremely good show in a little Off-Broadway theatre. They declined, saying that on that evening they wanted to see another show. And I said: 'You know that's not a very good show, don't you?' And they said: 'Yes, but we want to see it.' And I said: 'Why?' And they said: 'Because it's a hit.' That's when I began to notice the extraordinary degree to which Americans are attracted by 'success', in the sense of *public* success – what an extrovert means by success. That is, it's success measured only by the *impact* you have *on others* by virtue of your fame, glamour, wealth and so on. It has no connection with an introvert's view of success, that you've done something that's deeply satisfying to you personally. That's for the birds, basically. In as much as it's acknowledged at all, it's done so almost pityingly.

Robin I have to agree because I see the same thing there in my profession. In mental health work you see fashions developing one after another. Everyone wants to climb on the current bandwagon, until another one begins to attract more people and then it's 'all change'. It works against ideas of real quality being taken up and systematically developed.

John So it follows that in America, the very best kind of success is the most visible; hence America's obsession with show business. Michael Shamberg, my co-producer on *Wanda*, explains that it's the embodiment of the American Dream to see up there on the screen people from all walks of life who have 'made it'.

Robin I like that. It contributes to their willingness to have a go themselves, take a risk, try something new.

John But the nicest part of Americans loving success is that they are remarkably unenvious about it. Perhaps because Americans always seem to have felt that if you can't succeed in one place . . . well then you can always move somewhere else and succeed *there*. That's connected with their sense of space again . . .

Robin Which means they operate, far more than most other nations, on a philosophy of plenty. Which is enormously positive, and a major reason for their tremendous achievements.

John I can't help comparing it with the UK, which is an extraordinarily envious little island, with everybody trying to cut everyone else down to size, led by a pack of bright emerald-green Schadenfreude fans called 'journalists'.

Robin If you want people to be really nice and supportive to you in Britain, the thing to do is to fail, or at least *appear* to fail . . .

John Isn't that true! Fall flat on your face and everyone's ringing you up, helping you feel better. Only fair really, since you've made *them* feel so good.

Robin Our famous British 'modesty' is one way we try to deflect our fellow-countrymen's strong tendency to be envious of anything that smacks of success.

John But Americans love you if you're successful: it's *failure* they *can't* forgive.

Robin That's true. If you are not succeeding, no one wants to know you. You don't really exist . . .

John I suppose that's why winning has become so insanely important in the States.

Robin You remember all those quotes you used when we spoke to the American Family Therapy Association in Philadelphia?

John They're wonderful. They're from American sports team coaches. The famous one is: 'Winning is not everything, it's the only thing.' But here are some more. 'Nice guys finish last.' 'Show me a good sportsman and I'll show you a player I'm going to trade.' 'Show me a good loser, and I'll show you an idiot.' 'Without any winners there wouldn't be a goddam civilisation.' 'Defeat is worse than death, because you have to live with defeat.'

Robin Go on . . .

John And then I mentioned that several of my American friends couldn't really see what was funny about a book I'd found in New York called *Eat to Win*; and finally I showed a double-page spread from a Los Angeles magazine, advertising a weekend Buddhist seminar under the slogan: 'Buddhism gives you the Competitive Edge.'

Robin Of course, *that* audience was roaring with laughter. Many Americans see the absurdity of this fetish with winning. But it is a fearsomely competitive country.

John I remember an American psychoanalyst telling me about a patient whose problems with impotence they were able to trace back to his salary being too low.

Robin Well obviously this tremendous emphasis on winning has very unfortunate results socially. People at the bottom of the hierarchy are not only thought of as 'losers'; they think of *themselves* as such. Consequently, they become alienated from the culture.

John Yes, my American friends tell me that if you're poor and you live in a big American city you don't feel that you are a part of society – although it is still possible to do so in some small towns or in some traditionally agricultural regions. In such places, there's still a social fabric that hasn't been completely destroyed by the Winning Ethic.

Robin And inevitably people who are alienated from the culture through poverty will be antagonistic towards it, and may try to 'win' via the rules of an anti-culture – usually a criminal one.

John Then again, even the people who are successful are under a tremendous pressure to appear endlessly optimistic and up-beat. A New York friend in advertising tells me that there is only one acceptable response to the question, 'How are you?' It is: '*Never* better!' Anything less is considered defeatist, and the first sign of irretrievable decline.

Robin This Winning Ethic explains the huge popularity of sterile, one-dimensional creatures like Rambo and Superman and The Terminator, whose main personality trait is that they're unbeatable. But trying to emulate them would be a strain!

John I think everyone, when young, enjoys those comic strip heroes: but when I remarked that the odd thing about America is that adults stay interested in such figures, I was told I didn't appreciate what an important and influential part they'd played in the development of the culture. Perhaps that's why it didn't attract any notice when Bill Clinton claimed during his election campaign that, with the right changes, America could 'become the greatest country in the world, forever'. Can you imagine a European leader saying that?

Robin And there's a final aspect to this winning obsession: you can't make sensible judgements if you concentrate only on the up-side of situations. It's unrealistic not to take the down-side on board too; but that's difficult if your culture's pressuring you to tune out anything that might seem 'negative'.

John I think politicians in America find it almost impossible to give bad news. They have to foster feel-good notions: hence, any problems used to be blamed on Russia; and the moment that collapsed, the Japan-bashing started!

Robin Yes, it's easier to blame the Japanese for cheating, than to acknowledge that you're not as powerful or as efficient as you used to be. Or to talk about the budget deficit!

John Of course, the English are different. It's anything optimistic, full of hope, or uplifting that makes them uneasy. When, at the beginning of the Second World War, Winston Churchill told them he had 'nothing to offer but blood, toil, sweat and tears', I think most of them were quite relieved. I can't see the Americans warming to a slogan like that . . .

Robin Well, so far we've talked about the energy and the assertiveness and the aggression; and we've talked about success and winning and optimism. These can have positive effects, but tend to be taken to extremes, thereby upsetting the balance of emotions that characterise really good health. Any other important characteristics?

John One more. A great preference for simplicity. In every conceivable form. For a start, Americans tend to be straightforward and open in the nicest possible way, often to the point of naïvety – which I find extremely attractive.

Robin You really prefer it to cynicism and cunning?

John Yes, I've always been peculiar like that. So Americans frequently display an attractive guilelessness. But that of course can make them a little credulous, or gullible. Their culture encourages them to accept things without too much questioning – to be enthusiastic about ideas before they've really examined them. It's as though scepticism is considered a negative quality, something that inhibits the required positive approach. So I've often visited America and found people very enthused about a new attitude or idea. Then on my next visit I don't hear anything about it! And if I enquire what happened to it, people look at me as if I'm very out of touch.

Robin So they're rather healthy in being able to cope with change so well; but not so healthy about having a secure and independent sense of their own identity which isn't threatened if others don't agree. So they have fashions in ideas the way other people have fashions in clothes.

John The next aspect of this simplicity is their directness in communication. Which can be terrific, because you can get to the bottom of things quickly and sort them out. But sometimes the directness has a slightly uncomfortable 'earnest' quality about it – almost as though there's a subsidiary message: 'Please help me to keep everything absolutely and completely clear at all times, otherwise I get anxious.' No wonder they wrote their Constitution down before anyone else . . .

Robin They do like to keep their ideas safely nailed to the floor – until they turn them in completely for new models, that is. They don't like complexity or contradiction.

John So any kind of indirectness in communication makes such folk uncomfortable. And ambiguity and paradox are not just disliked and mistrusted, they're felt to be quite *unnecessary*; an attitude that can lead to simplistic thinking, as well as simplistic emotion.

Robin So lack of directness is taboo . . .

John Whereas, of course, it's all that the English are capable of. We *revel* in distancing devices – using funny voices, saying everything as though it's in quotes, allusiveness, not completing sentences and above all . . . *irony*. Simple direct speech is regarded as alarming and bad form – a kind of philistinism.

Robin By contrast, irony makes the Americans pretty uncomfortable, doesn't it?

John They're all at sea with it, Robin. To put it bluntly, it causes panic. Not among the more city-slicker types I'm acquainted with, of course: they find their fellow Americans' irony gap a bit distressing. In *Roxanne*, Darryl Hannah says something sarcastic to Steve Martin, and when he doesn't get it, she explains she was using irony. 'Oh, *irony*!' says Steve's character. 'No, we haven't had any of that round here since . . . oh, 1956 I'd say.'

Robin So communication is clear and direct and there's a lot of anxiety if it isn't.

John So the more 'regular' American prefers to keep things black and white. This tends to lead to a certain literal-mindedness, particularly in the area of religion. Fundamentalist Christianity, which is very widespread in America, seems to me to be based on interpreting *literally* what was intended to be understood *metaphorically*.

Robin That way of thinking is typical of a limited level of health, and it's found in all societies. But it's probably true that in the US, the emphasis on simplicity pushes more people in that literal-minded direction.

John Finally, this desire for simplicity can lead to an intolerance of diversity of opinion. Because when you desperately want everything pointing clearly in the same direction, it's pretty annoying when some people aren't.

Robin And if you feel anxious about feeling different and unapproved of yourself, you'll feel hostile towards anyone who behaves differently because it will arouse all your own anxieties.

John Nicely put.

Robin So, to sum up . . . you see the salient features of America as a great energy released by lack of social inhibition, which can overbalance into excessive aggression; a moral dimension to the possession of wealth; an excessive regard for success, especially visible success, which has led to insane attitudes about the importance of winning and also a refusal to see the down-side of situations, even when it's necessary to do so; and a simplicity which is attractive and which generates enthusiasm, but which can degenerate into literal-mindedness and intolerance.

John I have nothing more to teach you about the art of summing up.

Robin And of course all those characteristics, in greater or lesser degree, are present in what we've called individualistic societies. But what do you think it was that gave America this extreme version of the individualist culture?

John Well, the Puritans on the *Mayflower* were obviously the most determined dissidents – I mean, to get away from what they saw as the stifling restrictions of the Old World, they actually crossed the Atlantic! The Protestant work ethic flourished dramatically just because the early pioneers could be as Protestant as they liked and work as hard as they wanted; if a new establishment tried to control them they could move on, and on, until they came to the Pacific Coast. The land was so rich and empty that there really was some truth in the idea that poverty was a personal failure to have enough 'get up and go'. And of course the ideas of the French Revolution, Tom Paine's *The Rights of Man* and other seminal developments in political thought could simply take hold more quickly because there was less history to get rid of!

Robin So the American tradition has been the march of individualism. Now let's look at another tradition entirely.

John Yes. Japan. Highly successful but it's a society built on completely different values, isn't it?

Robin You had better fasten your seat-belt; the differences are extraordinary, beyond anything one can easily imagine.

That's one reason America and Japan are good choices for us to compare. They illustrate so well that, with nations just as with families, there is 'no single thread' making for healthy functioning, but many different recipes drawing on a number of common ingredients together with some unique additions. But let's start with a symbolic contrast. You said that in America a city dweller who's poor doesn't feel a part of society. Well, in Japan, even the road-sweepers have a sense of contributing something towards Japanese society. And yet, despite this strong communal sense, the Japanese have nevertheless overtaken this great competitive American society in one area after another. In the seventies, they'd captured the lion's share of the market in motorcycles, cameras and electronic consumer goods. By the early eighties, they'd outstripped the USA in steel production and car manufacture, and they were building half the world's ships. Then a few years later, they'd captured 30 per cent of the US car market, they were out-producing the US in semiconductors, and they were making microchips that were nine times more reliable than the best American ones. They're now the world's largest bankers . . .

John OK. OK. Even allowing for the fact that they're near the peak of their growth cycle, and Western countries are well past it, it's still phenomenal. So what do they know that we don't?

Robin Well, they have a great sense of cohesion, of being like a big family where everyone feels they should stick together and help each other and put the national 'family' first. They even talk of themselves as 'sticking together like glutinous rice'.

John How has that feeling arisen?

Robin They have a long history of isolation from the rest of the world, which has a number of effects. For a start, they're very

much one tribe. Ninety-seven per cent of them are united by
blood and culture and language and race. There's been no
major mixing with other races for twelve hundred years!

John There's no other advanced nation with comparable 'racial
purity' . . .

Robin Nothing like it. In this respect they couldn't be more
different from the United States. And it's the same story
culturally. After 1603, the Shoguns shut Japan off from contact
with the outside world, until the American Commodore Perry
arrived in 1853 with his 'black ships', and pressured them into
opening up to trade.

John So they're culturally homogeneous almost beyond our
comprehension.

Robin They are indeed. They have a tremendously strong
feeling of being quite different from everyone who isn't
Japanese.

John I believe they get very uncomfortable if they hear fluent
Japanese being spoken by a foreigner?

Robin So I'm told. Now, in addition to this isolation, the
Japanese have always felt they were under some kind of threat.
First, they have a large population packed tightly into a few
small islands, most of them mountainous, so there's always
been pressure on food supplies; second, they have few
resources or raw materials to speak of, so life has always been
hard; third, they've suffered frequent earthquakes, floods,
typhoons and other natural disasters; and finally I suppose it
doesn't make you feel any more secure living next door to two
giants called China and Russia.

John And any group of humans under threat will tend to sink
their differences and swim together to survive . . .

Robin So all their values emphasise the primacy of the group
over the individual. And this leads to something that Westerners
find bewildering: the Japanese actively dislike communication
that is too direct and clear!

John Really! Why?

Robin Because it might lead to confrontation, argument and
other difficulties in achieving consensus.

John Yes, OK. Oddly enough that makes a kind of sense. I
suppose if everyone in a group does spell out clearly what they
all think, differences become more obvious.

Robin So, like members of a family, the Japanese communicate through non-verbal signs, or 'belly language' as they call it. In this way, they can feel out others' attitudes before any clear proposal is put forward.

John Hmm. It's just struck me that this is how *we* handle people who are very touchy . . .

Robin But they see this behaviour as strength, a sensitivity towards other people. Indeed a *lovingness* which is threatened by Western reason and logic, which they see as 'cold', 'dry' and 'intolerant'.

John Wait a moment. Are you saying . . . that the Japanese don't subscribe to the idea of 'logic'?

Robin That's right. They're not keen on it.

John Holy mackerel! So . . . it must be rather difficult discussing things with them.

Robin If you try to construct a logical argument, yes. To give a famous example: they didn't want to import American skis, so they said Japanese snow is different from American snow!

John So it would be quite tricky to show them that anything they were doing should be changed. Tricky as in 'Forget it'.

Robin Right. Of course they've absorbed a lot of Western patterns in sports, clothes, music and so on, but such changes are pretty superficial. The Japanese view themselves as special – as essentially different from other nations, and not answerable to any general principles of conduct beyond Japanese views. Indeed, they deliberately avoid any examination of their culture. It's theirs and that's it.

John In the sense that it's superior, not capable of improvement?

Robin Yes. So there's an enormous resistance to foreign values of any kind that question their existing system. A few years ago a government survey found that two-thirds of the population didn't want to mix with foreigners and intended to avoid them as far as possible. And of those who said they positively would like to meet foreigners – just 25 per cent – only 4 per cent were actually doing so!

John And aren't they very tough on Japanese children who receive part of their education abroad and return to Japan?

Robin Indeed. They tend to get rejected and bullied at Japanese schools both by teachers and other children; they're made to feel contaminated, and special schools have had to be established to remould them into acceptable Japanese. The industrial system also regards foreign education generally as a handicap and seeing such applicants as potentially unreliable and trouble-making, often won't give them jobs.

John But psychiatrically speaking, this is very unhealthy, isn't it?

Robin Don't forget we're not talking about individuals, so you'll never find a society as healthy as the exceptional families we talked about. On the whole, they will be mid-range. But it's true that the Japanese as a group do show characteristics which in the West are found in the 'enmeshed' families lower down the health scale. Indeed, Takeo Doi, Japan's best-known psychiatrist, has described the Japanese state of mind as 'a conciousness of helplessness'! *But*, unlike our enmeshed families, the Japanese appear to have *a strong sense of their individual identity despite their group-awareness*. And this more negative aspect of the way their society functions is balanced by different qualities that make them seem healthier than we do in some other respects.

John But to be blunt, isn't it rather paranoid – this sense of being under threat, which is then compensated for by a feeling of superiority over other nations which means that you can't be compared with them, and can't learn anything from them?

Robin It's more like 'can't learn anything from foreigners which would improve the *essential* nature of Japanese society'. Remember how much they've learned from the West technologically. You see, the Japanese have managed to preserve their values more intact than other Eastern countries, because they've never allowed themselves to be dominated and exploited by the West. They saw the danger by the 1870s and quickly bent all their energies towards catching up in material progress. Now they're all worried that the Japanese worker will develop the British Disease – erosion of the work ethic – though perhaps we should now call that the American Disease, or even, more recently, the German Disease – and they complain that the old trust and codes of honour which governed business ethics in the past are vanishing under the influence of American business values! But as far as possible information coming into Japan is selected to preserve existing social values.

John But don't they go to great lengths to check up on marriage partners to make sure they're not Korean or anything? Explain to me why this isn't good old-fashioned paranoia.

Robin Well, it is paranoid, at least in the broad sense in which we're using that term. But it's a response to social custom, like the paranoid attitudes that develop in any country during a war, for example. It's expected that people will check up on proposed marriage partners, the same way we expect people who marry to have fallen in love. When social expectations change I think people will act differently. Interestingly, where only a small number of Japanese are living in a foreign country, they enjoy normal social relations with the natives. But when the expatriate community grows to a certain size, they revert to this exclusive behaviour, and become far more isolated from the local society than communities of Americans or Europeans abroad.

John So there's nothing insurmountable in their psychological make-up that prevents them from enjoying normal social relations with non-Japanese?

Robin Not at all.

John The paranoia's cultural, not individual . . .

Robin That's what I'm trying to say. But let's not concentrate too much on these negative aspects.

John It's hard not to, since we're all envious of them. Never mind. Well, I'm beginning to see how their history has made them so separate and cohesive. So how does this very communal culture of theirs work?

Robin Well I warn you, it feels strange to all us individualistic Westerners. But there are two central themes to it: the first is the primacy of the group over the individual, which I've mentioned; the other is the all-pervasive feeling of hierarchy.

John Well, let's take the subordination of the individual first. Give me an example.

Robin Take the economy. Whereas in the West, we almost automatically think of what will benefit the consumer, in Japan it's the opposite: the question is: 'What will benefit the Japanese *producer*?' Consequently, many of their markets are shielded from foreign competition, with the result that the Japanese consumer, who earns about the same income as their American counterpart, in very recent times needed to work five times as long to buy rice, nine times as long for beef, and three times as long for petrol.

John So the power of their economy doesn't give them a very high standard of living?

Robin Worse than that. A lot of Japanese feel quite poor and you can see why. Their houses are mostly tiny, with about a third of them still not connected to sewers; the trains are jam-packed; the road system is hopelessly inadequate; Tokyo has one-fifteenth of the park-area of London per person; welfare provision is poor; there's no great flourishing in any of the arts; they work so hard they're lucky if they're home long enough to get eight hours' sleep, and they're only allowed two weeks' holiday, and usually end up taking only *one*!

John That explains what I read about a Japanese television company that was making a documentary comparing the lives of a Japanese family and an Italian family on the same income. They abandoned it half-way through as the television network decided that the Japanese viewers would never believe how much better the Italians lived.

Robin They could hardly have made a more unfortunate choice than Italy. There's no country where people know better how to enjoy life. They seem to be very healthy in that respect, even if many aspects of their society appear quite chaotic.

John So why do the Japanese put up with it? Is it because they have the security of lifetime employment with their corporation?

Robin Not really, because only 30 per cent of them enjoy that. The vast majority of Japanese work for quite small companies, without great security.

John So why don't they elect someone who'll translate their economic success into better lifestyles?

Robin Because they *don't think* like that! Like any system, all the aspects of Japanese culture reinforce each other. This is how the system works, and the system works this way because this is how everyone thinks. So although they're inevitably changing under the impact of foreign ideas, the change is very slow, because it's resisted by every aspect of the system.

John So are they thinking: 'This makes Japan great, so let's not change anything'?

Robin I'm sure it's partly that. But remember they spent many centuries when any lapse from absolute obedience could mean instant death, so it was dangerous to think at all. Western democracy was introduced less than fifty years ago and it will probably take another generation before ordinary people get used to the power and freedom they now possess.

John OK. So tell me how they produce the people who keep this phenomenal economy ticking over.

Robin Well, stand by to have your liberal prejudices shaken. Let's start with the Japanese educational system. One authority says its purpose is 'to shape generations of disciplined workers capable of performing reliably in a rigorous, hierarchical and finely tuned organisational environment'.

John Won't the ants get jealous? I'm sorry, but it does sound a bit chilling.

Robin Not, apparently, if you're thinking of the common good of Japan. You see, after the Second World War, they went in a quite different direction from many Western countries. They based their education system clearly on merit. They designed a system like our grammar schools, with very high standards. Those compete with each other for the best pupils on the basis of their university entrance results. There's no interest in ideas about equality; everything is aimed at establishing and maintaining a hierarchy of merit. There's intense competition among all the pupils to make it to the top, and tremendous pressure on them from parents and teachers alike. The poor students facing university exams are the most anxious category of people in Japan! Not much health at this stage, I'm afraid; the suicide rate in teenagers, and even children, is cause for national concern.

John But the ladder to success is accessible to *everyone*?

Robin In theory, yes. In *practice* . . . the system is so tightly organised that getting to the best schools and universities is vital for future success, and poor families can't afford the expensive private schools that get pupils into the fastest rising streams.

John So the rich *are* at an advantage?

Robin Yes, but no matter what school you're talking about there's a fierce pressure on all children to study – even at kindergarten. School hours and terms are much longer than in other countries; in fact, by the time they finish school, Japanese children have done an extra year of schooling compared with the West.

John So the Japanese spend much more on education.

Robin Surprisingly, not at all! They spend almost exactly the same percentage of GNP as we do in Britain. And the average size of classes is about fifty-five, even in the top schools!

John Fifty-five! That's impossible! How on earth can it work?

Robin Well for a start, the teachers have a highly respected status in society. But, more important, there's the most extraordinary discipline. The whole system tends to *suppress any kind of spontaneous behaviour*. With the result that the children become very obedient and self-disciplined.

John They accept it.

Robin They have to. Also, it fits with the rest of Japanese society.

John At home the children see their mothers being very deferential to their fathers, right?

Robin Yes, it's a very traditional arrangement, where the wife is expected to serve the husband. But it's traditional also in the strict division between their roles. So despite the outward deference the wife shows him, she is actually very much in charge as far as the home and children are concerned, and she is the one exerting the main pressure for school achievement. So you see, the aims of Japanese schooling could not be further removed from the original sense of the English word 'education': that is, to bring forth and develop the powers of the mind. Japanese educational tradition has always involved rote learning and imitation. Pupils are not taught to think for themselves at all – in fact, spontaneous reasoning is suppressed. They learn the facts. And that's about it.

John But they're taught to *think*.

Robin Well, they're not taught to think logically in the way we would expect; nor how to ask the right questions. Indeed, they are taught *not to ask any questions at all*. There is little interest in originality.

John . . . This is extraordinary.

Robin One of the first foreign teachers in Japan, an American missionary called William Griffis, wrote that to teach a boy to think for himself would be to do precisely what it was the teacher's business to *prevent*! An investigation by the Japanese Federation of Bar Associations shows that most schools they investigated specified how pupils should walk, stand and sit. There were even regulations about how high they should raise their hands, and at what angle. So the degree of discipline is truly extraordinary. Yet the Ministry of Education sees most problems as due to *too little* of it!

John What can one say? I just have to keep reminding myself it's a completely different value system from ours, at the very deepest level. *And . . .* that it *works*.

Robin Partly because of the great importance placed on education. So, as far as absorbing information is concerned, the Japanese are astonishingly well educated. They have an illiteracy rate of less than 1 per cent, compared with 7–9 per cent in the States. Nearly everyone continues their schooling after the age of sixteen – twice as many as in the UK. As Robert Christopher says, the system produces 'a labour force that combines intelligence and work discipline to a degree unmatched anywhere else in the world'. And this manifests itself in other ways, too: there's a staggering interest in adult education; the newspapers, which have huge circulations, are of a very high standard, more like our Western 'quality' papers; and almost everyone seems to be studying and learning as hard as they can, no matter what their age. As Christopher puts it: 'The Japanese educational system trains people to get maximum mileage out of such native abilities as they possess.'

John I find it bewildering that a system that inhibits curiosity can teach people so effectively.

Robin I think you have to understand the Japanese attitude to discipline, which we'll talk about in a moment.

John But how can they be as intelligent as they are, if they're not taught to *think*?

Robin Well first, it's only certain kinds of thinking, underpinning particular types of intelligence, that they are short on. I mean exploratory, original, creative, 'lateral' thinking. And second, in industry they do involve everybody and draw on the intelligence of the whole system.

John . . . So what about their lack of creativity?

Robin Well they are famously uncreative. Take Nobel Prizes. They've won only five, compared with Britain's sixty-five and the USA's one hundred and fifty-three. And it's certainly true that Japan has not yet originated 'epochal' technologies – the kind that spawn whole new industries. But remember what we said about business – a lot of success comes from efficient application of *minor* technological improvements.

John Discipline is more effective than flair. How depressing. So how do the Japanese react to all this discipline? Do they rebel when they get out of school?

Robin Absolutely not. Japan's an astonishingly law-abiding society. It's very safe: there are over one hundred times as many armed robberies in the United States as in Japan, and thirty times as many in Britain.

John But isn't organised crime rife?

Robin They have a well-developed Mafia, or Yakusa as they're called. But it's as though the government accepts it as the price for restricting and controlling *un*organised crime! It reflects a practice going back to the Shoguns, who gave responsibility for keeping order on the road between Kyoto and Tokyo to the organisations that maintained gambling and prostitution along it. Nowadays, the unwritten rules of the system enable the hundred thousand Yakusa gangsters to run protection rackets, prostitution and similar illegal businesses, provided they don't carry guns or deal in narcotics. They don't even bother to hide their identity; they openly maintain offices and publish company brochures!

John So the Japanese bring crime within the system. They socialise it.

Robin Exactly. But I really need to emphasise how much the cooperative nature of Japanese society reduces the impulse to commit crime. For example, at airports, no one guards their belongings at the baggage claim. There I was, clutching my hand-luggage for dear life and keeping a foot on my duty-free, while the belongings of my fellow travellers were scattered on their trolleys all over the hall, with nobody keeping an eye on anything.

John So what are the police like?

Robin Well the tradition is 'benevolent authoritarianism'. There's no doubt about their great power, but they exercise it leniently, and display a friendly and helpful attitude.

John A bit like the old archetype of the British bobby?

Robin Yes. Very similar to that, but each one even more part of the neighbourhood in his little koban or policebox. They are very aware of what's going on, but the attitude is benign. The emphasis is on deterring crime rather than chasing it. Generally speaking, people are let off if they confess their misdemeanours and are sufficiently apologetic.

John So they really practise reform rather than punishment?

Robin That's the principle behind the whole legal system. They try to avoid sending anyone to prison if they can possibly help it. But a confession is essential, as a first step towards acceptance and a return to society. If people don't confess, quite extreme pressure, possibly to the point of violence, is alleged to be used to force it.

John And if they do confess . . . ?

Robin If they clearly show that they are *not questioning the system*, and that they feel shame for breaking the rules, then the job of the police is done. Most of the accused never go to court and, of the ones that do, and are found guilty, only about 4 per cent go to jail!

John Good heavens! So what do they do to the 96 per cent?

Robin They use fines, suspended sentences, or a kind of probation that seems to work very successfully in their society.

John It's absolutely admirable. But much easier in such a homogeneous culture.

Robin And that's what they work to preserve. So consensus and conciliation is always preferred. This means that litigation is frowned upon, with the result that the number of lawyers and judges is very small. The United States has twenty-five times as many lawyers as Japan, and Britain ten times as many, proportionately speaking.

John OK. So we've seen how the Japanese system leans heavily towards 'the subordination of the individual to the group'. Now what about the other major idea which you said underlies the Japanese system – 'hierarchy'?

Robin Well, the Japanese have a sense of hierarchy that's hard for us to understand in the West.

John What's so different about their version?

Robin In Europe, under the feudal system, obligations and loyalties went both ways between leaders and followers – right?

John Right . . .

Robin Well, in Japan the obligations went only one way: they were all on the follower to be totally obedient to the leader. Basically, loyalty has always been an ethic of *submission*.

John . . . The leader doesn't have to do *anything* to earn it?

Robin No. Japanese appear to feel obligation and indeed, gratitude towards superiors, regardless of what is received from them.

John That is odd. And it means, doesn't it, that there's no reason to upset the system if the people at the top don't deliver the goods – the goods aren't expected anyway.

Robin But there's an even stronger reason for not upsetting the system. Which is that the Japanese sense of hierarchy is so strong that it pervades everything – in a way that it's hard for Westerners to understand. It's because they don't really see that there is an alternative way of doing things.

John Because they were cut off for so long from other cultures, other models?

Robin Exactly. One way to explain the Japanese view of hierarchy is by saying that it's a bit like the power of the parent in a very isolated one-parent family, where the children don't ever see another adult. Even if the parent wanted to be democratic, and to help the children to be liberated, it would be extremely difficult for the children to achieve it because they wouldn't have any other model they could use for comparing and criticising the single parent's values and ways of doing things. You see, most of us become independent by witnessing independence in others, and in adolescence by sometimes playing one parent off against the other. We make an alliance with Mum, and pick off Dad. Then when we feel more equal to Dad, we make an alliance with him, and pick off Mum. But right from the start, we see that they are two different people, that they disagree about some things, and we see that neither of them is God, always and absolutely right. Now, the Japanese had no knowledge of any other country or form of government for hundreds of years. So they couldn't criticise their rulers because they had nothing to compare them with. They had never known anything different.

John But it's not just a sense of hierarchy, it's an extraordinary acceptance of authority, isn't it?

Robin Yes. I can't tell you where the attitude started. I'm just trying to explain why it has been so hard for them to escape from it.

John Is this why there's no real opposition in Japan? I mean it's been a one-party state since the War, hasn't it?

Robin More or less for the whole time since then. The Liberal Democratic Party is really just a coalition of political cliques who take it in turn to hold office. But the rest of the world assumes that Japan must operate democratically, when the truth is that by Western standards, it's a pretty corrupt system, using gerrymandering and bribery. But the Japanese don't deny our assumption that they have Western-style democracy; they encourage it.

John And the opposition doesn't object because they can't really imagine an alternative!

Robin This all explains something else very important about the Japanese – why they are so bad at fitting in with other nations.

John I don't see how you get to that last conclusion.

Robin Well as I explained, because of its isolation, Japan doesn't seem to have any awareness of itself as one system among many. So they automatically apply this idea of hierarchy to the world at large . . .

John With Japan at the top of the tree, you mean?

Robin Naturally. In fact, this was a fundamental element in Japan's war with the USA. The day they attacked Pearl Harbor, the Japanese envoys had handed a message to the American Secretary of State which said: 'It is the immutable policy of the Japanese government . . . to enable each nation to find its proper place in the world,' which really meant exactly that – all the nations arranged on a tidy squash-ladder with Japan as Big Brother. And, the day they lost the War, they quite consciously settled down to beating America economically! The government called management and unions together and they all started to plan together.

John Yes. They often behave as though they don't really want to join in the community of nations, don't they?

Robin They probably realise that, if they did, it would change them and at the moment that's the last thing they want. And a further reason why other nations have problems dealing with Japan is because they can't figure out how the Japanese system works, so they don't know whom they should be dealing with.

John What's wrong with dealing with the Prime Minister?

Robin His power is much less than that of any head of government in the West. The cabinet meetings themselves are brief and largely ceremonial, to rubber-stamp the decisions of the top bureaucrats.

John The *bureaucrats*!

Robin Yes, they have tremendous prestige and it's accepted that they're central to the running of Japan.

John . . . So why can't you find out which bureaucrats you need to deal with?

Robin Because there isn't a clear decision-making structure or process among them. There's just a balance of forces maintained by groups of them, jockeying for position and power.

John So you can't find out who's running things?

Robin In *The Enigma of Japanese Power*, which provides a wonderful look under the surface of Japan, Karel van Wolferen says: 'The system is elusive . . . The Japanese who participate in it cannot get a conceptual grip on it, much less change it.'

John Oddly enough, that makes a kind of sense to me.

Robin How do you mean?

John Well, there's a contradiction between these two principles of yours. If you mix 'hierarchy' with 'subordination of the individual to the group', what happens to the people who are rising to the top of the system? The more senior they get, the less they look as though they're subordinated to the group.

Robin Ah. I hadn't spotted that . . .

John It explains something I read in a very clever management book by John Mole called *Mind Your Manners* in which he says of the Japanese manager: 'The higher he rises in a company, the more pains he will take to hide his ambition and capability and not to be seen as a forceful leader.'

Robin I see what you are saying. They've evolved a system to cope with that contradiction in their values. It's the way they have coped with a double-bind.

John Then again, it fits in with something else I've noticed. If you look at the history of Japan, the person who's in charge is never really in charge, because there's always an *éminence grise* standing behind him, and usually another éminence, who's even grisier, behind *him* as well.

Robin I believe that's true. Apart perhaps from the time they were transforming Japan right after Commodore Perry, it's always been the same story: the 'leaders' aren't in charge, and nobody can tell you who is.

John So what sort of people make up these groups who somehow, between them, run the place?

Robin The ruling class is made up of the bureaucrats, the top businessmen, and part of the Liberal Democratic Party. But don't think of those as separate! For example, the most powerful LDP members are mainly former bureaucrats; and many bureaucrats join the business world as senior executives late in their lives. And almost all those bureaucrats have been through the law department of Tokyo University!

John My God, it's an old boy network!

Robin Absolutely. Theoretically it's open to anyone, but in practice you have to start in the right kindergarten! So they tend to be from the same family background. And they intermarry, too.

John Well, well, well. Right in the middle of this most bewildering of societies is a good old-fashioned Establishment.

Robin But a *highly educated* one! And it works brilliantly – like a nervous system. Important information is dispersed over the entire network literally within hours, through the 'grapevine'. And of course the sharing of values helps to soften friction among parts of the system.

John Well, I'm beginning to see why there's such a degree of consensus about what is needed to make the whole nation successful.

Robin Van Wolferen says: '. . . it has no strong leadership, yet it creates the impression abroad of a purposeful giant bent on economic conquest of the world'. So . . . do you think you're beginning to understand how it works?

John No. But that's the point, isn't it?

Robin I think so!

John What's hardest for me to get my mind around is . . . how they can cope with the lack of clarity – how logic can be so disregarded.

Robin Well, try this next thought for size. Are you ready?

John All ears.

Robin For the Japanese, reality is negotiable.

John . . . Excuse me a moment. I have to lie down.

Robin I keep repeating the point that in the West, people were always aware of different forms of government and ways of doing things. Therefore, they were able to compare different methods; and, once you start comparing things, you get *the idea of abstracting general principles against which different systems can be judged*. So you develop the idea of objective standards, and *you develop logic as the way of applying them*. As somebody said: 'Schooling in logic is as old as Western civilisation itself.'

John Go on.

Robin Well, the Japanese had nothing with which they could compare their ways of doing things. In any case, because they value cohesion above any other quality, *the Japanese are not interested in finding an accurate view of reality; they want a formula that everyone can agree on*. The word *Tateme* refers to this agreed version of the truth – a fantasy, but one that everyone has agreed to accept.

John It's sinking in. They adjust their view of reality to what is socially desirable. And logic is a threat to that, because it would lead to differences of view.

Robin Yes.

John No wonder negotiating with them drives Westerners crazy.

Robin Well, they're only trying to keep foreigners happy by saying what they think they would like to hear! I wouldn't be surprised if they gave different weather forecasts, depending on who asked for them – rain for farmers; sunshine for those heading for the beach.

John But what happens when there's a noticeable discrepancy between *Tateme*, the agreed version, and real . . . er, for want of a better word . . . reality?

Robin It's accepted, even if it's big! These discrepancies are not just built into the system, they're *essential* to the way it functions.

John . . . Well I can see that if 'truth' is as relative as *this*, people are not going to get stuck on points of principle!

Robin It's another aspect of the system that ensures there's so little disagreement. Everything is making it hard for people to form separate points of view. So there's no real opposition, no debate, no effective pressure groups, consumer movements, unions or even a women's movement of the kind we have in the West.

John . . . But even so, there must be *some* dissent . . .

Robin There is, and the system takes it very seriously and goes to great trouble to incorporate it or to diffuse it.

John Well, you can see why the society is so cohesive. It's impossible to rebel!

Robin The great expert on Japan, Edward Seidensticker, says: 'The key to understanding Japanese society is . . . the Japanese have not been taught to say no.'

John But if you did manage to say 'no' by accident, they'd all be telling you that you weren't really disagreeing with them, anyway. I see what they mean about 'glutinous rice'. Just talking about it makes me feel constricted . . . it's as though I can't feel separate . . . I have no space, no freedom . . . but I suppose that's exactly how a Western individualist feels in a very communal society.

Robin Yes, in the West we prize freedom, in the sense that our ideal is to be without restrictions, external or internal. The Japanese attitude is the complete opposite. For them, life is duty.

John . . . You mean, they could not imagine a life separate from obligation?

Robin No, the Japanese live their lives by properly discharging their obligations; both in a trivial sense – they spend an unconscionable amount of time and energy repaying every favour they've received – and in the important sense that they do not rest until they have carried out all their major responsibilities.

John Take an extreme example – love! In the West, we see the essence of pure love in being that it has 'no strings attached'; ultimately, we want to be loved for ourselves, rather than for what we do. What would the Japanese make of that?

Robin They would find it unimaginable, because they feel that love *is* a network of obligations. That's why the bit in the American Declaration of Independence about 'the right . . . to the pursuit of happiness' is incomprehensible to them.

John But does that mean that they don't really experience obligations as burdensome?

Robin I know it's very hard for us to empathise with, because in the West we experience discipline initially as a series of rules imposed on children by society, originally through their parents. So we think of discipline as frustrating children's natural tendencies, and we expect this to lead to anger, which then has to be kept in check by more social sanctions.

John Whereas the Japanese . . . ?

Robin They view things more positively! They think of human nature – or at least *Japanese* nature – as basically good and well intentioned. So they assume that people will do the decent, socially responsible thing if they're left to themselves, unless something has gone wrong with the machinery.

John . . . So they don't see being virtuous as a fight against naughty impulses?

Robin Not at all. Their view of human psychology is Eastern. They view the mind, the emotions, and the body as equally important, equally capable of being responsible, and each with their own different form of intelligence.

John So the intellect does not have to act like a dictator to ensure good behaviour.

Robin That's right. Therefore, the important thing for the Japanese is to coordinate these different parts of the self, not to have one part imposing rigid control and frog-marching the other parts around.

John So that means that they see self-discipline as something that *enhances* their being, rather than restricting it.

Robin That's it. They view discipline as something that expands their capacity to live fully.

John *Difficult* . . .

Robin Then again, think of a Japanese individual's relationship to their group. All the emphasis is on harmony. They say, and truly believe: 'The nail that sticks up must be knocked down.'

John So there's simply no room in Japanese society for a separate individual with views of his or her own?

Robin Not really.

John So would they understand what we mean by 'conscience'?

Robin No, because Japanese are not expected to take their cue from an inner voice, because such a voice would imply that they hold moral principles different from those of the group to which they belong. So it's no surprise that the great theme of Japanese films is of somebody's personal desire being sacrificed in the service of some greater cause.

John In fact a happy ending would be the end of civilisation as they know it. But then, if you're Japanese, it's *easier* to do your duty.

Robin Easier than for us, because their culture is encouraging it in every way. And especially because their culture is still much closer than ours to what I would see as a real, alive spiritual tradition.

John What kind?

Robin One that's deeply rooted in Buddhist and Confucian ideas that still permeate Japanese society and deeply affect vast numbers of people who'd claim they have no conscious religious belief at all.

John You mean, their religious values have come down to them in their mother's milk, as it were? They've been picked up more or less unconsciously.

Robin Yes; so in a sense, they're living on spiritual capital. They're reaping the benefits of the religious understanding and observance of previous generations, without quite realising the enormous value of the heritage they've been given.

John Just as in the West, certain Protestant values were still part of the culture long after the beliefs themselves had run out of any real steam.

Robin That's right. Protestant values that emphasised honesty, hard work, effort and persistence, played a large part in early British and American industrial success. But the homogeneous, cohesive culture in Japan will have enabled their spiritual tradition to have an even more profound influence.

John Yes, I read a Jesuit priest's account of how he stood up to torture in the Tower of London in Elizabeth I's reign, and at the end of it I realised that religious faith quite simply reaches parts that other beliefs cannot reach.

Robin And it's not just a question of belief. The spiritual tradition I'm talking about means the Japanese take it for granted that becoming virtuous is not something that you can achieve just by wishing for it, or by deciding to accept some set of beliefs – any more than you can learn to drive a car or play the piano by simply wishing you could, or by determinedly believing you can.

John In contrast to the quite widespread American attitude that you can acquire complex skills quite rapidly if only you're enthusiastic enough.

Robin Well, the Japanese understand that such things require continual hard work on themselves.

John Is that why corporations send their executives off to spend long periods at monasteries? It would be considered astonishing here.

Robin That's right. But the Japanese realise that, with the right study and practice, you can get to know yourself, and learn the complex skill of integrating your mind, your body and your emotions so that you can involve your whole being in the effective performance of your chosen task. Which is what they mean by 'sincerity' – a very different understanding of the word from ours.

John So their brilliance in cooperating and working as a team is a result of them spending their lives training themselves towards that purpose, guided by the entire culture.

Robin And as a result they can run rings around amateurs like us, who think it can all be achieved by reading books on management, telling people what they ought to be doing, and then assuming everyone will get on with it.

John Ssshh!

Robin Well, we're at least explaining why books alone, and head-knowledge, aren't enough. Still, there's some news to cheer us up a bit in the West. Things *are* changing a little in Japan. People are spending more, imports are increasing and Japanese industry is concerned that younger executives are wanting to spend more time at home with their children – a dread disease they call 'myhomeism'! Also, two-thirds of younger people now say that the purpose of life is 'to enjoy it'. In fact, the South Koreans have started to call the Japanese 'lazy'!

John We've been talking about the Japanese almost entirely as a society. But what are they like as individuals? Does all this inhibition on individuality restrict the quality of life from a Western point of view?

Robin I believe it does. The level of control that's required simply puts a bit of a damper on enjoyment.

John Do they seem to you any less happy than we are?

Robin No, that isn't my impression at all. They are justly proud of their system, which certainly works in so many ways better than ours, and their sense of playing a useful part in such a successful society gives them satisfactions that are denied to us. So they seem content and genuinely committed to what they are doing, getting real pleasure out of it, but . . . rather restrained and low-key, as if it's all rather hard going.

John Do you find them friendly?

Robin Very friendly and kind, and they smile a lot. I like them immensely. But they aren't exactly fun. It's something to do with the fact they can't let go, go a bit wild, let their hair down, throw their cap over the windmill. Unless they get roaring drunk, that is. That's the one socially approved way they can vent their frustrations – though the rule is: 'Not a word about this when we're sober again.'

John Perhaps they're frightened that if they 'let go', they'd stick out and get hammered down.

Robin That's a part of it. Another big part is that they're immensely preoccupied with how other people will view them. The whole culture is built on that kind of concern, so they spend all their time carefully preserving their self-respect . . .

John Not 'losing face'?

Robin Yes. After a certain age, if a child arouses social disapproval, even the parents will join in the ridicule, along with outsiders. So they fear failure acutely. This is why *individual* competition reduces their performance so badly.

John And yet they love to compete in teams.

Robin Yes, but Americans who have played for Japanese baseball teams remark how anxious the Japanese are to be approved by their team-mates, and how severely they all react to failure of the team. But it's not just a fear of losing. They get very upset and depressed if they're seen to be in the wrong or merely to have made a mistake.

John Despite all the support they're receiving from the rest of the group?

Robin They won't get support in those circumstances. So they deal with this fear by pretending they can do absolutely everything well. For example, they'll pretend they speak English perfectly, when they can't at all. Which is only too evident from the instruction book of any piece of Japanese equipment.

John The humorist Bill Bryson has a Japanese eraser which bears the legend: 'Mr Friendly Quality Eraser. Mr Friendly

Arrived!! He always stay near you, and steals in your mind to lead you a good situation.' He says that Coca-Cola cans have the slogan: 'I feel Coke & Sound Special,' and has seen a carrier bag showing yachts on a blue sea with the message: 'Switzerland Seaside City.'

Robin So 'saving face' derives from an intense fear of being made to look at all silly – perhaps because ridicule plays such a large part in the way they train children.

John And all these fears of making mistakes and looking foolish will mean it's very hard for them to be spontaneous or playful.

Robin Yes, they're even earnest about their games – they approach golf-practice as though they're designing a new Toyota.

John . . . It's fascinating to realise that this tremendous cooperative spirit still has so much individual insecurity lurking inside it.

Robin That's probably what puts a damper on fun and enjoyment. Soon after I returned from Japan, I had dinner with a Scottish psychologist who'd spent some years in Tokyo. We were in a very lively Italian restaurant in London where the waiters are exuberant, make jokes and sing snatches of song, and there are huge Italian families all having a good time. As we talked about Japan in the middle of all this racket, I realised that I was feeling very boisterous and talking loudly too, waving my arms about and feeling very mischievous and full of fun and life – suddenly feeling very free after the general constraint I had experienced in Japan. It was a wonderful feeling of no longer being expected to hold myself in, but having the physical and emotional space to feel marvellously expansive. I wanted to take great deep breaths. My companion said she felt just the same.

John It's such an extraordinary contrast with America, isn't it? About the only thing the two countries have in common, apart from being economically so successful, is their relative isolation: it's enabled them both to develop in such strikingly different ways, which is why they're at the very ends of the individualistic/communal spectrum. Otherwise they're polar opposites. Japan is hierarchical; America quite consciously anti-hierarchical. America is an immigrant culture; Japan literally wouldn't understand the notion of someone immigrating. Japan is orderly and inhibited and restrained; America is a bit disorderly, and extrovert, and unconventional. America's very creative and takes things to extremes; Japan is highly orthodox, and avoids all excess. Japan is safe but not fun; America's fun and really quite unsafe. America worships youth; Japan respects age. Japanese women are deferential; American women the most assertive in the world. America believes in truth, and that society's safest against corruption and tyranny when as many people as possible are trying to find out the truth; the Japanese see it as a threat to harmony. The Japanese are enormously polite and formal; the Americans don't worry overmuch about tender sensitivities and are famously informal. The Americans love to compete; while the Japanese are scared by competition as individuals. The Japanese strive for consensus; the Americans make a hero of the person who follows his conscience against the dictates of the crowd.

Robin When you summarise it all so concisely the differences seem even more extraordinary; the cultures could hardly be more opposite to one another.

John That may be partly because the extreme individuality at the heart of American society is often obscured by the fact that many Americans become very conventional – as a way of dealing with the anxiety that all that separateness would produce. So, on Sunday mornings, you see thousands of rugged, slightly overweight individualists in jeans and baseball caps and red check shirts loading identically clad families into inter-changeable station wagons. As Mark Twain said: 'In our country we have three unspeakably precious things: freedom of speech; freedom of conscience; and the prudence never to practice either.'

Robin You see the same contradiction among the Japanese, but there it's in reverse. Many of them report that their secure and ordered society allows them to feel great individuality and freedom within the framework it provides.

John Just as stuffy, respectable, uptight old Victorian England was famed for its eccentrics.

Robin Nature ensures that the balance is always struck in one way or another. But you're right, these compensatory feelings and behaviours obscure the basic reality – one society is highly individualistic; one is extremely communal.

John Of course we've almost completely ignored the factor of *size*, haven't we?

Robin Right. It's not difficult to see how many American traits developed, given all that space for people to be expansive in;

whereas the Japanese – and British – characteristics often clearly derive from folk being crammed together.

John But we can't do much about *that*, as we try to dream up our ideal society, short of encouraging tectonic vivacity . . .

Robin True.

John . . . There's no question that parts of *both* cultures are very attractive, aren't they? I want some of the characteristics of Japan, and some of America. But I just don't know whether you can get a balance between the two that gives you the *best* of both.

Robin Yet it must be *possible*! Remember, the 'very healthies' combine the capacity to be very separate with a very strong communal spirit. In addition, we all need to look for a balance, because it seems that the more extreme either of these two opposing tendencies becomes, the more the most undesirable side of either tendency emerges. I mean, the extreme of individualistic behaviour must be the Ik; the extreme of the communal way must be the failure, during the Middle Ages, to achieve a single improvement on Aristotle.

John And we both suspect, don't we, that America would be stronger if it could find more cooperative and less compulsively competitive behaviours; and that Japan would benefit from more individual creativity and a greater openness to 'foreign' values.

Robin Agreed. So, let's talk about the sort of mixture that might work best. Obviously it'll be different for each country, an acceptable compromise for that particular culture – more communal for the Swedes, more individualistic for the Italians. But what do we, as Brits, like about communal cultures?

John Well, I'm drawn towards the very positive sense of connection which people experience between one another in such a society. This brings involvement, both in the sense that a person offers support and service to others in the community, and also because he or she can enjoy receiving the same in return. And that's attractive, this feeling of give-and-take, of mutual cooperation. Also, I sense we'd feel better about our society if we had less out-groups within it – people excluded from any real participation in the way it runs. But I can see it would also bring much greater demands on us, which might not be so enjoyable.

Robin Yes, but remember that in a communal society such demands might be experienced as much less difficult.

Relationships wouldn't feel as competitive and perilous, so you wouldn't be distancing yourself so much. In addition, because of the deeper involvement with others, everyone will experience more often that life-enhancing satisfaction we get when we work with others towards a common aim. So the demands might be enjoyable and rewarding to meet. That's certainly been my experience when engaged in worthwhile joint ventures with others, however much I initially resist giving up my freedom to follow my own inclinations.

John . . . It's unfair isn't it? I mean, paranoia works!

Robin How so?

John Well, take Japan. Please. They have a pretty paranoid attitude to the rest of the world; they're distinctly racialist; they don't know the meaning of the word 'immigration' and so they finish up with a society of tremendously strong common values and minimal conflict. It's rather the same with Switzerland or some little islands like Jersey. Very tough on immigrants, very high on social order. Lovely places to visit but they wouldn't want you to live there. Whereas the dear old USA made itself into a racial melting-pot with its fantastic attitude to immigration, and now it's paying a dreadful price in terms of the fragmentation of its society.

Robin But you're forgetting that we're looking at the question of *balance*. Agreed, the US does have great problems, but look at its creativity and energy – its problem-solving capacity. Whereas . . . well, what are the *dis*advantages of communal societies?

John I find this difficult to think about. I know one would feel quite different if one had been brought up in a communal society. But I suppose I feel oppressed by the need to conform, by the 'ant-like' activity – and the fact that most individuals don't live particularly well, for no real reason other than the desire to make Japan the biggest anthill. What's that alarming expression they have about a nail?

Robin 'The nail that sticks up must be hammered down.'

John Awful. Though I suppose quite a few Western military men wouldn't think it *that* bad. But it seems such a negative response to anyone's individuality – like a particularly virulent form of envy.

Robin That somehow doesn't feel right; I didn't get that impression in their company at all. But of course, it would be a perfect social structure for *avoiding* envy, because everyone's got his or her place in the scheme of things and differences in status are either denied or minimised, or are traditional and non-negotiable. In neither case is there enough possibility of change for envy to be a meaningful option.

John And in communal societies life tends to be such an endless process of discharging social obligations. The consideration for other people I admire, of course, but the formalism of its expression makes it feel rather empty and meaningless to me – as though the avoidance of offence is the main purpose of existence!

Robin And where that kind of social conformity is extreme, there may be a loss of energy, exuberance and enjoyment even though the society as a whole is achieving great things.

John Yes, it's the feeling that there is no respect for an individual's *different* contribution that bothers me, which is reflected in the famous lack of creativity among the Japanese. My friends in design tell me they're still basically hopeless. And I remember Helena Norberg-Hodge saying that Ladakhi society lacked a strong aesthetic sense – they don't seem to get the pleasure from beauty that we do. It all reminds me of what Burckhardt said about man discovering the beauty of nature as he discovers himself as a separate entity.

Robin I recently asked an artist who had spent some years in Japan about the aesthetic sense there. I'd always thought this to be very highly developed. But she said that though there is a celebration of the beauties of nature, like the annual viewing of the cherry blossom, for the majority it's very much a ritual – the 'right thing to do'. She told me a story of having found a very beautiful little grove of cherry-blossom. When she told her Japanese host he looked in the guide book, and said that her grove wasn't mentioned. He was therefore not interested in going to look at it!

John But wait a minute. Do you think we are being a bit petty, even envious, carping on about this amazingly successful system just because the folk are a bit less self-indulgent than we are?

Robin No, because I think that what we've been discussing are symptoms of a much deeper malaise. After all, the Japanese political system is enormously corrupt, and all these facets of their culture that we've been describing means it's almost impossible for them to do anything about it.

John That's right. In the autumn of '92 there was the fourth major political scandal in a couple of years, where almost all the top politicians were found to be implicated, not only in vast-scale bribery but also *in trading favours with the Yakusa* – the organised crime syndicate! Uproar!! For a bit . . . and then what happens? One resignation . . . and *nothing else, because there isn't an alternative*! At this moment of revelation of truly appalling corruption, the opposition is even more hopeless than usual – almost as though they were making sure they weren't a credible alternative, because if they were things might actually change.

Robin Which the entire social system is brilliantly designed to prevent!

John But my basic problem here is this: I can't describe what I don't like about communal cultures except by talking about what I like about individualistic ones – so I have to talk about lacks: of initiative, of curiosity, of creativity and so forth.

Robin All right, so let's move on to what we do like about individualistic cultures.

John Well, it's a kind of personal independence, isn't it? It includes the ability to think things out for ourselves; and then a certain kind of toughness, a healthy disregard for any social pressure to conform, which we also need if we're to act on the principles we've chosen. That's apart from the pure pleasure of creating something new, and not just following well-worn grooves of thought.

Robin All of which gives each person great freedom to grow and develop, according to their unique potentialities.

John And of course in a society like this, you can enjoy the richness and variety around you. It's stimulating, intriguing, and constantly challenging – you can always be learning more than you could in a more standardised culture.

Robin Just like in a healthy family or marriage, where each person is relatively separate and independent, and thus brings more richness and diversity to the whole. And then there's the enjoyment that comes from accepting the challenge of reconciling those differences.

John And the fun of playing games and trying to win, while knowing it actually doesn't matter if you lose. And the great joy of experiencing beauty, natural, artistic *and* personal. And, of course, humour, which seems to rely on an ability to stand back from society and see from this position of greater detachment, how absurd much of it is.

Robin Which is how it gets improved! . . . I think that's a fair representation of the advantages of a more individualistic society. Now . . . what about the *dis*advantages?

John Well many years ago I came across an absolutely wonderful book about this. It's called *The Fear of Freedom*, by Erich Fromm, and everything I've read since just seems to be footnotes to it!

Robin I remember enjoying it when I was training in psychiatry. Can you summarise what he says?

John I'll try. He points out, of course, all the *good* aspects of the original move in the West towards a more individualistic way of living. But then he concentrates on analysing the negative effects. Basically, he shows that historically, as people felt more and more isolated and doubtful, they experienced a higher and higher degree of anxiety and insecurity. This gave rise to a number of character traits which accompanied the development of capitalism: a fear of 'wasting time' and a consequent frenetic filling-up of time with activity; the viewing of efficiency as a moral virtue; the drive constantly to increase one's capital, while never stopping to enjoy what it can buy, and an omnipresent competitive attitude. All of these, he says, contributed to the development of the famous Protestant work ethic. And all of them, he claims, basically arise from anxiety and are therefore essentially neurotic, despite all the gains they bring to society.

Robin There's something very profound here which I think we need to go into more deeply later on, when we look at values and the part they play in the way society functions. I'll just say here that I think Fromm is talking about a fundamental psychological change that came about as our society became more individualistic: we largely lost a deep sense of our own being, which, when we *do* experience it, gives us a sense of connection or communion with others and with the world generally. As we lost this, our awareness moved outwards to become focused on more superficial parts of the self. And once this happens, *our sense of identity no longer comes from what we are*, from our awareness of our being, our inner life, from the fact we exist! It comes instead from *outside* ourselves. We begin to feel *we exist only insofar as we are reflected by other people*: when we are noticed; when we are admired; when we achieve. In other words, we begin to live according to how we see ourselves reflected by others. Thus we become enormously over-dependent on the opinions of those around us.

John Yes, Fromm says that in a highly competitive society we all feel a 'constant lingering anxiety'; and that, as this is unpleasant for us, we're always wanting to do away with the various things that are making us anxious. So we constantly experience feelings of hostility towards almost everyone around us – but we repress and, of course, rationalise these, often into feelings of *moral disapproval*!

Robin It's true that a threat to our reflected image arouses the fear and defensiveness and hostility you're talking about – all of which we have to *conceal*! And in fact we've already described this in Chapter 1 as typical mid-range behaviour – how we all keep feelings of this kind hidden from others under the guise of good manners, and sometimes from ourselves, too. So we learn to pretend concern for people when it's not genuine, and to be 'nice' to them to their face, and then much more critical of them behind their backs.

John So all this hostility arises directly from our feelings of insecurity, doesn't it?

Robin Yes. In moving from an inner to an outer self-awareness, a basic security is lost. Incidentally, Fromm's observations tie in with the way Colin Turnbull describes the lack of a truly cooperative spirit in the Western world, which, he says, 'establishes division rather than unity, segmentation rather than integration, competition rather than cooperation. The focus is upon a number of discrete, separated individuals rather than on a single corporate group.'

John . . . I don't have much difficulty acknowledging what he says. At my English public school in the fifties, there was endless talk about 'team spirit', but we weren't actually shown *how* to work as a team, nor how to communicate, other than in a stiff, purely task-orientated way. To discuss our feelings would have been thoroughly deviant, so our cooperation was largely based on ESP.

Robin That's typical of individualistic societies. There's little or no provision to help children and young people understand, step by step throughout their development, how to fit constructively and enjoyably into social groups or to make transitions from one life stage to another. They're just thrown in at the deep end without being taught to swim.

John Yes. Until I witnessed my generation's children struggling with leaving school and going out into the world, I never realised how badly we fail them.

Robin It's an extraordinary lack in our social structure – and we don't even notice that it's missing!

John So, to sum up, the down-side of individualism is that at a deep level people often feel beleaguered, and consequently hostile. And competitive. Or to put it another way, the average person doesn't feel a very high degree of trust – which, given the fact that almost everyone else holds that attitude too, is entirely appropriate!

Robin So most of us are, at some level, constantly on the watch to make sure that we're not being out-manoeuvred; and most of the time we use others as instruments to get what we want, rather than treating them as whole persons. Under these circumstances it's much harder, of course, to maintain much real friendship or intimacy. And as we humans need supportive emotional contact if we are to feel good about ourselves, the behaviour I have just been describing simply fuels the insecurity that causes it in the first place.

John And looking at it from the level of society . . . there just isn't sufficient cooperative feeling to enable the huge problems of society to be handled in a really effective way.

Robin That's right.

John Well, we've been going on rather a lot about the *drawbacks* of an over-individualistic society . . .

Robin Well, only because that's the kind that affects *us*!

John True. Nevertheless . . . although it might be easier to be happy in a communal culture where one felt very integrated in and supported by the society around one . . . and although it might therefore be tougher to be comparably happy in an individualistic culture . . . I can't help feeling that it might somehow be more of an achievement to attain real contentment in our kind of society! Perhaps I suspect that the greater challenge might eventually bring the greater maturity.

Robin Yes, we've 'eaten of the tree of knowledge' and so we've been chucked out of the Garden of Eden. But the positive side of this is that we are no longer children, so now we can start to grow. That's true even if, to reach our *full* development, we have eventually to find our way back to that more open and trustful way of living that we lost in the course of our childhood.

John Well, we've been ambling through some different cultures, to see if we can get an idea of the balance we'd like, in our ideal Liberal Democracy, between individualistic attitudes and more communal ones. Now *I* don't have any doubts that we've gone too far in an individualistic direction, that we've lost too many of the valuable aspects of a more cooperative way of living . . .

Robin I agree. So we've achieved our aim!

John Right. Of course we can't say *how* far we should move! That's infinitely too complex. But at least we're sure we're too individualistic. But here's the problem. There's a general trend throughout the world towards *ever greater* individualism. Everywhere traditional groupings are breaking up, and traditional communal cultures being discarded. The level of tension and anxiety is rising, and that always increases the tendency for people to take the attitude we used to describe as 'I'm all right Jack, pull up the ladder'. So, Doctor, how can we reverse this tendency towards greater individualism, and get back to a healthier balance?

Robin I want to deal with that at length in our final chapter, which is all about change. So now I'll merely say this. Whether we're talking about an individual, a family, an organisation, or a community . . . we can't change *ourselves* in any fundamental way.

John Really? Why on earth not?

Robin Just for now let's say that any attempt to do so is like trying to lift yourself by your own boot-laces. Or to use a different image: to try to change yourself, or for a society to try to change itself, is only shuffling the same pack of ideas and attitudes that gave rise to all the problems in the first place. You see, ultimately it's *values* which have to change, *because it's only by changing people's values that their behaviour changes in an organic and enduring way.*

John And you're saying that radical changes in values come about . . . *how?*

Robin Only by contact with other, different systems, whereby new information comes in and combines with what we've already got.

John Well we certainly need new values which are going to encourage more cooperative feeling and behaviour. Right?

Robin And that means we need to find values of two slightly different kinds. First, cooperative, integrating values, as you suggest. But second, values that will lead us Westerners to a deeper sense of personal security, which will in turn facilitate more cooperative attitudes.

John . . . I've just had an idea! Next, let's talk about *values*!

Robin You've a mind like a scalpel sometimes, haven't you?

John It's the comedy training.

Afterthought: Money Makes the World Go Round

John I've been speculating that countries seem to go through economic cycles that are very closely related to psychological cycles.

Robin How do you mean?

John I mean if things go well, they get pompous and arrogant and, as we all know, pride comes before a fall. And then after the fall, they get more humble and realistic, and buckle down again, and start improving. Just like people. Except that with nations you can't say there's a beginning or an end to the process, because it just repeats, goes round and round like a Ferris wheel.

Robin Describe it.

John Well, let's take as the starting point the bottom of the cycle. The most obvious example is a disaster like the Germans and Japanese faced when they lost the War. There's a terrible depression in every sense of the word. Then comes acceptance of the situation. Then a realisation that you have to go back to the drawing board and start building again, because there's no alternative if you're to survive at all. So you work hard, and put everything you've got into the effort to save the situation. Everything's in the melting pot, so you're very open to new ideas. So there's new thinking everywhere, new ways of organising and doing things, and a lot of new inventions.

Robin Perhaps that's why most of the inventions which have brought industrial success were made at the bottom of these cycles, during the economic slumps. It's the same in wartime when a similar sense of desperation has dramatic effects on technology – like the jet engine, rockets, guidance systems, and nuclear power in the last World War – which can then be put to peaceful uses.

John Now a nation that's just experienced disaster tends to have few illusions. In fact, they have a healthy, realistic view. There's an attitude of humility, of thankfulness and appreciation for what they've still got, and a sense of obligation to society, to pull together for the common good. So there's a very favourable situation for economic success. A creative atmosphere in which people are willing to let go of old habits and try out anything new, plus a prevailing attitude of determination, together with a willingness to make sacrifices if it will lead to future improvements. So labour costs will be reasonable, productivity will be high.

Robin Exactly the situation in Japan and in Germany after the Second World War.

John So at this point in the cycle success is practically inevitable! The economy slowly begins to pick up. Life is hard, but people begin to see that their efforts are bringing success. Confidence grows, too.

Robin So there's nothing to stop the upward trend.

John Nothing. So on it goes. In a decade or two, they've got half-way to the top of the cycle. The economy is booming, it's a time of success, the words 'Economic Miracle' are heard. I have a feeling that this is the best time of all.

Robin I think that's probably right. At this mid-point, people are beginning to enjoy the fruits of their labours, but they can still remember the hard times so they're grateful for what they've got, and can appreciate it because they can compare it with the time of poverty from which they started. And they're still realistic; they know the good times they are enjoying depend on their combined efforts, on continuing to innovate, to work hard, to stay ahead of the competition. So the situation is still healthy.

John Indeed, they begin to criticise the 'fat cat' nations for being lazy, and complacent, and failing to innovate!

Robin And they haven't acquired fat cat attitudes themselves yet, so their success continues . . .

John And continues. In the mid-nineteenth century Britain looked unstoppable. Ralph Waldo Emerson wrote about us in *British Traits* in the same way that we talk about the Japanese now – 'What *is* it that these people know, that we don't?' A bit later in the century it was Germany's turn, then America's.

Robin At this stage of the cycle it's hard for anyone to imagine the success will ever end.

John I suspect that this is where the South Koreans are now.

Robin And then . . . ?

John And *then* . . . it all begins to go wrong. Everyone becomes more and more affluent. There seems less and less necessity for sacrifice and struggle, hard work, thrift, cooperation in the common cause. And the hard times of the past will never have been experienced by the majority of the population. Now only older people, those who went through the deprivation of the last slump, will be able to compare the affluence they're experiencing at this point with the previous painful economic failure – and remember the *struggle* it took to achieve it.

Robin And the majority of them no longer have any kind of influence politically or in industrial affairs.

John So at the top of the cycle the majority of the population thinks that the affluence has always been there, or at least, that it always *will* be. They will feel it is their right, their natural place in the world to be privileged to enjoy a higher standard of living than everyone else. Frankly, Robin, the nation has got 'swollen-headed'. They've got the idea that they '*know how to do it*' while others don't – that their success is due to their being intrinsically more special than other nations or races . . . *and* that they'll continue to gather the fruits of their past efforts without having to try harder than others.

Robin If the prevailing mood at the bottom of the cycle was depression, the mood now is the opposite to that . . .

John . . . Mania?

Robin Yes. Which means you're expansive, over-confident, arrogant, contemptuous of others. A swollen ego, focused on self-interest and short-term successes and satisfactions, unable to tolerate frustration, seeing itself as the centre of everything, unable to consider the needs of others or fit into and be a part of a group, trying to get what it wants in ways that will lead to the destruction of the economy and society, even itself. In a phrase, out of touch with reality.

John And therefore out of touch with the way the world is changing, and unaware of the changing responses required. So, now, you get a period when the economy is beginning to go wrong, but nobody notices, because they think they know it all, and can't imagine their ideas are getting outdated or that they could possibly be making any mistakes.

Robin And part of the problem is their past success! Their present strong economic position obscures the fact of their incipient decline and enables people for many years, or even decades, to avoid facing it. Even when there's strong evidence that the economy is going downhill, the people who point this out will be unpopular and disregarded, while leaders who continue to put forward a false, rosy picture are more likely to be listened to and elected to office.

John Like the Tories, who ran their 1992 election campaign on the slogan: 'Recovery is just around the corner. Don't let Labour and the Liberal Democrats mess it up.' And *were elected* on it.

Robin I don't think *any* of the parties fought the election on a clear statement that we were in a major slump which would continue to get worse whatever policy was followed. As a result, the country as a whole hasn't yet faced that truth and begun to make the necessary psychological adjustment to it. And it's quite natural really – people don't like acknowledging that things are going wrong – it's *alarming*.

John So to go back to our cycle: as our theoretical swollen-headed nation begins to decline, they'll become condescending towards nations which are doing better economically, or blame them for 'cheating' in some way – complaining about 'unfair' practices when they're just making better products, or whingeing about Japanese trade barriers long after they've been dismantled.

Robin While clinging to unrealistic expectations of a high standard of living! But the consequences of their foolish behaviour will confront them with increasingly painful experiences. The gap between their expectations and what actually happens steadily *widens*. And as this happens, the underlying mood of unease and depression deepens. For a long time it's been covered over by the manic behaviour, but slowly there's a growing realisation of the need for change – and *for humility*!

John In other words, like a mid-range person, the nation needs a severe crisis to force it to change. So very near the bottom of the cycle, the nation is brought up against reality, and realises it has to begin again.

Robin Exactly. Because all nations will be on average mid-range.

John . . . Well I'm wondering if we reached this point in Britain in late 1992. I sensed some change when we came out of the ERM – as though the last illusions that we could go on in the same basic way were shattered.

Robin We're getting closer to that point, but I don't believe we're there yet because people are continuing to 'hope for the best' when they should have been preparing for the worst; though of course this is exactly what your theory predicts. But I still find it extraordinary that so few people in leadership positions recognise where we are, because there is in fact a well-known long-term economic fluctuation which fits the pattern you describe. It's called the 'Kondratieff cycle'; it takes about about fifty to sixty years to run its course; and the last bottoming-out was the 1930s slump. So the present one has come along pretty well on time, and we, or at least our leaders, should have been prepared for it. Davidson and Rees-Mogg, in their recently published book *The Great Reckoning*, have given a very clear account of what to expect.

John Well, let's hope what I'm saying about cycles is right. Because if it is, we may be in the right psychological state to start the long haul back.

Robin It would be nice to think so. The reason we don't grasp this economic cycle is that it is so long compared with the human life-span that by the time the next depression is approaching, the people who can remember the last one clearly are already senior citizens, or at least no longer in positions of power and influence, and in any case a minority.

John Well perhaps this time around, we'll be able to sustain for longer those basic virtues that we learn over and over again in the crisis at the bottom of the cycle, where we learn to count our blessings, appreciate what we have, become less selfish and greedy, think more of others, and begin to pull our weight again.

Robin Let's hope so, but for that to be possible a way would have to be found to transmit this knowledge to younger people who can't remember, and don't want to hear about it!

John Because they think they know it all. This whole cycle reminds me of the kind of cycle that individuals seem to go through. A tendency in the late twenties and early thirties to think you've got it all sorted out; followed by a few mid-thirties disasters, which make you a lot nicer. Then a tendency to ossify in middle age, because once again, you think you know it all. You stop taking in new ideas and start looking backwards rather than forwards, and that's when you start to decline. Then, if you're lucky, another personal crisis which shakes you to the core and upsets all your certainties, so you can start re-thinking.

Robin And as a result, really take off again.

John So . . . the most dangerous moment is when we're at the top, when we're doing best! Because that's the moment we're most likely to think we 'know it all'.

Robin So the question is: when we are in this manic mood at the top of the cycle, can we arrange some way of being reminded of the danger coming, to bring us back to earth and alert us to the actions needed? Knowing the manic state, I don't think it's possible. In that mood we don't want to hear. Therefore, I believe we have to look instead for ways to *avoid becoming* so manic – too high in ourselves – despite the success. And that can be one function of value systems. And we'll discuss these in the next chapter.

John This cycle seems so obvious, so much a commonsense reflection of how people are, that I get very puzzled when I look at situations where it's *not* operating! That is, where economic relationships seem frozen, as has happened between the First World and the Third.

Robin Well, that relationship is frozen because at present the Third World is economically dependent on us; and therefore also subject to our cycle; just as the moon is subject to the earth's orbit. One result is that the less-developed countries of the world are getting poorer. For example, by 1990 the average income per person was lower in over forty nations than it had been in 1980. The average income of Latin Americans had fallen by 9 per cent, that of Africans by 25 per cent. And life expectancy fell in nine African countries. During that period vast sums were lent by the affluent countries to the Third World at high rates of interest they simply couldn't afford. Eventually the flow of money from North to South actually *reversed*, flowing uphill, as it were, from South to North, from poor to rich! Now the Third World owes over a trillion dollars. The banking system is in crisis, because the debtor nations can't pay it back – which is as crazy as expecting a terminally ill patient in hospital to give blood transfusions to the doctor! And the Third World's debt stops them from beginning to build decent lives for their people, and therefore fuels very unhealthy and destructive belief systems, which are a danger to the First World. So *everybody's* threatened.

John So everybody is behaving in a way that is counter-productive in terms of everybody's long-term interests. Seriously, why do people lose their brains when they try to find a solution to this problem?

Robin Well, we both lost our brains when we first talked about it! You remember, in order to understand the problem better, we tried some role-playing: you argued the case as a representative for the under-developed countries, and I took the side of the developed countries. And what happens between the two sides actually began to happen to us. I've got the tape of the conversation, so I'll play a bit to remind us both.

(The tape starts)

John's voice If you're the rich country and I'm the poor country, then as long as I continue repaying interest to you, I can pretend that we're equals in a business deal. And if I'm an emergent Third World country, then more than anything I want to feel I'm being treated as an equal by the developed countries – otherwise I am acknowledging an inferior, colonial, parent/child relationship. So because I want your respect, to be treated as your equal, I have to deny my weakness and carry on paying interest. I can't afford to pay it, but the price of not paying the interest is to admit my inferior position.

Robin's voice Well, as one of the more enlightened members of a First World country, I have to agree that you have been exploited in the most iniquitous way by my countrymen and other 'developed' nations. And you are still being exploited;

we are continuing to take advantage of you. We robbed you during your colonial past, and now we are lending back to you the money we made from processing the cheap raw materials and labour you provided and from the trade you had to carry on with us. We are now allowing you the use of that money, *but* at usurious rates of interest; and so, I have to admit, we are robbing you twice over.

John's voice It's hardly better than slavery . . .

Robin's voice In fact, the situation is really very much the same as when we enslaved you, except that in many ways it is better for us. We can now feel very much easier about the economic inequality, because we can deny that we are abusing you. We can flatter ourselves that we are treating you as if you are fellow human beings, in every way equal to us, because the extortion is disguised as a business relationship. You are not shackled with irons and whipped to work harder, but we still have the same power over you. Except that now we've been rather more clever. In the past we had power over your bodies, but you still had freedom in your minds. You knew that you were doing everything under duress, and you could say: 'I am a free man who is enslaved.' You were free to see the injustice, to despise and hate us, to wait secretly for the day when you could escape or overthrow us.

But now, we have somehow persuaded you to share our way of thinking about things and to believe that in order to be equal to us you have to enslave yourselves to our *values*. So you are doubly enslaved: enslaved first in the old sense of being in our power financially and materially; and enslaved even more deeply by accepting our rationalisation of the extortion, even to the degree of believing that allowing us to screw you gives you membership of a superior club, puts you closer to the superior plane you imagine us to inhabit. You have now joined in the double-think whereby we are able to exploit you without admitting we are doing so, even to ourselves. So we can even feel quite justified in robbing you, believing that we are helping you to learn the economic facts of life. And you will continue to hand over the money, to preserve your own self-image as equals.

John's voice Well, when you were imperial powers and we were colonies we tended to see you as parents and ourselves as children, so we accepted your value system as a parental, grown-up value system.

(Pause)

Robin's voice So, tell me John. What does it feel like being over there on your side of the table, in the Third World.

John's voice It's very odd . . . I feel lost . . . something's happened to me psychologically . . . I've reached the point where I just can't think . . . I have this funny kind of feeling that it's *your* problem . . . I feel completely helpless. And what is very weird is that I can't remember having had that kind of feeling before in all the time we've been writing together.

(The tape ends)

John I can remember feeling that. It was extraordinary. I just felt there was nothing I could do, and that it was entirely your responsibility to find the solution. And yet *I* was the one in the real doo-doo . . .

Robin And I felt the opposite. You had tuned out, but I couldn't stop talking and kept on lecturing you, without giving you a chance to answer. And it just went on and on like that, with both of us behaving completely out of character, for more than an hour.

John So what was really going on? Why did we get so trapped in those roles?

Robin I think the explanation is very clearly there in what we said. The imperial powers justified their conquests, and their right to rule their colonial possessions, by persuading themselves that they were completely superior in knowledge, values and virtue – more 'civilised' – and therefore had the duty to manage and educate the colonial peoples. In other words, they saw themselves in a parental role, and the indigenous folk in a child role. So it was their responsibility to take over, tell the 'natives' what to do, educate them in Western ideas, teach them how to work hard, and decide how much pocket money they should be allowed. Confronted with superior weapons and other technology, the colonised peoples swallowed these ideas. So that even when they finally won their freedom, they still treated many Western values as if they were superior, and therefore tried to copy us, lock, stock and barrel, rather than returning to what was good – and often much better – in their own traditional cultures.

John You mean it's the same old split between the 'parent' and 'child' parts of the personality?

Robin Yes. As colonisers, we projected all *our* childish bits onto *them*, and then called them 'lazy', 'irresponsible', 'feckless', 'ignorant', 'unreliable' and 'only interested in enjoying themselves' . . . while we in the more developed countries assumed the corresponding grown-up-and-know-it-all role, lecturing and admonishing them, nobly bearing what used to be called 'The White Man's Burden'. And before long *they* came to buy a lot of this thinking, too!

John . . . I've just realised something very obvious. This personality split must be what happens *between the rich and poor within a country*, too. The rich tend to feel they are entitled to their wealth because they see themselves as having more grown-up attitudes, while they view the poor as being responsible for their poverty because they say they are childish, irresponsible and unwilling to work. And the poor tend to accept some of that role; expecting, like children, that someone else will solve their problems and give them things.

Robin Yes, if they don't see what's happening they both get locked into those opposite roles. So you see, once this personality split has happened, both between the rich countries and the poor ones, and between the rich and the poor in any particular country . . . it mirrors in people's psychology the very problem they're trying to solve.

John And that's especially the case in Britain, isn't it, where you have a powerful *class system* reflecting this split, with a middle class pretending it's very grown-up, while so many working-class folk have come to feel they're helpless to improve their lot?

Robin Which is magnified and perpetuated by the two separate educational systems, state and fee-paying.

John So are you saying that it's this parent/child psychological split that is really preventing progress being made in matters to do with poverty – both at the national and international level?

Robin Yes, I am. The idea is not very palatable to either side, because it implies – I believe correctly – that responsibility for the problem is shared by both rich and poor, so that *both* have to change to find a solution. Which means that each side must give up its paranoid blaming of the other. Unfortunately, blaming is so much easier than accepting responsibility, despite the enormous costs!

John But look, isn't there a basic economic problem too? In any free-market system, unless we do something actively to prevent it, the rich always get richer and the poor get poorer. The more wealthy the rich become, the more they gain in power and are able to corner an ever greater share of everything that's going. They accumulate more and more possessions, and the more they accumulate, the less they are able to use them all, because they can't buy more hours in the day and they can only eat so much. But even so, they don't seem able to stop. So don't you have to introduce some redistributive principle? Forget any moral justification for it. I'm talking about two reasons that are pure *realpolitik*. First, if the poor are getting poorer, in the end they'll become so deprived and desperate that they'll have to resort to force. And that can't be 'put down' in a modern democracy in the way it could in the last century. And second, if you don't actually create a revolt, you at least create an underclass so alienated from the rest of the nation that it can never be properly integrated again, which becomes a social cost which is much, much greater that the redistribution would have cost in the first place . . . in addition to which the *rich* are having to spend most of their tax-savings on security equipment. And everything I've said applies in spades to the North–South Divide. So . . . what can we do? Or, at least, where can we start?

Robin I agree that some kind of redistribution is essential. All societies that are good to live in already have measures to bring it about at least to some extent; and where governments try to reverse that arrangement, as recently in Britain and the USA, the increasing polarisation and alienation you are speaking about grows. But unless the *psychological* aspect is understood, at least by governments and those advising them, redistribution can have negative unintended consequences and won't be sustained. In the US at the moment, for example, even the Democrats are concerned that the present welfare arrangements, intended to combat poverty, have created a culture of dependence, perpetuating poverty and alienation from mainstream society; and this has in turn aroused understandable resentment and resistance in those who have to meet the bill. So a more constructive and enduring approach to redistribution requires that much more attention is given to understanding and changing the psychological aspect of these relationships. It's no longer a question of only increasing or decreasing the payments.

John What you mean is that redistribution is necessary, but it's as wrong to achieve it by force as by hand-outs, which entrench the parent/child dependence. What's needed, obviously, is our old friend equality of opportunity, I suppose?

Robin Exactly, and not just as a slogan. It's only in a genuinely equal society, where everyone has equal access to educational and other advantages, that the *good* inequalities – such as progress of *deserving* wealth creators, who in turn create jobs for others – can possibly emerge.

4 The Price of Everything and the Value of Nothing

John Everything we've been talking about has been leading us towards *values* – the ideas which give us our feelings of what life's about, what matters most, what's good for us and what harms us. Presumably, we're now going to relate different value systems to different levels of mental health?

Robin Yes. But let me start by asking you a question. Thinking back over what we've said so far, what would you say are the most important indicators of real mental health?

John Off the top of the head, I'd choose two. The most compelling measure of health seems to be the degree to which you face reality; that is, the degree to which you perceive it, and accept it. Then, parallel with that, there's the extent to which you behave inclusively – that is, try to include: other people, new ideas, and your own perceptions and feelings, rather than exclude them. But I suspect that's really just an aspect of facing reality – which is, after all, inclusive!

Robin Well, let's examine the idea of 'reality' a little further. Man's achievements are due to his extraordinary capacity for *abstraction*. Without it neither our science, nor our art, nor our literature, nor our philosophy could exist. All our most positive achievements arise from this gift for abstraction; that is, for simplifying things by selecting out those aspects of reality that we want to concentrate on, while ignoring the other aspects as if they didn't exist.

John And, of course, all our values are abstractions, too.

Robin Yes. They originate from our experience of reality, but we can choose which set of values to follow. However . . . the snag is, all our most negative qualities also come from the same gift.

John Tell me what you mean by 'negative'.

Robin I mean madness, crime, evil – everything that's unhealthy. All of it arises when we get hold of the wrong ideas – in other words, when our abstractions have gone wrong, when our simplifications have ignored aspects that were important.

John So your point is: this capacity of ours for abstraction is completely double-edged.

Robin Completely.

John So what determines whether we use it positively or negatively?

Robin The easiest way to answer that is to look at the scientific method. Recapitulate, please.

John OK. A scientist observes certain available facts and then 'abstracts' a theory that fits them. Then he carries out further experiments to test the theory. If it holds, he regards it as 'true', but only in the sense that it's 'the best to date' for explaining and predicting what happens. So, when some new fact is observed which the theory doesn't cover, he has to go back to the drawing board to try to come up with a new theory that covers all the old facts, and the awkward new one too.

Robin In other words, science works when theory is constantly being measured against reality, and corrected by it.

John Agreed. So?

Robin So the essential feature of the scientific approach is that facts come first, theories second. Theories are adjusted to facts, not the other way round. It's the same with maps. If you look at a map, and then at the piece of territory it's supposed to represent, and on the territory there's a river, and on the map there isn't . . . which would you rely on?

John I'd tear up the territory. Sorry! I panicked . . .

Robin You ignore the map – if you don't want to fall in the real river and drown! So the principle is – never confuse the territory with the map. The map is only an abstraction, an approximation. It shows only what is of particular interest to the person using the map. Even that's only roughly represented, with most of the detail excluded.

John Especially one-way systems.

Robin Especially them. But it can't have everything. If a map included *everything* it would actually *be* the territory itself.

John As Michael Frayn once said, a truly complete history of the Hundred Years' War would be the Hundred Years' War.

Robin Which would take another hundred years! So . . . we've got to simplify things, so we've got to abstract.

John Hard to pick holes in any of this.

Robin But the problem comes when we move from ordinary maps to our famous 'mental maps'. We must have these mental maps, because we couldn't operate in the world without them. We wouldn't know what to do – because they're our guides to how the world works, and how we work, and how we relate to the world. And, of course, they're abstractions in the same way. They're never comprehensive, and sometimes parts of them are wrong. They're not reality.

John I sense that you're about to say something interesting.

Robin Here it is. To answer your question: whether we use our capacity for abstraction positively or negatively . . . depends on whether we make reality primary, or the map primary.

John . . . Ah.

Robin Everything hangs on that.

John . . . You know, that's very good. In fact, it sends shivers down my spine. Bloody obvious, of course . . . and yet I've never heard it put quite like that.

Robin Incidentally, I'm not saying the connection between reality and our abstractions about it isn't two-way. They interact – our perception of reality depends on the ideas we have about it. But we can improve both through a process of gradual correction. If you are constantly open to 'reality', if you're always checking your mental map, your perception of 'reality' will slowly clarify. But that all depends on your fundamental orientation being towards the primacy of reality, of your experience.

John So if being in contact with reality is a measure of good mental health, that means that, at the lower levels, people will *prefer* their map to the real world. In other words their belief system will run them, and they'll have no interest in checking it against reality. In fact they'll reject any bits of reality that intrude by accident.

Robin Yes, people like this are completely out of contact with reality. They have withdrawn into fantasy, the kind of insanity you get in lunatic asylums; or in Nazi Germany, where a particular crazy idea led to six million murders.

John Right. Whereas at the top level . . . could you say that the healthiest people are in effect taking a scientific attitude to their own lives?

Robin It sounds a bit strange, doesn't it? But it's right. Very healthy people are constantly interested in adjusting their maps to reality, in testing their ideas. Which is 'scientific'. And that's why they're more in touch with life.

John As you've put it before, they're the right size on their own maps! So they don't under-estimate their own importance, just as they don't over-estimate it.

Robin Right. They're not 'selfish' in that sense. That's because a truly scientific approach makes you aware that you're part of a whole, part of something bigger. And that's the most important realisation of all because it diminishes our egotism.

John All right. Enough of them. What about *us*? Where are we regular mid-range folk? Somewhere between physics and fantasy?

Robin Exactly. We're arranged along a spectrum of 'degrees of contact with reality' – some a bit more, some a bit less. In many ways we may be very practical and efficient. But underlying everything, there's a basically egocentric attempt to dominate and coerce other people, in order to make the world fit in with our desires.

John We're more *selfish* than the really healthy.

Robin More egotistical, yes.

John But surely we *need* a degree of egotism, don't we? We need to value ourselves, to develop self-esteem and self-respect if we're to be reasonably well-functioning human beings, and therefore useful members of society.

Robin Certainly. The 'Ego' is necessary. So I suppose that 'egotism' could mean being aware of yourself, and giving validity to that awareness. But *normally* 'egotism' means not giving equal importance to the wider perspective – the one that comes into view as you zoom out from your concentration on yourself, and see yourself in a broader context as part of a community.

John So in the wider perspective your ego is still there, but it's taking its proper limited place among all the other egos.

Robin And once you've seen reality in that balanced way, it's much harder to be egotistical in the old way. It makes absolutely no sense! It's so obviously ridiculous!

John . . . Now does all this imply that the problem for us mid-range folk is that our egotism gets in the way of our perception of reality?

Robin *That's* it. Either through ignorance, or because we're deliberately restricting our awareness of others – turning a blind eye to information that contradicts our map of the world. That's what makes us egotistical, to a greater or lesser extent. Compared with the very healthy, that is . . .

John But of course it seems *normal* to us, because most of the population are like us.

Robin Exactly. That's why it's 'normal' to see so much harmful egotistical behaviour; ranging from greed and power-seeking and engaging in the rat-race, down through unscrupulous business practices and destroying the environment, right down to actual criminality and violence.

John So, to sum up: the more primary reality is to us, the more accurate our mental maps are, and the healthier we are.

Robin Right.

John Now how do 'values' fit in here? Are they contained in our mental maps too?

Robin Of course. So let's talk about how we build up the value systems that guide us – in other words, how we draw our mental maps. What do you think we usually construct them from?

John Well, primarily from our experience. That's what guides us most strongly. I mean obviously we never have enough experience ourselves, so to fill in the gaps we have to rely on advice, which is based on the experience of other people. But it's not the same, is it? We always give our own experience more weight.

Robin Yes, it's the most direct connection we have with reality, so we can be more sure of it than anything we've been told. It can also have the strongest influence because it's always tinged with more feeling. We haven't just understood something with our head, we've understood it with all of ourselves, so it carries a special conviction.

John So does that make our own experience the best guide for drawing mental maps?

Robin Well, until we've had *enough* experience, other people may know better, but we can never be absolutely sure of that. So ultimately the only safe way is to check out everything important ourselves.

John Well, let's take fidelity. I know that's something you believe in strongly, but you also think it's a good idea for young people to have sexual experience before they marry, right?

Robin I don't *advocate* it, of course; it has to be each person's own decision and responsibility. But yes, my experience of treating couple relationships does suggest that people are more likely to be fully committed and develop increasingly enjoyable sexual relationships after they marry, if they have had a chance earlier to have other sexual relationships. Unless it's against their religious convictions, of course.

John Why is that?

Robin Well, if people are faithful to their partner just because somebody – even a religious leader – told them to be, they're always going to be struggling against temptation.

John Because there will always be a part of them speculating about what it would be like? Wondering whether it might not be slightly terrific, although still wicked, of course.

Robin Yes, that kind of fantasising's almost inevitable.

John So there'll be quite a lot of energy expended in trying to repress the fantasies, too.

Robin Exactly. So the fidelity won't be truly 'whole-hearted'. There's a split. Now I've always found that such a person will have a fear of becoming really turned on sexually even with their committed partner, because they're frightened that if they actually took the brakes off, they might not be able to control themselves when they met someone else they found attractive. So, for safety's sake, they keep the brakes on all the time; which of course limits their capacity to have a fulfilling relationship with their spouse.

John And that'll mean that a bit of them remains unsatisfied, and that'll fuel the fantasising.

Robin Whereas . . . if you've learned from experience that trying to run two relationships rapidly degenerates into a French farce . . .

John And after a time, a rather unfunny one, lacking real spontaneity because of all the lies you have to hold in your head . . .

Robin . . . And that it's not only complicated and rather hard work, but that it eventually brings a lot of unpleasant – if foreseeable – consequences, and *also* wrecks the possibility of having a really good relationship with *either* of the people involved . . . well, if you've learned all that, you won't waste much time on dreams about affairs, because you *understand* why they don't work . . .

John In other words, you'll be faithful to your partner because you really *want* to be!

Robin You won't waste much time imagining affairs because you're permanently cured of the idea that they are 'fun'. And that makes possible a much more complete commitment to your spouse, because it's no longer the result of a struggle against temptation, it's based on real understanding. So you can now let yourself go sexually with your partner, without worrying that you might be opening a Pandora's Box.

John So you're saying that partners who are faithful because they are 'obeying orders' will be committed only with the more moral 'good' part of themselves, and not with the more 'racy', more 'animal' part of themselves. Which will make it harder for them to live up to the values they espoused when they made their marriage vows.

Robin Whereas *experience* will bring a higher degree of integration. You can give more of yourself to the relationship, because more of you is convinced that it's a good idea!

John I agree that this kind of experience gives a deeper understanding. But you can also have an experience which is powerful in its effect on your value systems but which *limits* your understanding. If a Belgian immigration officer insults you, it can affect your view of his fellow citizens. Or, much more serious, childhood sexual abuse can put someone off sex for life.

Robin Indeed. But you're giving examples where a person has one bad experience and avoids having any others that might balance and correct it. Whereas I'm simply saying that a person who experiences a number of sexual relationships has a better chance of finding out that novelty soon palls, that affairs are shallow and unsatisfying compared with sex in a long-term committed relationship.

John Yes. OK, that makes sense. Now a corollary to this occurred to me a few years ago. It's this. If you try to work out why any particular moral rule exists . . . I don't think you can *really* understand why it grew up in the first place, until you've *had* actual experience in connection with it. You could never foresee all the nasty consequences that the moral rule is intended to avoid, if it was just presented to you as a slogan.

Robin So a good principle is this: *until* you've had enough experience, *pay attention* to injunctions!

John Ah! You mean, break them only after serious consideration?

Robin Yes. Don't assume there aren't good reasons behind moral rules. But, equally, it's important to know, as you grow up, that just accepting an injunction unquestioningly can bring problems. Ultimately, it's just practical advice which should be explored for deeper understanding.

John Like scaffolding, a temporary structure upon which you can build something more solid and useful. OK. So our experience is the strongest force in shaping our behaviour, while injunctions and advice are not really so persuasive.

Robin Nevertheless, we have never got enough personal experience to construct a mental map. There'll always be huge blanks in it. So what else can we use?

John Well apart from advice, and observing what happens to other people if they behave in a particular way, there's books, plays and films and novels, newspapers, television, lectures, seminars, classes . . . and that's just *how* the information comes to us. The content itself is . . . endless. I can't think of a word that covers it all.

Robin The trouble is, there isn't one. Or at least there wasn't. That's why I like the idea of a Greek psychologist called Charis Katakis. She's taken a word we're all familiar with – 'myth' – and given it a wider meaning. Roughly, she uses it to mean the ideas and stories that enable human beings to cooperate and work together as a society.

John What, anything *at all* that has value in helping people to live more harmoniously?

Robin Yes, it can include any kind of abstraction which fulfils that function, from the Ten Commandments to nursery rhymes. It's a wonderfully broad concept.

John Broad is a good word. But does it include ordinary myths too, like Prometheus stealing fire?

Robin Absolutely. What Katakis means by 'myth' includes: all the ideas that make up ethical systems, both religious and non-religious; any information about how to organise ourselves, like laws and regulations, politics itself, social psychology, management studies and even books on etiquette; and also all the smaller-scale ideas that unify us in minor ways, like proverbs, folklore and fairy tales. A Katakis myth embraces anything at all that guides our social behaviour, by giving us pointers on how to live together, how to reconcile our own needs with the needs of our society. Of course, I'm probably simplifying her idea and interpreting it rather more broadly than she would do, for our purposes here.

John So, as we try to construct our mental maps, we first use our experience, and then we supplement that with information from what Katakis calls myths. Then we'll have a reasonably complete map which will guide us how best to fit in with others.

Robin And also how to live a happy and fulfilling life.

John Hang on, isn't that *two* things? One about society, and the other about the individual.

Robin Yes, but they're very closely connected. We've agreed that a healthy society is one which makes possible the development of healthy individuals. The other side of the coin is: the more that people develop individually, the more they'll be able to give back to society. So in looking at Katakis myths, we'll expect them to have the two aspects: the first is to provide a basic structure for society, enabling people to live together with as much cooperation and harmony as possible; the second is concerned with the growth and maturing of the individual, enabling each person to understand and organise their life by finding a greater harmony within themselves.

John Fair enough. But these Katakis myths . . . I mean, they extend all the way from scientific knowledge to fairy stories. Can you really call scientific knowledge a 'myth'?

Robin It fits this definition completely – abstractions that enable groups of people to cooperate in a common task. Also, although scientific knowledge is expressed in as unambiguous a way as possible, so that the maximum number of people can agree on what it means, philosophers of science have now shown very clearly that much of this 'agreement' is possible only because of shared perceptual habits within a particular culture; it's these shared cultural perceptions that make certain assumptions seem 'obvious' or 'commonsense'; but they're really describing cultural habits, which are sometimes deeply ingrained and associated with strong emotions.

John Yes, I'd forgotten that. Assumptions like these are defended with the same sort of passion that people feel for their native language.

Robin And of course that's why any radical innovation in science is resisted in the same irrational, emotional way that religious dissension is rejected by the orthodox believer.

John Agreed. But there's still a tremendous difference between the kind of information we get from a scientific theory, and from a parable.

Robin Yes, but remember that we live our lives at different levels. Most of our life is spent at a relatively mundane level, where a spade is a spade, and there we only need the more factual, scientific aspects of Katakis myths. But some of them deal with individual growth. And the closer we get to psychological, and indeed spiritual ideas, the more these have to be conveyed in a symbolic way – using material that's more mythical in the ordinary sense, because only that can convey the complex, paradoxical, two-sided nature of the reality we're interested in at that level.

John Yes, all right. I see we need the whole range. But now here's the big question. With all these different myths about, how do we know whether they're good and useful, or not? What's the criterion for judging their *value*?

Robin By how effective a myth is in helping to integrate human behaviour.

John In both helping individuals to become more integrated, and in helping groups to become more cooperative?

Robin Yes, its effectiveness at both those levels. And there are two aspects to that effectiveness. The first is: how *inclusive* is the myth? Is it just helping some people to integrate and cooperate better, but excluding others? In Katakis' thinking, the more inclusive a myth is, the better it is. Exactly the quality you described as a sign of health in the individual.

John And the second?

Robin The second is: how *persuasive* is the myth. How much does it actually affect people's behaviour? Obviously the more it does, the more highly it's rated.

John So Katakis is saying it's better to have a way of organising people that includes everybody than one that just includes a tight little group of power-seekers, right?

Robin Yes. You see, *Mein Kampf* would be considered a myth by Katakis, but of course it would rate very low down on the scale. It's a myth because it contains some organisational principles, which is better, as we said in Chapter 3, than absolute chaos, no myth at all. But it's very, very low in value, because it included only supporters of the Nazi party and excluded and did immense damage to other members of that society, not to speak of the damage to other societies. The Nazis were the only ones 'integrated'.

John The same low value would obviously apply to any system based on some kind of supremacy, racial, tribal, class – even male and female chauvinism. So the more comprehensive the myth, the better it's judged to be . . .

Robin Think of Christ's parable of the Good Samaritan, where He intentionally chose a member of a group that his listeners would be prejudiced against, in order to emphasise how widely he was defining the group towards whom neighbourly feelings were appropriate. Katakis would put the highest value on a myth like this.

John All right. Now let's look at the other aspect – how effective a given myth is, in the sense of influencing people's behaviour.

Robin Obviously all these myths will vary hugely in their persuasiveness. Some may really affect our behaviour. Most we just shrug aside or forget, because they have no impact on us.

John What's making the difference?

Robin Well, remember the greatest influence on us is our experience, because it's so coloured with *feeling*. Now although myths can never be as persuasive as experience, the more they engage our feelings, the more they affect us. That's why so many of these myths, especially the religious ones, tap into our basic feelings about the family. By expressing so much of their information in terms of fathers, mothers, brothers and sisters, they evoke deep and powerful emotions first laid down in us when we were very small and dependent.

John So when we talk of 'Our Father' that automatically releases emotions connected with the expectation we have of a parent.

Robin Yes, that he will love us, and that he will love our brothers and sisters too! And if we believe that God cares about people that we don't much like normally, that may help us to try to be friendlier towards them.

John Yes I see that. But only a small proportion of myths release these family feelings, surely?

Robin If you reflect on it, a lot of them do. Think of the powerful emotive force released by the idea of a 'Mother Country' or a 'Fatherland'. Socialists call each other 'Brother' or 'Sister' . . .

John True. And groups often refer to themselves as a 'family' . . .

Robin But over and above arousing family feelings . . . the myths that engage our emotions most effectively come in the form of *stories*.

John Ah! In the same way that if we learn something from novels or films or poetry, it has a deeper impact than learning it from a book of philosophy or psychology? Because it's not so 'dry', it involves our feelings more?

Robin Yes. After all, learning from stories is the nearest that words can bring us to actual experience. We get involved in the characters. We get absorbed in the situations. We care about the outcome. We may identify with a character, we feel it could be us trying to achieve something but not knowing how, finding out the hard way, failing and then perhaps finally succeeding. At the end, the story has given us some of the feelings we would get if we had gone through the experience described, and it may inspire us to take on a similar challenge ourselves.

John Twenty years of Video Arts training films have been based on this thinking. We've always maintained that film is a rotten way of putting across ordinary information, but a very good way of changing people's behaviour – *if* you use comedy or drama to involve the audience, because then you can affect them at the gut level from which behaviour arises. In fact our CEO Peter Robinson was always quoting the old Chinese saying: 'Tell me and I'll forget. Show me and I may remember. Involve me and I'll understand.'

Robin Lovely! In fact there's a kind of paradox about how best to convey a 'message', isn't there? Where it's clearest, as with a simple instruction, the listener has no sense at all of 'experiencing' it, so it actually has less impact. But where the message is wrapped up in a story in a less explicit way, it can make a much stronger impression.

John Is it because, when you have a story, behaviour is linked to its consequences, so that the hearer can *make up his or her own mind* whether the behaviour is desirable?

Robin Exactly. It's left to the hearer to decide, when they've digested all the consequences. Indeed Christ ends many of *His* parables by saying something like: 'Which was better?'!

John So, a story that leaves us free to think about it, will affect us more deeply than an injunction.

Robin Indeed. Giving us the space to allow the penny to drop, allowing us a private moment of choice, makes the effect of that choice much more powerful than if it is forced upon us. We've chosen it in a much deeper and more enduring way. It's our own.

John It has more of the quality of an experience.

Robin Exactly. It touches our emotions in the same way.

John And parallel with that, somebody telling us what to do, or just making plain assertions about what is or is not the case, can put us on our guard and arouse our resistance.

Robin Right. But everyone loves stories, and the information they convey can get past our suspicions and defences.

John Less is more, as they say. Not a technique much used by politicians.

Robin Luckily – or they'd have more power over us!

John You know, everything you're saying reminds me of my experiences in therapy! Shrinks don't tell you what to do. They may ask you questions that help you discover more about your feelings about something, or possibly about the consequences of a course of action, but they never express a preference themselves. They always let you choose.

Robin That's certainly what they should have been trained to do. Because decisions will then come from the patient, not the therapist.

John And even if they have a sudden insight into some aspect of your behaviour – if they make a connection that you haven't seen yet – they don't explain it to you! They wait until *you* can make the connection yourself. Obviously it has a greater impact then.

Robin And also, if some information is given too soon, before the person is ready, it may only arouse their defences, so that they find it more difficult to see the truth of it for themselves.

John Yes . . . so, although we've been talking about the way in which some myths have such a powerful effect, we're also discussing much more general principles about the way in which information needs to be conveyed to folk, if they're really going to take it on board.

Robin Yes, and especially where that information encounters ingrained attitudes and emotional resistance. Of course, the more that information is aimed only at the intellect, the less feelings need to be involved in conveying it.

John OK. So, to sum up, we've been talking about what makes a myth – in the Katakis sense – persuasive. Because that's the second of the two aspects that determine any given myth's value; the first being its inclusiveness.

Robin That's it.

John Well now Robin, a tiny little point has just occurred to me. Why's it all working so *badly*?

Robin Come again?

John Let me lay out my argument. I think most people try to base their behaviour on the values they hold. I don't mean it's very conscious most of the time, but nevertheless people don't want to do what they themselves consider to be 'wrong'. They like to be able to justify their behaviour and feel what they've done is 'all right'.

Robin Agreed.

John Well obviously we're getting our values from what Katakis calls myths. Now I know there are a few nasty myths, which advocate excluding people of different race or culture or class or whatever and of treating them distinctly less well than the people who are included by such myths. But my point is that most myths that we encounter are pretty inclusive – to put it another way, the world's greatest thinkers and creative artists and spiritual leaders tend not to be bigots. In fact you could claim that most values in the West are derived from Christianity, and you don't find anything more inclusive than the words of Jesus Christ. And yet despite these myths, Robin, the world is not a very harmonious or cooperative place; it seems to me to be characterised by constant squabbling, even where there isn't actual violence.

Robin Ah. Now that leads us on to rather an important point, perhaps the most important that I have to make in this chapter. It is this: people interpret each myth according to their level of mental health.

John . . . Let's get this straight. You're saying that exactly the same myth will be understood by different people in different ways?

Robin That's the way I think it works.

John And that's not because a person consciously and cynically misuses a healthy idea to justify their unhealthy behaviour?

Robin No, it's because they genuinely believe the myth justifies their behaviour. You see, even if they could see that other interpretations are possible, the only one that would 'feel right' would be the one that fitted into all their other values and attitudes.

John I've just remembered that in Chapter 1 you said that each level of mental health believes itself to be the best possible.

Robin Yes, that's right. This is the same idea, put a different way.

John So let me get this right: a less healthy person will take a healthy idea and turn it into something less healthy?

Robin Absolutely. And vice versa too. A more healthy person brought up, say, in a Stalinist society, will behave in a way that's healthier than the norm.

John I suppose this is all obvious really . . . but I've never heard it explained quite like this. I certainly realised years ago that no idea is incorruptible – we all know what's been done in the name of Christianity . . .

Robin And look at politics. One of the most influential books of all time is Plato's *Republic*, which enquires into the nature of justice and says that it is the obligation of the state to provide it. Yet Sir Karl Popper has shown that Plato *can* be regarded as the first in the tradition which led to the Fascists! As somebody said: 'An idea is not responsible for the people who hold it'!

John So it's obvious why values that seem absolute and obvious, like freedom and democracy, have been argued about so much and described in such different ways. Each view reflects a different level of health!

Robin So we begin to see why there's such a divergence of opinion in the world!

John I'm intrigued. I want to explore this. Let's take some myths and see how they would be interpreted at each different level of mental health.

Robin Rather than look at one particular myth, let's examine a basic value about which there'd be a whole cluster of myths.

John All right. Let's start with a value that's at the centre of the cooperative purpose of Katakis' myths – loyalty to a group.

Robin All right. Each person will bring their own family attitudes and feelings to their interpretation of myths about loyalty. So if they come from a very unhealthy family, they'll feel that the group should all hold practically identical views, and that anyone who questions these views is a 'trouble-maker' who is being 'disloyal'; they'll feel hostility towards outside groups, and a disregard for the rights of such 'outsiders'; and they'll feel intense and demanding dependence on all the other members of the group.

John And you're saying that they will therefore inevitably interpret any idea to do with loyalty in a way that supports these basic attitudes.

Robin Yes.

John In other words, loyalty, to unhealthy people, is simply paranoia dressed up and relabelled.

Robin That's what it amounts to, seen from a level of health above it. Remember the Mafia refer to the requirement of silence about all their crimes as '*omertà*' – honour! And of course it does represent a higher level of health than *dis*loyalty, where everyone in a society is betraying everyone else. It just isn't very *inclusive*, it's bad news for everyone outside that little group of people who are at least loyal to one another.

John Now I'm puzzled. People from healthier families will interpret 'loyalty' as allowing much greater freedom to group members to be separate and different. And they'll be basically positive and trustful towards people outside the group. So does that mean that for them the concept of 'loyalty' isn't that important?

Robin Well it depends what you mean by 'loyalty'! Of course, they'll feel a greater emotional commitment to people inside the group and will consequently be prepared to spend more time and energy on them. But they won't feel there's a rigid distinction between the sort of people who comprise their group, and the sort of people outside it. Their loyalty will be more *inclusive*, so the difference between their loyalty to people within the family, and people outside it, will be more one of degree. And then they'll be much more tolerant of criticism within the group, and more positive towards ideas about how to change the way the group operates.

John I've never seen before just how 'disloyal' they're bound to look to the paranoids!

Robin Of course . . .

John I'm also thinking there's a special form of loyalty called 'patriotism'.

Robin Well, that'll be interpreted in exactly the same way. Except that in a group as big as a nation one aspect of unhealthy behaviour becomes even more obvious. Unhealthy 'patriotism' not only involves antagonism to foreigners, it requires almost the same degree of hostility towards any fellow countrymen who don't hold similarly xenophobic views! Otherwise a wide spectrum of views would be permissible, and that would feel very unhealthy.

John It makes me think of the slogan of a few years ago: 'America – Love it or Leave it'. In a way, a clever bit of verbal manipulation; you don't immediately see that the sloganeers have defined 'America' as only themselves. The Tories always have a big Union Jack up at conferences for the same purpose.

Robin So when very paranoid people talk about 'patriotism' they're using the term to describe the process by which they deny the parts of themselves they find unacceptable, and project them onto all the people who are either 'foreign', or 'unpatriotic' compatriots.

John . . . It's odd, but there's a problem here. It's that healthy loyalty feels less passionate. But I suppose you realise healthy loyal people will be out there *doing* good, whereas the more passionate 'loyalists' will be merely *feeling* good.

Robin When you say 'less passionate' I think you're talking about external appearances. A person whose emotions are very polarised and partisan may appear to be feeling a lot. But the emotion is crude, vehement, and the person generating it may be incapable of anything more subtle and varied. More healthy people feel more, not less, but in the sense that they are more responsive to a wider range of richer feelings. So it's as if they don't have to turn the emotional volume up to a deafening level, in order to hear anything at all.

John Well let's look at another value almost everybody would accept as good – honesty.

Robin There's a lot of different forms of *that*!

John True. Well let's take, say, 'telling the truth', and 'keeping promises'. How are they going to be interpreted differently?

Robin Well, before you can tell the truth, you have to know what the truth is! So the healthies are at an immediate advantage, since they have a more realistic view of what's going on around them, and what they're like themselves. In addition, they'll really 'believe' in honesty; because they believe that openness works, that it's not dangerous, but on the contrary is positively beneficial. So healthies will interpret a myth like 'Honesty is the best policy' not as an injunction but as a simple fact that's obvious from their experience, and do so in such a way as to encourage telling the truth in a wider, more open way about a more complete range of topics.

John Makes sense. What about less healthy folk?

Robin Well it's more difficult for them to tell the truth in any objective sense, because for a start they're tending to project all their faults onto other people, and to blame everyone but themselves for anything that goes wrong. So, unlike the more healthy, they don't even know what the truth is. But in addition, because they see the outside world as basically hostile, they'll feel morally justified in 'doctoring' the truth in order to defend their own interests against all these unfriendly forces. Even with people close to them, and knowing they've been at fault about something, they'll tend to deny it because they feel that they have to present a faultless front in order to be acceptable. Finally, to give truthful and helpful criticism to people close to them would be very difficult too because it would feel 'unkind' and 'disloyal'.

John So in a very large number of circumstances it will not feel safe or 'right' to unhealthy people to tell the truth.

Robin Exactly. So although they'd agree in principle with many myths encouraging truth-telling, if you pressed them further they would attach a long list of conditions which would render the principle less and less meaningful.

John So where does that put us mid-rangers? To what extent will it feel 'right' to us to tell the truth?

Robin Well it'll depend how much we've got behind the screen – we'll certainly defend that. Otherwise we'll probably be pretty straight with people that we trust – subject to our basic, mid-range, egotistical, manipulative attitude in our dealings with the world! That will often lead us to be 'economical with the truth', while carefully avoiding telling direct lies, which would make most of us genuinely uncomfortable.

John Most of us will maintain a Secretary-to-the-Cabinet level of veracity most of the time.

Robin And a slightly lower level when we're filling out our insurance claims. Because, reassuringly, that's *normal* . . .

John OK. What about keeping promises, or 'sanctity of contract', as lawyers and street-traders call it.

Robin The attitudes to this show why we say that people we can rely on have 'integrity'.

John How do you mean?

Robin Healthier people have more 'integrity' because they are more psychologically integrated – they've included more of the 'bits' of themselves; they haven't denied them and split them off.

John Which is why less healthy people are less good at keeping promises?

Robin Let's take an example. Why don't you want to keep some promises?

John Because . . . I don't feel I made them really seriously . . . or circumstances have changed . . . or it wasn't really part of a deal, I just made an agreement which I now regret because it's really inconvenient . . .

Robin That's right. The trouble usually arises because one part of us makes a promise, and a different part of us has to carry it out.

John Expound.

Robin Well imagine we want something. It might be anything from borrowing money, to a momentary desire to feel that we are an outstandingly saintly human being. So we make a promise – to repay the money soon, or to do a special favour for someone. But a few days later, when we have to carry out the promise, we're in a different mood. We're not anxious about money any more – we've got it now! And we don't need to feel good about ourselves today, because we've already given ourselves that quick fix when we made the promise. And yet here's this damn commitment we made – except that it doesn't really feel as though we made it! Not exactly anyway, it was all a bit vaguer than this – a lot vaguer, come to think of it!

John So a change of mood completely changes our feeling about the promise.

Robin Yes. Whereas a more integrated person will be more conscious of what they're undertaking when they make a promise. You could say that the part of them that does the promising is more integrated with the rest of their psyche, including the parts that are going to find the promise difficult to fulfil. So they've taken the future resistance and desire to backslide into account at the start, and when the times comes for them to carry it out, they will feel much more completely committed.

John This is right. I've seen this process in myself, and I also observed it a few years ago when I began to have some spare money and I loaned a fair amount of it to quite a few people. It was quite astonishing how little came back! And you could trace the change of mood. At the beginning there was frequently a degree of desperation arising from the need for the money; then for a very few days after the loan there was tremendous gratitude; then the gratitude cooled a little, but there was still a great deal of warmth; and then there was quite a change – the money now felt more like theirs, and I could sense they were distancing themselves from me, partly because of our embarrassment about the position they'd originally been in, and more because of the anticipated inconvenience of having to repay it; and finally there was the stage when it was their money and I'd become just an irritating reminder of some vague obligation that would only spoil their life! Being so English I was myself too embarrassed ever to bring the subject up; it served me right – I got back less than 10 per cent of what I loaned. But to see the pattern repeated in different people was an education.

Robin Well, this is a good example of the other side of the equation. Though you were very generous, *you* didn't anticipate and allow for the fact that *they* might not allow for their resistance and therefore behave as they did. Also, if you feel they are not keeping their side of the agreement, but don't openly and honestly tell them so, misunderstanding is possible and never gets sorted out. You would have helped them a second time, and maybe preserved the relationship, if you had told them to cough up!

John But does all this mean that a less healthy, less integrated person will interpret a simple myth like 'you should always try to keep your promises' much more narrowly, with many more conditions attached, as we saw with 'telling the truth'? Or does the 'interpretation' really show only in the actual performance – or rather the lack of it?!

Robin Unless the borrower is intending to default – that is, like a confidence trickster – it's more a matter of lack of self-awareness and so not being able to be honest with themselves: 'meaning' to repay but gradually 'rewriting the script' so that they convince themselves that the original agreement didn't stipulate repayment, or at least not yet, or only when you asked for it – which so far you haven't – or only if you hadn't made so much money yourself since the loan was made that you probably don't *really* need it back. But in a healthier person, their professed values and their actions will be more integrated. So their behaviour will stay closer to the reality of any agreement they make.

John All right. So far we've been talking about comparatively vague, if heroic, values like 'loyalty' and 'honesty'. But what about all the mundane organisational principles that Katakis might include in the category of 'myth' – like traffic regulations. Can a 'No Left Turn' sign be interpreted in different ways?

Robin Well obviously the more the myth conveys detailed practical instructions for carrying out activities, the less difference there will be in the way people respond to them. But with traffic regulations, less healthy people are likely to interpret them according to the letter of the law: they will believe that a 30 mph speed limit will give them permission to do that speed even in a crowded area where 20 mph would be more sensible. They'll tend to drive forward when the light changes to green, even if it's a bit dangerous, because it's their 'right' to do so.

John A more healthy driver will be more flexible in responding to the spirit of the law?

Robin Yes, understanding that the thinking behind the regulations is to reduce the danger of accidents, or to keep the traffic flow moving.

John But a healthier driver might feel more relaxed in breaking a regulation if it was safe and didn't inconvenience other drivers?

Robin Probably, and similarly a healthier police officer will use his or her discretion, being tough on those drivers who are not considering the safety of others, while turning a blind eye to trivial contraventions. A less healthy police officer, on the other hand, might regard the slightest infraction as a collapse of the moral order, or may just be a 'little Hitler' using the law to enhance their personal authority in the cause of feeling better about themselves.

John Or perhaps they want to go home but haven't yet bagged enough victims to satisfy a quota set by an unhealthy superior.

Robin Yes. The level of health of any person in a hierarchy will influence the behaviour of those below them in the pecking order.

John So the healthy behaviour is to look at the thinking behind regulations; the less healthy behaviour is to take a literal and inflexible interpretation of the letter of the law. It sounds to me a general principle of mental health.

Robin That puts the principle in a nutshell.

John How does all this apply to the world of sport, where the main value is 'sportsmanship' – trying to defeat the opposition 'within the rules'? That's a phrase capable of several interpretations . . .

Robin Well, I would say the healthy attitude to games, apart from the sheer pleasure of physical activity and practising skills, is in contending with a worthy opponent, who stretches you because they're a 'good match' for you. The unhealthy, paranoid attitude is to regard the opponent as an enemy who must be defeated, and if possible, humiliated and wiped out.

John Basically, the more tunnel-visioned the focus on winning, the less healthy?

Robin Basically, yes. Winning-at-all-costs is a pretty non-inclusive value!

John So the unhealthier they are, the more cynically players will operate the rules, and even condone cheating.

Robin You see, to someone at this level losing feels like being wiped out, exterminated. They don't see that there is greater pleasure available if the game is played in a different spirit – and much less anxiety and fear, too!

John We're talking about integrity again.

Robin Yes. A healthier person knows that the result of the game is only a part of the activity. So they're also concerned about behaving in a way that reflects their personal values, that maintains their friendship with their opponents, and that maximises their enjoyment!

John It's to do with the Affiliative Attitude, too, isn't it? Some of the most touching experiences of my life have been moments of great sportsmanship. You know how electrifying it is in a big game, when one player suddenly acts in a way that shows that he or she knows that 'playing fair' is more important than winning. Because this respect for the rules honours the fact that the players share a common culture. It reminds everyone that what divides the players is less important than what unites them. And when a player demonstrates this, the change in feeling in the crowd is a truly wondrous thing. A wholly different atmosphere suddenly fills the stadium. All the narrow, partisan anxiety goes and the crowd now roars their support in a new warmer, fuller, more generous way. Still wanting to win, but at the same time knowing that their opponents are 'all right', and that ultimately the game is what matters.

Robin And with the paranoia gone, it all becomes more fun! Unfortunately, in recent years, a more obsessive attitude towards winning has been spreading throughout all sports. I'd guess that the tennis players of the late seventies and early eighties were in the vanguard.

John It always struck me that there were certain key players who were considered exciting to watch primarily because they polarised the crowds – you either loved them or hated them. Which was a good thing commercially, but a bad thing for all young people looking for role models, because this paranoid polarisation of the crowds seemed to me to reflect a similar split in the minds of the players involved.

Robin And of course it's a vicious circle. If players are sufficiently divided in their own psychology to polarise the crowd like that, the crowd in turn will encourage that split and be disappointed if players don't behave badly and abuse the referee. So the paranoid pattern gets more and more difficult to escape from and, as you say, young people eventually come to see it as 'normal' and copy it. I think sport and games were much healthier for people when winning was kept in perspective. The old British ideas of 'fair play' and 'good loser' were thoroughly admirable ones, and came from a much more mature and integrated philosophy of life.

John It suddenly strikes me that we've been discussing all this without mentioning the huge increase in the amount of money that winning brings nowadays. Perhaps 'money' is the value I should be asking you about above all others! It's a huge aid to social cooperation, yet, unlike the other values and myths so far, it seems to me fundamentally morally neutral. I mean by that simply that it facilitates the exchange of goods, without being exactly good or bad in itself. Yet there are a million myths about it, and an enormous amount of people's values and behaviour are determined by it. How do you see the different levels of mental health interpreting good old amoral money . . . ?

Robin It's a huge subject. But let's look at it in the light of the three indicators of health we've already discussed. First, unusually healthy people see the world very clearly and realistically. So they are more likely to see exactly what money is – it's a means of getting the things you need to give you the life you've decided will satisfy you best. And healthy folk will be clearer about what's really satisfying too, so they'll have a pretty accurate idea of how much money they need. And they won't be likely to waste much time on making more than that!

John So people are not behaving healthily if they spend a lot of time acquiring more money than they really need.

Robin No.

John . . . Well if they do, it must be because of the symbolic value that money has for them.

Robin That's right.

John Well there are several possible aspects of that: for some people, money is primarily a symbol of their power or status – their position in the hierarchy; for some, especially a certain kind of Puritan, possession of it conveys actual moral Brownie points; and for some who've suffered from real poverty in their earlier lives it's symbolic of security against a return to that deprived state.

Robin And not just financial poverty. For many people who have lacked love and emotional security in childhood, money comes to be a substitute, a source of security and gratification over which they can have complete control. It's one reason many people never feel they have enough; it never meets the real need.

John Are there any specifically psychiatric insights into the compulsive accumulation of money that you've found particularly interesting?

Robin I've never come across a person like that who was happy!

John So is it fair to say that the more a person's search for money is compulsive, and based on some symbolic value they're unaware of, the lower the level of mental health they're manifesting?

Robin Yes, I'd acccept that.

John So that's money looked at from one aspect of health – realistic perception. What's the second aspect that sheds light on Lucre?

Robin Our old friend, 'integrity'. This simply means that healthy people will apply the same values to the money-making part of their lives as they do to their personal lives; they won't treat them as separate compartments.

John So the cynical 'Business is Business' attitude won't apply?

Robin No, even if the workplace sometimes feels a bit fierce, the healthier people will try to hang on to their values.

John But there are always a few really nasty people out there in the business world, aren't there? I've met two myself . . .

Robin Plenty of them. But remember that 'healthies' are realistic. They'll take all necessary precautions if they have to deal with somebody they judge to be unscrupulous – but that'll be true of the rest of their lives too.

John Nice to think some of the best medieval attitudes are still around. And what's the third measure of health that illuminates attitudes towards money?

Robin The most obvious one – the Affiliative Attitude. Healthier people will be generous with any money they have to spare, spreading it round in rather the same way as they spread their warmth and friendliness and goodwill.

John It's interesting, isn't it, that there's such a dislike of someone who won't stand their round of drinks! But I guess people intuitively sense that it reveals a person's deeper attitude towards their friends.

Robin Behaviour like that usually reflects a general tendency, doesn't it? If it's persistent, it's likely to show in other aspects of the person's behaviour. You'd probably hesitate to get into a financial relationship with someone who takes advantage when they are given too much change in a shop.

John There's one final aspect of Money-as-a-Value that I want to pursue – materialism. I can't quite get my mind round it, despite all my own materialistic tendencies! Let me tell you a story. David Puttnam once told me that the first three people he lunched with after he took over Columbia found different ways of telling him that they were worth over a hundred million dollars. He thought about it a lot and came to the conclusion that they were not just trying to impress him with their power; he felt that they were trying to establish a sense of worth with him, and that money was just about the only way in which they knew how to do this. Of course a corollary to that is that they may have felt, on some level, that they would come pretty low down the hierarchy if their worth was measured by any other criteria! What do you think it is that causes people to try to base their self-esteem on their material possessions?

Robin Well, as you say, they must feel impoverished of other qualities if they have to make so much display of their bank balances. Though you, and Puttnam, are speaking here about the USA, and Los Angeles in particular, and the film industry specifically. And among people concentrated in those localities, as we know, money is a generally accepted measure of status, for reasons you've spoken about in Chapter 3.

John Are people *driven* to acquire wealth because they really are unable to see the importance of other values?

Robin Not necessarily. Some might acquire wealth in order to have the freedom and resources to do other things – either for their own fulfilment or for others. But if they are *just* concerned with making money I would expect them to be very impoverished in other respects. And to be unaware of their general poverty.

John So, to adapt Oscar Wilde, a materialist is someone who knows the price of everything and the value of nothing?

Robin And is unaware of how much they don't know!

John So would you say that materialism is a species of the narrow literal-mindedness that characterises a less healthy approach to interpreting values?

Robin Yes, I would. A limited view where you don't see the wood, just the trees.

John Well, I'll attempt a rough summing-up so far. We've been looking at the idea that each person interprets the world according to his or her level of mental health. And it seems to me that the unhealthier we are, the more literal-minded we are in our interpretations of the letter of the law, as it were; and the healthier we are, the more influenced we are by the broader idea that lies behind the specific formulation of the myth that we are interpreting.

Robin That really catches the essence of it.

John . . . Something's just struck me. People are always going on about values *changing*, aren't they? You know, 'People used to believe in X – they don't any more.' Or, 'Folk used not to bother about that – now it upsets people.' But it's not so much that the value itself changes, is it? Nobody ever said loyalty was 'bad', or that oppression was 'good'. So it is really the *interpretation* of a value that changes over time, isn't it?

Robin I think there are two aspects to it. First of all, those values that people complain we're losing have not basically *changed*; they've been the same throughout history. And I've no doubt that the complaints that we are losing them have been repeated throughout history too. But the second point is that there *are* swings in the degree of respect we have for them, and in how narrow and literal, or how broad and subtle, our understanding of them is at any given time. It corresponds to the swings in society between attitudes which emphasise a more narrow, selfish and short-term approach to life, and the more inclusive 'traditional' values which look at society as a whole and consider the welfare of all classes and of future generations.

John Now there's only one more thing I want to ask you about values. And it's absolutely huge! Or maybe it isn't . . .

Robin What are you talking about?

John The R-word.

Robin . . . Religion?

John Yes.

Robin Why are you being so coy about it?

John Well if we have a really serious discussion about religion at this point, most of our readers will just throw the book in the wastepaper basket, won't they? I mean, it's just not allowed as a serious topic these days. Even a trivial interest makes you suspect, unless you're trying to rise in the Tory party hierarchy.

Robin I think this has changed tremendously since the 1960s. In the fifties when I was training in psychiatry I can remember chatting with a group in the hospital dining room and having the most frank and detailed discussion about sexual perversions – which in those days would have produced a shock-horror response in mixed company outside. I found myself thinking that it would produce a similar shock-horror response in my colleagues if someone started to talk equally openly about spiritual experience! But since then surely it has become steadily more open and accepted. No one thinks twice if a person talks about meditation, or going on a retreat. I think you're being a bit old-fashioned!

John Perhaps. But for those of our readers who regard religious matters as being beyond the pale, and who may therefore be irritated by the superstitious cant, metaphysical waffle and ethereal gobbledegook coming up, here's a suggestion: *skip to page 308* where perhaps you'd like to make a cup of coffee while the rest of us catch you up. We'll return to real life then. Goodbye. See you soon . . .
   Good riddance. Now, Robin, I want to ask you about religious values, because most people would agree that our secular values are either derived directly from them, or at least heavily influenced by them. Although actually it's just an excuse for me to find out if this idea about different-interpretations-at-different-levels-of-mental-health applies to religion too.

Robin Why do you want to explore that in particular?

John Well, I've become rather interested in religion recently, and naturally I'm embarrassed about it. I mean most people are prepared to forgive me for having had therapy; but if I now start admitting a serious regard for religion they'll think I've really cracked up.

Robin I know you're exaggerating in search of comic effect, but . . .

John But I'm not! Or not much, anyway. You must know what I mean, Robin. You mention at a British Dinner Party something about a 'force' in the cosmos, and if people twig you're not talking about gravity, their smiles become fixed and their eye movements more rapid.

Robin You think people are that uncomfortable about religious ideas?

John I don't think it, I know it. Most people in Britain feel that the versions of religion on offer are not really of much interest to bright people. And if this is hurtful to the Churches I would make two points. The first is that the truth of what I'm saying is reflected in the low numbers of people attending church at a time when so many folk are looking around for something meaningful; and second, I'm *not* talking about *individuals* in the Church at all – I usually find them open and ready to engage and struggling upwards in a way I admire – no, I'm talking about the institutions themselves and the party line they put out, this mixture of platitude and mumbo-jumbo that they wave at us like a stick.

Robin You sound pretty annoyed about it.

John I suppose I am. Because now that I know there's some really good stuff around, yes, I do feel angry that so much of what we hear from the orthodox religious sources doesn't strike most people as being very interesting. That's why I and all my friends were put off it at school. What we were taught then simply made no sense to us. And what was intelligible wasn't intelligent. The words in the gospels had a strange resonance, yes, but nobody could talk about the stuff in a way that we could connect with, or that we could actually apply to our lives!

Robin Were you confirmed?

John Yes, in the same way that I joined the Army Cadet Corps. When I was preparing for confirmation I was told about concepts like Christ being the son of God, and the Forgiveness of Sins, and the Life Everlasting; then I was expected, after a decent period of soul-searching – about two days – to assent to them, despite the fact they were quite without meaning for me. And all this time we poor teenagers were hearing sermons every Sunday so breathtakingly half-witted that the only valid response was reading, sleeping, or invading the pulpit. So when I left school it never ocurred to me to go near a church. Except for weddings, of course. In fact, my image of religion for many years was a mental picture from a friend's wedding in the late sixties. I was standing in a pew next to Marty Feldman, encircled by large confident women in strangely flowered hats, who started each verse before everybody else did, to show they were regulars, and who held the last note far longer than the rest of the congregation, too, to confirm their superiority. And as they trilled away about the troops of Midian prowling and prowling around after dark, I stood there with the tears rolling down my face, so weak with laughter that I really could have fallen to the floor at any moment. 'Christian, up and smite them!' they warbled ferociously, 'Smite them by the Virtue of the Lenten Fast'. And what reduced me to this state was not just the sheer zaniness of it all, but, much more than that, the thought that these good folk could believe that what they were doing was something that pleased God. Any God, I felt, who would seriously approve of what was going on in that church would be out of His infinite mind.

Robin And you thought that this kind of thing was the only available option.

John In my ignorance, I did. Now here's the ironic bit. It was only when I began to do some background reading with the other Pythons prior to writing *The Life of Brian* that I slowly began to discover stuff that was really fascinating. And from then onwards I've met more and more people and read more and more exciting stuff that's pointed me in an interesting direction. So I'm hoping that what you'll tell me will persuade some of my highly intellectual friends that there are approaches to religion that are a bit more rewarding than the aforesaid.

Robin Well to start with, religious ideas are certainly subject to the same interpretation by different levels of mental health as the other values or 'myths' that we've been discussing. In fact, all the great world religions seem to be constructed in a remarkably brilliant way as if they are designed to be useful to people at every level of health, according to their capacity to understand.

John So a religious idea will be interpreted by a person in a way that fits in best with their existing psychology?

Robin Yes, and it can therefore support them in functioning at the best level they're capable of, given their limitations.

John All right. So let's start working through the different levels of mental health and see what basic religious attitudes correspond.

Robin Well, take people functioning at the least healthy level first. They'll understand religion as a collection of rules, of rewards and punishments, of threats and promises, all enforced by a powerful and frightening God.

John The kind of extreme, black-and-white thinking that's found in young children?

Robin That's exactly what it is. The thinking of such people has got stuck at that level, and though it's normal in a very young child, it's obviously unhealthy in an adult.

John Rather paranoid in fact.

Robin Oh yes. Quite extreme, violent and punitive.

John And how is God experienced?

Robin He's seen as a terrifying, domineering, bad-tempered dictator, who wants everyone to spend their time admiring him and telling him how marvellous he is.

John A kind of ethereal Saddam Hussein.

Robin Not so far from that, in a way. So naturally people holding this view feel they have to do lots of things to keep Him sweet, so that He won't get into a bad mood and blast them with thunderbolts, or boils, or rivers of blood.

John A bit like the church congregation in *The Meaning of Life*, who, when invited to praise God, all chant 'Ooooh, You are so big', and 'You're so tough and strong, you could beat anyone up, especially the Devil', and 'We're all really impressed down here' before singing Hymn 42, 'Oh, Lord, please don't burn us'. I can remember, even as a nine-year-old, thinking that God couldn't be so stupid that he wouldn't see through such blatant buttering-up.

Robin Of course the point about praise is not that God needs it or that it's good for God – which is ridiculous, I agree – but that we need to give it and it's good for us to do so. You see, if we are to have the right kind of relationship to the universe we must see how dependent we are on it, how tiny and helpless we stand in comparison. Then we'll have a healthy respect for it, which will lead us to care for the world and all the life in it, instead of exploiting and destroying the environment in the way that we are doing at the moment. In other words we need to have a sense of awe, of wonder, of love for the creation . . . then we can praise it as a lover praises his beloved.

John Granted. But at this lower level isn't praise seen as flattery, as though making God feel very important will put Him in a good mood?

Robin Something like that. And even when He's seen positively, it will be as a sort of headmaster at a cosmic school prize-giving, awarding halos and entry-tickets for heaven to those who've done their homework and haven't been caught smoking behind the bicycle sheds.

John All right. Now let's move up to the mid-range level, our lot. How do we treat the whole business?

Robin Well we won't of course have such extreme attitudes; we'll have a much more balanced view and see God as basically more benign and compassionate. But we'll still tend to see religion as a set of rules. For people like us, religion is more like a container that enables life to be lived with minimum confusion and anxiety.

John You mean it's a little similar to the mid-range marriage: it's an arrangement that props us securely in place; it confirms our views rather than provoking us into examining them?

Robin Exactly. Our lot will see belief in the dogma as the important thing.

John With God still as a conventional authority figure.

Robin Yes, someone who makes the rules and judges people on how well they keep to them.

John In other word, rather as a human being might behave if he was promoted to God!

Robin Yes. Like a stern and distant but loving parent. Then as we get higher and higher in the mid-range – which, remember, is a pretty wide spectrum – God is more and more seen as the essence of love, a friend and guide who is there when we seek to contact him, but who wants our commitment to be given only out of a condition of total freedom. Which would then of course be a commitment from the whole of our being, rather than just from the part that fears authority, or wants to be approved.

John So here God is viewed as the *essence of everything we value*, but still as a kind of person.

Robin Yes, someone who cares about us in a parental sort of way, but someone with whom we can have a relationship.

John And now – the moment we've all been waiting for! Tell me about the third level – the people at the top end of the health scale.

Robin As we're both basically mid-range, trying to answer that question is a bit like trying to imagine the view from the summit of the mountain from half-way up . . . but insofar as I've had moments of glimpsing what it is to be more healthy, and maybe even have become a bit healthier through understanding the ideas we've been talking about, I think I have some idea . . . I *guess* that really healthy people understand religious myths not as rules or commands, but more as information, as a kind of instruction book which helps people in their spiritual understanding and development.

John You mean . . . taken in this way, religious teachings give people insight as to where they are spiritually, and what they have to do to make progress?

Robin Yes, with the basic aim of helping them to feel more connected with everything round them.

John Connected with other people, or connected with whatever it may be that's 'out there'?

Robin Both. Connected with the universe we're all part of.

John So, for the 'most healthies', myths are information – not orders. Almost suggestions, which they are then left with, free to use as they wish?

Robin Well, let's say to experiment with. To see if they can learn from any experiences they gain from trying out the ideas.

John Like at university, where you are trusted with more freedom to explore and make your own decisions, rather than having to obey school rules?

Robin I think so. A more grown-up relationship, where the religion is treating you as a young adult, rather than as a child.

John So the value is placed on discovery and understanding, rather than upon unquestioning obedience.

Robin Yes.

John And how is God seen at this level?

Robin Well let me put it like this. I suspect that God is experienced not really as a person, but more as a feeling, a direct awareness, that the universe is ordered and meaningful. We said in Chapter 1 that the 'most healthies' have a real sense, most of the time, of being connected with the universe; and I suspect that in the moments of their highest experience, they have a sense of actually being part of that order. People who've experienced that sense of connection find it totally fulfilling. One doesn't need anything else.

John Well this is already making sense of a few things for me. And it's giving me a much better way of explaining what Monty Python's *Life of Brian* was supposed to be about! You remember the film was attacked by various religious groups on the grounds that we were making fun of religion, and indeed, of Christ Himself.

Robin The protests were particularly strong in America, weren't they?

John Yes. In New York we were condemned by groups that were Jewish Orthodox, Jewish Liberal, Catholic, Lutheran and Calvinist. As Eric Idle said, at least we'd achieved some good – we'd given them the first thing they'd been able to agree on in 2000 years. But our serious point was that we were only making fun of the way in which some people *follow* a religion, not of religion itself. But our critics seemed quite unable to separate the idea of the supreme value of Christ's teaching from the idea that some people might misinterpret that teaching.

Robin If they were from a lower level of mental health they'd be unable to allow that there are other possible interpretations.

John So the way I can explain our position now is to say this: there are different ways of following Christ – which correspond to different levels of mental health – and therefore it's quite legitimate to make fun of the less healthy ways, not least because they actually *conflict* with His teaching! The Inquisition was not an example of 'Blessed are the meek'.

Robin Maybe, but to see the film from your point of view would have forced your critics to acknowledge that they were unhealthy. And as I've pointed out, the unhealthy way of dealing with such painful truths is to defend yourself and react violently. So they acted true to form and attacked you, proving you were right. You proved your point; or rather, they proved your point for you. You can't expect them to admit it as well.

John Fair enough. But could we have done it differently, and presented the idea in a more acceptable way?

Robin You can't expect it to be accepted by those people who attacked it. You didn't make it for them, but for healthier people. And the fact that it was attacked served a useful purpose by demonstrating that your criticism of the sheep-like crowd in the film was actually the way such people behave. I don't know what you're complaining about. To get everyone to behave as if they agree with you, you'd have to be Hitler!

John Ah! I see what you mean. I'm displaying my own low level of mental health, by expecting them to *agree* with me! *Touché*. Back to real religion. And that means for most people not just the teaching or dogma, but what they actually do to practise their religion: assembling in a holy place, praying, chanting, performing rituals and so on. So how do the different levels treat religious practice?

Robin Well, at one level, rituals can be seen as no different from many kinds of group behaviour and the need to reinforce the identity of that group, by wearing a badge, dressing similarly, obeying group rules, singing songs together, and so on. Both that aspect, and the regularity and familiarity of the practice, have a kind of 'security blanket' effect. But so far as the more religious aspect is concerned, well, I'll start at the bottom level again. As we said just now, for the least healthy, religion is based on the kind of thinking typical of very young children. And young children have difficulty distinguishing fantasy from reality, wishes from deeds. So at this level, religion is valued as magic – as a means of making wishes come true, without acknowledging scientific laws and relationships of cause and effect.

John You mean at this level we believe that we only have to repeat a prayer of incantation, or perform some other prescribed routine, in order to make the world do what we want.

Robin Yes, and when you're thinking like this, whether or not your wish comes true seems to depend only on how strongly you believe in the procedure!

John Then again, the wishes are usually highly personal, aren't they? There's not usually much consideration of the effect they'd have on other people, if God granted them.

Robin That's true. When religion is used in this way, the wishes are always very partisan – that He'll make it rain tomorrow for the sake of our garden, even if it spoils everyone else's day on the beach. Or that God will make sure our country wins the World Cup, or the war.

John My father told me a National Day of Prayer was organised during the Second World War and that it coincided with a great military disaster. So they didn't have another.

Robin Which at least showed an admirable if belated contact with reality! Another common use is to pray that we'll be let off all the naughty things we've done today so that we can have a clean slate when we start doing naughty things tomorrow.

John Put this way, it does sound like the more primitive animist religions, doesn't it?

Robin Yes, but *all* bodies of religious knowledge are used in this way, by people at this level of mental health. It may be that more primitive religions specially lend themselves to this kind of thinking, and indeed may be used only in this fashion. But all the great world religions are treated like this too, because it's the only way that some people can understand them; if you like, it's the way those people *need* to understand them.

John So this magical approach to religion means that apart from repeating the spells, you don't have to make any other effort to achieve the desired result.

Robin Except that you have to *believe* in it deeply as well. Which is why such 'magic' sometimes actually works in situations where 'suggestion' can have a powerful effect, as for example in psychosomatic illness.

John OK. Now how does this magical approach differ from the value placed on religious practice by mid-range folk?

Robin Well, although we'll display a little of this magical kind of thinking, mid-range folk will be much more aware that what we desire will come to us through our own efforts.

John Like the old Puritan battle-cry: 'Trust in the Lord and keep your powder dry'?

Robin Exactly. In ordinary matters, the middle-rangers believe in hard work and planning. But, in moments of crisis . . .

John Ah, yes! Moments when your own efforts can't make any difference, like the times when you're waiting for the result of a cancer test. Then we – I mean, I – become much more child-like. Then I want to influence the physical world by magic, and make deals with God.

Robin And if it helps us to cope at a difficult time when our level of health has dropped temporarily, why not? It may be appropriate to what we need in that state.

John . . . Thank you for saying that.

Robin Sometimes we need to be kind to ourselves!

John Now . . . what about the Chosen Few, the Mental Health Freaks, the Psychic Gold Medal Winners. What's the attitude to religious practice at the top of the tree?

Robin I would guess that it's very largely aimed at achieving greater understanding. After all, the top level of health – which implies a truly scientific attitude – always seeks to *understand*. And remember what that word really means – to

'stand under', in the sense of seeing yourself as part of
something much bigger, infinitely more important than you
are.

John . . . As opposed to . . . ?

Robin Well, the rest of the time, we're fundamentally
egocentric – we're attempting to dominate in order to have
our own way and fulfil our personal desires, to impose
ourselves.

John Basic mid-range behaviour?

Robin Yes. Let's call that 'overstanding'. When you're
'overstanding', you're only really interested in what you're
getting in the short run; you're out for your own immediate
advantage, because you're not giving validity to other
people's interests; and also, you're ignoring most of the
consequences of your actions, as if you could somehow
control them! So for example, you're greedy for money, for
economic growth, and you don't see all the complications you're
going to create by, say, building atomic power stations, or
cutting down rainforests. And then the results will
eventually come round in a circle like a boomerang and hit you
– or your children – in the back of the neck.

John So the greatest value religion has for the very healthy is
that it increases their understanding. *How*?

Robin Well the key is this: they study the teachings of the religion, treating them not as commands, but as psychological information.

John All right, I need an example. What about the most basic of all religious values, 'Good'?

Robin All right. Let's start with the 'normal' attitude. How will our lot, the mid-range, treat the idea of 'Good'?

John Well the mid-range attitude of religious folk is to value highly the view that God judges people on how well they keep his rules. So they'll inevitably always be watching themselves and others, and judging every thought and feeling against those rules, to see if it's 'Bad'.

Robin So there won't be much spontaneity, joy and fun about. Now if people approach religion in this more rule-minded way, their fundamental aim inevitably becomes: Get rid of the 'Bad' – Enhance the 'Good'. So they'll be trying, all the time, to deny the negative feelings that we *all* have – anger, envy, jealousy and so on. In fact, many of them will actually feel that they've got rid of these negative feelings *altogether*! Of course, all they've done in reality is to *pretend* that the feelings aren't there – they've merely concealed them from everyone, even themselves. As we put it in our first book, they've put those emotions 'behind the screen'; and you know what happens next!

John Yes, the denied emotions are projected onto other people, who are then 'seen' as displaying them. Then the people doing the denying can attack those 'bad' feelings, by condemning the people who appear to be carrying them for them.

Robin This is what the basic mid-range approach is all about, trying to feel that you're 'Good'.

John I can certainly see this operating in myself most of the time. I mean, the tendency to judge – both myself and others. I try to fight it a bit, but it seems deeply ingrained. But are you saying that this way of operating will be found, in some form or other, all the way through the mid-range of mental health?

Robin Yes, though it becomes less intense as you go up the scale. So to give an overall picture: at the bottom level, you get people who don't just want to judge others; they want to persecute and punish them too, and they may rather enjoy that! As you move up the scale, getting healthier, people's feelings towards those different from themselves will pass from hatred, through suspicion and resentment, to moral disapproval and a desire to 'save' them. And finally at the upper end of the mid-range, people are thoroughly kind and compassionate, trying to be aware of their own faults, and struggling with them so that they can genuinely forgive them in others.

John That's how they avoid judging others?

Robin Well, they do their best not to, at least. After all, if you look in the sacred texts, there are enough warnings! Think of 'Judge not, that Ye be not Judged'. A clearer hint couldn't be given that what you condemn in others is also going to be present in you, too!

John And then there's Jesus' 'Don't point out the speck in your neighbour's eye, when you can't see the plank in your own'.

Robin As you see, the idea of denial and projection existed long before modern psychology! And the same idea is present in the New Testament in all the stories about the Pharisees. They represent people who are denying their nasty bits to enable them to feel 'better' than others. But it's made clear that the ones who can 'enter the Kingdom of Heaven' are the ones who are willing to admit their faults and see themselves clearly. As in Christ's tale about the publican who was collaborating with the occupying troops and ripping off his own people, and the upright Pharisee, who both go to the temple to pray. The Pharisee congratulates himself in public for his worthy conduct, while the publican beats his breast and says: 'Lord, be merciful to me, the sinner.' Christ declares the 'bad' publican to be good, and the 'good' Pharisee to be bad.

John In effect this is teaching healthy family behaviour, isn't it? It's encouraging us to acknowledge our faults and accept our ambivalent feelings – to get stuff out from behind the screen and stop projecting it onto others! It's all working against the tendency to split things up into 'Good' and 'Bad'.

Robin That's what understanding does for you!

John Yes, this all fits in with an observation of mine. I used to think that very good people would spend a huge amount of time making sure they were 'being good'. But now I've met some, it's clear they're not thinking in this way. In fact they're completely the opposite – they're the *most* relaxed and accepting kind of people . . .

Robin That's right. They don't feel the need to be judging and checking so much. Look at happy, contented, good-humoured forms of society. They're much less concerned about rigid moral demarcations than uptight societies. Compare Ladakh with Calvin's Geneva.

John So let's take this on a bit, into the way people behave towards each other. Take the value most of us would regard as the highest in this department – 'Love Thy Neighbour As Thyself'. What's the kind of 'understanding' the most healthy will apply to this?

Robin Well first, what's the least healthy interpretation?

John As a command, I suppose. 'Love Thy Neighbour As Thyself, or Thou Art For It'. Not an interpretation likely to sort the Balkans out overnight.

Robin No. But if it can at least be understood as a command to give others as much consideration as you give yourself, it can help to increase harmony in society.

John But will it? First of all, loving your neighbour as much as yourself is pretty difficult – practically bloody impossible, I'd say. You might as well have a commandment that states, 'Thou shalt fly', or 'Thou shalt move backwards in time'.

Robin True. But even trying, and discovering how difficult it is, can surprise and shock us into really wanting to make greater efforts – to struggle for the kind of personal change and deep self-knowledge that could make it possible.

John Yes, but we'd have to move one rung up the mental health ladder to think that way, wouldn't we? Meanwhile, if I'm trying to love my neighbour as much as myself, and failing dismally, I may feel bad about that, and start blaming the neighbour for not being more lovable, and making me feel bad about it. So, taken as an order, it might cause more harm than good, mightn't it?

Robin Of course it can be understood wrongly, as in the joke about the boy scout who was late for a meeting. He excused himself by saying that he had been told that boy scouts should help people, so he had been helping an old lady across the road. The scoutmaster said: 'But you're *very* late,' and the boy replied: 'I know, sir, but she didn't want to go!'

John So now tell me how the 'very healthy' will interpret this. How do they take 'Love Thy Neighbour' . . . as *information*?

Robin By looking at it as a law of human psychology.

John . . . What law?

Robin Roughly this: to the extent that you face and accept your own psychology, including all your weaknesses and faults . . . to *that* degree will you be able to accept and love others. And conversely: to the extent that you love others, to that degree will you be able to love yourself.

John . . . Yes, that feels right. Even if the original was punchier. The healthy families behave so generously to others, not because they're making a fantastic effort to be morally good, but because of their spontaneous open-heartedness, which comes from their acceptance of all the different aspects of themselves. Right.

Robin So if you understand 'Love Thy Neighbour' in this psychological way, you're getting some information about *how* to do it – which you don't hear otherwise. You're being told that loving yourself means accepting your 'bad' parts; that if you can accept them in yourself, you'll accept them in other people; and that then you have a genuine chance of being able to love others.

John Of course if you do take it simply as an order, at least it gives you an excuse. 'No, I don't love my neighbour, but fortunately I dislike myself equally. I have fulfilled the moral law,' and am therefore irreproachable. I'm sorry. I digress.

Robin You see, if you're mid-range and therefore haven't accepted all your own faults, you're likely to deny them and project them onto the people you're supposed to be loving, which creates a sense in you that you're *different* from them. And that makes it *impossible* for you truly to love them. You might be able to feel *something* for them – tolerance or pity – but it wouldn't really be *love*. Whereas if you take 'Love Thy Neighbour' as psychological information, you can start to try to put it into practice. And as you discover its truth, you'll change in a positive way which actually enables your love for your neighbour steadily to increase.

John Any other psychological advice contained in these five little words?

Robin As a matter of fact, there is. It's made clear that the essential thing is to aim to love your neighbour as much as you love yourself – not necessarily more!

John Good point. It is odd, isn't it, but we seem to think that *more* than equality is required . . .

Robin That's important, because once you've grasped this idea and started facing your own limitations, you really can begin to give equal validity to other people. You truly sense they are all as important as you. Then you can 'love your neighbour as yourself' – and that's all that's suggested.

John Yes . . . and without this information, and the changes it could bring, 'Love Thy Neighbour' can only be an aspiration, more to do with good manners and self-control.

Robin Which of course is better than bad manners and lack of self-control! But no matter how decent the person is, or how hard he or she tries, they won't be able to love in the way that's meant. *And*, they also won't know what's getting in the way.

John . . . I find this oddly convincing. But, take 'Thou Shalt Not Kill'. Now, can you interpret a value like that as 'psychological information'?

Robin Well, first, on the literal, factual level it means what it says, of course. Though even there people understand it in

very different ways. A really strict Jain will use a little brush to sweep the chair he's about to sit on, in case he squashes an insect; and cover his mouth to avoid harming one by breathing it in. At the other extreme, in some religions it's regarded as perfectly all right to kill unbelievers in crusades or 'holy wars'. In between, most of us would agree that the commandment refers to murder, but that it doesn't include killing to defend one's country, or family, or even oneself, against attack. Now on the psychological level, the meaning is in fact simpler and clearer. It refers to the psychological truth that if we hate and harm others in our thoughts and feelings towards them, this will inevitably poison the whole of our emotional state.

John The whole of it? Not just our feelings towards them?

Robin No, the whole of it.

John . . . You mean, you can't encourage a negative and unpleasant thought without having other similar thoughts appear?

Robin That's right. If you observe your inner world carefully, you'll see that allowing a single intense feeling of hate or violent self-pity – let alone nurturing it – can sometimes contaminate your internal atmosphere for the rest of the day!

John I know what you mean. If you feel someone is behaving unreasonably towards you, or even if somebody's merely carved you up badly while driving, you can let the business – no matter how small – prey on your mind in a way that takes you over; so that for the next few minutes, or hours, your whole view of the world is coloured by it . . .

Robin One driver makes you angry, and you start taking revenge on all the others!

John . . . But you can't *stop* aggressive or self-pitying thoughts from popping into your head, can you?

Robin No. But you can decide whether you're going to make light of them, or whether you're going to cherish them and nurture them and let them grow until they're really big.

John We talk about 'nursing' feelings like this, don't we – caring for them as though they were prize vegetable marrows. Look at mine, it's huge!

Robin Exactly. That's how we can 'kill' in our minds. And if we habitually indulge in such destructive feelings we become increasingly dominated by them. Moreover, we will have a poisonous effect on those around us even if these negative attitudes are never consciously expressed or acted upon.

John You mean if we're harbouring them, but trying to conceal them, we'll express them *anyway*, in ways we're not aware of.

Robin And others will register them at some level, and will be affected by them, and will probably be unable to avoid responding in some fashion, thus setting off a vicious circle of negative feelings.

John Yes, I see. But if we take 'Thou Shalt Not Kill' as psychological information, we may be able to stop the vicious circle from even getting started.

Robin Exactly. And the moment it starts is the easiest place to do that. So the smallest destructive thought really needs to be tossed aside straight away, or its power may grow.

John So, to return to our general theme: people at the top level of mental health take myths as psychological information, because this slowly brings them what they value very highly: the deeper understanding of their own psychic machinery which allows them more and more to practise the value contained in the myth. Whereas in the mid-range we tend to take myths as rules which emphasise the idea of Good and Bad: this can lead us to try to get rid of 'Bad' emotions by denying them and projecting them onto other people or groups.

Robin That's a fair outline.

John This doesn't put Fundamentalism in a very good light, does it?

Robin How do you mean?

John Well, everything you've been saying implies that it's a manifestation of a fairly low level of mental health, doesn't it? For a start, Fundamentalists call for a literal interpretation of scripture, and as we saw when we were discussing secular values, focusing in on the letter of the law is a characteristic of the less healthy. In addition, wise people tend not to exhibit literal-mindedness, so it seems singularly inappropriate to assume that this is the vein in which great spiritual teachers are speaking. Then again, whether we're talking about Christianity, Islam, Judaism or Hinduism, the values of Fundamentalists seem aimed at making themselves feel better by placing all negative and destructive emotions in people with different beliefs, and enjoying the golden glow of self-justification that results.

Robin Maybe. But you need to contrast it not only with the manifestations of religion at the levels of health above it, but also with the values of the level below. Just as a totalitarian political system at least provides some order and stability in a society that has degenerated into total chaos, so even a Fundamentalist value system can be a tremendous improvement in a society which was previously completely corrupt and where all values of human decency, honesty and respect had been lost. In fact, I think religious Fundamentalism tends to arise in just such situations of extreme moral decay or deprivation where only an extreme and rigid kind of correction can restore some sort of order.

John I can accept that so far as parts of the Middle East are concerned, given the level of poverty and desperation in much of it. But is it really true of the Bible Belt in the United States?

Robin Fundamentalist attitudes are always present in a proportion of any society, because there's always a proportion functioning at that level of health. And it may be more striking in the USA just because in other parts of the country there are such extreme attitudes in the opposite direction, towards complete permissiveness and self-indulgence – 'having it all'. On one of my visits to Texas a resident explained that church attendance was high because 'we ain't gonna let ourselves be Californicated down here'. And I really liked it there. I found California exciting, but also frightening because so many people seemed completely off the wall; there was no sense of stability and values were completely superficial. But I found ordinary people in Texas still very influenced by traditional values – neighbourly, warm, direct and straight.

John All right, I agree that it's better than *nothing*! But it's hardly the *best* interpretation of Christ's teaching, is it? You know that simile: 'As rare as a Fundamentalist who loves his enemy'?

Robin I don't believe you can talk about one level of interpretation as 'best'. It doesn't make any sense psychologically.

John *Doesn't* it? Look . . . the Inquisition did largely miss the point of 'Love Thy Neighbour', didn't they? Wasn't burning heretics 'worse' than being tolerant towards them? Or are you saying it genuinely is a valid, alternative interpretation of Christ's teaching?

Robin You're making the same mistake again. How people see 'better' and 'worse' depends on the level of health. And given the level involved, I'm sure many Inquisitors had convinced themselves that they were torturing people for the good of their souls. Just as the headmaster of my public school, who in most respects was a really wonderful man, probably felt it was necessary to beat boys for misdemeanours just as the other headmasters did. I don't believe he enjoyed it.

John I'm not sure that their victims would have found that equally persuasive. Surely the consequences were 'worse' from their point of view . . .

Robin I'm not saying I condone it in any way at all. It was a complete misunderstanding of the Christian message and human psychology, But I think you are still forgetting that these different ways of understanding value systems are all a 'natural', inevitable consequence of the levels of health of the people concerned.

John . . . You *really* don't feel you can talk about a 'best' level of interpretation of a myth? Isn't it 'better' to be 'healthier'?

Robin No. That would be like saying it would be best if everyone won the Olympic Games. Your view would only make sense if everyone was exactly the same, and that's not the way the world works. The point is, each person interprets the prevailing myth or religion in a way that is appropriate for them – the best understanding they can manage.

John . . . And you're also saying that no matter what level they take it on, it will still be useful to them.

Robin I do think that's so.

John . . . You've just made me think how much worse the Inquisition might have been, if they hadn't been Christians!

Robin Well, ponder the point. In really chaotic social conditions, people can have their limbs tied to bent trees by the local overlords so they can be pulled to pieces, just for the fun of it. And today, there are reports of South American drug barons regularly sending their henchmen out to capture young girls so they can all rape them as part of the evening's entertainment. But the important point I'm making is this: at the higher levels of mental health, people are mature enough to bear uncertainty, to think for themselves and to take more responsibility for their lives; so they will view religious ideas in a corresponding way. But if others are not comfortable with that amount of uncertainty, they'll understand the information as commands to be obeyed, because they function better that way and feel happier when there's someone telling them what to do. It's like children needing clear guidelines, firm limits within which they can feel their emotions are safely contained. Such people will simply be better suited by understanding myths as supporting them in keeping the lid on their emotions. And, of course, if they later change up to a higher level of health, their understanding will change accordingly.

John . . . Of course I've just realised what I've been doing.

Robin I wondered when the penny would drop.

John You rotten old shrink. You were waiting until I saw it myself, weren't you?

Robin I thought it was a good illustration of the points I'd been making.

John There I was, *judging* the *Fundamentalists*! Making the same mistake towards them that I was accusing them of making towards others . . .

Robin That's right. To spell it out, it doesn't make sense to judge and condemn those members of society who use religious ideas to judge and condemn others – in fact, if you do so you are obviously just joining them and misunderstanding religious ideas in the same way. Criticising, attacking or even making fun of them may make us feel a bit better temporarily, but it just locks them more tightly into their paranoid, black-and-white attitudes. In the long run they can only change, and we can only help them – and ourselves – to change, through understanding. Which means understanding ourselves, and seeing that in some part of us we are exactly the same as them.

John And that was my other mistake. Pretending all the

intolerance was in them, and thus avoiding seeing the intolerance in myself. Totally forgetting your 'Love Thy Neighbour' point. Oh dear, I'll never get to heaven now. I'd better sum up. All these Very Healthy Folk, these Golden Goodies, are taking their religious teaching as psychological information – as an instruction booklet, as you put it. This way they get to understand themselves better, and as a result can begin to behave better towards others.

Robin Which will gradually increase the level of health of people around them.

John But this isn't the only purpose behind this approach, is it? Presumably there's also a purpose that's more to do with the 'spiritual' – which would be a higher purpose, a *higher value still* for those who believe in such a force.

Robin Fair question. Well, I have to make a bit of a leap now, so I hope I can take you with me.

John Don't worry, I'll crawl doggedly along behind.

Robin You may fall in the river if you do.

John Why?

Robin You'll see.

John You're getting all mysterious, aren't you? Still I suppose it's an oracle's perk.

Robin I have to refer back to what we said about the most healthy people: that they have a strong sense of connection with the cosmos.

John You called it a feeling of being 'plugged in'.

Robin Yes. Now of course, we can't help being a part of the universe; we're part of it whether we like it or not!

John Agreed. It's not in fact a matter of choice. Not even for a Tory.

Robin No, but there's an element of choice in whether we *recognise* the fact. And therefore in whether we *feel* we're a part of it and so have that sense of connection, of belonging.

John And most people don't carry that feeling with them most of the time, do they? I don't, and I admit that in my capacity as a spokesman for the mid-range.

Robin No, the majority of us don't have that same sense of connection that the very healthiest folk experience more fully: a deep emotional feeling of being involved in the whole cosmic set-up, connected with it in a harmonious and pleasurable way.

John You've called it 'a sense of the universe as a giant support-system'. And you're saying that this feeling is something that the 'most healthies' are experiencing most of the time.

Robin Yes. And of course it's affecting the way they *think* too.

John So, are you hinting that this kind of feeling is some form of 'spiritual experience'?

Robin I believe it's the most basic form of it, yes.

John . . . Have you had any kind of spiritual experience yourself?

Robin Yes. An awareness of that kind has slowly developed over the years, and there have been particular occasions when that understanding seemed to deepen.

John Can you describe what they're like?

Robin The trouble is, it's extraordinarily difficult to describe to someone who hasn't experienced something similar themselves.

John The ineffable is in fact ineffable? Well, try and eff it anyway.

Robin I'll try. And prepare yourself for an anti-climax. It's a deep sense of the way everything is connected which you can't really put into words at all, because you're not really seeing anything new; you are just realising there's more significance in what you have been seeing all the time. But of course that will mean nothing to someone who is seeing the same facts, but not the pattern, the significance of the whole.

John I don't follow.

Robin Remember that story of the blind men who are all exploring, by touch, different parts of an elephant. They can't see the whole beast; they each think they have a different animal in their hands; and they speculate on what these different animals are like. Now if one chap suddenly gets his sight back, he'll see the elephant, and he'll understand that his limited perception had prevented him from recognising it before.

John Ah yes! And if he then tells the others about this discovery, they won't believe him. They'll say: 'We can't see any elephant. You're imagining it. You're being unscientific and going beyond the facts.'

Robin Yes. That's exactly the difficulty in talking about this subject. Or to use another analogy, it's as if we have blinkers on, like a horse, so we don't get a full picture. Imagine that we are looking all the time through little tubes, so that you and I, say, can see little bits of this room we're in, but never the whole room or the design and shape of it, or the relationships of one thing to another. A spiritual experience is like those blinkers coming off. You're getting a completely different impression of the world, but if you try to explain it to someone who's still got the blinkers on, you can't mention any detail they aren't aware of already and they don't know what you're talking about. You just end up speaking about the clarity and vividness of the impressions you're getting but can't convey what's new, 'the big picture'. In fact, when I opened up to this kind of experience for the first time I asked someone to write down the world-shaking profundity I felt I had come in contact with. The next day I discovered that I had said: 'Everything is exactly like it is, only more so!' Which in fact is quite a good description of a higher state of consciousness, but pretty useless to anyone who hasn't experienced it!

John Does that mean that you didn't 'see' anything unusual like angels or pink elephants? It was only your *perception* of what you saw that was extraordinary in its vividness?

Robin And its *connectedness*. Seeing the 'whole picture' made complete sense of all the bits of which it was composed, bits that were rather meaningless when viewed separately. What I mean by 'the bits' is the fragmented way we see the world in our ordinary state of consciousness; and by 'the whole picture' I mean the way you see it all fitting together when you're in that different state of consciousness which people call a 'spiritual experience'.

John Afterwards, how much were you able to retain?

Robin I couldn't of course go on experiencing the world in that vivid and connected way any more, though I can remember having done so and have had similar experiences since. And I have never lost the certainty that the world is actually like that, that it's designed to be as it is. I know it is 'all right' even at times when I haven't felt all right myself.

John A lot of people are very sceptical about this kind of thing, and feel these experiences are either partly imagination, or actual hallucination, and that the sort of 'sense of connection' you're describing is illusory. What can you say to them?

Robin Nothing really. If you begin to have this kind of deeper awareness, you know it's real, as I know for myself now. It has the force of experience, which as we said earlier is the most persuasive there is.

John Freud called it 'oceanic', and thought it was an emotional recall of the infant's experience before it had begun to separate psychologically from its mother.

Robin Yes. He sounded a bit rueful that he didn't experience it himself. And *before* I'd experienced it, I used to argue with people who had, trying to prove to myself that I wasn't missing anything. So you just have to report your own experience and leave it be, let people come to it in their own time, and hope they'll be lucky.

John All right. Now will you spell something out for me. What exactly is the *value* of an experience like this?

Robin It's certainly good for you in the sense that you gain a great sense of confidence and meaning.

John Ah. Say more about 'meaning'.

Robin Well, seeing 'meaning' is just understanding how things connect with one another, how they relate. It's seeing where you are, where you fit in, how everything fits together. And the overwhelming sense of connectedness you receive conveys a deeper understanding of the world we live in: you feel its order, its structure as a whole, its meaningfulness.

John Even though you can't really express in words what that 'meaning' is?

Robin Well, all the great spiritual teachings *are* expressing it. That's *exactly* what they're trying to convey. But, as I've said, you can only be confident of the truth of ideas on that great scale when you've *seen* them for yourself, when you're in a more awakened state of consciousness.

John The way you're talking about this kind of experience, it's hard to see how it differs from scientific knowledge.

Robin It doesn't really. Except that scientists are looking at 'bits' – physics, chemistry, biology and so on – and not seeing the whole picture, the whole elephant. Otherwise, yes, it's really all about discovering and testing things by your experience.

John You seem to take for granted the fact that the universe has order, a meaning, a structure. Do you believe this as a result of these experiences?

Robin I do now, yes. I've just seen that it *is so*. But until I saw it for myself, it meant nothing to me. Now I see that it's all of a piece, like those sticks of rock-candy which have the name of the town where they're made running all the way through them. In a sense, the right structure of society, the way it has to function if it is to promote the greatest welfare for all, is implicit in this sense of the order of the universe. So if we could perceive this order more directly, and become connected with that structure by direct experience of it, we would see what it was necessary for us to do, as members of society, for it to function at its best. And of course we'd be motivated to follow that magnificent pattern without the usual need for rules or rewards and punishments.

John Hang on. I see what you meant about 'taking a leap'! Are you really saying that the structure of the world, the meaning of life, the way we can function most harmoniously . . . is all staring us in the face . . . but . . . that we can't see it because we've got blinkers on, except when we're having these 'experiences'?

Robin Yes, that's exactly what I mean. Or putting it in other words, using computer language . . .

John And losing half our readers, including me . . .

Robin May I remind you that you've been talking about 'finding out about computers' for years and the great day gets mysteriously put off again and again?

John I've decided they're contrary to nature. Nevertheless I shall investigate them in my next incarnation. Do go ahead, please, and express your idea in this charming computer language of yours. My daughter can explain it to me later, when she gets back from the Brownies.

Robin Well, using that kind of analogy, I believe that we do in fact possess the 'hardware' with which to perceive this deep structure and order in the universe. However, I also believe that this particular bit of our mental equipment is almost always 'switched off'; it's 'switched on' only in moments of intense emotion and shock, like a birth, a bereavement, or some other profoundly important event.

John I think I know what you mean. At moments like that I can feel that my sense of what is important shifts and I become much more aware of what really matters to me. And then soon after, I move back to my everyday values and find it surprisingly hard to recapture this different perception about the real priorities in my life.

Robin That's just what I'm trying to describe.

John But hang on. You used the phrase 'switch on' just now. That suggests that the experience is all, or nothing. But you're not saying that, are you? The experience can be weaker or stronger. These pesky 'super-healthies' seem to be having a weaker version of it most of the time, we mid-rangers might very occasionally get a brief taste if we're lucky. But we're all merely getting a hint of something really huge, aren't we?

Robin Indeed. And I'm sure that anything I have experienced is only a faint shadow of what's possible. But even that can transform your life.

John Spill the beans, buster.

Robin My first experience came as a result of taking part in a research study, during my psychiatric training.

John What sort of research?

Robin Into LSD!

John . . . Are you telling me, Robin, that your first experience was *drug-induced*?!

Robin Yes. But I had such massive blinkers on at that time that I doubt if I would ever have allowed myself to have a 'spiritual experience' without a bit of 'chemical dynamite' to blow them off. So the drug temporarily stripped off some of my blinkers, and encouraged me to take this side of life more seriously, to investigate it.

John I think some of our readers may have their confidence in what you've been saying rather shaken by the revelation that you were experimenting with drugs, Robin.

Robin *I* wasn't doing the experiment; the hospital was. This new drug was being used in the USA as an experimental form of therapy, and one of the senior doctors wanted to test it out on some ordinary people first, before trying it on patients. So I volunteered, together with some other trainees, to be a 'guinea-pig' for this purpose and report the effects of receiving it.

John Did it make you want to take the drug again?

Robin No. For me it was like seeing a wonderful distant land from the top of a mountain. You knew that no matter how many more times you went up the mountain to look at it again, you still wouldn't really get any *closer* to what you'd seen. To get to it you had to go back down and make your way along the ground, which I've been attempting to do ever since. So I'm enormously grateful for that glimpse the drug gave me of what was possible!

John So your subsequent experiences weren't brought about by drugs?

Robin No.

John Did they vary much?

Robin That first experience was different from anything that came after because there was, first, the effect of the drug – like the brilliant sparkling colours and the impression that everything was wobbling – and second, the less blinkered view of the world the drug opened me up to. I have since repeatedly had the second type of experience, but since I haven't ever taken a drug of that kind again, not the first.

John Tell me about another one.

Robin It's a pity I had to start with that drug-induced opening to a deeper perception of the world, because I think it's leading you to expect more strange visitations. As if you're asking me: 'Have you seen any good flying saucers lately?' But the truth is much more simple and 'ordinary'. In fact, once you get a glimpse that your view of the world is normally blinkered, and that it's possible to see it more clearly, your interest naturally turns in this direction and you begin to notice things you ignored before. Just as, if you go to painting classes, you start paying more attention to shapes and colours and their relationships; they were always there to be seen, but you didn't see them before because you weren't paying attention. Similarly with this 'spiritual' interest, once you see that you have been missing something important, a steady interest grows and you look inside yourself more. And step by step, you gradually realise how accurately the great religious teachings describe what you are now observing. For example, you see *for yourself* the fact that if you hate others, you poison yourself; and that when you see your own faults, you can be compassionate about those of others. And as you see more and more of these truths for yourself, the world begins to make more and more sense to you.

John All sounds rather ordinary.

Robin It is and it isn't. Remember my insight into the 'secret of the universe': 'Everything is exactly like it is, only more so'! The experience is ordinary in the sense that 'everything is exactly like it is . . .' – that is, the details of the world don't change at all. But the '. . . only more so' bit transforms everything. In a more immediate physical sense it shows itself through a more intense awareness of everything around one – the beauty of trees, flowers, the sky, other people; and also of oneself, a vivid and immediate sense of being very alive – you experience *yourself* at the same time as you experience things around you. And along with this, you sense the connectedness, the wholeness of everything together. All of which, when you experience it, is immensely enjoyable.

John Do you feel this all the time, or intermittently?

Robin Both! I'll try to explain. Over the years this kind of deeper awareness and sense of connection has increased, so that to some measure it has come to be more frequently touched – to do so is more 'normal' and 'ordinary'. But it fluctuates. There are times when it seem to be nearer, more easy to contact, and more rich and intense. And in between it can seem further away, more of a struggle to attain to, even though you still feel nearer than you were in the past. Now, if you meditate regularly, and your interest draws your thoughts more in this direction, the moments of stronger consciousness become more powerful, and you feel generally closer to the possibility of it in between.

John What sort of help do you need to bring about this change?

Robin You can read about it in books, but you easily forget about it and don't sustain the search, just like it can be hard to stick to a diet or take adequate exercise or recreation. And you get it wrong: you soon misunderstand something and end up making the opposite kind of effort to what is necessary. So you need a guide, a spiritual adviser of some kind who is really like a coach – someone who has already achieved what you are aiming for and can see what you need to do next, and where you are going wrong. Usually you will join some kind of group for this help, and working with others not only makes it easier to remember your aim and work towards it, but seems to generate more energy of the kind you need. Certainly, my strongest experiences of what it's like to be more conscious, more 'all there', have been while meditating and working with others over a period of time; especially when one is helped by being with others to sustain some unusual effort over an extended period. For example, carrying out a physical activity like building, not only all day but all night as well. At times like that a wonderful stillness and quietness can descend upon you, in which you're given for a time a profound awareness of being alive, in a living universe. Of course there are many routes up the same mountain, and other people will find they're helped more through prayer, and other activities.

John Does it involve some kind of change in your understanding, as in psychotherapy?

Robin Well yes. This more direct perception of the nature of the cosmos is almost always accompanied by a much clearer perception of oneself, of one's own nature.

John Ah, I see. You can't see the world in this more profound way without seeing yourself more objectively too.

Robin That's it. During that first experience through LSD, a colleague who was not taking part in the experiment came into the room, and it was as if I could see right through him in a psychological sense. I could see all his faults and limitations – and can remember what I saw – but *I didn't feel critical at all*. In fact I felt great affection for him, for exactly what he was. At the same time, I seemed to lose all my own defences and need for self-deception, so that I could see my own faults clearly and accept myself despite them too. This seems to be a common experience – many similar ones were reported by the great psychologist William James in his book *The Varieties of Religious Experience*.

John But if you can suddenly see things about yourself that are ordinarily 'behind the screen', isn't that painful?

Robin It can be. There are occasions when your understanding goes through a kind of 'gear-change'. You feel stuck for a time and then suddenly all kinds of observations 'come together' and it may feel as if you've received a fresh vision of things. But if you reflect, you often realise that the new picture was building up over a long period, but couldn't be completed until one last insight was gained, one final bit of the jigsaw. And the key insight is usually a fact about one's own character that contradicts one's picture of oneself, which is therefore painful to see. Sometimes this kind of insight can only be attained in a situation of strong emotion or stress, or with the help of someone who understands much more than one does oneself.

John Can you describe an occasion like that?

Robin For me a very profound one was on a 'retreat', where the person in charge somehow made me aware of the ways in which I didn't consider the effects my actions would have on others, by clearly noticing it but not giving me a sense that I was judged or condemned in any way. Instead, I got a feeling of immense support. It was very painful, a crash course in unpleasant self-knowledge. But it was also wonderful; I felt loved and cared for in a way I had never before experienced.

John I think I have *some* notion of what you've been describing. But one thing puzzles me. To what extent was the experience *'spiritual'*?

Robin It was the heightened awareness and especially the sense of *connectedness*. I saw with inescapable clarity how everything we do affects other people, and how little I was aware of the effects, and how much harm that unawareness does to others. The profound detail of the insight, and of the chains of cause and effect stretching out in all directions from one's unconsidered actions, together with the compassionate yet relentless way I was brought to see it all, was such a clear demonstration of everything I had read in the great religious traditions. I was brought to experience what they were all talking about.

John So it was a profound realisation of how everything affects everything. A bit like Buddhist ideas about everything in the universe being connected in the cause and effect relationship of 'karma'.

Robin Exactly. And it had a profound effect on me. I have never forgotten it, and it seemed to give me a greater strength to face what I was being shown.

John So, to sum up, these direct and very clear perceptions of how the cosmos works have the following value. First, they are overwhelmingly persuasive: whoever experiences them 'knows' they are true. Second, they bring a sense of meaning and hence of security. Third, for a person who is religiously inclined, they bring a sense of direct contact with the spiritual force in the cosmos, which must, of course, be the highest possible value for him or her. Fourth, they give a deep sense of connectedness through an infinite network of cause and effect: this helps develop a deeper appreciation of how we might behave better towards other people. Fifth, they are available at very reasonable prices from Harrods Spiritual Capers Department . . . I'm sorry, I shouldn't have said that. Seriously . . . what's the effect on people generally of an experience like this? Does it change them noticeably?

Robin There isn't necessarily a major immediate change, but the insights gained can never be forgotten, so the experience seems to start people on the path of changing their life in a healthier direction. Not that it's easy of course! It's often a hard struggle to apply the new knowledge and to live in accordance with it.

John Do you think this is what is meant by 'a moment of conversion' in the conventional religious sense?

Robin It can be. The decision to move to a new philosophy of life – that is, the arousal of an overwhelming desire to do so – is usually a sudden opening to its truth. And often we've been resisting this idea for a long time, but the new information we've been getting has been chipping away to loosen our attachment to the old way of looking at the world, and then one day we can no longer maintain our old ideas in the face of the steadily accumulating evidence. At this point there's a sudden collapse of the old ideas, revealing the new ones which have been building up all the while. And yes, that's what religious people often call a conversion, an awakening, a rebirth.

John I was struck, reading James' book, by the struggle that usually preceded the moment of revelation. People reported a feeling of increasing stress that became quite unbearable, and which they simply couldn't handle by using their ordinary lifelong way of operating. And then they all had the experience of suddenly just 'giving up'! And that was the moment that they received their extraordinary experience.

Robin Which nicely illustrates the fact that what stands in the way of a deeper understanding of things is not a lack of knowledge, but an inability – or rather an unwillingness – to see what is in front of our eyes.

John But what is really 'giving up' or 'letting go' is the 'Ego', isn't it? Our normal everyday Ego – the thing that limits our perception of reality by screening out the bits about ourselves that we don't want to acknowledge. And we can't screen off those bits without also screening out a huge proportion of the rest of the information coming at us from the universe. It's our Ego that keeps the hardware switched off!

Robin Indeed. So these experiences are less likely to happen if we're denying a lot of our own faults by sticking the emotions connected with them behind the screen. If we wear blinkers to avoid looking honestly at ourselves, the same blinkers prevent us from seeing the deeper reality about the world we live in. So we are more open to this greater awareness of the world – provided we're ready in other ways – in those moments when our defences are down.

John All right. But as such experiences mean seeing yourself more clearly, then the less healthy you are – the more there is behind your screen – the more painful the revelation's going to be.

Robin That's true. So if people are very unhealthy, a revelation of this kind may 'blow their mind' to the extent that they can go crazy and lose contact with reality altogether, because they're simply not ready to stand so much truth about themselves. Or if they don't fall apart, the information they've received may get distorted and turned into something else in their minds, sometimes in a harmful or dangerous way – as when someone begins to think he's a kind of messenger from God who has the job of bumping off anyone who doesn't agree with him.

John And how will this kind of spiritual experience affect our mid-range group?

Robin Well in fact, I'm sure the majority who have an experience of this deep contact belong in the mid-range group, because there are so many more of us. But it may be painful, depending on how much we've got shoved away behind our screens.

John The one very limited experience of this kind that I've had was, oddly enough, more a total shaking-up than a cause of great pain – not so much a revelation of badness, but of triviality. But it had a vividness that gave it a terrific impact; it was much more unforgettable than any other ordinary experience.

Robin I think it's the shaking-up that counts – shaking us out of our habitual attitudes.

John And finally, our pals, the Moral Toffs, the people at the highest level of mental health. Presumably they'll find such experiences less painful and tend to have them more frequently?

Robin I think so. Although, as I said, these profound experiences can occur to anyone, the general rule is: unusual mental health goes together with a capacity to experience at least some degree of this deeper sense of connection. So, other things being equal, they're likely to see more, and to see it more often. And as they're more aware of their faults and limitations, this won't be so painful.

John . . . I'm wondering if many of our readers are slack-jawed at the two of us chatting away quite seriously about mysticism. I'm not sure how safe it will be to visit Weston-super-Mare in future.

Robin Yes, but these 'altered states' have been written about all over the world, at all periods, by thousands of people who've experienced them.

John Even by such respectable GCSE authors as Tennyson and Wordsworth and Coleridge – sorry, he was a druggie – and Chesterton and Yeats. And Blake, of course.

Robin And all the descriptions are remarkably similar, that's the surprising thing.

John And yet in my own Christian education, nothing of any of this was mentioned. The focus was on theology – on the map, perhaps one could say, rather than the territory.

Robin Well a preoccupation with theological beliefs is usually a substitute for spiritual experience, and can even stand in the way of it.

John It was a tremendous help to me to discover a few years ago Aldous Huxley's description of the two different ways in which religion can be approached. He speaks first of 'the religion of immediate experience – a religion, in the words of Genesis, of "hearing the voice of God walking in the garden in the cool of the day", the religion of direct acquaintance with the divine'.

Robin Wonderful!

John It sends shivers, doesn't it? Then Huxley contrasts this with the normal Western approach, which he calls, 'the religion of symbols, the religion of the imposition of order and meaning upon the world through verbal or non-verbal systems and their manipulation; the religion of knowledge about the divine, rather than direct acquaintance with it'.

Robin Go on.

John Well, Huxley's words gave me the confidence to pursue a line of thought that ran counter to my culture. I've updated it to something like this: I have a cat called Bernie. We have a very affectionate relationship, but to be brutal, I am a lot more intelligent than he is. In fact, I could say that my cat doesn't really understand me. His idea of my purposes in life would be, frankly, unreliable – probably worse than a London gossip columnist's. So I wouldn't want anyone to rely on Bernie's account of 'what I'm really like'.

Robin He's not planning a biography of you?

John Not yet. Now here's my point. If I use the word God to mean 'whatever's really going on' . . . I bet that the gap in intelligence between God and me is rather bigger than the gap between me and Bernie. So I honestly don't see the point in trying to describe what He's really like, or what He's up to because, frankly, he's right out of my league, Robin. I could not possibly fathom Him. Or Her. I mean, I'm sure Bernie suspects I'm *really* after mice. But I can conceive of the possibility that I might have an experience, a very slight kind of contact, a sort of divine pat, which would be important to me. And it might even be worth talking about *that*. But the *Trinity* . . . what do you think, Bernie?

Robin He doesn't seem to be listening.

John But coming back to the deeper, more connected experience of the world you were talking about, it doesn't seem to play much part in Western religions. Eastern religions seem almost to give it primacy.

Robin It's true that the experiences we've been talking about wouldn't seem at all odd to people from many other parts of the world – nor even perhaps to Christians of the Russian or Greek Orthodox variety. It's simply that in the West, this understanding of religion – which is often called 'mystical', or sometimes 'esoteric' – that is, concerned with the 'inner' meaning – has been rather pushed out of sight. But it does exist in writings stretching from St John's Gospel through Meister Eckhart and the author of *The Cloud of the Unknowing*, through Mother Julian of Norwich and St John of the Cross, to Thomas Merton and Bede Griffiths in our own day.

John If it's as beneficial as you say, why don't more people get involved in it?

Robin Because there's a huge obstacle right at the start. This mystical, esoteric understanding of religious teachings regards our ordinary waking state as mostly made up of imagination, as more like a kind of waking dream where we see others according to our expectations and prejudices rather than as they really are. But the trouble is that our lives don't feel like a dream; we think we're fully conscious already, so we don't realise we've been living mostly in imagination until we're aroused or startled into a more alert and attentive state, as we are in the kind of experiences we've been discussing. At *that* moment we're really awake, seeing things more objectively. But very soon we're back in another dream *imagining* we're continuing to be more alert and attentive! So it's extraordinarily difficult to escape from this self-deception, unless someone who's already more awake startles us out of these waking dreams by some kind of emotional shock, or gives us tasks to do which bring it home to us by the fact that we can't do them.

John Do you think this is what Plato's talking about in his myth about those people in the cave, their necks chained so they can't turn their heads, who think they are seeing the real world but are actually looking at the shadows cast on the cave walls by the fire behind them?

Robin I think so. Though the same idea is expressed in different ways in the different traditions. For example, Christ talks very directly about this fact that we're normally living in this state, which he calls a kind of death in which we are only half-alive, and says he comes to awaken us to 'life in all its fullness'. And the Hindus talk about 'maya', the Buddhists about 'sensory experience' as the obstacle to clear perception.

John And part of this 'waking dream' you're talking about is our false ideas about ourselves, our avoidance of seeing what we're *really* like?

Robin Yes, that's the basis on which the dream is built! And the more unhealthy we are, the more we're constantly polishing our self-image, noticing the bits we like and sheering away from the bits we don't. To keep ourselves 'looking good' we spend a lot of time 'rewriting the script' after any encounters where we don't perform according to our fantasies about ourselves. Obviously, all this self-deception interferes with our ability to see the outside world accurately or to be clear about our place in it. Until something shocks us out of it, we can't even start.

John I cannot quarrel with you about this. For several years now I've felt that a fundamental purpose of religion must be to help us strip away bits of our ego – 'Blessed are the poor in spirit'. This is because I simply can't believe we can experience anything important while we're pretending to be somebody we're not! As Christians put it, we need to be 'like little children'.

Robin In the sense that young children haven't yet learned to join in the self-deception we've all been taught by the time we're adults. As in that story of the 'Emperor's Clothes' where the little boy is the only one to see and express the truth straightforwardly.

John And such a child-like state makes these 'experiences' more likely? And vice versa?

Robin It's a circular process, I think. So although these feelings can begin to occur to people at any level of health, I believe that this greater sense of connection that they bring leads people to become more mentally healthy over time, more integrated inside themselves, less blinkered. And the other way round: the more mentally healthy and open to the truth we become, the more possible it is for us to have this experience of being connected with everything, at least in a very basic way.

John All right. Robin, we've been meddling in mysticism. Are you now prepared to reveal why some time ago you became all mysterious and sibylline and pythonic. You remember, when we got to the subject of how the 'most healthies' approached their religious teachings and practice?

Robin I wasn't trying to avoid the question. It's just that there's not much detail in the *research* on exceptionally healthy families about the nature of the 'transcendent value systems' they are said to operate by, beyond the fact that they find their 'meaning of life' in something beyond themselves and their families. My own impression is that the researchers themselves have very different attitudes towards this aspect, and don't investigate it very closely. After all, they don't claim to be exceptionally healthy themselves, so their own values are likely to affect their judgement. Also, at the time a lot of this research was done, too open a focus on the 'religious' aspect would have led many of their colleagues to reject the findings as a whole.

John Have any of the researchers committed themselves to a view about it?

Robin You'll remember meeting Bob Beavers, one of the main Timberlawn researchers who later became President of the American Association for Marriage and Family Therapy. He has been interested in this area, and recently said: 'In the years of studying family patterns, I have come to be impressed with one particular skill of an optimal family which up to now I have not stated publicly. This skill is as follows: to be able to know one's boundaries very well and operate accordingly, and then . . . to be able to abolish those boundaries and to become free – free of the limits of one's body, free of the limits of ageing and death . . . a person must let go of his ego, self, and share in a larger identity in order to be free of biological linear identity. . . . Optimal family members can switch, flexibly identifying with the larger world at times and then becoming quite clear as to being a particular individual.'

John All right. Let's see if I've got this straight. You're saying that the very healthiest folks are more likely to be drawn towards the so-called 'esoteric' understanding of the great religions. An esoteric tradition will enable a person to become more aware of his or her true self, to gain the self-knowledge which brings an increased likelihood of having these experiences we're talking about, which are often described as 'mystical' but which you're saying are clearer perceptions of the world.

Robin Yes, I *think* that's probably so. But as I've said, I'm basing that view not just on the research findings, which are still scanty, but on a combination of what there is, together with my professional experience of what happens when people become healthier, and my own personal experiences of the relationship between health and spiritual understanding. You're making the link between mental health and spiritual experience a lot tighter than I'm comfortable with. I've no doubt, as I've said, that good mental health, and the real sense of spiritual connection we're talking about, are linked. Each promotes the other. Healthier people do seem to feel a greater emotional sense of connection and belonging, and that sense of meaning and connection is a vital part of health. But I think that *something else* is required, before a person wants to *devote their life* substantially to a quest for deeper spiritual understanding. Some sense of vocation is probably needed, a willingness to sacrifice many other things to this search. And the more you've got – even in the way of health and happiness – the more you've got to lose! Of course it's possible that this is the highest form of health there is. But I don't think we can answer that on the basis of your knowledge or mine. I said before that for mid-range people like us, even trying to understand optimal health is like trying to imagine the view at the top of a mountain from half-way up the side. So I think that for us to talk about high spiritual development is like trying to imagine the view at the top of Mount Everest from base camp.

John All right. And whereof one cannot speak, thereon one must remain silent. So let's forget about 'spirituality' now, and welcome back at this point all our readers who think religion is a load of old rubbish.

It's nice to have you back with us, infidel heathen scoffers. And my next question to the notorious quack Dr Skynner is completely secular: how would you summarise the *purely psychological benefits* of religous practice at the most healthy level?

Robin It seems to me that an essential purpose of all the great spiritual traditions is to help us to be more whole, both within ourselves, and within the society we live in.

John In other words, the aim is integration?

Robin Yes. It's even there in the language. The words 'whole', 'healthy' and 'holy' all have the same root. They're all expressions of the same idea.

John Well this whole chapter has been about how we get our feelings of Value, and we've heard that the more *inclusive* a myth is, the greater its value. So whether we're talking about religious rubbish or secular sense we're back to integration again. That's what we come to at the end of every chapter! At the end of Chapter 1, you said how important it was for us to be able to integrate our parental part, our adult part and our child part – our Super-ego, Ego and Id – so that they were all available to us. At the end of Chapter 2, you pointed out how the healthiest organisations pass as much power and decision making as possible down the chain of command, thereby encouraging each employee to develop his or her autonomy, treating him or her as a whole human being and maximising his or her chance of real personal integration – as well as integrating all the parts of the organisation by insisting almost obsessively on communication. And at the end of Chapter 3 you laid out exactly the same principle with respect to a very healthy society. So it's hardly surprising we're back to it at the end of the chapter on Values. So please spell out why integration seems to be the ultimate value, the greatest expression of mental health.

Robin Because it's the opposite of *dis*integration, which is the expression of mental *ill*-health. In *Families*, I said that mental health, like physical health, is a matter of balance, of all the different parts of us operating harmoniously together. Disease and disorder mean that the balance is upset and some parts of us have too big an influence, others too little. For example, if our emotions get unbalanced in one direction we may get too excited and over-confident – mania; or in the other direction, despondent and lacking in energy – depression. Health is a balance between extremes of this kind. But if one part of us gets split off, denied, lost to us . . . our health is gone.

John We're unbalanced, we've disintegrated.

Robin Remember, one name for the Devil is 'Diabolos' – which means the divider, the splitter-into-fragments. Integration brings illumination and understanding. Disintegration brings darkness and meaninglessness.

John So does that mean that our degree of fragmentation is, as it were, a measure of our evilness?

Robin No, it's one step more complicated than that! It's not fragmentation itself that produces evil. It produces problems, yes, but not evil. It's the *denial and avoidance* of the fact of fragmentation – which is a deliberate, purposeful further fragmentation – that creates evil. If you can *see* fragmentation in yourself you are already connected to the problem, aware of it, and therefore moving towards integration.

John Which is why healthier people are more aware of their fragmentation than less healthy people?

Robin Exactly. Or to put it another way, once you see evil in yourself *as evil* it becomes hard to sustain it. The acknowledgement of it is the first step towards healing it, because it then becomes connected with other feelings that oppose it and want to change it.

John So evil is the avoidance of seeing that you are fragmented, split, sick?

Robin Yes. And because of that, if we want to remain evil we have to destroy anything good, *anything at all*. Because its existence would remind us, by contrast, of our own evil – and that would be a step towards integration and health! So true Evil seeks to wipe out anything Good, because Good will eventually include and balance and integrate the quality which, in isolation, creates Evil. Think of the concentration camps where the Nazi guards not only abused the prisoners but tried to make them perform evil acts too, to drag them down to their own level.

John . . . So all we have to do to increase our health is to become more aware of ourselves.

Robin And the same is true of the health of any group to which we belong – we all need to develop more awareness of the group.

John So this is why Katakis says that 'inclusiveness' gives a myth its greatest value.

Robin Right.

John . . . So what can any of us do to increase our degree of integration?

Robin Sit still.

John . . . Was I fidgeting?

Robin No, that's what you have to do. Sit quietly.

John Oh . . . that's *all*?

Robin Well you might meditate, or contemplate religious 'myths', or pray, but being quiet is the best start! I'll explain more in Chapter 5, when we talk in detail about what people can do about changing their level of mental health. But for now, let me say that just 'being quiet' helps us to be more 'together', more whole. Remember how I've explained repeatedly that most of our psychological problems come from *denial*, from not facing the truth about ourselves . . .

John I seem to recall something like that, yes.

Robin Well, remember this avoidance of the truth is a very *active* process. For example, we keep ourselves busy, and fill our minds with other things, in order to keep any painful emotions and memories at bay. Well, if we sit quietly, relax, let our emotions subside and clear our minds of thoughts, this avoidance can't go on. For a moment there's space, and openness, so we begin to be aware of the parts of ourselves we're denying. But because we are relaxed and calm, we can face what we were formerly avoiding without getting agitated or upset. So we can become more integrated, more complete.

John This ties in with the other measure of health, doesn't it – facing reality.

Robin How?

John Well, the territory is more important than the map, isn't it. You're saying the best thing we can do to integrate ourselves is 'study the territory' – *face our own experience*, without distractions.

Robin Yes . . . And let the information cure us.

Afterthought: The End?

John Do you realise we managed to talk about religion without even mentioning death! Yet for many people religion is mainly about the after-life and doesn't make any sense without it . . .

Robin But we're in good company in not making it the main issue. In those lectures William James gave in 1901–2 which became his book *The Varieties of Religious Experience* – it's still by far the best thing we've got on the subject – he apologises at the end for leaving it out altogether!

John But for Christians and Jews the idea of resurrection is absolutely basic, surely. And Hindus and Buddhists believe in reincarnation . . .

Robin Yes, there's increasing interest in that. Not least because there's been a lot of recent evidence from people who've been judged dead by ordinary standards, and then been revived, which has certainly made me think again about some kind of continuation after death. But first we need to talk about death, and the part it plays in our lives, before we get to the actual business of dying.

John You mean our lifelong awareness-that-we-shall-surely-croak?

Robin Yes, the whole way we approach the fact that our time here is limited.

John Talk about it.

Robin Well, when I began working with groups of patients during my training, I noticed after a year or so that the most important difference between those who were getting better and those who weren't lay in changes that were happening with the former lot in the kind of feelings and attitudes you could call 'spiritual'.

John In the broad sense . . .

Robin Yes, nothing to do with religious belief of a conventional, orthodox kind. In fact, the growth of this more 'spiritual' attitude often involved breaking with the religious attachment they had clung to up to that point . . .

John . . . Breaking with the way you were saying less healthy people use religion?

Robin That's right. Some of those who improved certainly lost the notion that just believing in some idea, or going through ritual observances, would improve their lives in a magical way. Instead, this kind of childish attitude would be replaced by a real sense of being part of some greater design.

John The 'sense of connection' we banged on about *ad nauseam* in the last chapter?

Robin Yes. Anyway, I noticed that as people developed this sense, a number of other things happened as well. They became more contented, more happy, more able to involve themselves – to make commitments to others, to their work and to their lives generally. So they enjoyed themselves more, developed deeper and more satisfying relationships, and began to live more fully. And as this happened the symptoms they'd come about – which were usually to do with being unhappy, or unable to make relationships, or experiencing a lack of meaning and connection with life – all these difficult feelings would fade, like marks on the sand when the tide comes in and washes them away.

John And what was the connection between all this and their attitude to death?

Robin They seemed also to lose these fears of extinction that they came with. You see, healthy people, who are fully alive, fully involved, fully committed, don't fear death. They're too busy getting the most out of life, too fulfilled to waste time on thinking about it except where there's some practical purpose, like making a will, taking out insurance for their family, or thinking how they'd most like to use the limited time they can expect.

John But isn't it very healthy to live with an awareness of the fact we're going to die, and to ponder on it sometimes?

Robin Certainly. The Buddhist master Padmasambhava said: 'Those who believe they have plently of time get ready only at the time of death. Then they are ravaged by regret. Isn't that far too late?'

John So those of your patients who developed this sense of connection were able to concentrate on the fact they're alive, rather than on the fact they're going fairly short to be dead. They see the glass as half-full, not half-empty.

Robin Yes. And more than that. If we are full of enjoyment and deeply involved with others, we're not half-full but actually *full* of good experience, whether we're seven or seventy years old. But if we are worrying about losing what we have, we'll avoid or limit our commitment and enjoyment in order to reduce the pain we'll feel, if and when that loss occurs. Then we create feelings of emptiness and loss and our glass doesn't even feel *half*-full!

John Rather like throwing away your dinner, so you don't have to face the trauma of eating it all and then finding you've finished it!

Robin Exactly. Crazy! But it's what we all do.

John And you're saying the people in your groups who didn't develop something of this feeling of 'connection' didn't get better in the same way as the others.

Robin Not to the same degree. I remember one chap who seemed to personify, in an exaggerated way, the people who didn't get better. He had terrible fear of open spaces, and of death. He spent most of his time in the group trying to convince others that religion was all rubbish, but there was a feeling of desperation about it. At any rate, his hostility to religion and need to attack it, as if he was frightened it might get him and eat him up if it got too near, occupied most of his attention; in fact it seemed more important to him than his incapacitating symptoms.

John How do you explain it?

Robin It was all a fear of loss of control: one aspect of which was a fear of commitment to other people, in case he became too dependent on them so that they were able to control him. And he similarly felt terrified of any sense of spiritual connection with the universe because that would mean he felt dependent on it – that it had therefore got him under its control . . .

John But by cutting himself off, he could 'feel' he was in control of everything?

Robin Exactly. So, as long as he behaved like this, he was able to preserve a fantasy of being completely independent of everything – the ultimate outsider, lord of creation, master of all he surveyed. And he extended this idea *ad absurdum*: he feared committing himself to life because that would mean that it could be taken away from him and he would have to accept the fact of death.

John . . . Not being alive meant he felt he had control over death?

Robin Exactly. It doesn't make sense at all when seen by someone else, from outside. But for someone trapped inside this kind of thinking it all seems logical enough. To them, it makes sense to avoid living their life too fully, because then it will hurt less when they ultimately lose it.

John Like keeping the brakes on in a car to reduce the damage if you have a collision.

Robin That's the kind of thinking it's based on.

John And of course this attitude of 'stop-the-world-I-want-to-get-off' prevents a person from making the most of their life.

Robin That's right. Those who fear death, fear to live fully; so they are half-dead already by their own choice. And their terror of losing their life is, paradoxically, a fear of dying before they've decided to start living! Which they fear to do, of course, because of the fear of losing it eventually.

John Muriel Volestrangler couldn't have put it better herself. So . . . it's a Catch-22.

Robin It's such crazy thinking that I always have to say it to myself several times before I can get my mind around it! But once you *see* that's what it is, then you can just break out of it, and start living.

John But *how* do you 'just break out'?

Robin It's the same as walking.

John *Walking* . . .

Robin Tell me how you walk. What movements do you make to do it?

John You put one foot forward, and then the other, and off you go.

Robin No, you don't. That would be marking time, goose-stepping in place. You wouldn't move forward at all.

John . . . I'm embarrassed. I thought I'd mastered this.

Robin You *fall*.

John Oh *yes*! *Absolutely*! Yes! I knew that really . . .

Robin If you watch what you do when you walk, you'll find that you begin by leaning forwards. You actually let yourself *fall* – that's what the movement forwards really is. And then you save yourself by moving one foot forwards under the new changing centre of gravity. You do this over and over, but the movement forwards is always falling, until you decide to come to rest and lean back to bring the falling to an end. Try it. It's easier to experience the falling part if you walk backwards, which is less habitual, and where we notice the individual movements more easily.

John *Of course* you fall. Everybody knows that. But what's this got to do with death?

Robin Well, to live fully involves the same kind of movement as walking, but in a psychological sense.

John . . . You mean, not being afraid of falling forward into the future? Letting go, instead of trying to control things by holding back.

Robin Exactly. Going with the flow. Accepting what comes, being fully alive and aware each moment. Not trying to cling to the past. Then there's no fear, you embrace life with a 'go for it' attitude and extract every bit of experience and enjoyment there is. But of course, to do that is to *accept that you are falling forwards towards your death.*

John Which we're doing anyway. Refusing to accept it doesn't slow things down.

Robin No. And yet the fearful, hesitant, foot-off-the-throttle-and-always-on-the-brakes attitude *is* trying in some illusory way to stop time. And what I'm trying to convey by this image of walking is the attitude that can lead to really exciting, happy and productive living. Because living should be a constant dying to the past. Of course, we keep the past as a memory, inside us – even loved ones continue to live within us when we suffer a bereavement – but only if we stop clinging and let go completely of what is finished in the actual world.

John But most of us resist change, by clinging on to all kinds of things – to people, to our social group, to a particular place and time, to routines, and to attitudes, views, even to ideas about ourselves . . .

Robin . . . To whatever. It's all like clinging on to a teddy bear.

John All right. So you've explained in general how we're affected throughout our lives by the fact we're mortal. So, moving on . . . *as we get older,* we become *increasingly* aware that death is getting nearer, that our short span is becoming *even shorter* . . .

Robin Yes. We usually don't think much about death in our twenties, but in the later thirties and early forties we suddenly realise it's half-time. If we've coped adequately with the world of work and been reasonably successful, we feel it's been OK, but it can all begin to seem a bit empty. All the things that mattered to us up to this point – success, achievement, material possessions, the opinion of others – no longer seem worth so much.

John Mike Nicols told me that his brother, who is a doctor, says that he's never yet seen anyone on a deathbed who has confessed: 'I wish I'd spent more time at the office.'

Robin Beautiful! So, around this age, we begin to feel there must be something more, but we can't see what it is.

John So is this the essence of the 'mid-life crisis'? The first half hasn't seemed all that long, you feel you've wasted a lot of time, you're not very satisfied with what you're doing now either, and life suddenly feels very short? *And* you don't know what to *do* about it . . .

Robin That's why we feel depressed. It's a healthy reaction, a sign that we are re-drawing our map of the world, changing our values. And if all goes well at this stage, our disillusionment with the conventional stereotyped values we've been operating on leads to a turning back towards the inner world, and the deeper, unchanging satisfactions of life: exploring more deeply our relationships with people; attending much more to nature, beauty, art; and getting more interested in spiritual teachings and what they tell us about the meaning and purpose of life. Of course, we don't lose what's real in our education and experience! Our knowledge, skills, social competence and ability to do useful work and earn our living are all still *useful*! But we come back more and more to a strong inner life, where we become interested in exploring things and parts of ourselves that up to now we've neglected. We begin to do things that we personally value rather than things we feel we *ought* to do!

John That's exactly what's been happening to me. Projects I would have pursued almost without reflection a few years ago I now find quite unappealing – they feel pointless, as though I've 'done that' and won't learn anything from getting involved. Yet the pleasure I get from simple things, unconnected with 'success', is so enormous that life feels infinitely richer.

Robin That's what happens, *provided* this turning away from previous ambitions towards the inner life isn't resisted. Life does get richer and more enjoyable with advancing age. So in terms of how a person *feels*, it's as if one gets older until the forties, and then you begin to feel as if you're getting younger again.

John I'm certainly feeling younger *psychologically*. So is this something to do with the idea of a 'second childhood'?

Robin Absolutely. Of course, some people see this change as negative – getting less conventional and hard-working, more irresponsible. But others see this stage of life as much more interesting – more happy, more relaxed, more enjoyable, more fun.

John . . . And more *playful*.

Robin That's *right*! The key to the idea of a second childhood is that after forty we begin to rediscover something we had as children, but lost in our twenties – playfulness! You see, when we're born, we begin by being completely ourselves, not yet affected by other people and their attitudes and problems. We're real, spontaneous, natural, and fully alive. In the first few years life for us is *play*.

John Amusing ourselves and discovering things for their own sake, because *we're* interested. It all comes naturally.

Robin Yes. We're true to ourselves because we don't know any other way of operating. But from early on, we're learning what our family approves of, or disapproves of, or denies the existence of. By the age of four we are beginning to copy, imitate and take on the beginnings of the adult role. One charm of this age is the mixture of both, the way children are *playing* at being *adult*, wearing Mummy's high-heeled shoes, Dad's trilby hat.

John And getting praise for being more 'grown-up' as they learn to fit in.

Robin So this period is the beginning of the end of that early time where we are truly ourselves, living according to what our essence is. From then on the pressure of family attitudes, and then school, socialisation generally, and later the world of work and outer achievement, increasingly buries that fresh, essential part. We lose touch with it as we come under the control of all the other influences.

John And also we come to live by comparing ourselves with others; each person ceases to be unique, and is valued by others, and learns to value themselves, against some common yardstick. Everyone ends up wearing jeans, or bowler hats, and worrying about whether they're 'getting ahead', or 'falling behind'.

Robin Yes. And this burying of the original, spontaneous part, this alienation from our essential self, reaches its peak in our twenties and thirties. You only have to watch a few lager adverts to see what I mean.

John So this world of *work*, of achievement, of 'proving ourselves' . . . do you think it's in any way harmful?

Robin Not at all. It may sometimes feel rather boring to be with some people that age, or to remember how one was like that oneself, because our interests have changed. But it's a normal, necessary part of the growth process. We have to go through it. We have to learn how to deal with the world, earn our living and play a useful part in practical affairs. But we do lose something immensely valuable when we lose touch with that child-like, spontaneous, essential part that's able to *play*.

John And you're saying that we re-connect with that again as a result of realising, bit by bit, that our time on this planet is getting shorter?

Robin Re-connect, and appreciate it all the more for having lost it temporarily.

John All right. But I've suddenly realised something. We're talking blithely about 'play' . . . I'm not sure I understand enough what you're meaning by the word.

Robin Well there's a wonderful book on it called *Homo Ludens* by Johan Huizinga which seems to explore every facet. But the aspects I'll pick out are these: first, it has to be voluntary: the impulse has to come from within – you have to *choose* to play. Second, though in a sense it's 'not serious', it *is* serious in the sense that it's completely absorbing, we give it intense attention. Third, we give ourselves to it without our usual reservation or calculation. We're disinterested, free of ambition or preoccupation with 'success', because there's no profit or practical advantage. Fourth, it's about discovery, about creating order and understanding. Fifth, we also feel uncertainty and tension when we're engaged in it. The fact that it's spontaneous puts us at risk, and at risk especially of discovering ourselves more fully. And finally, like Plato, Huizinga sees play as putting us in touch with, and expressing, that deeper level where religious understanding is to be found.

John It all rings true, but it's getting more complicated! Can you simplify it?

Robin When we play, we are getting more deeply in touch with, and living out, the most essential, most real and unique part of ourselves. So the increased relaxation and playfulness of the second half of life and the greater interest in relationships, nature and spiritual matters which accompanies it, are all part of the same thing.

John And this goes on right to the end?

Robin As far as I can see it does, at least in those older people I've known who are healthy and happy. I can only speak for myself, and say that life has steadily become more enjoyable for me. I've felt increasingly free and relaxed and playful as I've got older, compared with how I remember myself before I was about fifty. So I think the movement towards greater playfulness and depth of enjoyment must continue and accelerate until the moment of death, because the awareness of limited time 'concentrates the mind wonderfully', as Dr Johnson said of the prospect of being hanged, and makes one increasingly aware that nothing else matters. The last part of one's life can be the most fulfilled and happy of all, even making up for all past unhappiness. After all, when you finally see the truth of something, the length of time during which you previously *failed* to recognise it doesn't matter.

John Is that really so?

Robin Of course. For example, if through some misunderstanding you come to think that someone you trust has betrayed you, and later you suddenly discover they haven't and that it was all a mistake, that moment of truth cancels out all the past unhappiness where you feared the worst. You now have a friend who has *always* been trustworthy, not a friend who *was* untrustworthy and suddenly isn't. Not only is the present changed, but the record of the past is also corrected, and you can now feel happy about both. I suppose you might kick yourself for making the mistake in the first place, but that's something else.

John So, Doctor, the distant approach of the Grim Reaper is really a cause for rejoicing, since it causes us to reassess our lives, to discard those of our attitudes that are holding us back, so we can move forward into a much more enjoyable, fulfilling and playful phase.

Robin The awareness can have that positive effect, yes.

John *Nevertheless* . . . while we've been writing this book, I remember how over and over again we've seen that death was at the centre of what we were discussing – and then we would forget about it for months, until we realised we had tuned it out again.

Robin That's because it's surrounded with so much anxiety, and it affects us as much as everybody else.

John I see. Um . . . well . . . *now* we have, in fact, reached the topic of . . . as it were, *dying*. We can't put off looking at it any longer . . .

Robin Well, we haven't *quite* got there yet.

John Phew!

Robin I know you'll think I'm changing the subject, but we need to talk about the period immediately before death – that part of life when we know we only have a certain short time to live.

John So what's known about that?

Robin Going back to the basic principles of what we've said about change, the knowledge that we're definitely going to die within a limited time means facing a massive change, a dramatic loss of hope and expectation. So the map of our world is suddenly useless, and unless we've been facing the fact of death and preparing for it earlier in life, we almost have to start again from scratch. So it's a huge stress, and after the initial numbing shock there'll be a lot of sadness, appropriate to such an all-important loss . . .

John Which if it's avoided, will lead to a freezing-off of emotion – that is, depression?

Robin Correct. As we discussed in great detail in *Families*, depression is a refusal to change, a clinging-on to previous expectations, the old map. And freezing-off the painful feelings simply means they don't get dealt with; though of course they are there underneath, and may express themselves in emotional or physical illness of some kind. So whether it's the impending death of a loved one, or our own end, what happens at this point depends on the extent to which the loss is faced. This process has been studied by a number of people, but Elizabeth Kübler-Ross, who made a life-work out of helping the medical profession to understand dying, noticed a series of different reactions which frequently seemed to follow one another, though they could overlap too.

John What comes first?

Robin First of all, as we've said, there's shock, numbness of feeling. People tend to deny to themselves that the sentence of death has happened. Then when that wears off, it's followed by anger . . .

John 'Why should this happen to *me*'?

Robin Yes. And the less down-to-earth the person is, the more likely they are to rail against fate, or blame the doctors, or anyone else available – or themselves by feeling endlessly guilty, which is really another version of the same thing . . .

John . . . Is this the feeling that they should be able to control the world, and stop anything happening that they don't like?

Robin I think that's what it's really about. It leads into a phase Kübler-Ross calls 'bargaining', which is still a hope of controlling the situation, but now by some kind of deal, rather than just an angry demand to have one's own way.

John I don't understand. Who are they bargaining with, Fate?

Robin Or God or whatever. When people react like this they are doing so with the Basic Bit of the personality we called the Child, understandably wanting some Parent to make it all better. But gradually, as reality is faced and the map begins to be re-drawn, there is sadness, grief, which as you said may be blocked and lead to depression. But if the pain is faced, the map gradually becomes re-drawn to accommodate the massive changes that have to be adjusted to, and then the final phase of acceptance follows. Now there's space for positive feelings like love and gratitude and enjoyment of life to return.

John This phase *really* does occur?

Robin It certainly does – provided the person finally gives up the demand to control this most uncontrollable of events. If you visit a hospice you'll be left in no doubt about how positive it can be.

John . . . And then, finally – Dead Parrot Time. Becoming an ex-me. Discuss.

Robin Well, as I don't need to tell you, the answer is: no one actually knows! Or if they do – people who claim to have lived previous lives and been reincarnated, for example – the evidence is accepted by some and disputed by others. Of course, it's part of the beliefs of every civilisation that survival of some sort occurs. But that just means it's part of the particular myth they operate by. And the myths are different, so they can't all be true, or the whole truth. So it's all still an open question.

John Excellent waffle. What do *you* think?

Robin Well, I'd always assumed that everything came to an end at death, and it didn't worry me. I've never seen any reason why I should be worth preserving, and I've felt content to enjoy life now, particularly relationships, and to develop my talents and grow through my experiences. But in recent years, I've begun to get a bit worried that there may be an after-life of some kind . . .

John . . . *Worried*! Why worried?

Robin I suppose because it means a massive re-drawing of my map – the same scale of change that *losing* a belief in an after-life would mean to someone who has always assumed it was true.

John What made you change your mind?

Robin Well first of all, the rest of the universe being the amazingly efficient place it is, I think it would be very odd if that more essential, spiritual part of us that I am certainly aware of wasn't recycled and put to further use. Then I began to discover that there's a lot of very strange evidence on reincarnation, which is hard to reject or find a different explanation for. I don't mean there's any clinching set of facts, just the scale of the research and the convincing detail of a lot of it. So that has made me more open-minded about the possibility, at least.

John Some of the cases investigated by Professor Ian Stevenson of the University of Virginia are extraordinarily persuasive.

Robin Nevertheless, for me the most convincing evidence that something continues after death is all the records we now have from many authors about what's called the 'Near-Death Experience'.

John That's where people who have been thought dead, with all the medical signs of having gone too far towards death to recover, then come back to life, and can recall what happened when they were near to dying.

Robin Yes. Some of the first accounts of it were reported to the Swiss Alpine Club by a geology professor, Albert Heim. As a keen climber he had some near-fatal accidents himself, and was surprised by his reactions. He found many other mountaineers had undergone similar experiences when they had been facing death, so he got interested and investigated it more closely.

John What did he find?

Robin The first thing was that there was no pain, or strong anxiety, or grief or despair, at the prospect of imminent death. Instead, they had all accepted their perilous situation calmly; perception was very clear; and time expanded as if a second became a minute, or a minute became an hour – there was all the time in the world to react, so any reactions were lightning-fast.

John That all seems stuff that would be developed for normal evolutionary purposes. The numbness you get after a severe shock, and the greater efficiency in reaction, would both have survival value.

Robin Agreed. But the other facts Heim found can't be explained quite so easily. For example, there was often a rapid review of the person's past life.

John Like the traditional idea of a series of flashbacks, a kind of Edited Highlights of My Life?

Robin Yes. And then they described hearing music and seeing scenes of transcendental beauty. Some saw a figure coming to meet them.

John Yes, the Darwinian explanation of all this would be in terms of the unconscious providing alternative entertainment to take the mind off present prospects.

Robin The opposite of what the explanation was just now? Anyway I just mentioned Heim for starters. Many other researchers have now investigated this near-death experience, in hundreds and hundreds of cases. The people they talked to all reported very similar experiences.

John Such as . . . ?

Robin They usually said that the moments when they were thought by the medical staff to be at the point of death – or actually dead by the usual medical criteria – were generally very positive. There was a sense of peace and well-being, an experience of beauty, joy, love. And coinciding with the medical signs of 'brain-death', about half of them reported leaving their body and seeing it from above, as if they were spectators at their own death.

John With no pain or anxiety?

Robin Certainly no pain. It was as if their physical suffering was now over. They often felt surprised, and wondered what would happen next.

John And what did?

Robin There would be a sense of movement at great speed through a black space, often described as a passage along a dark tunnel. But there would be an increasing awareness of a light at the end of it, and this would get brighter and brighter as they approached it. Then they would feel themselves entering a world from which this light was coming. What they experienced at this point seems to have been indescribable. Most spoke of great brilliance and surpassing beauty. And they felt some kind of presence – some kind of 'being of light' which was radiating love and compassion, and enveloped them warmly. Some even described this being as having a sense of humour!

John I *like* that! A warm-up man at the Heavenly Gates. But I'm not clear – this 'presence' was a person of some kind?

Robin People experienced it differently. For some who were members of a major religion, this guiding presence might be experienced as God, Buddha, Jesus. For others it doesn't seem to have had an identifiable form.

John So it was an entity which some people experienced in the light of their religious ideas. Now . . . what did they all *feel* about this experience?

Robin The whole thing was usually so positive that they wanted to stay, and didn't want to return to their life on earth.

John Why would they be *expecting* to return?

Robin They weren't. By this time they felt glad to be in this new world they had entered. But what happened next was this: they were told that their time to die had not come, and that they had to return to earth and complete their span.

John Were they told why?

Robin Yes. The reasons given would be either that others still needed them – their children, for example – or that there were things they needed to complete in their own life and development, something they had to learn which wasn't finished.

John And these reasons were too good for them to dispute?

Robin Yes, typically they accepted that it was necessary to come back and serve out their full term! But the point is that their motivation to return to life was usually selfless and had the sense of service to a higher purpose.

John So what was the longer-term effect of these near-death experiences as these people carried on with their lives?

Robin It seems to have been very positive. They describe feeling renewed, as if starting life again. They seem to have become more open and loving and compassionate. Material issues had become less important to them.

John Anything else?

Robin They usually felt a responsibility to develop their unused gifts and talents, especially to serve others. And it left them wanting to achieve a deeper understanding of life, to search for the purpose and meaning of it all. Their view of religion was usually changed; there was a greater sense of direct contact with some higher power. But this was accompanied by a more relaxed relationship to formal religious observance, as if that was less important than the direct inner experience they'd had a taste of.

John So a high proportion of these experiences brought a much stronger interest in spiritual matters.

Robin Indeed. A psychologist called David Rosen recently studied people who had tried to commit suicide by jumping off the Golden Gate Bridge in San Francisco, and failed.

John They missed the ground?

Robin I imagine most were aiming for the sea; anyway, they landed *relatively* safely.

John And lived to tell what tale?

Robin *Every* person reported during and after their jumps 'feelings of spiritual rebirth and unity with others, the universe and God'.

John Our old 'sense of connection'?

Robin Yes. As a result many of them underwent quite dramatic conversions.

John Perhaps the Church of England would do better if they incorporated some kind of bungee-jumping into Morning Service. So . . . how does the experience of a dummy-run like this change someone's view of death?

Robin That's one of the most striking effects. People who've been through this experience seem to lose their fear of death, and it leaves them with a greater conviction of an after-life.

John All very positive. A Doctor Pangloss like you must be pleased. But didn't anyone have a negative near-death experience?

Robin Some do. They seem to be very much a minority, though there's the question whether some people have a negative experience and then forget it. However, even where it's negative, they still have an experience of *some kind of continuing life*. But instead of the feeling of calm and acceptance, there's panic and a sense of evil, and then of entering a hell-like environment.

John Is there anything to suggest how people who have a negative experience differ from those who have a positive one?

Robin It's not clear to me from the accounts. But I would expect that they would be people who have harboured powerful negative emotions. There's some very interesting research by Grof and Halifax which supports that possibility, about the experiences of cancer patients who were given the hallucinogenic drug LSD. Many of their patients had positive experiences in some respects very like those reported by the people we've been talking about who came close to death. There'd be a sense of wonder and awe, of deep purpose and meaning, of vivid awareness of nature, and often the religious feeling of an 'oceanic' kind I've described. It could include a replay of their life, or in some cases even of past lives. And as with those who went through the near-death experience, their anxiety about death would disappear because it was no longer seen as the end of everything but as some kind of transition of consciousness. But *some* of these patients had very negative, hell-like impressions, with great pain and suffering. They seemed to be the ones who'd had very unhappy lives, such as being rejected and treated cruelly in childhood, and in later life they carried great animosity and bitterness, or other negative feelings, in response to that.

John So you suspect that the kind of near-death experience a person has may be determined by the emotional tone underlying their psychological make-up?

Robin Coloured by it, yes.

John Inevitably it carries echoes of religious ideas of heaven and hell.

Robin It does. But of course those ideas are understood differently by people at different levels of health. At a low level where thinking is very primitive and concrete, and the feeling tone is generally negative, religious teachings about 'heaven' and 'hell' are likely to be taken literally, as geographical places somewhere outside oneself to which one is assigned at death according to one's conduct in life. But for those who are more healthy, they are more likely to be seen as inner states of mind. That is, if we choose to nourish our negative emotions, they will steadily increase in power until in the end we find ourselves living in a self-created hell-like inner world, where we are at the mercy of our most violent and destructive feelings. While if we forgo the immediate satisfactions of such emotions, and struggle instead to relate to others in a more affiliative way, positive emotions will grow, negative emotions will gradually lose their power, and life will be experienced more like descriptions of 'heaven'. In some religious systems, like Buddhism, this kind of interpretation of 'heaven' and 'hell' is quite explicit. And all this makes perfect sense in terms of what I see in mental illness. Now in fact, even the negative experiences of this minority of cancer patients and near-death survivors often had a positive effect. A number of them came back from their 'trip' on the drug with a vision of how the awful events of life, which we see with our limited understanding as so unfair, all formed part of some greater scheme where events balanced up and everything seemed all right after all.

John The sense of things being *somehow* 'all right' and meaningful, which is the characteristic of 'mystical' experiences . . .

Robin That's right.

John I must say, I *like* all this stuff about near-death experiences. It makes everything more uncertain and much more interesting. Still, I feel the same about the Loch Ness Monster, too . . .

Robin Well the really nice thing is . . . we don't have to make up anyone else's mind about it!

5 All Change Please

John So far in this book we've been discussing what characterises unusually healthy behaviour for individuals and families, for organisations, for societies, and for value systems. Now I want to ask you a different type of question. If we accept some of this stuff, what can we do about trying to improve our level of mental health?

Robin As individuals, you mean?

John Yes; but also how we can help improve our families, any organisations we belong to, and the society we live in, too. The lot.

Robin Well, first of all, we need to get one thing clear. Changes in the level of people's mental health are happening everywhere all the time. In both directions. As circumstances change, our levels of mental health go up and down. For example, too much stress will tend to make us less healthy. But when circumstances improve, say, after three weeks' holiday when we're getting on well with our family, we'll be operating at a healthier level again.

John In the same way that the spirit in a football team deteriorates if they're on a losing streak? Then if they start winning again, confidence returns and the team's attitudes become more positive, cooperative and healthy.

Robin And similarly, people in a company will behave less healthily if they fear that the company's going belly-up and their jobs may be lost. The same with a society where people feel very threatened because unemployment is high, or law and order has broken down. So . . . none of the previous chapters should be taken to mean that anyone's level of mental health stays constant.

John Point taken. Now tell me what steps we can take to become a bit healthier.

Robin Let's start with a few basic principles on the subject of change. We are constantly changing, biologically speaking; our immediate environment is changing, in that we are regularly confronted with new developmental life-tasks – being weaned, leaving school, getting married, raising children, taking more responsibility at work, coping with retirement, and so on; and beyond that the whole world is changing around us as well. So we have to change constantly too, in the sense of continually revising our knowledge, attitudes and feelings – what we've called 'the maps of the world that we carry round inside our heads'.

John So how do we do this?

Robin Here's my basic proposition. Ready?

John Ready.

Robin If we are living in reality, and communicating clearly and honestly, life will change us automatically!

John . . . Without our having to do *anything* else?

Robin Yes, because the information we need in order to know how to live our lives is coming at us all the time. So if we are open to it and allow ourselves to be affected by it, we'll change inwardly to match the outer changes, and adapt continually.

John You mean, by staying in contact with reality, which is always changing, we'll maintain our level of mental health, rather than falling behind, getting out-of-date.

Robin More than 'maintain' it. We'll improve it.

John Why 'improve'?

Robin Do you remember what I said in those conversations we had in *Families* – that it's normal for problems to get better, unless we start pretending we haven't got them?

John Well hang on. You said that at each stage of development there are certain lessons a child has to learn – first how to love and trust, then how to fit in, then how to share with others, and so on. And that normally the parents will help the child to learn these lessons. But if they don't, the child can still pick up the lessons later on by seeking out a 'substitute emotional experience' from someone else – for example, if the father dies, finding a kindly supportive grandfather, uncle or teacher and seeking 'fathering' from them instead.

Robin And the child will automatically seek these substitute experiences, provided he or she doesn't deny needing them.

John Right.

Robin Now, next, do you remember one of the findings of the Harvard Study – that among the graduates they studied, by the age of fifty any ill-effects caused by a difficult childhood were hard to spot?

John So you're saying these Harvard Study men had sorted out a lot of problems stemming from childhood, by seeking out substitute experiences?

Robin To a surprising extent. By the time they were fifty, it seems that they'd found sufficient opportunities to get whatever they'd missed and so they'd 'caught up'.

John And they sought out those experiences because they were able to accept they needed to do so.

Robin Yes. Remember, a good proportion of them were particularly healthy. So they were probably more able than most of us to accept their limitations. That's the point. So these men are a very good example of how life changes us in the direction of greater health, *if* we're open to all its experiences. So getting healthy is normal!

John But it's only normal if you're healthy enough to accept you have problems!

Robin Let's put it like this: that the healthier we are, the easier we'll find it to admit there's something wrong with us. And the less healthy we are, the harder it will be to face our defects, unless life puts us under so much pressure that there's no alternative.

John So to sum up: we get healthier, by catching up on the lessons we failed to learn in childhood?

Robin Again, I think it's *more* than that. You see, as we grow up we're repeatedly moving out into bigger and bigger systems, all the time. So as we do, there's more and more opportunity for fresh information to reach us, new ways of seeing things which are different from the attitudes we were limited to in our families. So, provided we've been prepared for the change to each new bigger system by our experience in the smaller one before, and can therefore cope with the increased stress it brings, each move out into the wider world brings with it a wider perspective, a more inclusive view of the world, and so of greater health.

John The wider the perspective, the greater the health. That's got to be right, hasn't it?

Robin Of course that doesn't mean getting healthier is easy! No one in that healthy group in the Harvard Study got to fifty without some crises and difficult periods. But, and this is the central idea I can't repeat too often . . . *if we can stay in touch with reality, the truth will heal us.*

John A strangely optimistic thought . . . Now, let's come at

this from the less healthy end of the spectrum. If I'm not getting healthier, I must have lost contact with reality in some way.

Robin Correct.

John Why have I done that?

Robin You've got stuck in some rigid attitudes and patterns of behaviour. That's what stops the information coming in from the world – the truth – from reaching us.

John So how do I close myself off in this way?

Robin Well let's start with a couple of everyday examples. To start with, take a change that we're both aware of. Ageing.

John . . . Are you going to tell me this is an area in which I might be getting 'healthier'?

Robin Yes. Because of all the lessons I've learned, this is the clearest of all. Certainly for me, life has got steadily better from the age of eighteen months, which is the earliest I can remember, to the present time where, as you know, I clocked up my basic three-score-and-ten a few weeks ago. I have to say I didn't expect this and was surprised to keep noticing it every time another ten years went by, but it's true. Of course we're bound to lose some things as we go along, but we should gain others which more than compensate. For example, you lose the joy of drinking eight pints of Carling Black Label and being sick afterwards in the car park every night, but instead you can get more enjoyment from fine wines and keep more interesting company. You may not want to have sex so often, but you should enjoy it much more when you do because of the greater depth of emotion you experience as you get older. In fact, life should get altogether more rich and enjoyable, not least because you should have become a lot wiser and gained more control of your life and of yourself. You're less and less concerned about what other people think of you. So, living increasingly by your own values, you become more spontaneous and free in expressing your feelings and making relationships. Of course, all this depends on whether you remain open – ideally you should become *more* open – and continue to learn and grow. In other words, it depends on whether you 'let go' of the past all the time and let yourself 'fall forwards into the future', as I put it when we talked about death.

John I agree with you about life getting better. It's just that sometimes the noise of your body creaking distracts you from the joys of senility.

Robin Which is why we all have mid-life crises.

John Weekly.

Robin You see, a mid-life crisis is simply what happens when someone is clinging to thinking appropriate to an earlier age and life has to knock them about a bit to make them let go of it. Then they can begin to enjoy other pleasures.

John Like regularly seeing their friends at memorial services. All right. So that was one example of how we can close ourselves off from information from the world, by clinging on to outdated thinking.

Robin Here's another example – from the other end of life! How does a baby show that it would like to have something changed?

John It issues forth complaining noises of a crescendoing type.

Robin That's how a baby sends signals, yes.

John Signals?

Robin To make its needs known. Before it's able to use words.

John Ah. Yes. The noises are signalling: 'I want something changed'. It might be food, less heat, a new nappy, reassurance – the mother has to figure that out.

Robin Which can take time.

John As we have all observed on aeroplanes. So?

Robin The point is, this way of asking the world for what we want is normal and appropriate before we're able to talk. It's 'babyish', yes. But there's no alternative – for a baby.

John It's very good of you to defend babies in this way, Robin.

Robin Hush. Then they learn to talk.

John At which point they can express their needs in a way that mother will understand much better.

Robin Yes, with words, we can make clear what we want. And if we can't get it immediately, we can negotiate the best deal going, without needing to send out any more distress signals.

John The need for complaining noises has been superseded.

Robin So they should just vanish. But often they don't, do they?

John . . . How do you mean?

Robin Although people can express their needs easily, some get stuck and go on using baby-signals.

John You mean adults who whinge a lot, who send out whining, complaining, blaming messages to try and get what they want?

Robin Or who go on grumbling long after they've *failed* to get what they want – who continue to send out the distress signals even though it's pointless. So what's happened here is that baby-like emotional manipulation has taken over the person in a blind, automatic, completely unintelligent way.

John So when we whinge, we're hanging on to the way we expressed our needs as a baby.

Robin Exactly.

John OK. You've given two examples of clinging on to outdated and inappropriate behaviour. So next question: *why* do we get stuck? What has stopped us from being open to the world in a way that would have changed us?

Robin Let's widen that question a bit. I'm saying that all emotional problems are caused by hanging onto behaviour that was appropriate at one stage of our lives, but isn't appropriate any more. Now, you remember we've talked many times about how a person can put certain emotions 'behind the screen'. Do you recall the process?

John Well most families experience difficulty or discomfort with some emotion or other. So, as a child grows up in a particular family, it learns not to manifest that emotion because, if it does, the family disapproves. Therefore the child learns to hide the emotion from its family; unfortunately, it usually finishes up hiding the emotion from itself. In other words, the child learns not to notice when that emotion is aroused; it has put the emotion 'behind the screen'. Once it has done that, it is no longer aware of the emotion, nor of the fact that it has a problem with that emotion.

Robin Right. Now hiding the emotion from the family was totally appropriate behaviour originally because no child wants disapproval from its parents. The problem arises when the avoidance of the emotion continues in later life. For example, a child whose family couldn't cope with anger, and has put that emotion behind the screen, won't have it available at school when it needs to stand up for itself against a bully.

John Robin, the question 'What keeps us stuck?' has certainly been widened, no doubt about it. Any chance of your now answering it?

Robin There are two reasons we can stay 'stuck'. We'll call them 'Denial' and 'Dog Biscuit'.

John 'Denial', please.

Robin Well, as I've said many times before, an emotion only becomes a real problem once it's been put behind the screen. Because then, if we are in danger of experiencing it, or people around us display it, or even if they just start talking about it, it makes us very uncomfortable. And that increasingly influences our behaviour. We'll choose friends, and eventually a spouse, who will allow us to keep that painful emotion hidden away – people who won't challenge us in that area – and that's always because they've denied the same emotion themselves!

John You mean we become like people who are bound together by a need to conceal some secret they know other people would disapprove of. Like alcoholics or drug addicts.

Robin Yes, except that we can't acknowledge even to ourselves that there *is* a secret, because we've hidden it from ourselves as well. If the denied emotion does show at all it will be called something different. A weakness will be turned into a virtue.

John You're losing me.

Robin Let me give you a personal example. My family often used to tell stories about great-grandfathers who would throw the Sunday joint out through the window if it arrived late, or wasn't perfectly cooked. The tale was always listened to with mingled awe and admiration, as if these were wonderful strong men who dominated others and got what they wanted. I remember feeling that I would be more of a man if I was also able to behave like that, and that I wasn't quite up to scratch. I only realised much later that these ancestors of mine were just behaving like enormous babies.

John . . . You mean the family used to deny this behaviour was infantile by reinterpreting it as really macho. So what would have happened if somebody had started querying how manly these ancestors really were?

Robin There would have been increasingly strong disapproving signals sent out until the subject was dropped. That's how expression of the forbidden emotion is controlled, remember? By the non-verbal signals the family members send to one another. If anger is taboo, everyone will display feelings of intense discomfort and displeasure whenever one member expresses annoyance, unless it's kept very mild and apologetic. Or if sex is a forbidden and denied emotion, then anyone who is indiscreet enough to begin talking about it will be warned off without a word needing to be said. Mother will blush and change the subject; or father's lips will tighten, his posture will get more stiff and he'll rattle the newspaper he's reading; or if all else fails Aunt Agatha will drop the tea-tray. Children learn to recognise these signals so early in life that just the faintest trace of them, right at the beginning, is enough to steer them away onto some less uncomfortable topic. It all happens so quickly, so imperceptibly, that neither the family members sending the signals, nor the member they are directed at, are conscious of them at all.

John It's all happening, as they say, 'below the threshold of consciousness'?

Robin That's right. So no one is aware of the signals, even though they are having an effect. We therapists didn't see them either until we began, when we saw families, to have other therapists observing us all through one-way viewing screens. The observers were watching so carefully they were able to catch these little changes in expressions and postures, and then tell the therapists in the room with the family what was going on! And what eventually helped even more, was being able to make video-recordings, so that we could watch bits of family behaviour over and over again, in slow-motion, until the signalling system became clearer and clearer.

John So the family members all prevent each other from expressing the forbidden emotion, while being totally unaware they're doing so. They're not only avoiding the shared emotion; they're also avoiding seeing the way they're avoiding it!

Robin So they're really trapped. They've locked the emotion up and thrown away the key.

John And chosen spouses and friends who've tossed out the same key.

Robin So they can't rescue each other. Now once this completely automatic control system is operating, if one person takes a small step in the direction of becoming free of an habitual negative pattern, all the others will automatically increase their non-verbal signals to bring that person back into line. Until, of course, he or she joins in the hiding, or denying, of the emotion again. Then the warning signals can stop and the uncomfortable 'atmosphere' – because this is what an 'emotional atmosphere' means – will vanish and everyone will be more comfortable again. In this way the signalling system keeps everyone locked in the shared avoidance of the denied negative emotion, just like the thermostat on a central heating system keeps the house at an unvarying temperature.

John So that's how 'Denial' works to keep us stuck in some type of behaviour that's no longer appropriate. Now what's this second thing – 'Dog Biscuit'?

Robin Well this refers to how we teach a dog to beg. Each time he does it, we give him a biscuit; so he keeps on doing it, because it brings him the biscuit. In the same way, we can cling to inappropriate child-like behaviour because in the past it's been rewarded, and even in the present it still brings us some kind of pay-off. So we persist in it.

John And if our child-like behaviour brought us no pay-off at all, it would force us to change?

Robin It wouldn't *force* us to change. But if we stopped being rewarded for that particular reaction, after a time the reaction would just fade away.

John Just as the dog would eventually stop begging if we never gave him another biscuit.

Robin Yes. So if we've learned as small children to deal with others by emotional manipulation, then as we age, there will be no incentive for us to change our behaviour provided it still works.

John Hang on. What do you mean by 'works'?

Robin I mean, as long as people allow us to pressure them into giving us the response we seek, our manipulation is rewarded, and that keeps us stuck.

John And how did we get 'stuck' in this behaviour in the first place?

Robin Obviously we learned it in the family. First, there are the reasons why the child went on behaving this way; then, there are the parents' reasons for going on giving the dog biscuit.

John Start with the child's reasons.

Robin Well, we've agreed that sending distress signals is all the baby is capable of. But supposing, after it learns to speak, it discovers that sending distress signals *still* works?

John You're saying that if it finds it can 'get round' its parents, trick them into letting it have its own way – by having a tantrum, or crying or just allowing tears to well up in its eyes – why the hell should it abandon such a powerful bargaining counter?

Robin Quite. The child won't know the reason why it shouldn't.

John . . . Which is?

Robin That it will learn to become an unhappy grown-up.

John Come again?

Robin Well, you see, the baby didn't suddenly decide to play at being unhappy in order to manipulate its parents! That was its natural reaction. Now if, once it can use words to make its needs known, the parents go on being completely controlled by its baby-like distress signals – instead of helping the child to cope gradually with not getting its own way all the time – the child won't be able to find a more mature way of dealing with frustration.

John You mean, by rewarding the child with an emotional dog biscuit every time it becomes distressed, the parents are, in effect, training the child to go on using that type of negative emotion?

Robin Exactly. *Without realising* that's what they're doing, of course. So the child continues to believe it has to be unhappy to get what it wants. And eventually that becomes a deep-rooted habit – a basic part of that person's character.

John You mean it becomes an habitually depressed person?

Robin Yes.

John . . . But what's the person *now* getting out of being unhappy? What's the dog biscuit?

Robin Well, as they grow up, they will go on reacting with depression. And a lot of people – first the family and later on friends, doctors, fellow-workers and others – will give *enough* emotional dog biscuits – sympathy, worry, attention, feelings of guilt about not helping enough – to keep the habit going.

John I see.

Robin In addition there's something else going on. At some *deeper* level the depressed person feels that to give up such childish emotions – for instance, a feeling of self-pity for having been ill-treated, or of anger at the parents for not having loved them enough – would be giving up a claim for what the parents failed to provide; or at least what the depressed person *feels* they had failed to provide.

John . . . Interesting. You mean, it would be like tearing up an IOU and admitting the parents didn't owe them anything more?

Robin Exactly; cancelling the emotional debt. So to stop being unhappy would in effect be saying to the parents: 'I'm all right now, you can forget about me; you're free to go off and enjoy yourselves.'

John . . . so they remain unhappy, in order to keep their parents – or others – responsible for them?

Robin Something like that. Of course, the advantages of giving up the claim – by giving up the emotional problems which justify the claim – are infinitely greater than the imaginary losses the person would suffer. As long as a child – or a childish person – has to remain inadequate and unhappy in order to force others to look after it, it actually loses all the benefits of freedom and independence and has to just go on feeling rotten!

John Whatever it was that actually went wrong in the way the parents brought the child up just gets perpetuated?

Robin So if the parents really were hopeless, the child spends the rest of its life trying hopelessly to get something out of them that they couldn't give it in the first place, and won't be able to give it in the future! And even if they *did* change and become *able* to give something the childish person probably wouldn't recognise it or benefit from it . . .

John . . . because of being locked into playing this part, of someone suffering from having hopeless parents.

Robin Exactly. So they'll go on being seen as hopeless, even if they improve.

John And if they weren't hopeless to start with?

Robin The same. Such a person would never be able to take what they have to offer, because to do so would involve a total change in his or her way of dealing with life. By remaining inadequate and hopeless, the person can go on saying, in effect, 'I'm stuck and it's your fault.'

John So they *can't* change?

Robin Not unless some person who is not controlled by the family taboo – perhaps a family member who has escaped, or someone outside the family altogether – breaks the deadlock and starts the change off.

John By not giving the dog biscuit?

Robin That's it. By *not* automatically trying to rescue the person, or not giving them a lot of sympathetic attention, or not feeling guilty about not doing enough for them.

John All right. Got that. Now, that was 'Dog Biscuit' from the *child's* point of view. You said there was also a *parent's* side to this – why they *give* the dog biscuit.

Robin That's usually because they've had some difficulty in their own upbringing with the particular emotion by which the child is manipulating them.

John Ah. Maybe they have some feeling, say, that *they* should have got more support from their parents, so they're particularly sympathetic, or vulnerable to the same feeling in their own children?

Robin That's usually what it is, though the parents' reaction tends to be more of a *mixture*. If they haven't had the right kind of love from their own parents there will usually be a number of effects. First, their own childhood unhappiness will make them particularly anxious, sensitive and touchy on the subject of whether they are being good parents themselves. They'll be too worried about their own performance to enjoy their child in a warm and relaxed way, and they'll be vulnerable to any criticism or suggestion of failure especially from the child. Secondly, they'll probably find it hard to give to their own children what they've never experienced themselves; they may go through the motions, but it'll be done 'by the book', without real feeling; or they may *think* they are giving, but in fact do so in a conditional way that actually demands that the children should love *them* and make up for *their* own unhappy childhood. Or thirdly, they may even spoil what they do give, because they feel envious of their children having what they lacked, even though they've given it themselves. So, although they're often trying desperately hard to do a better job with their children than their parents did with them, it just doesn't work out the way they intended.

John So, the child uses a bit of babyish behaviour that the parent should really be weaning it away from; but the parent's sensitivity to it causes them to be 'manipulated' by it; this gives the child's behaviour the pay-off that keeps it stuck in the pattern; all of which operates more or less automatically.

Robin Yes, that sums it up. Of course the parents are aware that the child isn't happy, but they don't see how they are contributing to that.

John Because what the parents do to solve the problem actually prolongs it?

Robin And that's the first thing that we family therapists noticed when a whole family would come and talk to us. So we realised that the key to treating the family was *not* 'How did their problem start?', but *'What's stopping it from getting better naturally?'*! So we concentrated on trying to see what the family was doing, in the present, *that kept the problem stuck.*

John And when you'd figured that out, you could help them to stop 'helping' the person in that way. Very droll.

Robin Which usually meant convincing them to 'hold back on the dog biscuits'.

John Summing-up. You've been telling me the two reasons why we can get stuck in childish behaviour patterns. One is the 'Denial' process, where our family teaches us to put certain taboo emotions behind the screen. And the other is the 'Dog Biscuit' process, where outdated behaviour continues because it goes on being rewarded. OK?

Robin OK.

John Now . . . what I am confused about is the *relationship* between the two processes. Are they just two ways of looking at the same thing, or are they partly overlapping, or separate, or what?

Robin As you'll appreciate, I'm trying to convey in ordinary language ideas which are essentially simple once you grasp them, but where understanding is obstructed by the complicated psychological jargon in which they're usually expressed. But what I'm calling 'Denial' and 'Dog Biscuit' are actually two very different processes. 'Dog Biscuit' is just reward and punishment, which influences learning of all kinds, and is perfectly normal. It's 'Denial' that is abnormal, and causes all the problems – because it leads us to avoid facing reality and live in fantasy instead. But the two of them connect in producing the psychological problems we're talking about. Here's how. If a family has denied something, any member who expresses the truth will be punished; those who avoid the truth will be rewarded. So once this pattern is established, there's no escape – without outside help – because even seeing that people are denying reality will be denied and punished too. It's like a crazy school – you're rewarded for giving the wrong answer and punished when you're right. But let me give you an example of both processes in action, and how they connect, from my own experience. My very own experience, in fact, as I was the child!

John From your point of view first, or from your parents'?

Robin First, let's look at both the 'Denial' and 'Dog Biscuit' aspects from my mother's point of view. She had suffered the most painful kind of loss when her own mother had died when she was four, and she wasn't really helped to face her distress at that time. So she never mourned her mother properly, but learned to hide and eventually deny feelings of sadness in herself. As a result, she became unduly sensitive to these feelings in others, and responded in an exaggerated way when other people were unhappy. She would see much more distress than was really there, she'd over-react and give too much sympathy.

John Giving to others what she had really needed herself.

Robin Now, here's the situation from my point of view. I was the eldest in the family, and so an 'only child' until my next brother was born when I was four – the age at which my mother had been bereaved. I naturally got distressed when he arrived – jealous and miserable and difficult. But instead of just giving me a reasonable amount of support and comforting, while also letting me go through the pain so I could get over it, she tried to relieve my distress too much. So the normal distress reaction that all children of that age get to the birth of another child was *over-rewarded*; which meant I got 'stuck' with a proneness to sulking and self-pity.

John Because she gave you too many dog biscuits.

Robin Too many and for too long . . .

John Now, how does 'Denial' come in from *your* point of view?

Robin Well, my mother's over-indulgence of me was a result of her denial of her grief at her own mother's death when she was a child. She had put that behind the screen, and when I showed a similar – if less intense – grief at losing my exclusive relationship to her when my brother was born, it would have threatened to re-arouse her own buried feelings of sadness – more so, perhaps, as I was the same age that she had been when she lost her mother. So she worked overtime to counteract my distress, by giving me a giant, and particularly tasty, dog biscuit every time I looked sad, to get me to stop showing that feeling.

John Instead of letting you feel sad, which was an appropriate reaction to your loss of 'specialness', and supporting you through it.

Robin Yes. I was rescued from going through that normal feeling in a way that would have enabled me to get over the loss. But notice that there were two almost contradictory effects of that. I was rewarded with special attention from my mother whenever I felt feelings of sadness, which would have encouraged that kind of sad response. And at the same time she was encouraging me to conceal and deny those feelings, because they upset her so much. So I learned to put these feelings of grief 'behind the screen' too, as she had done.

John Ah. And after a time you were no longer quite aware of what you were up to?

Robin Yes. And once my awareness was lost, I was stuck with that pattern of behaviour. I really couldn't see it myself, so if others tried to point it out, I could truthfully deny that I was aware of doing anything of the kind.

John It suddenly all seems so *complicated* . . .

Robin Well I'm afraid it is – a sort of 'double-think'. That's the trouble. Once we learn to disconnect ourselves from our experience and then deny it in this way, we create enormous difficulties. Life becomes like a farce – which, as I don't need to tell you, is usually about someone trying to hide something from others and creating ever-greater complications in the process.

John It's worse. In farce you don't have to hide it from yourself. So . . . what was the long-term effect on you of trying to manipulate your mother by self-pity, while pretending – ultimately to yourself – that you weren't doing anything of the kind?

Robin It led to a tendency in later life to get depressed when I couldn't get my own way; and this of course caused difficulties in relationships, without my knowing why. It took a long time, years after I was grown-up and had begun to understand my own problems, before this buried sadness became clearer to me and I could start to overcome it.

John How did it become clear to you?

Robin It was a very long and slow process. But I remember when it finally became startlingly clear and the biggest change occurred. My late wife, Prue, came from a similar family to my own, where sulking was a favourite means of controlling others. And we both used it on each other. Now, as long as it worked we could never really see what was going on because we would comply with each other's manipulation before the signals of disapproval we were sending were strong enough to be recognised as *just sulking*. But Prue saw the pattern clearly before I did, and one day, when I was displeased with something she had done and was expressing this by withdrawing and being silent, she took no notice but went on being friendly and cheerful. What I then noticed was myself becoming *more and more irritable and sulky to a quite outrageous and ridiculous degree*!

John You mean, when sending the usual subtle sulking signals didn't work, you turned up the volume?

Robin Louder and louder! It was completely over the top . . .

John Because they weren't working.

Robin Yes. And this is what happens if the other person doesn't comply with the manipulation, but just goes on being pleasant and friendly. It's automatic. Your manipulation steadily amplifies until you can no longer avoid seeing what you're up to. In the end, you feel like a hooked fish thrashing about on the end of the line. In this case, I saw quite clearly that I was behaving like a ridiculous sulky child. And once I had seen clearly just what I was up to, I couldn't bear to go on being like that and it changed rapidly from then on.

John So we can't begin to see our manipulative pattern as long as the other person is controlled by it. While they give us the dog biscuit we remain blind to the way we're begging.

Robin Because they're complying with our non-verbal signals at a stage when they are still so faint that we don't notice we're sending them – or at least can't recognise them for what they are. It's only when the other person doesn't respond and our signals automatically increase, that we can begin to see what we're really doing.

John All right, so you've told us about 'Denial', 'Dog Biscuit', and how the two interact. Now nobody's perfect. So I assume we're all a *bit* stuck in childish and inappropriate behaviour, even if it mainly emerges when we are very stressed. So what can we do to get ourselves *less* stuck?

Robin Well, to return to my theme, all we need to do is just expose ourselves more fully to the influence of the outside world, and accept the feedback it gives us.

John Because it will inevitably push us towards facing up to the emotions we are trying to avoid?

Robin That's it. Everywhere – at school, at work, at play, in the newspapers and on the television – we will find other people who are not anxious about the particular emotion that was taboo in our own family. Instead, they'll be expressing it, and talking about things that arouse it. So if we don't shut ourselves off from contact with people or influences that upset us, the emotion that's been stuck behind our screen is always being encouraged to come out. In fact, it needs pretty hard work on our part to keep it firmly out of our awareness, by avoiding situations where it might crop up!

John And as most people won't be particularly susceptible or over-sympathetic to our signals, they won't be rewarding our manipulations with dog biscuits either.

Robin Here's the situation. As long as we are surrounded by our family, the taboo feelings will get pushed back behind the screen. Similarly, if we choose friends, and political attitudes, and religious views, which conform to the family pattern too, they'll help us to keep the taboo emotions under wraps. *Yet all the time*, the world beyond our circle of intimates is sending the messages that can free us.

John So there's two pressures pushing us in opposite directions: the outside world drawing our taboo emotions out from behind the screen, and our family and friends trying to shove them back again.

Robin Exactly. And that's why I keep banging on about

the fact that just mixing with a wide enough range of other people in ordinary life is usually all the help that anyone needs.

John But obviously, many people don't do this kind of healthy mixing. Why not?

Robin The problem is this: getting taboo family emotions out from behind the screen is at best embarrassing, and at worst quite painful.

John I remember from *Families* that the process can be difficult because, first, it may involve remembering things that were very painful and upsetting in themselves; and second, because even if what emerges into awareness is not intrinsically unpleasant we've been taught by our families to *believe* that it is – that it's 'bad' and 'destructive'.

Robin Indeed. So as it emerges we re-experience feelings of family disapproval – even if our family is far away! In addition, as the stuff starts to come out from behind the screen, we suffer the pain of realising that we have always been angry, or violent, or envious, or self-pitying, or whatever . . . when previously we have always believed that we were rather wonderful in being unusually free of such feelings. And that can make us feel pretty foolish about being less grown-up than we thought; and naturally, the older we are the more foolish it makes us feel. And *then* we discover that we can't change these deep-rooted habits immediately! We find it's quite a long struggle, and that makes it more painful still.

John So, as you often pointed out to me in the group . . . when we start on this process leading us to greater health, *temporarily we can feel worse*.

Robin Yes, when you've left the security of your previous adjustment, but haven't yet reached a better one, you have a difficult and uncertain time. Not least because, in that unfamiliar period of transition, you are more aware of what you may be losing than you are of the benefits you'll eventually receive.

John So the question of whether we will be brave enough to expose ourselves to the wider world is going to depend on how difficult that is for us: on whether it's merely slightly embarrassing but manageable, or whether it gives us more pain than we can handle.

Robin In other words, it depends on how healthy we are, which in turn is usually a reflection of how healthy our family was. Of course no family is perfect, and probably they all run away from some issues, or at least don't face up to them squarely. But, as I explained at the begining of this book, there's a tremendous variation in the degree to which families avoid facing reality.

John Folk at the top end of the mental health scale don't have much stuff hidden away behind their screens anyway, lucky devils.

Robin That's why it's not too difficult for them gradually to uncover what's there, by going out into the world – as the rest of their family is doing.

John Whereas the further down the scale you go, the more stuff you've got stashed away behind the screen, and the more painful it is to start getting it out. And if you haven't already pushed yourself out into the world, the huge pile behind your screen sits there undiminished, looking at you, making any attempt to start work on it terribly frightening. It's that Catch-22, isn't it? If you are healthy, you get healthier. If you're not, it's down the slippery slope.

Robin Well, there's some truth in what you are saying, though you're overstating it. I'd rather say that the further down the health scale you go, the more strongly the family will oppose attempts by any of its members to free themselves from the family taboo.

John So if you begin to get some insight into it, through contact with people outside your family, you must expect resistance from inside it.

Robin Yes. If you start talking about what you've learned, or even expressing the taboo emotion, the non-verbal signals from the rest of the family which normally prevent this kind of thing from happening will become more and more intense. You'll experience strong disapproval. Of course, if despite this you can keep on changing towards greater openness and honesty, the rest of the family are presented with a choice: either they have to see themselves more clearly too, or they have to distance themselves from you to avoid being affected and eventually changing as well.

John The fact that you're changing causes a crisis.

Robin Yes, it really puts the cat among the pigeons. Everyone will feel very threatened, and there will be arguments, emotional pressures, even separations and so forth. All of which naturally makes it tough for the person who's trying to change.

John Very tough. I mean, what they're trying to do is painful enough, even without disapproval and resistance from their family.

Robin So the result is that they often have to make several attempts, and experience several failures, before they gain the courage to sustain their challenge to the family 'cover-up'. And to succeed, they'll probably need support from outside the family, to encourage them to keep going against the intense family pressures to stop.

John Is this where therapy comes in? After all, we've been yapping on for ages about becoming healthier, and the word 'shrink' has never passed your lips.

Robin More often support of this kind will come from friends, or a teacher, mentor or spiritual adviser. But where the family taboo, and the pressures from the family to avoid exploring it, are intense, then the extra skills a therapist has may well be needed.

John All right. Let's assume that someone has a problem and they're unable to deal with it by your preferred solution of mixing with other folk in ordinary life. So they go to see a therapist. How do you describe what the therapist basically tries to do?

Robin Essentially, the therapist is trained to help the patient reconnect with those parts of their emotional life that they have learned to avoid and deny – in other words, the ones they've put behind the screen.

John And how does the therapist encourage the patient to get all this very threatening taboo stuff out into awareness?

Robin If you ask a number of therapists about that you will probably get different and rather complicated answers about their particular techniques, according to the kind of training they've had. But probably the most important thing is what they all have in common: providing a particularly relaxed and supportive atmosphere for the patient. This by itself will encourage the person to open up and begin to explore the problem more deeply than it's comfortable to do in the bustle of everyday life, or in the company of people who aren't sympathetic. Then, because therapists will have heard it all before from other patients, and ideally will have brought their own taboo family emotions out from behind the screen during the therapy that was part of their own training, they won't be made anxious or upset by anything the patient says or does.

Thus the patient slowly learns that the therapist is quite comfortable about emotions in general – and in particular is quite unfazed by the emotion that has been forbidden in the patient's family. Now, this relaxed acceptance of the taboo feelings by the therapist acts as a powerful reassurance that it's safe for the patient to face these feelings too. So gradually these begin to be explored openly, and thus gradually re-integrated into the personality.

John So on the first occasion that a trace of the forbidden emotion bubbles up, the therapist remains totally relaxed, and doesn't send the patient the 'squash that nasty emotion!' signals that their family did.

Robin Exactly. Let's imagine that the taboo emotions are anger and violence and destructiveness. One day the patient reports a dream in which, say, they've run over their old headmaster in a car. Instead of the usual shock-horror response to the idea of violence that the patient has always received in the family, the therapist nods in a relaxed way, and may even say, with a grin: 'Sounds as though you felt like bumping someone off – maybe it was me?' The fact that the therapist is completely unworried by manifestations of the taboo emotion means that the patient slowly gets the message that it's normal to have such feelings, and that the ceiling won't fall in if he or she expresses it.

John In your example, the therapist points out the taboo emotion. Wouldn't that alarm the patient?

Robin Well, stirring up the taboo emotion will always be alarming to the patient, but if they are helped to hang in there and face the fear, instead of avoiding it and hiding it behind the screen again, then the fear diminishes and they gain courage and confidence. But knowing how ready they are to face the fear more openly, and how to support them through that painful process, are the most vital skills a therapist has to learn.

John So you're saying that the main factor that helps the patient to become aware of the taboo emotions, and therefore to integrate them, is the relaxed and accepting atmosphere that the therapist provides.

Robin I believe that's the main thing that helps people to change. In my view, all the clever 'techniques' are secondary to that.

John What about meditation? A lot of people, and I'm among them, find it not only calms our emotions, but that it makes us feel more 'together'.

Robin I'm sure that's right. In meditation we're encouraged to relax, and to be open and accepting towards the thoughts and emotions that arise – very specifically not to judge them, but instead to drop our usual tendency to self-censorship, so that we don't suppress negative emotions in the way we normally do. Then the more we achieve this calm and relaxed state, and become aware of our thoughts and feelings by letting them flow uncensored, the more the experience becomes similar to what happens in good psychotherapy.

John Prayer could have the same effect?

Robin I'm sure it does, if we're talking about the kind of prayer in which you're trying to achieve an inner quietness and peace. But the support of another person may be essential, where someone is *very* anxious about bringing these difficult and painful emotions into consciousness for the first time. As I've said, it needn't be a therapist – just someone with whom the patient has a good relationship, and who is free of the family taboo, as long as they don't give the usual family 'shock-horror' response.

John Now what training makes therapists particularly good at not giving 'shock-horror responses'?

Robin They need to be comfortable with their own emotions, so that they are not only at ease with all the feelings that patients bring to them, but also have a belief, based on real experience, that facing the truth ultimately heals. Therefore they need to be reasonably healthy themselves; and while some therapists may just be blessed by growing up in an unusually healthy family, those less fortunate may need some therapy to sort themselves out first.

John And what other skills do shrinks need?

Robin A good therapist has particular skills in locating taboo emotions, and may succeed in uncovering these where other methods might fail. Also, they have to be good at not giving out dog biscuits!

John At not falling for the patient's manipulations, as the family has done?

Robin Yes. Because naturally the patient will try to control the therapist by sending out the same signals as he or she uses to control their family – and which were used by the family to control them. Believe me, a lot of these manipulations are very subtle and persuasive, and it's easy to get caught up by them and start behaving in the way that the patient desires; which of course would mean giving the patient the same dog biscuit which has always kept them stuck.

John So a therapist has to avoid getting enmeshed in the manipulation.

Robin That's right. The skill is to become aware of manipulative patterns, without falling for them, and also without condemning them; but just being interested in them.

John So 'not getting the dog biscuit' means that the patient's outdated behaviour pattern isn't rewarded, which helps it to fade away?

Robin Eventually, yes. That's part of it. But the immediate result is that the patient starts turning up the volume of the manipulation.

John Ah, like a fish thrashing around on a line, as you said.

Robin And that helps to reveal the denied emotion that all the manipulation is designed to keep concealed.

John It helps the patient to begin to see what is going on.

Robin Yes.

John But when the patient realises it's the forbidden emotion surfacing, that must be pretty frightening for them. They're not going to like that *one bit* . . .

Robin And that brings us to the main difficulty of therapy. On the one hand, the therapist is providing a supportive, friendly, accepting atmosphere. On the other, the therapist causes the patient to be confronted by the terrifying forbidden emotion.

John A supportive person who suddenly brings terror into the room . . . so, what's the trick?

Robin Balancing those two things – support and confrontation – in such a way that the patient is exposed to *as much of the fear as they can cope with*, without overloading them. If you are too sympathetic and protective, they never get to face the fear and overcome it. But you must never press them beyond the point where the fear becomes too great to bear, and they have to break contact. If in doubt, obviously you must always err on the side of safety.

John I remember your saying once that there were two things a shrink has to understand. The first is what the patient basically needs to go through; and the second, just as important, is the pace at which he or she should proceed.

Robin Indeed. The first part – 'what to do' – is the easier bit which you learn in your training; but the second – 'when to do it, and when to wait' – is something you go on learning for the rest of your life. And it's the same in family therapy as with individuals – the shrink must find a way to enter the family system and remain in contact with the family, but at the same time avoid colluding with that system: that is, avoid being changed by the family into accepting its rules, including its most central rule that the taboo family emotion must not be spoken about or even recognised for what it is. In other words, the difficult bit is drawing to the family's attention what it is that scares them so much – the emotions they are avoiding – without getting rejected and excluded by them in the process.

John Like a transplant that's got to be grafted into a body to save it, but which might get rejected if it's too different and is therefore treated like an enemy.

Robin Yes, and, as with a transplant, the main reason for a breakdown in therapy is the shrink's failure to handle that dilemma. You somehow have to hang in there, despite the fact that the family is bound to experience you as a threat to its stability and comfort.

John So what helps?

Robin In the jargon, it's called the 'therapeutic alliance'. The family or individual has to feel you're basically *on their side* even while you're in fact criticising something about the way they operate. The most fundamental requirement is that you should actually like them.

John That's most reassuring. Tell me about the 'liking' requirement.

Robin I think the key is to see what's good and worthwhile in people. If you do, they *sense* that and it will hold them through a lot of difficulties in facing painful truths.

John Is that always possible?

Robin Occasionally I have not taken people on because I can't find something in them that I respect. But when it happens I've usually found that the problems they're complaining of are connected with the fact that they are quite deliberately choosing to be dishonest and destructive, and that they have no real wish to change. If I sense this, I challenge them about it. Sometimes they then reject me; and sometimes they make it clear they've no intention of playing the game straight, and so I tell them I'm not going to take them on. Of course, they're always free to come back later if their attitude changes, because then we may be able to make progress together.

John How often do you not take them on?

Robin Personally, I find it's quite rare not to feel some liking and compassion even for very difficult people after I've spent an hour in their company. By then I've usually been able to see what they're like deep down. Because at root, we are all very similar.

John All right. Final question on this therapeutic approach you've been describing. Does it work for anyone with considerable emotional difficulties that can't simply be resolved by going out into the world in an open-hearted way?

Robin Well, the first thing to say is that the more healthy a person is, the easier it will be for them to accept therapy when they need it, and the more benefit they'll receive. It seems unfair, but if facing our weaknesses requires courage, honesty and realism, it will be more possible for people who have a lot of those qualities already. On the other hand, the more unhealthy a person is, then the more faults and weaknesses they have to face, with correspondingly fewer strengths to bring to the task. In that case the prospect will be more daunting: indeed, facing the truth can be overwhelming for them. But I must emphasise that some people who are very sick, who have a lot wrong with them, nevertheless have a solid core of courage, honesty and ability to love. With them amazing results may be possible. And yet a shallow, deceitful person who's suffering much less, may be unhelpable.

John You're talking about individual therapy?

Robin What I'm saying applies to all forms of therapy up to a point. But I should add that very much more is possible if you work with the whole family. There are so many more possibilities, and you are drawing on the *healthy bits of all the members*. Where one person is stuck or resisting, someone else may be more motivated or insightful at that moment. It's very rare not to be able to do *something* to help if you see the whole family together, and things often happen which seem little short of miraculous.

John But what can be done with people who can't be helped at all by the process you've described?

Robin A great French physician once described the duty of a doctor as 'to cure sometimes; to relieve often; to comfort always'. Even if the family resists attempts to help them understand how they are creating or encouraging the problem, they can still often have their suffering relieved by medicines; or by temporarily giving them a break from the burden through a holiday or hospitalisation; or by providing some alternative care and support the family can't provide for children by arranging special classes or clubs, or boarding school. Luckily some doctors enjoy this more practical approach, while others are mainly interested in bringing about deeper change by psychological understanding, and I believe that patients tend in the long run to end up with the kind of doctor that suits them. For example, I used to feel worried that patients who got sent to doctors who favoured drug treatments would miss out on the chance of understanding themselves better. Then one day I was visiting another hospital and was shown round the new outpatients department of the chief psychiatrist, who was famous for his interest in drugs and his hostility to psychotherapy. I was very relieved to find that all the people waiting there gave the impression of having severe problems and little capacity for insight; if they had come to me originally I would probably have been able to do little to help and would have felt like sending them to this department!

John So, to sum up: to become healthier, most people need only go out into the world, and allow their experience there to change them; some will need a therapist to provide the right atmosphere to allay their anxiety before they can unlock their emotional taboos; those who can't benefit from this kind of

360 All Change Please

guided insight can be helped by drugs and more practical methods. Now I want to return to a central paradox in all this: the fact that it's the healthiest people who are most interested in getting healthier.

Robin Well, it's not that the desire to get healthier will be the conscious motivation for most people – they'll just be drawn to situations that are challenging. But remember also that 40 per cent of all the men selected as exceptionally healthy by the Harvard Study received therapy at some point of their lives!

John So the people who've already got mental health want more, while the people who have less are fully satisfied?

Robin Well, let's put it this way. The further down the scale of health you go, the greater the dislike people feel towards change of any sort, because it's much more painful for them to face their defects. It's easier to cope by clinging to the belief that they're healthy already – in fact, healthier than anyone else – and then they can believe they don't need to change. Until, of course, they are brought up against reality by some new situation they can't cope with at all.

John So less healthy folk don't seek to change; they only do so involuntarily, if they're forced to by a crisis.

Robin Yes, a 'crisis' being a situation when they realise that their usual way of approaching things is not working; or to put it another way, a situation where it is less painful to change than to stay where they are.

John So this means that a crisis may have a very beneficial effect for them in the longer term.

Robin Oh yes. In fact the Chinese ideogram for 'crisis' means a mixture of danger and opportunity – which puts the whole idea very neatly. So almost anyone can improve their level of health given the right kind of crises, and the right kind of help.

John And that's why what's called 'a nervous breakdown' is often a good thing in the long run.

Robin Yes, it's often the first step on the way to greater health. Such a 'breakdown' is really the final failure of a lifestyle based on wrong principles, that was never going to work anyway. And once that way of living is seen to be hopeless, the person who has cracked up can start again, and with help, build a life on more solid foundations.

John It always fascinates me that the idea of a nervous breakdown, which so alarms lay folk – and of course the person who has to undergo it – is viewed by therapists almost with quiet satisfaction, as a step on the way to something better.

Robin I can't say I ever feel *pleased* about it. It can be so alarming for the person concerned. But I may see that they at last have a chance of finding solutions to their problems.

John And so to return to what seemed like a paradox but begins to look less and less like one . . . the most healthy folk are more open to change because they're more able to risk trying out new experiences and experimenting with different ways of coping with them.

Robin That's right. They'll find exposure to new and challenging situations attractive, exciting and pleasurable. But if we are less healthy, our psychological adjustment to our situation in life will feel more shaky to us, so we'll hesitate to expose ourselves to the possibility of change, for fear of losing whatever security we've achieved.

John I think sometimes we fear exploring new situations because our intuition tells us they will force us to deal with unfamiliar, uncomfortable and indeed alarming emotions. But more often I think we hold back from 'risky' experiences because we fear loss of control; we know we can't go through them without experiencing confusion, without entering the emotional unknown.

Robin But allowing ourselves to feel confused sometimes is absolutely necessary; it's part of the process of growing.

John . . . I remember your once saying that when people are *trying* to change, they don't change anything like as fast as they do when they *give up trying* to change. Is that connected with what we're saying about confusion here?

Robin Yes. You see, someone who is trying to change is almost always attempting to do so according to his or her *own* ideas of what changes are necessary for them. In other words, they are trying to use a machine that isn't working properly to mend itself.

John They are trying to change faulty ideas in the light of those faulty ideas.

Robin For example, in a therapy group people will often talk most sincerely about trying to change. But later it becomes clear that they want to change themselves, according to how they see their problem, not how the group sees it.

John So nothing happens, you mean? They just go round and round in the same old circles?

Robin Of course. Whereas, all that's necessary is to feed the information about your problems out into the group, and *let the group change you.*

John You simply need to take advantage of the fact that the other group members have a more objective view of you, because they are not denying certain aspects of the truth about you, in the way that you yourself are!

Robin Then you can get this invaluable feedback about what's wrong, or what's getting in the way. And of course *that* can be painful. But if you are open to it, this feedback actually does change you.

John I remember this well. You suddenly find the whole group looking at you and telling you very kindly but firmly that something you think is the case, is *not* the case. And this experience, of being told by an independent jury, as it were, that you are perceiving something incorrectly is *extraordinarily* powerful. After it I always had a period of complete confusion when I felt that I didn't have any idea of what was going on, or which of my responses was still valid. It's an experience that I still occasionally get and I now call it 'rewiring'! I feel I ought to put up a sign: 'Closed for Alterations'.

Robin Obviously you have to knock an old house down before you can build a new one in its place. And there's quite a lot of mess and disorder while you're doing it. It's exactly the same with changing yourself; the old structure has to crumble before the new one can form. This is what the confusion is about. So it's only when a person gives up trying to control the process of their own change that the system outside them can begin to change them.

John And although giving up trying to control the process takes you inevitably into confusion . . . in a sense you are moving up to a higher level in order to receive more information and to get a wider, more complete perspective.

Robin Yes, but talking about 'going up a level' sounds rather grand – as if you might be climbing upwards to a place where you feel you are more in charge of everything. But of course it doesn't *feel* like going up a level at all when it's happening to you! It feels like coming *down*, coming off one's high horse on to the firm ground.

John In fact the first few times it happened to me I felt it was quite humiliating. You feel inadequate, you're not in charge any more, you're lost, you don't know what to do, you feel a fool.

Robin And then I think you slowly realise it's only your Ego getting its nose rubbed in the dirt – learning that it can't control and understand everything in the way an Ego likes to!

John That's true. And you do get more used to allowing yourself to go down into that confusion. You slowly learn to let go and trust something in you to absorb the new information, and, amazingly, to somehow eventually make sense of it and integrate it.

Robin Yes. It's a kind of higher intelligence we're not ordinarily aware of. You see, it's the 'right brain' that sees new patterns and intuitively makes sense of things that our 'left brain' can't sort out. But in the West all our thinking has a left-brain emphasis – the logical-analytical-critical faculties. I remember an occasion when Prue and I were attending a conference on Science and Religion; everyone had already agreed that it was necessary for us to be able to move from our present predominantly left-brain mode to greater right-brain functioning, if many world problems were to be solved. So someone with a military background said: 'All right. We've got to be able to move from left to right brain. So what's the drill?' And of course with this attitude it's impossible, because it's a left-brained way of addressing the problem.

John It's very funny, really. Conjures up the image of the Army teaching soldiers to meditate. 'Squad! Let the mind go . . . *blank*! Now, on the command "Be spontaneous" allow images to arise in an undirected manner from the unconscious, *not yet Higgins, wait for it*!' So . . . what *is* the alternative to using the left brain to gain access to the right?

Robin The alternative is simply to see that the transition can never be made like that, and that the only way we can get there is to allow ourselves to feel confused, to accept we can't do it from our ordinary clear-minded 'I'm-in-intellectual-control' thinking. We have to be able to bear feeling lost, feeling 'all at sea'; then, if we can just stay with that feeling of inadequacy, and not try to achieve intellectual understanding yet, we find ourselves automatically moving more into the right brain, in spite of – or rather, *because* of – our confusion and puzzlement. And then, given time, new understanding will emerge.

John We have to learn to 'let go'.

Robin Yes.

John So it's not really enough just to put ourselves in the way of new people and unfamiliar experiences; we've also got to be prepared to allow ourselves to feel any confusion that results from this?

Robin Of course.

John I wonder if this is why some of the people with the finest intellects often seem emotionally less developed.

Robin Go on.

John Well it's always seemed to me that folk who acquire vast quantities of knowledge often do so almost as a kind of defensive measure, because they are very uncomfortable if they are not in mental control of every situation. So I'm wondering if perhaps that need to try to dominate with the intellect, to keep control – to 'overstand' as you've put it earlier – is the very thing which prevents these folk from allowing themselves the feelings of confusion that would enable them to grow in all those directions connected with *feeling*, where they're not so developed.

Robin That's certainly my impression.

John . . . Well I must admit I do see ever more clearly why very healthy folk change so easily. First, they approach their lives almost scientifically in the sense they're always revising their hypotheses, their mental maps; that means regularly accepting the periods of 'not-knowing' which that entails. In other words, they feel a lot more comfortable than we do with this kind of confusion you've been describing. Second, since they tend to be in contact with some transcendental feelings, some sense of the universe as a support system, that's going to help them deal with the anxiety that always accompanies such periods of confusion.

Robin In addition, the fundamental idea conveyed by all religions is that we are part of a greater design, under a higher authority, and that we really know very little and have very little control over anything. This emphasis on our real 'humility', if we allowed it to influence us, would protect us against the 'hubris' we experience when we try to control everything, and would leave us open to a continuous process towards deeper understanding of the kind I've been describing.

John So I want you to sum up for once, for the benefit of any reader who is interested in changing.

Robin Well, the problem is to free ourselves from the automatic habits and attitudes and avoidances which are locking us into our present lifestyle – because they are what prevent change from occurring naturally. As I've said, even our present ideas about how we need to change will only take us round in the same old circle. So what's required is to open up to a wider range of life-experiences, and to allow the feedback we receive to change us – first by dissolving our old, ineffective habits of thought and feeling by throwing us into confusion; after which there's space for a new understanding to form. And it will help if we can do all this without the intention of 'succeeding' or 'achieving' but just for the sake of *learning*, letting the world teach us.

John All right. Two final questions about change as individuals. First a subjective one. Robin, there are so many different activities in which we could engage. Is there anything that might indicate the sort of thing that would be particularly beneficial to us individually? Do we need to take on what we dread the most? Should I become a mountaineer, or even a morris dancer?

Robin You'd probably learn something very interesting from just trying a bit of climbing, if that's a particularly uncomfortable idea for you; which doesn't mean you need to become Chris Bonington. Going against a deep-rooted fear or resistance can often break a habit and prove very liberating. You might find out that the fear has a very different meaning to what you assume; in my own case I discovered that a deep anxiety about taking risks in physical activities had more to do with my mother's worries, and was really a fear of what might happen if I was too *bold*! Through this, I got back in touch with that boldness and began to enjoy exciting sports.

John And you're not a bad wind-surfer for a seventy-year-old.

Robin So, the object is to learn more about yourself, after which the right changes will happen automatically.

John So second and last, an objective question. What would you say were the ultimate objective criteria of whether something is helping us to become mentally healthier?

Robin The ultimate criterion is whether it is taking us towards an increasing integration of the various parts of the personality: an increasing connectedness and communication between them, which will lead in turn to a greater contact with, and understanding of, the reality outside ourselves. When that's happening your life gets better, your relationships improve, you become more effective and successful, you stop worrying so much and enjoy life more. But that's looking back later. As you're going along you may feel at times that you're getting worse. So you have to trust that the truth heals, that if you are learning more about yourself, meeting a wider range of people and learning to get on with them, and taking in the feedback they give you, you're going in the right direction. Of course, it helps to have contact with others who as far as you can judge are healthier rather than less healthy than yourself – though of course that's a bit uncomfortable – and also with people who are trying to grow and change, perhaps just through informal friendships, or maybe in some kind of therapy or consciousness-raising group. As I don't need to tell you, this is exactly what groups do so well, and it's why I took up group therapy as my own main interest.

John Well let's now move up a level, and talk about improving the mental health of the sort of institutions we examined in Chapter 2 – companies, schools and hospitals. How much impact can an individual have?

Robin It obviously depends on the size of the institution. If you have a very small organisation, or a very small department, then one very healthy person joining that group, even in a subordinate position, can make a big difference.

John That's true. It's not just that such a person does their job well; they also inevitably 'set an example' by being cheerful and uncomplaining and conscientious.

Robin Of course some of the less healthy people in the group may even respond negatively to that at the start! But if the healthy person interacts long enough in an affiliative way, more and more of the group will be affected and tend to emulate them.

John I've noticed that, after a time, as standards improve, it throws a spotlight on to the weaker members of the team. As others get better, weaknesses are thrown into starker relief, and it becomes much harder to ignore them, both for the rest of the group, and for the weak links themselves.

Robin Yes. The general standard goes up, so they become more noticeable. Then either they improve too, or the whole group will eventually make it clear that it doesn't want to go on carrying them; or the person concerned will get so uncomfortable that they will find an excuse to move to another organisation, one more compatible with their level of health.

John But at the moment, we're talking only about small groups. What about big organisations?

Robin There, any real improvement in the way the organisation functions can only be achieved by the leadership.

John And do I assume that such an improvement will entail the introduction into the organisation of the ways of functioning that we described as healthy in Chapter 2?

Robin Indeed.

John And the leaders are the only ones who can do that because they're in charge.

Robin Hang on . . . what do you mean by 'in charge'?

John They're in control. Right?

Robin Let's look at that idea more closely. You see, I don't think it's useful to think of the leadership of a really well-functioning organisation as being in *ultimate* control of it. The whole organisation is really under the control of the external world.

John Just like a living organism in the natural world, you mean?

Robin Go on.

John If it's to survive, its behaviour has got to be appropriate to its environment.

Robin Yes, it has to be 'responsible' in the basic sense of the word: that is, it must respond appropriately to the conditions in which it finds itself. Now, the leadership's function is to enable the organisation to be 'responsible' in this sense. First of all, it must ensure that the activities of the different parts of the organisation are connected and coordinated with one another. And after that, it must relate the whole set-up to the outside world. The leadership is the link between the organisation and the world around it.

John Because it's the outside world – and not the leadership – that decides whether to go on using the organisation's products or services?

Robin Precisely. For example, it's the management's responsibility to maintain an early warning system which will alert them if the company is heading for trouble financially, and then to work out what action needs to be taken for the enterprise to survive. But it's not exactly that the leadership has to brandish a big stick in order to get those changes implemented. Rather, the leadership has to draw everyone's attention to the big stick that the outside world is waving at the whole organisation, which threatens everyone's income. Some members of the workforce may resist the changes because they're only concerned with their immediate advantage and won't face the danger that they could lose their jobs altogether if they don't compromise. But by making the danger clear to the majority, a good leader can use the crisis to push through vital changes which are in everyone's long-term interest.

John I like this perspective – that the big stick is 'outside'.

Robin In short, the leaders' job is to help the organisation to respond appropriately to its environment by seeing that relevant information about the outside world is received rapidly and circulated widely; and then, having given everyone the opportunity to contribute their intelligence, the leaders must coordinate the feedback from the various departments so that appropriate responses are decided on and carried out efficiently.

John In other words, the leaders keep their organisation constantly in contact with reality, so that it learns from and adapts to the world around it.

Robin In a nutshell. It's essentially the same principle as the one we've been talking about, whereby individuals and families stay healthy or become more healthy.

John It's a very different way of thinking compared with the old-fashioned view of leadership, where a 'boss' might be very surprised to be told he wasn't in charge.

Robin Well, let's call this exceptionally healthy way of leading others something like 'The New Leadership'.

John Snappy if banal.

Robin For clarity's sake, let's contrast it with the kind of leadership that was taken for granted in the last century. Obviously, we're taking the two extreme poles on a spectrum of leadership behaviour. So all real organisations will fall somewhere between the two extremes.

John I will forgive you some caricature if you will lighten my darkness.

Robin Let's take the old-fashioned leadership first. The underlying assumption is that 'the boss' knows best. So naturally all the other people in the organisation are treated as less than complete human beings. They are regarded as different animals, as inferior species. He wishes to use only a very limited range of their skills, so most of their abilities are of no interest to him. Basically, he uses his staff as instruments to carry out his orders. There was a nice example of this mind-set when one senior figure in a large company, where more worker-participation was being urged, described it scathingly as 'letting the monkeys run the zoo'.

John So all the control is seen as concentrated at the top.

Robin Yes, the boss takes all the decisions and tells everyone else what to do – with everyone of course saying: 'Isn't he a genius' – to his face at least. Now, this kind of organisation can function, albeit not with great efficiency, provided the boss functions. But the moment he stops, the organisation collapses because there's nothing to sustain it. The whole thing is unbalanced because all the intelligence controlling the organisation was contained in him.

John I was in a film called *Clockwise*, written by Michael Frayn, which was based on a real school which had a headmaster exactly like the man you describe. He was a dynamo! Everybody went on about how fantastic he was. He did everything! Then he left and the school collapsed. No one had the slightest idea what to do, because he'd never allowed anyone else to understand how the school operated.

Robin A lot of Western firms are like that because of our emphasis on the individual, in contrast to the Japanese where group decisions and consensus are more valued. For example, during the twenty years that Harold Geneen was chief executive of the giant American firm ITT, the company became one of the most efficient and profitable in the US. But he seemed unable to help subordinates to grow to fill his shoes, and since he retired the company has slipped down the scale in terms of profitability. Of course, he was a most exceptional man, and while he was there his methods were highly successful in economic terms at least. But his need to control everything meant that this success left the firm when he did. Of course, most bosses who prefer this way of managing don't even have the justification that their firm is particularly successful.

John Considering how many people still admire this style of leadership, it makes me wonder what its advantages *are*.

Robin I would say that the main one is that it makes the boss feel important. He's carrying tremendous responsibility since he won't let anyone else have any; but he's compensated for all the stress by feeling immensely powerful and breathtakingly 'decisive'. He can bark orders out at people and have them all dashing around in a frenzy, and nobody dares breathe a word even if they're sure that he's making terrible mistakes.

John Or even if he's robbing the pension funds. OK. Advantages of old-fashioned leadership: the boss feels Really Impressive. And if he really is a genius it will work for a time. Now, what about the disadvantages?

Robin I'll shorthand them because they're a recapitulation of what we've been saying so far. The boss gets inaccurate information, since negative feedback will all be filtered out before it gets to him, because everyone knows he doesn't want to hear it. Then as long as the boss uses only his own intelligence in taking decisions, he will never get to hear of any better ideas that might be circulating. His decisions will be carried out by people who've not been given a real understanding of the thinking behind them, so there's a good chance they will be misunderstood and executed wrongly. And since all decisions are taken by him, every question has to be passed all the way up the hierarchy and then down again before any action can be taken, which means the organisation's responses are slow. Meanwhile, the employees are not being treated as whole human beings, so they're not strongly motivated, except by fear, which makes them behave defensively. And as they're never consulted, they'll probably be subtly obstructive when dealing with decisions they disagree with.

John Pray continue.

Robin Very well. The place will fall apart if he's not there. He won't groom a successor, because the organisation could only be run by someone exactly like him, who'd have been fired years ago because the boss couldn't have stood the competition. Instead, he'll surround himself by yes-persons; so when he makes mistakes, as he inevitably will, there'll be no voice to point them out and he'll go further and further off course. He'll decide what customers *ought* to want instead of finding out what they *do* want; so he'll rely on advertising to persuade people to buy what he's made, rather than making what will sell . . . can I stop?

John Yes. So . . . you could say that the organisation pays a pretty startling price for making the boss feel so good.

Robin In the long run, huge. Now if we look at the New Leadership, the key assumption is 'others know best'!

John Others?

Robin Well, at least about those aspects of the work that they're closest to. So it's taken for granted that the great majority of the decisions in the company should be taken by people other than the Leaders, because they'll be much better qualified to take those decisions. As a result, people are treated as complete human beings; all of their knowledge and skills are used by the organisation, while their emotional needs are also taken into account. So they tend to be highly motivated, and to be able to contribute and to achieve much more.

John Now wait a moment. I'm worried about this 'others know best'.

Robin It's perfectly simple. By virtue of their vantage point at the top of the organisation, the Leaders are going to have a wider, more encompassing view of how the company is doing. So certain overall strategic decisions are best taken by them. But all the other decisions are delegated by the leadership as far down the hierarchy as possible, as far as is consistent with efficiency. Control is dispersed throughout the whole system.

John I like the sound of all this, but it just feels a bit idealistic.

I mean, I know a lot of training is moving in this direction, but how far has it developed in the real world?

Robin You don't get much more 'real world' than the US Army. Doctrine there emphasises decentralisation and passing responsibility down through the ranks. You remember how amazingly efficient that army was in the Gulf War?

John Somebody said: 'No army has ever moved so much, so far, so fast.'

Robin You see, General Schwarzkopf did not tell his commanders exactly how any of this was to be done. He simply indicated the broad thrust of his strategy and the main targets that he wanted to attack: the lines of communication and supply up the Euphrates Valley, the Republican Guard, and of course Kuwait City. And then, according to a commander at the briefing, he simply said: 'OK boys, this is what I wanna do, now you think about this and tell me how I'm gonna do it'! And, in fact, the British and American generals have conducted their planning in this way since the Second World War.

John So when you say the philosophy is 'others know best', you mean that New Leaders basically set the strategy and then get their subordinates to use their various close-to-the-ground expertises to carry it out.

Robin Yes, provided the system has been set up properly, almost all the decision making can then be delegated.

John And the New Leaders can put their feet up, and have a game of darts.

Robin That's right. If the strategy's been made really clear, the New Leadership won't have a lot to do except to check that everything's ticking along. And to be available, of course, if there's an emergency.

John Well let's just examine those two aspects.

Robin As far as keeping an eye on everything is concerned, you'll remember that back in Chapter 2 I said that in the healthiest companies, control is exercised by means of a few strictly enforced economic 'regulators'.

John That's how the Leaders know if the organisation is drifting off course, yes.

Robin Because the main threat is always bankruptcy. So the regulators are all to do with finance and budget, to enable the Leaders to spot the slightest hint of something going wrong early on – so they'll see a danger before it's dangerous.

John So they're monitoring this key information all the time. And investigating any blips.

Robin Now if the work group whose figures have blipped can put things right again on their own, that's just fine with the New Leaders; if not, the Leaders may have to step in, sort things out, and make sure the group is back on the right track again before handing control back to them.

John It occurs to me that the Leaders might step in for two relatively separate reasons: one, because the group is getting it wrong; two, because outside circumstances are changing faster than had been assumed when the overall strategy had been set.

Robin Well that brings us neatly to the second aspect – what I referred to just now as 'an emergency'. What I mean by that is – the unexpected! A crisis, in the sense of something that's not been planned for.

John None of the Leaders had anticipated it when they set up the systems or laid down strategy.

Robin So in an emergency, the Leaders have to step in again, shorten the reins so to speak, and take command until the crisis has been handled. At which point the organisation will have learned to handle that kind of crisis in the future.

John Ah! So next time the Leaders may not need to step in because the crisis won't be 'unplanned-for'.

Robin That's right. The better the organisation's been set up, and the more experience it gets, the better will be its systems of predicting what's going to happen, and for reacting to it when it does. So the more the organisation learns, the less the Leaders need to take control. Each crisis will teach the organisation something new to incorporate in its structure in order that it can deal with such unexpected events better in the future. So the organisation's life will consist of a natural ebb and flow between longish periods when things are running more smoothly with no need for central control, and then times when things go unexpectedly wrong, when strong action is necessary to bring things back into balance.

John It's like a driving instructor, isn't it? Leaving everything possible to the student, because that's the way the student learns fastest, but stepping in when there's a real danger. And hoping they won't need to step in the next time that particular danger occurs.

Robin Exactly.

John And you're saying that these crises, when the Leaders have temporarily to take over, will nearly always be of a financial kind?

Robin Well obviously that's the most crucial one in commercial enterprises, although within the governmental system the threat might be that the organisation will be closed down if it's not doing its job properly by criteria that are not merely financial.

But there's one other set of circumstances when the Leadership may need to step in: where the crisis is not necessarily a threat from outside – though it may be caused by that. And that's where there's a crisis of confidence in the organisation.

John Ah, you mean where people all suddenly get worried for reasons that are psychological rather than primarily financial?

Robin Yes. I had the chance of observing this when I was at the Day Hospital at the Maudsley Hospital, where I used to advise on organisational problems. When it was all running well, in a healthy way, the leader – the consultant psychiatrist – left decisions as far as possible to the staff and delegated everything he could. He was always there in the background, in a supportive role when requested, but not interfering more than was absolutely essential. It usually ran smoothly, with a high morale and general sense of responsibility, and everyone was happy. But when there was a crisis, people expected him to take charge in a firmer, more direct way, to be more authoritative and tell people what to do to resolve the crisis.

John What happened if he didn't?

Robin If he hesitated to be authoritative, there'd be signs of demoralisation and he would be increasingly criticised by the majority of the staff. Now the crisis might be financial; or it could be something like a big turnover in staff, or someone committing suicide, or a particularly difficult and provocative patient.

John The staff becoming too stressed . . .

Robin So by taking more direct control for a time, the consultant would carry the responsibility which for the moment was too much for the less experienced members of staff. He had the confidence to do this because of his great experience and expertise, though he didn't necessarily do anything they couldn't have done, and indeed he often didn't really *do* anything extra at all! When the load of responsibility and consequent anxiety was lifted by him in this way, everybody would get their confidence back, and begin to cope, and then he could relax the reins again. So there was always this oscillation between times when the consultant could delegate and let the authority pyramid flatten, and times of crisis where the pyramid would be automatically re-established.

John Did people feel it was inconsistent?

Robin When I first went there I think everyone, including the consultant himself, thought there was something inconsistent and wrong with this fluctuating behaviour on his part. But the longer we looked at it, the clearer it became that this fluctuation was necessary and right. It was simply a question of matching the degree of control to the needs of the situation.

John So, in a corporation, New Leaders may take tighter control simply for psychological reasons, like too high a level of anxiety.

Robin Yes, because besides financial difficulties, organisations experience the same kind of crises that I've just been describing in the hospital. There may be a big turnover of staff, a major change in the organisational structure or in working methods, conflict between heads of departments and so on. Temporarily, the boss might need to take tighter hold of the reins to provide whatever degree of order and security people feel safe and comfortable with.

John I see. Now we've just been talking about the rather unusual circumstances under which New Leaders temporarily take control. But the general rule is 'control is dispersed as far as possible'.

Robin Yes, the New Leaders are dispersing everything as much as they can: information, understanding, power, responsibility, prestige, the ethical principles on which the organisation is run – so that all of it comes to exist as a living force within each one of the sub-groups, and within each one of the individuals. And one of the most beneficial results of that, of course, is that the organisation is tremendously stable, because no one person is that important.

John The Leaders are consciously not making themselves 'indispensable'. Wonderful!

Robin So, if a New Leader retires, a replacement will be relatively easy to find, because the organisation has been continually bringing people on by delegating decision making to them, and by sharing information so openly. So promotion will be less of a step into the unknown than it would be in a more authoritarian organisation.

John A New Leader is in effect working to put himself or herself out of a job!

Robin That's right!

John This New Leadership stuff is full of paradoxes, isn't it? For example, unless there's a crisis, the most successful New

Leader will seem to lack old-fashioned leadership qualities, because they deliberately won't be exercising them!

Robin In fact, they'll be practising the new kind of leadership most effectively when they're exercising the old kind least. Because that's what makes other people develop those qualities themselves. This is why it's so difficult to pin down the key features of leadership in a very healthy company.

John You'll only see what's traditionally meant by leadership when a New Leader has to step in to provide some that he or she hasn't yet succeeded in exporting to subordinates.

Robin True. A crisis will reveal what's normally only in reserve.

John All right. We've been discussing at length how the healthy company characteristics can be introduced into organisations by the practice of what we've called the New Leadership – that is, by dispersing control as far as possible throughout the organisation. Now, if the leaders start to do this, what happens? How does everyone else in the organisation react?

Robin The main difficulty is in getting people to accept the idea when they first encounter it. Leaders, managers, supervisors, they're all used to 'being in control', and giving up some of that control makes them nervous for a while, even if they're getting more power delegated down to them too.

John I had to deal with this problem in writing a training film. Basically, we were trying to persuade managers to 'coach' their subordinates: which means not giving them orders; but instead, outlining the problem that has been delegated to the subordinate, and then discussing with them the possible ways of solving it. The key to this kind of coaching is that the manager behaves as an equal, at most asking questions which draw the subordinate's attention to possible consequences of the latter's ideas. That's all the manager does! Of course, this requires the manager to accept that the subordinate may make a mistake! Or, perhaps even more alarming, that the subordinate may come up with a better idea than the boss! So, after a lot of consultation we decided we had to spend half the film reassuring managers that the ceiling wouldn't fall in if they started to behave like that.

Robin It's a very natural response, and you have to allow for it. A second difficulty, of course, is the fact that this way of working is more demanding; that is, to work in an organisation like this where you're offered more responsibility and involvement requires a higher degree of mental health.

John Right! It can be easier, even if it isn't as satisfying, having other people tell you what to do.

Robin Bound to feel safer, if that's what you've been used to in your family, and your school, and your previous jobs. So the transition to a more free and open structure will inevitably arouse anxiety at first. It's like first riding a bike, after being taken about in a pram or in your parent's car. But once you get used to it, of course it's a lot more enjoyable and fulfilling.

John Then, of course, managers are much more accessible in a healthy set-up. That makes their life tougher in a way, because with everyone in such direct contact, their authority will have to be based on *real* knowledge and competence and achievement! In a sense, they're publicly on trial all the time. In the old-fashioned company structure, people who didn't really deserve respect could maintain their formal authority by staying distant and relying on their rank, keeping themselves apart in offices with closed doors, separate dining rooms and headquarter blocks.

Robin Indeed. This healthier way of working makes it harder for people to conceal areas of incompetence. But to compensate for that, because the atmosphere is *geared to learning*, people are given every opportunity to work on their weaknesses, instead of spending the same amount of energy concealing them. What it comes down to is that all of these 'disadvantages' are related to the stress of coping with more change, but eventually it results in much greater confidence and higher motivation.

John All right. Now let me ask something that's been at the back of my mind for a long time. If you use these very very healthy ways of operating with lots of delegation and consultation, what happens when there's a major disagreement between individuals or groups within the organisation – you know, where they're locking horns and disagree totally on something really important? What does a good leader do then?

Robin Then you have to integrate the different views.

John But is that always possible?

Robin From my own experience of studying the operation of groups of many kinds – from therapy groups and training groups to companies, and even groups of bishops trying to improve their pastoral work – I'd say that the blending of the

380 All Change Please

different views of the group members into a synthesis is automatic, *if* the right conditions are provided.

John Really? So what are the right conditions?

Robin First, the leader has to trust the group process and serve it, rather than trying to force agreement – or accepting disagreement too quickly. Second, the leader has to make sure that enough time is made available for this process. Third, the leader needs to bring out the reasons why each individual sees things differently. My experience is that if this is done, a more inclusive, integrated understanding tends to emerge. The new understanding that results will make sense of the disagreements – it'll explain why the divisions are inevitable and each valid in a limited way. In other words, all the different views, fully understood, will come to be seen as vital elements of the more comprehensive view that each participant acquires as a result. And this in turn will suggest a decision that would either resolve or accommodate the different views.

John Let's put it the other way round. What stops people reaching a sensible compromise?

Robin The discussion usually gets stuck at a stage where two people, or two sub-groups, can't see each other's point of view. It's almost always because there's too much at stake, too much to lose. At that point there's a tendency to polarise, to dig in and each fight his or her own corner in a blind way, not wanting to listen to any more argument in case they get talked out of seeking, or holding on to, some advantage. So instead of taking a wider, longer view, each side narrows their view, losing sight of the whole picture. And this, of course, increases the polarisation and disagreement. It's then the group leader's role to sustain the discussion past this sticking point.

John But how can the leader do this?

Robin For this to be possible, the leader must be open to seeing the opposing views without joining any of them. The participants must sense that they have a fair referee, a leader who is interested only in the welfare of the whole group.

John Well, that means that the leader must really have an open mind. He's got to be neutral.

Robin Certainly. That's the only way he can preserve a protected arena where debate can continue.

John But a top businessman once said to me that any chairman going in to a meeting should know what decision he wanted on every item on the agenda. That's not an open mind.

Robin I'm not saying he shouldn't have definite views of his own. Indeed, he won't be able to be neutral if he's unclear about where he stands because then he'd be biased without realising it – he wouldn't be able to discount his bias.

John Oooh, that's clever!

Robin So what I'm saying is that he has to put the welfare and collaboration of the group first, and his own view second. And I must emphasise this again: the leader's got to have the confidence, based on experience, that if the discussion can be sustained past the point of polarisation, the conflict will eventually clarify and be resolved.

John Can you give an example?

Robin That'll naturally be from the kind of work I do. One situation arose when I first started seeing whole families together, in clinics where staff had in the past seen the members of a family separately. There was a lot of resistance to this new approach from members of staff who had a heavy investment in work with family members one at a time, because they were highly trained and respected in that approach. They knew they'd have to begin all over again from scratch if they took up family work. So they took up the position that family work produced superficial, temporary change, while their work was aimed at a deep, lasting alteration of personality which family work couldn't achieve. Which in fact was nonsense; but using this argument, they sought to separate themselves from the new methods, resisting change in their own work and leaving the new and difficult work of seeing whole families together to the rest of us. This split also happened at the Tavistock Clinic, except that the division there persists to this day.

John Why didn't the division persist at your clinics?

Robin Well, I had to accept the polarisation to some extent, in the sense that you can lead a horse to water but you can't make it drink. But I refused to accept a polarisation as far as *communication* was concerned. So at first some of us worked with families, and some didn't, but I made sure that all of us met regularly together and discussed the two forms of work and the results we obtained with them. And I made sure that both methods, individual therapy and family-group therapy, were applied to some cases.

John What happened?

Robin At first there was a lot of resentment that they were forced to listen to each other's views, and I was aware of enormous hostility towards me for quite a long time. But the therapists who worked with individuals eventually began to do some work with families too.

John It worked. You won.

Robin No, I didn't win. Because the continuing communication not only led the people doing individual therapy to be more open to the group method; it also led to my facing the fact that in some cases the group method was not effective, and individual methods worked better. Or sometimes both together were needed for success. Which led me in turn to be more respectful of the skills of the colleagues who worked with patients one at a time. So neither side won. But the *work of the clinic* certainly won. We kept all our old skills, but we also began to combine our different skills in ways that were much more powerful, and enabled us to help patients and families that we had all failed with before.

John So your contribution was to keep the discussion open, when some people wanted to separate themselves off in order to avoid it. It must have been difficult to keep doing that when there was a lot of resentment about, especially since you didn't know it was going to lead to a constructive good result.

Robin Well, as I say, I have confidence coming from long experience, that if you encourage good communication, and respect everyone's contribution, it will always produce a better result than a solution imposed by a leader or a sub-group.

John And the Tavistock Clinic didn't have this confidence?

Robin Maybe. Or perhaps there was no one there who had the power to insist on sustained and open discussions – it even may have been against their philosophy to provide that kind of authority-structure. But I did have the power to make people meet, and I believed it was right to use it for this purpose. You see, we're back to the idea of using the intelligence of the whole system. If the leader really believes this intelligence is far greater than his own, then he'll see his main responsibility as creating the conditions where that combined intelligence can operate. So he'll encourage people to talk freely and share their views, by ensuring that they all feel safe to do so, and by making them realise that all their views are valued and effective in forming the decision.

John Fair enough. Well that's eased my main worry about this New Leadership: whether it can resolve a really basic disagreement within the organisation. And ironically it does so, not by imposing a solution by virtue of its authority, but by using that authority to force the warring parties to find a solution themselves!

Robin That's it.

John I'm relieved because there's so much I like about these New Leadership ideas. But I've always been worried about how authority can be imposed, as it sometimes must, without it being done in an 'authoritarian' way! And now I've seen a chink of light.

Robin Now let me ask you something. You've had some experience in business. What attracts you to these ideas?

John It's the way they specifically aim to reduce the amount of egotistical behaviour that's acceptable.

Robin Go on.

John Well the fact is that in many organisations, egotism is practically institutionalised! Yet everybody knows it causes most of the cock-ups. You know, people trying to pretend they're more knowledgeable than they are, or that they're more experienced than they are, or that they can predict the future far better than they actually can. Now it seems these New Leaders are acknowledging the reality of the limitations on their knowledge, capacity and powers of prediction. And of course that's what makes them, and their organisations, more rational and more scientific.

Robin Yes, it comes down to living more in contact with reality, under its discipline, and less in the personal, self-aggrandising fantasy you're calling 'egotism'. And of course, if they are dispersing this style of leadership throughout the organisation, everyone else is encouraged to behave in a less egotistical, more scientific way, too.

John . . . You know, the more I think about all this non-egotistical behaviour, the more I wonder . . . what's the key quality that differentiates these New Leaders from their subordinates?

Robin I think it's the ability to take a more comprehensive view.

John Ah. A wider perspective.

Robin Yes, as though they're looking at the world from a greater height, seeing more of the terrain below, observing more of the connections between things, and therefore having a more complete awareness of the way the company works and of the external conditions which affect the company's operations. In other words, they'll be steering their ship with a much more accurate awareness of its abilities and limitations, and of all the rocks and channels to be navigated.

John Which is simply saying again: they're more in touch with reality.

Robin Indeed. They're able to hold the whole thing in their mind. While, of course, working to disperse this understanding of the total system throughout the company, to enable everyone to grasp as much as possible.

John Well, if they're dispersing this quality of being-in-touch-with-reality throughout the organisation, what they're actually dispersing is their own excellent mental health!

Robin That's what the New Leadership is about.

John In fact . . . it suddenly seems obvious . . . leaders like this are, in an absolutely fundamental way, behaving like therapists, aren't they?

Robin Go on.

John Well, they're always trying to make the organisation more integrated, aren't they? They connect all the parts of it together by insisting on open communication, so that conflicting parts of the organisation can't stay separate – they're forced to communicate and resolve their conflicts. *And* they may use crises – big sticks – to bring about change! It's exactly what shrinkery's about!

Robin Let's just say that whether we're talking about an individual, or a family, or an organisation, many problems arise when the parts of the system become disconnected and act at cross-purposes, instead of cooperating harmoniously towards a common goal. And when that happens help may be needed from someone who can bridge the disconnections and enable its various parts to operate in a unified way, without losing their rich diversity. In the case of individual or family problems, that person may be a therapist; and in the case of an organisation it will be the leadership, or if the leadership gets stuck, an external consultant. But as you say, in either case their aim is the same – greater integration.

John And then . . . they take your advice about how to become healthier.

Robin How do you mean?

John They get everyone in the organisation to play a bigger part in facing and relating to the outside world – and to respond to it, and be changed by it . . .

Robin . . . Yes, that does describe what happens . . .

John Well now we need to move up a level and talk about change on a much bigger scale – that of society. And I particularly want to hear what you have to say about this, because you once wrecked my old view of politics.

Robin . . . When?

John When I was in that therapy group.

Robin What did I say?

John It wasn't what you *said*. But one day I was sitting in that room looking around at the others in the group and I had this thought: 'These are some of the most professionally competent people I know – very successful businessmen, top lawyers, heads of hospital departments – and we're all here because we don't enjoy our lives very much and we want to learn how to do so. In other words, we *want* to change, we've got your wife, Prue, and you *helping* us to change, and we're not stupid, and yet our progress is . . . well, the word "imperceptible" leaps to mind. And yet, out there in the political world everyone's dashing around trying to change the country. *Now* . . . if we can't change *ourselves*, what hope is there for politicians who are trying to change *other people*?' So here's a nice simple question to start with, Doctor. To what extent can we actually make society better?

Robin Well, the big changes being pressed on society the whole time are the result of a mass of interacting forces, like a turbulent river rushing down a valley. We sometimes imagine that we can control our own society, but the truth is that we're like swimmers being swept along in that torrent, with just enough power to be able to face the way we are being carried.

John In other words, not much.

Robin That's right. But, if we are realistic, if we accept that we're at the mercy of the river and have little control over where it's taking us – that we can't stop it or swim upstream – then we are clearer about the little bits of choice we do have, so we can at least swim in a way that gives us a slightly better chance of avoiding the rocks. Or we can do better than that . . .

John Get in a boat?

Robin Yes.

John I'm pretty hot on aqueous metaphors . . .

Robin Then if we can get the crew organised, and all paddle a bit, we can improve our chances of missing the rocks even more.

John Yes but that raises the question of the captain. To what extent is anyone actually in charge in a democracy?

Robin I know what you mean. There's an old story that when Harry Truman was about to hand over the US presidency to Eisenhower, he expressed sympathy for how different Ike would find it from being a general in the Army; 'Poor old Ike,' Truman said – as near as I can remember it – 'He'll say "Do this", and "do that" – and *nothing will happen*'!

John And nowadays many political commentators feel the reason why American presidents spend so much of their time on foreign policy is that they feel they might actually *accomplish* something! This quasi-confidence does not seem to extend to their own society, towards which there's a feeling of powerlessness.

Robin In foreign policy it's always a shared decision. You can blame the other government if things don't work out according to your aim. Whereas at home, failures are the ultimate responsibility of the president.

John So do you think a leader, or a group of leaders, can really improve the way a nation functions? As opposed, that is, to pretending they're responsible for movements that would have happened anyway – like Mrs Thatcher claiming she'd caused the collapse of the USSR.

Robin Well yes. Improvement is certainly possible in limited areas; but there are probably always penalties and unanticipated side-effects, so one person's improvement is often another person's impoverishment. And the more local the change you're attempting to bring about, the more chance there is of succeeding, partly because you can have a better idea of the obstacles, and can engage the interest and cooperation of more of the people concerned. I don't believe you can hope to change the world in any general sense, though it will change despite us anyway and we can at least adjust to it, in the way I described in that analogy of being carried along by a torrent. And of course, all improvements are reversible – what's gained can easily be lost. But local improvement *is* possible.

John So we can *really* talk about a leader helping to improve the general level of mental health in a society?

Robin Certainly. I'm sure everyone would agree that some leaders – Hitler for example – can drag the general level down by operating according to the most unhealthy principles. And a leader who is able to operate in a more healthy way, and sets that standard for his government, and thereby sets an example to the whole population, can raise the general level at least while he or she holds power. Of course, the average level of mental health will be quite a lot lower than the very high standards obtained by some families and a few organisations. I went through World War Two, serving part of it in Canada and the US as well as in Britain and on active service abroad, and I certainly experienced the powerful effect Churchill and Roosevelt exerted in uniting their countries, and the Allies generally, and drawing out the best efforts of everyone to achieve victory. It's one reason why so many people who lived at that time, which was dangerous and very hard in a physical sense, speak with nostalgia about the sense of purpose and solidarity we experienced then.

John So if a political leader is to achieve this, what kind of attitudes and qualities will he or she have to possess?

Robin We've described them when we were talking about healthy families and organisations. Valuing and respecting others; an ability to communicate in a way that everyone can follow; willingness to wield authority firmly, but always for the general welfare and with as much consultation as possible, while handing power back to the people when crises are over; a capacity to face reality squarely; flexibility and willingness to change when circumstances require it; and belief in values above and beyond the personal, or considerations of party.

John Now when we were talking about the New Leaders, you said that their primary job is making their organisation respond appropriately to the outside world; that is, they integrate the organisation; and they relate it to the outside world. Now what *differences* do you see between this kind of leadership and really healthy political leadership?

Robin I think the differences are mainly of degree. The main requirement is a capacity for healthy functioning in the ways I've just outlined. But a political leader needs to understand and relate to the wider range of levels of mental health you find in a nation, compared with an organisation where the range will be more limited and a higher overall level can be maintained.

Also, a leader needs an acute awareness not only of what
choices for change can be taken, but also of the pace at which
that change can actually be implemented. I'm not talking just
about people's natural conservatism; there is usually a strong
conflict of interest among a nation's citizens between those who
advocate and perhaps benefit from taking the most intelligent
action to cope with the current challenges, and those who are
mainly concerned with hanging on to the advantages and
privileges they possess under the status quo. The compromise
required between adjusting to, and resisting, changes is much
more difficult to handle than in a company where those who
don't like the change can leave, or be sacked. And finally the
politician needs another skill to a greater extent than an
organisational leader: namely, the power of persuasion, since it
is the main influence politicians have on the electorate. And
here a good understanding of psychology, in a practical sense,
will enable them to use the currents of public opinion to
manage healthy change. In particular, they must be skilled at
using crises as a way of persuading people to accept necessary
change, because they are then more willing to accept it and
indeed become more unified to deal with the problem.

John All right. Now the umpteen-million-dollar question. Why
don't we get this kind of leader?

Robin Well, I agree with you. We don't. The democratic
structure should be the best way of ensuring that the interests
of the widest number of people are served, but it usually
doesn't work out like that.

John Why not?

Robin Because, for the democratic system to work at its best,
it needs a fairly healthy electorate – people who take
responsibility, are well informed, and can think for themselves
and reach independent conclusions.

John People with minds of their own who can take a
longer-term view . . .

Robin *And* who can see beyond immediate personal
advantage . . .

John So what stops us from being healthy in this way?

Robin I think it's the highly polarised nature of our system of
party politics.

John . . . Yes, well most of the people I know basically regard
that as a joke.

Robin Why?

John Because the parties almost always behave in a way that is depressingly tribal, and which often seems quite irrelevant to solving the country's problems.

Robin Basically I think the effect of people banding themselves together in self-interest groups, and then largely allowing their leaders to think for them, is to produce a less healthy population.

John But it's hard to see a better way of functioning democratically than the present party system, isn't it? We're not about to advocate a one-party state, or the rule of a philosopher-king . . .

Robin No. Whatever better alternative the future may reveal, we have to start from the system we've got now. We can't start, as the Irishman recommended to the traveller, from somewhere else. So any change for the better has to be a modification of the present party system, even if we don't like it much.

John And yet it has so many disadvantages. You know how occasionally you can suddenly see something with fresh eyes, and it strikes you as thoroughly odd. Well I realised only a few days ago that if a young person thinks 'It would be terribly interesting to spend my professional life trying to improve the way in which my country is run,' they have to *join a party*! That means, at an age when you really have almost no experience whatsoever of how anything actually works, you have to make a choice between two or three pre-packaged political outlooks. Think how many people are excluded from public life by that.

Robin George Bernard Shaw said: 'He knows nothing; he thinks he knows everything – that clearly points to a political career'!

John And by the time you've really qualified to make such a choice you're excluded because you should have started fifteen years earlier! And *then* . . . worst of all, once you've joined a party, you are supposed to be committed to its 'line'. It's regarded as tribal disloyalty to question anything too much – from Nuclear Deterrence to Whales, from South Africa to Animal Rights, it's all laid down. I sometimes feel that it would be only the truly power-hungry who would, at the age of twenty, submit to such intellectual humiliation.

Robin Our system certainly offers no encouragement to people to give *real* thought to these matters. Instead, the choice you make as a young person is really based upon the particular cluster of attitudes that you've experienced in your own family – basically, either an acceptance of or a reaction against that cluster, rather than an intelligent, independent view. We've often talked of how we build up in our mind a map of how the world works, and how essential it is for real mental health that we should all keep revising that map in the light of new information. Well, the party political system is built around people who have very little wish to revise their mental maps of the world.

John Indeed, their 'beliefs' mean they have tremendous difficulty taking on board ideas that are out of line with their habitual way of thinking. They appear to be almost innately unable to express doubt, to be open to the possibility that their view may not be right. Examining their own maps is of no interest at all – they're only interested in selling them to others.

Robin Well, if your security depends on clinging to a particular set of ideas, as a toddler clings to a teddy bear or a security blanket, you feel more normal if you're surrounded by a lot of people doing the same.

John One senior British political correspondent told me that the politicians he knew were with very few exceptions vastly more vain and pompous than average folk. Do you think our present system encourages this – that people get involved in party politics as a way of avoiding questioning their mental maps, and staying inflated by feelings of omniscience?

Robin Yes, I think many do. The best and most healthy probably have a desire to serve the community without too much of a hidden agenda. They're not mainly seeking something for themselves and they don't take it all too seriously. But I believe that people operating on 'passionate belief', who are very keen to change other people – whether it's stopping people hunting and shooting, or making others work harder for less money – have opted for changing the world so that they don't have to change themselves.

John Instead of facing their own problems and sorting themselves out, they want to make everyone else fit in with them?

Robin So they don't need to feel there's anything wrong with themselves, yes.

John So their 'passionate beliefs' actually allow them to run away from their personal problems?

Robin Usually. You see, there's a common misunderstanding. It's often thought that strong political views are held by 'strong' people. But I find that it's people with a rather weak sense of themselves who need strong views.

John . . . You mean, they use their political views to give themselves a stronger feeling of identity?

Robin Yes, as a prop to support themselves. Whereas truly confident people don't need to hold on to views so tenaciously – they're much more comfortable about constantly revising them.

John I'm thinking what science would be like if it was conducted like politics. People would decide what the laws of the universe were in their late teens, and would spend the rest of their lives systematically abusing any people or evidence that supported different theories.

Robin Of course, even in science the greatest obstacle to progress is that many researchers do become emotionally identified with their ideas.

John You mean, instead of trying to find things out, they start trying to prove that they are 'right'?

Robin Yes, and getting very upset if some other scientist questions an idea that they have always taken for granted.

John Yes, I know that happens. But science, the glory of Western Civilisation, has progressed because most scientists see most of the time that what they are doing is a *process*. That is, they understand that if they really respect and adhere to the scientific method, they will get nearer and nearer to the truth. And what's fabulous about this approach is that it demands humility because you must acknowledge the possibility of your own error; it demands that you treat truths as provisional, operative only so long as the evidence supports that conclusion; it demands the capacity to examine evidence disinterestedly. Yet all of these attitudes are absent in the political arena, where what is widely regarded as impressive in a politician is the kind of behaviour we described as typical of the old-fashioned boss. So whereas scientists know that they're heading in an approximate direction, and that if they stick to the right process they will get closer and closer to their target, politicians do the opposite: they state what their target is and then try to get there by distorting the process which might have shown them that they shouldn't be trying to get there in the first place. It was very hard by the end of Mrs Thatcher's reign to remember she'd been trained as a chemist.

Robin A fine speech. I think you're practising to be a politician. But I'm afraid it's true.

John I suppose *some* 'passionate beliefs' are all right, but I'm not *sure*. A 'passionate belief' in Freedom or Justice is harmless enough, except that in practice it usually gets coopted to support highly partial policies. I'd certainly allow a 'passionate belief' in the scientific process but that wouldn't wow them at the party conferences. A 'passionate belief' in the importance of self-knowledge? A 'passionate belief' in the complete bloody uselessness of 'passionate beliefs', perhaps?

Robin It depends on the *motive* for holding it. A passionate belief in free speech, as where Voltaire is said to have declared: 'I disapprove of what you say, but I will defend to the death your right to say it', is quite different from a passionate belief in persecuting people you disagree with. The first supports a basic principle of health, the second is a manifestation of highly unhealthy functioning.

John So where do all the usual passionate beliefs *come* from?

Robin Well, before you took to the soap-box, we were saying that in joining political parties, people are influenced more by the emotional attitudes they grew up with in their family, than by any real experience of how the world works.

John Oh yes. Now is that connected with why political parties always seem to display a Right–Left polarisation?

Robin Absolutely. Because, if you think about it, the Right-of-Centre parties are based on values associated with the *traditional* role of the *father* . . . and the Left-of-Centre parties on the *traditional* role of the *mother*. So whether people identify with one side or the other will be influenced by their experience in the family they came from.

John Ah. That's why parties on the Right say fatherly things: 'Get yourself together, pull your weight, stop complaining, stand on your own two feet, pull your socks up, on your bike and there's no such thing as a free lunch'?

Robin Yes. Essentially, the traditional father values people differently, and *rewards them differently, according to how useful* a role they play in the group.

John And making money is viewed as more useful than caring for people.

Robin It's experienced as a higher priority. And because there's a heavy emphasis on fitting into the group, and keeping the rules, the basic attitude is pro-authority. In a confrontation between police on the one hand, and students or demonstrators or trade unionists on the other, the Right instinctively sides with the police. After all, the traditional father believes that it's good to be tough with people, and to say 'no' to them. It 'makes a man of them', as they say!

John And the emphasis on conformity means that the Right is uncomfortable with too much diversity; often tends to feel the national culture is threatened by 'alien' elements; and also values creativity less than being practical and business-like, art less than spelling.

Robin On the other hand, the Left-of-Centre parties, being based on the traditional mother-values, emphasise the importance of accepting and *loving everyone equally and unconditionally*, for their own sake, regardless of ability and even perhaps of how much effort they make. Also, the traditional image of the mother sees her as protecting the children against the harshness of the father's demands, and sympathising with their problems and difficulties.

John And traditional mothers make sure everyone gets equal shares so there's no jealousy, don't they, and they encourage everyone to be nice and kind to each other, and they like to see children pursuing activities that they enjoy, even if they are more creative than practical.

Robin By the very nature of that traditional role, they'll feel more comfortable expressing loving feelings; so they'll be more inclined than the father to say 'yes' and spoil them a little.

John So all of those attitudes tend to underlie the political attitudes of the Left.

Robin The Left instinctively sides with the underdog, with students or demonstrators against the police; encourages diversity by supporting ethnic cultures, while tending to belittle the value of the traditional majority culture; and emphasises 'teaching *children*' rather than 'teaching *subjects*'.

John In a sense, the traditional mother is slightly undermining the traditional father?

Robin The *traditional* mother and father, yes. Because the idea that men and women have different and conflicting values is *part of* that tradition.

John OK. Now one thing's puzzling me. Surely it's a good thing to have all these different views expressed? To reach the right decision, you need to consider the tough, meritocratic, economically realistic aspects of an issue, and the more tender, egalitarian, socially-conscious ones, too.

Robin *Absolutely*! In a healthy family where the parents play a more equal part and share power they will automatically bring both these aspects into their decision making. And in forming national policy, it's by hearing views based on both the 'traditional fatherly' and the 'traditional motherly' values and by being able to find the right balance between them that correct political decisions can be taken.

John So what's the problem?

Robin The problem is not the divergence of views – which is good. It's the fact that this diversity is expressed through *rigid* party allegiances and reduced to a few polarised, over-simplified attitudes. It's all ritualised. It's not real. It certainly isn't drawing on the intelligence of the whole system.

John So when big political decisions are being taken, the cabinet's judgement of how much value to give this or that aspect of the matter will depend on which particular cluster of emotional experiences the ministers shared in their childhood?

Robin Yes. So the ability to balance all the arguments in the national interest is much diminished because whichever side is in power embodies a one-sided view of affairs.

John All right, that's clear. But there's another odd aspect here. Communists, on the left, the 'mother's side' as it were, are *just* as authoritarian as the 'fatherly' Fascists.

Robin Yes. We need to see that as the political views of either the Right or the Left become more extreme, they become equally authoritarian. Because what extremists of both the Right and the Left have in common is their high degree of paranoia.

John But they need to conceal from themselves just how similar they are, don't they? So they attach different labels to the same kind of institutions and behaviour, to hide the fact that they're the same personality types. Nevertheless . . .

Robin Go on.

John Well, it's as though these two political tendencies, Left and Right, Stock-Mum and Trad-Dad, diverge and go in opposite directions . . . but somehow end up meeting again. It's as though political positions should be plotted on something more like a circle than an axis because the two sides seem to join up round the back.

Robin Yes, it is a kind of circle. That's because, in looking at political attitudes, we're dealing with *two* dimensions at right angles to each other. On the front–back axis, as it were, we're going from healthy to unhealthy; and on the right–left axis, we're going from traditional father attitudes to traditional mother attitudes. See?

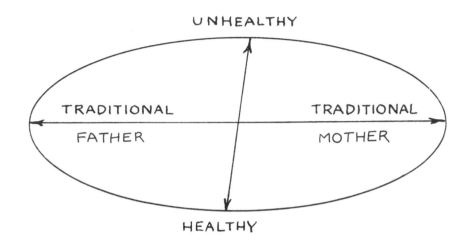

The male has to be on the right, otherwise he'll feel he's losing his marbles.

John So the people are *facing out* towards us, the *healthiest in front*.

Robin Yes. Now, if we start plotting different politicians' positions on these two axes, you'll see we get a circle. Give me some well-known politicians who are moderates, fairly close to the centre.

John Well, allowing that these 'moderates' are power-seekers . . . On the right, Major, Hurd and Heath. On the left, Smith, Blair and Healey. Then Paddy Ashdown and Roy Jenkins.

Robin Well, this is very, very rough, of course, but I'd put them in the kind of positions in the diagram below.

John So you're putting the most moderate people in the healthiest positions?

Robin I'd rather say their moderate attitudes! I don't know what the people are like in themselves. You disagree?

John Absolutely not! Just clarifying.

Robin Temperamentally, you see, these politicians seem quite like each other. They're very much in touch with reality. Their views are more worked out, in the sense that they've been able to change their mental maps in the light of new experience – because they're capable of being genuinely interested in evidence that doesn't confirm their standard positions. They don't have to hang on to their views for fear they'd be disorientated without them.

John And they don't have to hate their political opponents.

Robin That's right, they don't need enemies onto whom they can project all the destructive feelings they have to deny in themselves. These people will know when they're angry or envious, and they'll be able to take responsibility for such feelings and handle them. They'll be able to acknowledge their mistakes, without always having to blame others.

John But despite their similarities they have clear differences of view.

Robin True, but they also have large areas of agreement on fundamental principles. They can take a wider view than the less healthy view of their colleagues, because they can listen to, understand and respect different opinions; they can change their own positions as a result of what they learn; and they could negotiate sensible, workable compromises between their different positions, *if* the extremists in their own parties would let them! Which they *won't* . . .

John It's very much like the parents in a healthy family, isn't it? They accept their differences, and are quite happy about them, but there's a lot of overlap, and they listen to each other easily and reach joint decisions all the time that they're both happy with.

Robin They see their differences as complementary rather than as causing division and antagonism, yes.

John All right. Now, if we move a bit from the very healthy position at the front towards the back, in the direction of a slight loss of healthiness, the diagram suggests that people in this position become either more traditionally-Right-and-'fatherly', or more traditionally-Left-and-'motherly'.

Robin Yes, as their views become a little less healthy, they become more of a caricature of the old-fashioned father and mother positions, as expressed through political attitudes.

John Rather like the more mid-range families, where we find old-fashioned, role-segregated marriages where the partners maintain some distance and independence by being deliberately very different from each other – 'Men are men and women are women and never the twain shall meet.'

Robin Yes. So as we move from the most healthy political views to the more mid-range ones, we get more 'political role-segregation'. Mid-range folk are more apt to deal with difficulties and stress by using paranoid thinking – albeit a relatively mild version of it – so we're now dealing with politicians who will divide people up into 'them' and 'us', and who will always need someone to blame when things go wrong. They are that much less in touch with reality, and their views are less worked out, and more an expression of their fixed emotional attitudes. They are views that they *need* to hold, emotionally speaking. Now the majority in both the Conservative and the Labour parties will of course be mid-range folk, so the *average* attitude will be more polarised, more prejudiced against the opposing party, and therefore less able to see the whole picture and to work out sensible compromises than the healthiest people in each party can.

John So they'd find it almost impossible to conceive of sharing power with the opposing party.

Robin Indeed. In fact, having power is partly viewed as an opportunity to punish the other lot.

John I remember Tony Benn saying of Mrs Thatcher: 'While she's been in power, she's looked after hers, and when we get into power, we'll look after ours.'

Robin It's just like the polarisation in traditional marriages. The rigid and antagonistic attitudes on each political wing prevent any mutual understanding, dialogue or negotiation, and ensure that each side reaches conclusions on the basis of only half the facts.

John So am I right in thinking that you would put, say, Mrs Thatcher and Tebbit about half-way back on the Right wing, and Benn and Skinner half-way back on the Left?

Robin Yes; I'd agree with that.

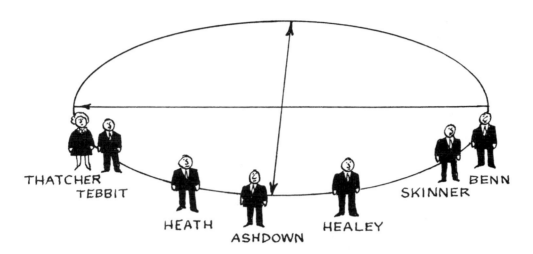

THATCHER
TEBBIT
HEATH
ASHDOWN
HEALEY
SKINNER
BENN

John Now, these people in the half-way-back position on Right or Left; how fair is it to describe their attitudes as 'paranoid'?

Robin I'm not talking about 'paranoid' in the sense of mental illness here, but a tendency to polarise, and criticise others for faults you can't face in yourself. And of course, whatever tendencies individual politicians may have in this direction are greatly magnified by the political party system.

John I agree the system makes it worse, but folk like these hardly seem to be working against it, do they?

Robin Let's say they'll feel better when they are blaming their opponents. And might become increasingly uncomfortable if they stopped.

John OK. Now let's move much further back towards the really unhealthy position occupied by the views of Hitler and Stalin. Now, at the back they're very close to each other because, as we've said, the Stalinist Communists and the Nazis were both very highly authoritarian and completely paranoid.

Robin But that also reflects how close together they are on the male–female axis! Remember what we said in Chapter 1 about the very unhealthy families?

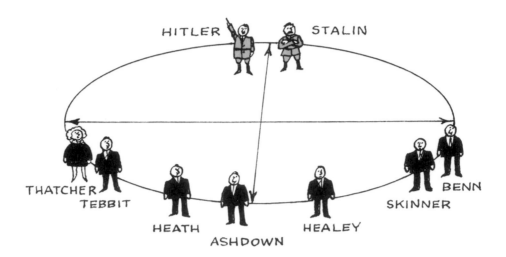

John What?

Robin There's extreme confusion among the couples about gender! Because they've not developed clear and separate male and female identities, which means there's much indistinctness and overlap, and therefore great rivalry. They're always competing for power.

John Fighting like cats and dogs . . . or Fascists and Communists.

Robin That's right. Members of these extreme parties hate each other because they need to do so if they are to function at all. If their opponents suddenly disappeared, they'd have to take back all the violent emotions they'd projected onto them, and they simply couldn't do that. They'd go crackers – even more crackers than they appear already.

John It's an extraordinary set-up, isn't it – two more or less identical groups, each using the other as a scapegoat for their problems, as dustbins to contain all the nasty feelings they can't admit in themselves.

Robin Yes, and just as in the sickest families, each side regards itself as absolutely right, and prides itself that its views are so 'pure' that any disagreement is seen as contamination and defilement. So anyone with different ideas is not just 'wrong', but an enemy to be attacked and if possible destroyed.

John So as you move towards the back of our diagram, you get sick, very paranoid people who are violently authoritarian and who blame their mirror-images for all the evil in the world.

Robin Yes.

John . . . Now, moving to the *front* of the diagram again . . . we're saying that the attitudes of the folk there are the healthiest. But that doesn't mean the *policies* of the Centre are necessarily the best, does it? I mean the centre position shifts all the time, doesn't it?

Robin Remember, how healthy the views are is measured against the fore-and-aft axis of the diagram: most healthy at the front, least healthy at the back. The side-to-side axis measures the extent to which the views are more traditionally paternal or maternal, where one side is not necessarily any more or less healthy than the other. It's true that the parents of healthy families are able to share power and collaborate well in child-rearing, but each gender will bring different viewpoints and values to the task. And those differences and disagreements are valuable, as long as they are reconciled each time. They are a source of richness and diversity, which you would lose if the parents were a pair of neuters who took an identical, middle-of-the-road attitude to everything. In the same way, I think difference, disagreement and debate are important in making the right political decisions, because then we explore a whole range of possibilities and, by comparing and choosing among them, bring about the changes in the consensus you've mentioned. I don't think there's any special merit, or greater health, in being exactly in the *centre*.

John Now . . . one other thing strikes me strongly. All these folk at the front have a lot of other interests in life beyond politics, don't they? They have what you'd call 'real' lives – what Denis Healey refers to as 'hinterland'. Whereas . . . the further the others are placed towards the back of the circle, the more completely obsessed they are with politics.

Robin Yes, with power. You see, those with the healthiest views have much less need to control other people, for the reasons I've just explained. So they are less interested in power for its own sake, and more concerned to share it as far as possible, to empower other members of society. Further, when they believe change is desirable, they try to bring it about by persuasion, instead of just imposing it. By contrast, those with less healthy views further back in the circle show a greater preoccupation with power, because they need it in order to force everyone else to fit into their distorted perception of reality.

John Which leads us to a rather nice paradox: the people we should give power to are those who need it least.

Robin And under the present system, alas, those we're usually *least* likely to get! Although the ones towards the front of our diagram are moving in the right direction . . .

John But they're *held back* by all the others! Because that's how our system works. You gain influence in your party by giving all your time and energy to it – which you're much more likely to do if you're obsessed with power and have no other real interests. So it's the people with the *least* 'hinterland' and the *most* power-lust – the activists – who have a disproportionate influence, forcing the more healthy and moderate ones into taking up more extreme positions than they would otherwise.

Robin Which in turn polarises everyone further and encourages more extreme views than most people would ordinarily hold.

John Not least because British newspapers take it to be their job to act as party cheerleaders. Especially nearer elections, when most of them become Conservative propaganda sheets: for which dereliction of duty their scrofulous editors receive knighthoods. There was a good political joke recently. After John Major had resisted calls for David Mellor's resignation by saying that he did not intend to let the popular press select his cabinet, a letter in the *Independent* noted that as they had got him elected in the first place, it was merely a logical extension of their influence.

Robin Yes, the press reinforces the political polarisation – though they are really only reflecting what's there.

John Well, I believe that the result of all this polarisation is that government in Britain is not very good. Mainly because British governments take decisions that are always partial: they are the result of partial consultation, partial exchange of ideas, and above all partiality, or bias, towards the interests of the part of the nation that votes for that government. In a nutshell, government in this country largely consists of the imposition of minority views on its citizens, a very large proportion of whom feel entirely unrepresented in the political process.

Robin Go on.

John Whereas, when we discussed the kind of decisions that really work, we saw that they are reached by a careful process of open discussion, where divergent views are welcomed, which leads to actual widespread agreement; or at the *very* worst to the taking of a decision by a leadership which is felt to be acting for the benefit of the whole system.

Robin Agreed.

John I know that some people will find this absurdly idealistic. But I'd claim that Mrs Thatcher proves my point. She came to power more dedicated to changing the system than any other recent Prime Minister. Yet if you look at the changes she made that really worked – limiting trade union power, encouraging entrepreneurial activity, selling council houses, application of monetary limits – she had a general consensus for them, which she'd helped to create by her own persuasive powers.

Whereas the changes she made later without bothering to create a consensus – look at the poll tax – have either already been reversed, or are seen not to be working well and will soon be revised.

Robin I think that's also true.

John So if we're making one point about decision making in this entire book it is this: *partial decisions don't stick*. Instead of solving problems, they simply perpetuate the disappointing process in our political set-up, by which each decision is never what is really required, but always an over-reaction against the previous partial decision. A pendulum, a process of endless alternating over-compensation, ever repeated.

Robin I can't say I disagree with any of this, but I don't yet see why you're hammering away at it.

John Yes I *know* I'm banging on about it, but it's because I'm *worried* about what's happening! Just let me quote from the last chapter of Anthony Sampson's *The Essential Anatomy of Britain*. He says in 1992 'the gap between government and governed looms wider than ever, and Britain is run by one of the most centralized and least accountable systems in the industrial world. . . . The British in the last decade have seen concentrations of power which the Victorians never dreamed of. . . . The middle ground . . . has been eroded. . . . Town halls and provincial cities have been by-passed. . . . Parliament . . . allows still more decisions to be taken by party-machines, the executive, the cabinet . . .' So do you see why I'm worried? By every measure of health we've been discussing, Britain is becoming *less* healthy – more authoritarian, more polarised and partial. So what can we do about it?

Robin We have to have *people who are less partial*.

John . . . You feel we have to start with *people*, rather than with measures like proportional representation.

Robin Yes, I know you've always been keen on that. I'm not so sure.

John It seems to me that it would be in accordance with the principles of better decision making that we've been discussing, if the House of Commons represented the views of the British people in roughly the proportion in which they are actually held. Whereas our system means that three-fifths of the electorate have voted against the programme of the party exercising power.

Robin Obviously we should aim for the best structures, ones that facilitate healthy functioning as far as possible. And PR *may* be the best one. But I believe that whatever kind of structure you have, its effectiveness will be limited by the level of the health of the people taking part in it.

John Well, that's true. The Soviet Union under Brezhnev in fact had a written constitution that was quite liberal.

Robin This doesn't mean I'm against trying to find the best political set-up! But I'm primarily interested in how the general level of health of those operating within it might be improved.

John And *how* might that be achieved, Sagacious One?

Robin I believe we need a lot of people who can speak out independently, ignoring the 'party lines' and expressing themselves openly and personally. Of course, if they know what direction is healthy, and what direction is unhealthy, that will help even more!

John But, are you really suggesting this kind of openness could bring together people who hold widely different *political* views, and achieve constructive agreement?

Robin Let me tell you about some very interesting recent work done by a group of family therapists in the US. They'd noticed something that we've already talked about: namely, the many similarities between highly polarised political controversies, and the way people communicate in unhealthy families. So they tried applying family therapy principles to see if they would improve communication about polarised political issues. And they started by choosing a real 'hot potato': whether or not women should have the right to have a pregnancy aborted if they wish.

John Which, in the States, is about as polarised as an issue gets. So how did they proceed?

Robin Participants from both sides of the conflict were brought together and after they'd all met, they were encouraged, one at a time, to explain their views in some detail, while all the others just listened. They were asked to talk not just about their views, but about the life experiences which had influenced them to form their opinion on the matter – and above all they were asked to speak in as *personal* a way as they were willing to do. In other words they were helped *to speak for themselves as individuals*, relying on their personal emotional experience and *expressing any doubts and reservations* they might have about their chosen view.

John So they were discouraged from just trotting out the 'party line' – from speaking 'for their side'?

Robin Or from just repeating the views of the leaders of each faction, yes. This emphasis on, and respect for, the uniqueness of everyone's views was the central principle of the discussion. After the participants had presented their views in this way, about half-way through, they were invited to ask questions of one another – *subject to one vital condition*: that the question came from *genuine curiosity*, from a real desire to understand, and not as an attempt to persuade or argue.

John So what was the result?

Robin There were a number of these discussions and they seem to have worked so amazingly well that it surprised the family therapists who'd arranged them! The participants showed that they were able in these circumstances to communicate in a respectful and non-polemical way, quite unlike what would normally happen on a political platform or television debate. Indeed the participants themselves were surprised at their own lack of anger and defensiveness. They all said they'd valued the experience and felt they'd become more open-minded and thoughtful as a result – even if they'd retained many of their original views on the abortion question. In fact, they began to realise the extent to which they had all been in the grip of stereotypes – stereotypes being exactly what the party political system produces. And the therapists themselves came to feel the same about *their* own attitudes! They realised that in the national debate on the topic, 'the rhetoric of the controversy had belittled valid concerns, denigrated noble values, and obscured rich and complex truths'.

John Well I can't deny that this all confirms my own experience – that if I use rhetoric, people simply move to that mode and rhetoric back at me, and we get *nowhere*; but if I speak from my personal feelings I immediately receive a matching response which leads to much more profitable discussions.

Robin Obviously this experiment needs to be tested with a much wider range of people, and with much bigger groups than these therapists used. But the fundamental conclusion for me is this: when people are encouraged to think for themselves, as individuals, they do so in a much more healthy way than when they form their conclusions by modelling them on those of a leader, or a group consensus. The trouble is, as we've seen,

that only healthier families feel confident enough to
encourage independence and freedom of expression in their
children. So, unfortunately, the childhood family experience
of the great majority of the population will make them feel
uncomfortable about expressing truly independent views in
public. It will feel wrong and seem likely to lead to rejection;
while on the other hand, falling in with the current consensus
of a group will feel right and reassuring and give a feeling of
security. So it's not surprising perhaps that a majority of
people tend to polarise into groups or parties where they feel
comfortable and safe.

John So, psychologically speaking, an improvement in the level
of mental health requires us to find some way to counteract the
effect of this general training most of us have received, which
encouraged us not to be separate and independent.

Robin I think that's what we need to work on, yes.

John But that's not made any easier in Britain by a loutish
popular press which falls on any kind of genuinely open
emotional statement with all the coarse contempt of a
playground bully.

Robin In my experience of treating bullies, they are actually
scared stiff themselves except when they manage temporarily
to feel a bit better by making someone else feel even worse. So
again, the problem is to find a way to make such people more
confident and secure, so they are not so scared at the prospect
of facing their own emotions.

John So, Doctor, what might be done to encourage more open
and individual expression in public?

Robin Before I answer that in general terms let me tell you
about one way my colleagues and I have found we are able
to help people to do this. It's a course called a Large Group
Experience and we've been running it at the Institute of Group
Analysis for over twenty-five years now as part of our training
programme.

John What's its aim?

Robin Just what we're talking about. Giving people the ability
to feel confident about expressing a divergent view in the face
of a large crowd.

John And how many is large?

Robin At the moment it's 200. But 120 is ideal because if you arrange everyone in three concentric circles they can all hear each other even if they speak in a normal voice.

John And what happens?

Robin Everyone just comes in and sits where they like. And the staff – about ten of them – scatter themselves around.

John And?

Robin Well it's all completely unstructured.

John . . . So what do people talk about?

Robin Anything.

John . . . *Anything*?

Robin It's Liberty Hall. They might discuss whether the course is good or bad or whether they should be discussing people's family backgrounds or just sticking to professional issues; or politics or cricket or Shakespeare or sex . . .

John . . . But what's the *point*?

Robin The point is that at the start the assembly always splits into violently polarised sub-groups.

John . . . *Whatever* they're talking about?

Robin Whatever they're talking about. And it's this polarisation that we want people to see and study.

John . . . So everyone starts off behaving like political parties.

Robin Exactly.

John What do the staff do?

Robin We chip in when we feel like it, to comment on the *process* that's going on – how everyone continually gets locked into these crazy polarised sub-groups. And gradually the increasing understanding changes the process.

John In what direction?

Robin People gradually begin to speak for themselves, independently of the polarised sub-groups. They'll often say afterwards how frightened they were both before and while they were speaking, but whatever they say, the fact that they have had the courage to speak up is usually admired and welcomed. And people come to realise that their fear was based on some deep fantasy that the group will be hostile and annihilate them; so this experience of facing the fear usually gives them enormous confidence about speaking their mind in other big groups too. And as the bolder spirits in the group start to speak up and stand firm against their fear of group disapproval, it provides an example for others, who gather courage and eventually do the same. I've always been amazed at the extent of the change that takes place in participants.

John How much do the staff have to *control* the group?

Robin Well we wouldn't hesitate to take control firmly if necessary, though I can't remember any occasion when we had to do so in any serious way. But the most important influence we have is the example *we* set. If staff members express views independently of the staff group as a whole, and disagree with one another in front of everyone else, it seems to provide a powerful model for participants to take on board and begin to emulate. On the other hand, in the early days when the staff were quite anxious, we tended to try to present a united front to the course, and that didn't work so well! It made the participants anxious – so there weren't such positive changes.

John So let me get this clear. The participants in this exercise learn to speak out in a more individual and personal way. And the reason they overcome their deeply conditioned fear of doing this – which all mid-range folk will share – is twofold: they gain an understanding of how polarisation tends to take over by actually observing it happening there in the large group; then they are helped to break free of the power of that polarisation by the example set by the first folk who are bold enough to speak individually.

Robin That's it. And of course we talk about that so they not only see it, and do it, but reflect on it and understand it with the mind.

John So, switching back to the political context, you're saying that the most important requirement is for more people to speak out individually, avoiding becoming polarised, and trying not to slip back into the usual party political points-scoring ritual. And you really believe that this could have an important effect?

Robin I believe it might happen more easily than you'd think. As with families and organisations, small changes can have a very big effect, *if* they're the right ones. So it may only take a few people speaking more personally to get the ball rolling. For example, remember the occasions when you and I have talked together to big audiences of the caring professions. Well, each time we've spoken to a room full of shrinks and social workers, I've been astonished to see how people I know to be quite guarded and anxious about revealing any personal problems, have opened up and talked about their family backgrounds, and their anxiety and weaknesses, in an amazingly frank way. And that usually followed directly from your talking very openly about yourself, and giving them that example. You see, you wouldn't have noticed it so much yourself, because you didn't know these people, and therefore didn't realise how differently they were behaving from the way they usually do.

John . . . Well, we certainly do get some startlingly open conversations going, where people seem to speak in a more real way than normal. But remember one thing! I'm extremely careful before *I* speak to a group like this to make sure that there is no one from the popular press present. I couldn't talk in the way I do if a tabloid was poised to take advantage of that trustful atmosphere.

Robin I'm not saying that people could actually *learn* to do it in a public arena like parliament, any more than you'd choose the Cresta Run for your first shot at tobogganing.

John So where can they learn?

Robin Well the first step is to *recognise* that this is the problem!

John And the second?

Robin I've told you about the group-work Course we started. There are now similar courses replicating it in Britain and throughout Europe. And this is an understanding that needs to spread organically, like a seed. Nevertheless, such courses are now being incorporated more and more into the educational system.

John Really?

Robin Really.

John Good Lord. In my schooldays, if anyone had suggested dropping a vital matter like trigonometry, in favour of a soft, fringe, rather girlish subject like 'How Human Beings Think, Feel and Behave', most of the governors would have thought the Vandals were at the gates.

Robin I think you might be surprised at how much British schools are beginning to move in this direction. For example, since 1985 the syllabus for all the senior-year pupils at Harrow has included a course on human relations, which as well as more formal input involves attendance at the kind of open group discussions we used as part of the group-work course I've just talked about. The consultant the school first engaged to advise them about setting up the scheme was Miss Win Roberts, who had been Head Social Worker at the clinic where I was Director, working with me to develop family therapy back in the 1960s. She later attended the group-work course, and the groups at Harrow are modelled on it. So in one way or another, the knowledge about healthy family and group functioning is now a standard part of the education of everyone who goes through Harrow. Other public schools have since become interested in, or are already developing, similar types of group experience; and Harrow itself has expanded the scheme to include participation by three local schools for girls. At present the course there includes thirty-three such groups, each with eight members – four boys and four girls – plus the group leader. And you'll be reassured to know that one of the school governors is a consultant to the course and takes a deep interest in it!

John That is hugely encouraging. If these ideas can get into the mainstream of thinking they may eventually reach politicians and the media. Certainly if the newspapers could ever be influenced by them I think it would make a crucial difference.

Robin Well as I don't need to tell you, Harrow turns out a good proportion of future cabinet ministers and members of parliament, as well as other leading figures in society. So at least they will all have had just the kind of preparation we are advocating. But you're right, if people in the media could enjoy similar benefits it could have a crucial effect.

John So, to sum up . . . *for the very last time in this book*! You believe that if people can speak more individually it will help progress to be made towards solutions of social and political problems. *Provided* that what each person says is based on their individual feelings and life experience, and that it includes their areas of doubt; and *provided* that their questions should be for the purpose of furthering their understanding, and not to make points; and *especially* if they have an understanding of the principles of healthy functioning.

Robin Yes. I've been saying that people who are attracted to politics are often trying to change everyone else, as an alternative to the real need to change themselves. And we've agreed that this is a very unhealthy and ineffective way to go about the management of public affairs. But I know from experience that we can work to become healthier and make life better for ourselves. If we do so, it usually has a knock-on effect on other people with whom we're directly involved, and the influence extends far beyond what we expect. That has certainly been true of all the groups I have observed over a lifetime of working with them. And the larger the group, the more the benefit has multiplied and accelerated the growth of the individuals comprising it – *provided always that the leaders, like everyone else, are facing their own defects and trying to become more healthy too, rather than trying to change others.* So if we each concentrate on changing ourselves and becoming more healthy, I believe the entire society will benefit in an enduring way.

John I know you're right, but it always feels so . . . *small-scale.* As if we ought to be able to do it more quickly than that!

Robin I appreciate that feeling. But on the large scale of society no one person, and no one group, has enough knowledge to change one thing without creating more problems than they solve. Artificial change, through power, on the basis of theory, either makes things worse, or alters things in an artificial way that can't be sustained. But if each person will take on the responsibility of trying to be open to all the information available, and to the views of others, and allow it to affect and change them, this will bring about gradual changes in the whole society which are organic, and vastly more intelligent than any one individual can hope to grasp. Then the change will be appropriate, the right compromise for the circumstances at that time, and once it takes place it will be stable.

John But surely people can 'club together' to do something. Ferdinand Mount has recently pointed out the extraordinary achievements of voluntary organisations in the last century, before the state began to encroach on their activities.

Robin Of course. As individuals change and grow in understanding, they will join together quite naturally on the basis of common interest to apply what they have grasped. That's how all the understanding of groups and families developed – and, may I point out, it's exactly what has happened to us in coming together to write this book!

John Well, I suppose what you're saying is encouraging. That we *can* improve society – a *bit.* Last question: how much better can we hope to make it?

Robin Well, to me, the wider question of whether it's possible to have *continual* improvement in human life is a bit like asking if you're ever going to finish the washing-up or the dusting or the weeding for good. Or to win at motor-racing, tennis or chess completely and finally. Or to totally conquer climbing Mount Everest. What do you do after that? Sit on the top of Everest for the rest of your life? Watch soap operas instead of playing games? The whole point is to wipe the slate clean every time so that you can start afresh. Because *it's the game that's interesting*. And I think life needs to be taken like this – as a game which should be engaged with playfully, and which certainly ought to be enjoyed to the full.

John Funnily enough, that's a spirit I think the English used to have. Certainly the French were always saying that we treated life like a game. I feel that's a profoundly healthy attitude – that it's not the arriving that matters, it's the journey. And that gives me a chance to quote my favourite 'last words', spoken by an Englishwoman towards the end of the eighteenth century. Just before she expired, she announced: 'Well, I must say, it's all been *most* interesting.'

Further Reading

An excellent outline of much of the research on healthy families is provided in *Normal Family Processes* by F. Walsh (Guildford, New York, 1982). The books about the Timberlawn research on exceptionally healthy families are *No Single Thread* (white middle-class families), *The Long Struggle* (black working-class families) and *The Birth of the Family* (effects of birth of a child to families at different levels of health), all by J. Lewis and others (Brunner/Mazel, New York, 1976, 1983 and 1989). The generalised research results tend to make the healthiest families appear too perfect, and the chapter entitled 'Two Families' in *The Long Struggle* (above) gives a more detailed picture of an exceptionally healthy family, and of a dysfunctional family, which brings the flaws in the former, and the differences between the two, more to life. *Successful Families* (Norton, New York, 1990) by R. Beavers, the main theorist of the Timberlawn group, amplifies the conclusions and applies them practically to treatment. The long-term study of Harvard students is described in *Adaptation to Life* (Little, Brown, Boston, Mass., 1977) by G. Vaillant. *We Two* (Aquarian, Wellingborough, 1992), edited by R. Housden and C. Goodchild, is a study of eight successful couple relationships, as seen separately by each partner of each pair. The chapter entitled 'Frameworks for Viewing the Family as a System' in Robin Skynner's *Explorations with Families* (Routledge, London, 1990) outlines his view of normal family development and includes a tabular summary of the Timberlawn research, while his first text, *One Flesh: Separate Persons* (Constable, London, 1976), reaches similar conclusions about health from a clinical basis.

We have found the following particularly helpful in understanding humour and laughter: *The Expression Of The Emotions In Man And Animals* (Murray, London, 1904 – Popular edition) by C. Darwin; *The Attitude Theory of Emotion* (Johnson Reprint, New York and London, 1968) by N. Bull; *The Act of Creation* (Hutchinson, London, 1964) by A. Koestler; *The Psychology of Laughter* (Gamut Press, New York, 1963) by R. Piddington; *Laughter (Le Rire)* (Johns Hopkins University Press, Baltimore, 1980) by H. Bergson; and 'The South Bank Show' – Arthur Miller interviewed by Melvyn Bragg. The healing power of humour is described in *Laugh After Laugh* (Headwaters, Philadelphia, 1978) by R. Moody and *The Healing Heart* (Norton, New York, 1983) by N. Cousins.

Corporation Man (Pelican, London, 1975) by A. Jay and *Understanding Organizations* by C. Handy (Penguin, London, 1976) are good introductions, as also is the latter's *Understanding Schools as Organizations* (Pelican, London, 1986). *Fifteen Thousand Hours* by M. Rutter and others (Open Books, Wells, 1979) is an account of research on what makes for successful schools. *In Search of Excellence* by T. Peters and R. Waterman (Warner, New York, 1982) was a best-selling study of successful American companies, and *The Winning Streak*, by W. Goldsmith and D. Clutterbuck (Weidenfeld & Nicolson, London, 1984), is a similar study of British companies. *The Art of Japanese Management* (Penguin, London, 1982) by R. Pascale and A. Athos compares Japanese and American management methods. *Guide to the Management Gurus* by C. Kennedy (Business Books, London, 1991) and *Makers of Management* by D. Clutterbuck and S. Crainer (Papermac, London, 1990) both provide concise outlines of management theories and their originators. Accounts by successful industrialists such as *Don't Ask The Price* (Weidenfeld & Nicolson, London, 1986) by M. Sieff of Marks & Spencer; *Making it Happen* (Fontana, London, 1989) and *Getting It Together* (Mandarin, London, 1992) by J. Harvey-Jones of ICI; and *Made In Japan* (Collins, London, 1987) by A. Morita of Sony, help to add flesh to the theoretical bones. *Practical Thinking* and *Handbook For A Positive Revolution* (Jonathan Cape, London, 1971; Viking, London, 1991) by E. de Bono facilitate the necessary re-thinking; *Small Is Beautiful* and *Good Work* (Abacus, London, 1976 and 1979) by F. Schumacher are seminal books proposing an approach to production that is sustainable and puts human values first.

The Human Cycle (Paladin, London, 1985) by Colin Turnbull compares some traditional and modern societies and the ways in which they prepare, or fail to prepare, young people to play a responsible adult role. His study of the Ik, summarised in our text, is *The Mountain People* (Paladin, London, 1984). Two other excellent general introductions to the study of cultures are *Man On Earth* (Penguin, London, 1988) by J. Reader, and *Societies At Peace* (Routledge, London, 1989) by S. Howell and R. Willis. The healthy culture of Ladakh is richly captured in *Ancient Futures* (Rider, London, 1991) by H. Norberg-Hodge and *A Journey in Ladakh* (Flamingo, London, 1984) by A. Harvey. The development of the individualist ethic and capitalism are traced in *The Protestant Ethic and the Spirit of Capitalism* (Allen & Unwin, London, 1930) by M. Weber; *The Discovery of the Individual* (University of Toronto, 1972) by C. Morris; *The Origins of English Individualism* (Blackwell, Oxford, 1978) and *The Culture of Capitalism* (Blackwell, Oxford, 1987) by A. Macfarlane; *Europe and the Rise of Capitalism* (Blackwell, Oxford, 1988) by J. Baechler and others; and *The Fear of Freedom* (Kegan Paul, London, 1942) by E. Fromm. More recent or anticipated developments in Western society are set out in *The Pathology of Power* (Norton, New York, 1987) by N. Cousins; *The New Realities* (Heinemann, London, 1989) by P. Drucker; *The Age of Unreason* (Harvard Business School, 1989) by C. Handy; *The Next Century* (Morrow, New York, 1991) by D. Halberstam; *The Disuniting of America* (Norton, New York, 1992) by A. Schlesinger; *Amusing Ourselves To Death* (Methuen, London, 1987) by N. Postman; *The Culture of Contentment* (Houghton Mifflin, Boston, Mass., 1992) by J. Galbraith; *Money and Class in America* (Picador, London, 1989) by L. Lapham; *Understanding the Present* (Picador, London, 1992) by B. Appleyard; *The Essential Anatomy of Britain* (Hodder & Stoughton, London, 1992) by A. Sampson; and *The End of History and the Last Man* (Hamish Hamilton, London, 1992) by F. Fukuyama.

Good outlines of Japanese history and culture are to be found in *The Japanese Mind* (Pan, London, 1984) by R. Christopher; *Inside Japan*

(Sidgwick & Jackson, London, 1987) by P. Tasker; *The Japanese Achievement* (Sidgwick & Jackson, London, 1990) by H. Cortazzi; and *More Like Us* (Houghton Mifflin, Boston, Mass., 1989) by J. Fallows. *The Anatomy of Dependence* and *The Anatomy of Self* (Kodansha, Tokyo, New York and San Francisco, 1973 and 1986) by Takeo Doi are best-selling studies of the psychology of the Japanese by one of their most eminent psychiatrists. We have also drawn heavily ourselves for information on a work of extraordinary scope and psychological perceptiveness, *The Enigma of Japanese Power* (Macmillan, London, 1989) by K. van Wolferen, who has lived there since 1962; some of his findings are not altogether welcome in Japan, but *The Sun Also Sets* (Simon & Schuster, New York, 1989) by B. Emmott, which assesses Japan's economic future, is in broad agreement except for the recommendations about American–Japanese relations.

The long ('Kondratieff') economic cycle is well described in *The Downwave* (Pan, London, 1983) by R. Beckman, and its consequences for the depression of the 1990s are detailed in *The Great Reckoning* (Sidgwick & Jackson, London, 1992) by D. Davidson and W. Rees-Mogg.

Excellent introductions to human value systems include *Myths To Live By* (Bantam, London, 1972), *An Open Life* (Larson, New York, 1988) and *Transformations of Myth Through Time* (Harper & Row, New York, 1990), all by J. Campbell; *The Road Less Travelled* (Arrow Books, London, 1990) by M. Scott Peck; *Ronald Eyre on the Long Search* (Collins, London, 1979) by R. Eyre; *The Varieties of Religious Experience* (Fontana, London, 1960) by W. James; *The Human Situation* (Chatto & Windus, London, 1978) by A. Huxley; *A Handbook of Living Religions* (Penguin, London, 1984) by J. Hinnells; and *The Pocket World Bible* (Routledge, London, 1948) by R. Ballou. And good introductions to 'esoteric' or 'mystical' approaches to spiritual experience include *A Guide for the Perplexed* (Abacus, London, 1977) by F. Schumacher; *The English Mystics* (Kyle Cathie, London, 1991) by K. Armstrong; *Water Into Wine* (Fount, London, 1985) by S. Verney; *The Second Penguin Krishnamurti Reader* (1970) ed. M. Lutyens; and *The New Man* (Stuart & Richards, London, 1952) and *The Mark* (Vincent Stuart, London, 1954) by M. Nicoll.

The meaning of 'play' is explored in *Homo Ludens* (Routledge, London, 1949) by J. Huizinga. The experience of ageing is well described in *I Don't Feel Old* (OUP, Oxford, 1990) by P. Thompson and others, and *The View In Winter* (Allen Lane, London, 1979) by R. Blythe. *Death: The Final Stage of Growth* (Prentice-Hall, London, 1975) by E. Kübler-Ross describes well the stages of adjustment to be undergone. Most books on bereavement do not discriminate between the reactions of more and less healthy individuals, but *Dimensions of Grief* (Jossey-Bass, San Francisco, 1986) by S. Schuchter is excellent and records the frequent experiences of psychological growth. *Return From Death* (Routledge, Boston, Mass., 1985) by M. Grey surveys near-death experiences, and *The Human Encounter With Death* (Dutton, New York, 1977), by S. Grof and J. Halifax, reports on the experiences of cancer patients under LSD. Evidence of reincarnation is examined in *Cases of the Reincarnation Type* and *Children Who've Remembered Previous Lives* (University Press of

Virginia, Charlottesville, both 1987) by I. Stevenson; and in *The Tibetan Book of Living and Dying* (Rider, London, 1992) by Sogyal Rinpoche. The last presents Eastern wisdom about life and death, and approaches to meditation, in a form which is readily understandable by Western readers.

The Discovery of the Unconscious (Allen Lane, London, 1970) by H. Ellenberger is a marvellous description of the early development of the major depth psychologies, set against their social and scientific background; *The Complex Secret of Brief Psychotherapy* (Norton, New York, 1986) by J. Gustafson extends this to the most recent developments; and *Awakening the Heart* (Routledge, London, 1983), ed. J. Wellwood, relates Eastern and Western approaches to self-knowledge and therapy. Robin Skynner's own attempt to integrate individual, group and family methods, and analytic, behavioural and systemic approaches is set out in *One Flesh: Separate Persons* and *Explorations with Families*, mentioned above – and also, of course, in our *Families and how to survive them*, all of which contain suggestions for further reading. Leadership and change are dealt with in many of the books about organisations mentioned above, while Robin Skynner's own ideas, including those on the constructive management of the dynamics of large groups, are explained more fully in *Institutes and How To Survive Them* (Methuen, London, 1989; Routledge, London, 1991). The approach to group exploration mentioned is described in *Group Psychotherapy: The Psycho-Analytic Approach* (Penguin, London, 1957) by its originator, S. Foulkes, and more recently in *The Evolution of Group Analysis* (Routledge, London, 1983) ed. M. Pines. Voluntary initiatives are examined in *Clubbing Together* (W. H. Smith Contemporary Papers, No. 12) by F. Mount. The article on the application of family and group therapy principles to political discussion, 'The Citizen Clinician: The Family Therapist in the Public Forum' by L. Chasin and others, appeared in *Newsletter of the American Family Therapy Academy*, No. 46, Winter 1991, page 36, and the research continues at the Public Conversations Project, Family Institute of Cambridge, 51, Kondazian Street, Watertown, MA 02172, USA.

Index